ROUTLEDGE LIBRARY EDITIONS: THE FRENCH REVOLUTION

Volume 1

THE INTERNALIZED REVOLUTION

THE INTERNALIZED REVOLUTION
German Reactions to the French Revolution, 1789–1989

Edited by
EHRHARD BAHR AND THOMAS P. SAINE

LONDON AND NEW YORK

First published in 1992 by Garland Publishing Inc.

This edition first published in 2016
by Routledge
2 Park Square, Milton Park, Abingdon, Oxon OX14 4RN

and by Routledge
711 Third Avenue, New York, NY 10017

Routledge is an imprint of the Taylor & Francis Group, an informa business

© 1992 Ehrhard Bahr and Thomas P. Saine

All rights reserved. No part of this book may be reprinted or reproduced or utilised in any form or by any electronic, mechanical, or other means, now known or hereafter invented, including photocopying and recording, or in any information storage or retrieval system, without permission in writing from the publishers.

Trademark notice: Product or corporate names may be trademarks or registered trademarks, and are used only for identification and explanation without intent to infringe.

British Library Cataloguing in Publication Data
A catalogue record for this book is available from the British Library

ISBN: 978-1-138-66567-5 (Set)
ISBN: 978-1-315-54584-4 (Set) (ebk)
ISBN: 978-1-138-67310-6 (Volume 1) (hbk)
ISBN: 978-1-138-67311-3 (Volume 1) (pbk)
ISBN: 978-1-315-56213-1 (Volume 1) (ebk)

Publisher's Note
The publisher has gone to great lengths to ensure the quality of this reprint but points out that some imperfections in the original copies may be apparent.

Disclaimer
The publisher has made every effort to trace copyright holders and would welcome correspondence from those they have been unable to trace.

THE INTERNALIZED REVOLUTION
German Reactions to the French Revolution, 1789–1989

Ehrhard Bahr
Thomas P. Saine
Editors

GARLAND PUBLISHING, INC. • NEW YORK & LONDON
1992

© 1992 Ehrhard Bahr and Thomas P. Saine
All rights reserved

Library of Congress Cataloging-in-Publication Data

The Internalized Revolution : German reactions to the French Revolution, 1789-1989 / edited by Ehrhard Bahr and Thomas P. Saine.
   p.   cm. — (Garland reference library of the humanities : vol. 1661)
   Papers presented at the public colloquium "German Reactions to the French Revolution, 1789-1989," which was held in 1989 at the UCLA.
   Includes bibliographical references and index.
   ISBN 0-8153-1144-3
   1. France—History—Revolution, 1789-1799—Influence—Congresses. 2. France—History—Revolution, 1789-1799—Foreign public opinion, German—Congresses. 3. Public opinion—Germany—Congresses. 4. Authors, German—19th century—Political and social views—Congresses. 5. Authors, German—20th century—Political and social views—Congresses. I. Bahr, Ehrhard. II. Saine, Thomas P. III. Series.
DC158.8.I67   1992
944.04—dc20   92-25174
                                                        CIP

Printed on acid-free, 250-year-life paper
Manufactured in the United States of America

CONTENTS

EHRHARD BAHR
Introduction   3

GONTHIER-LOUIS FINK
The French Revolution as Reflected in German Literature
and Political Journals from 1789 to 1800   11

W. DANIEL WILSON
Internalizing the Counter-Revolution:
Wieland and the Illuminati Scare   33

ZWI BATSCHA
Kant and the French Revolution   61

BERND WITTE
The Beautiful Society and the Symbolic Work of Art:
The Anti-Revolutionary Origin of the Bildungsroman   79

KLAUS L. BERGHAHN
Gedankenfreiheit: From Political Reform
to Aesthetic Revolution in Schiller's Works   99

THOMAS P. SAINE
Georg Forster and the Mainz Revolution   119

JENS KRUSE
The French Revolution and the German Romanticists   149

GÜNTER MIETH
Hölderlin and the French Revolution   163

JEFFREY L. SAMMONS
Heinrich Heine: The Revolution as Epic and Tragedy   173

HERBERT S. LINDENBERGER
The Literature in History:
Büchner's Danton and the French Revolution   197

ARLENE A. TERAOKA
Race, Revolution, and Writing:
Caribbean Texts by Anna Seghers   219

EHRHARD BAHR
Models of the French Revolution and Paradigm Change in
Contemporary German Drama: Peter Weiss and Heiner Müller   239

EHRHARD BAHR
Bibliography: A Select Checklist   253

Notes on the Contributors   259

Index of Names   263

THE INTERNALIZED REVOLUTION

EHRHARD BAHR

Introduction

BECAUSE GERMANY DID NOT HAVE A REVOLUTION of its own during the eighteenth century, the French Revolution was embraced as part of the German intellectual heritage. Friedrich Schlegel, for instance, juxtaposed the French Revolution, Fichte's *Theory of Science* and Goethe's novel *Wilhelm Meister's Apprenticeship* and called them the greatest events of the age (*Athenäum* fragment 216, 1798). This claim is characteristic of Germany's perception of political events in terms of their philosophical and literary repercussions and the intense intellectual discussions of the French Revolution. Summing up the effect of the Revolution on his generation, Schlegel declared the French Revolution to be "the greatest and most remarkable phenomenon in the history of states," "an almost universal earthquake, an immeasurable inundation in the political world." For Schlegel it was "the model for revolutions," "the Revolution *par excellence*" (*Athenäum* fragment 424, 1798). Johann Gottlieb Fichte considered the Revolution important for the entire human race ("A Contribution to a Correction of the Public Opinion on the French Revolution," 1793), and Johann Gottfried Herder wrote in 1792 that nothing had ever occurred that was comparable to the Revolution (*Letters for the Advancement of Humanity*). Friedrich Hölderlin suggested that the idea of the French Revolution should be imported to Germany, though it would not have to be a political idea, since he believed in "a future revolution of ethics and imagination" (letter of 10 January 1797 to Johann Gottfried Ebel). As late as 1822/23 Hegel recalled the French Revolution as a "beautiful sunrise," explaining that all rational beings had participated in celebrating this epoch: "A sublime emotionality prevailed, an intellectual enthusiasm thrilled the world, as if the Divine had been reconciled with the world" (*Lectures on the Philosophy of History*, 1822/23).

It was Heinrich Heine who developed the idea of an elective affinity between German philosophy and French politics. In an 1831 essay he asked his countrymen to compare the history of the French Revolution with the history of German philosophy and declared: "You will notice that it is as though the French, who had to conduct so much real business, during which they had to stay awake, had invited the Germans to do their sleeping and dreaming for them: German philosophy is nothing but the dream of the French Revolution." Heine considered the German break with tradition in the realm of thought to be comparable to the French break with political tradition: "Kant was our Robespierre," he exclaimed ("Introduction to Kahldorf on Nobility in a Series of Letters to Count M. von Moltke," 1831). Heine developed this line of argument further in his book *Concerning the History of Religion and Philosophy in Germany* of 1834.

There are enough quotations to support Heine's thesis, even in French historiography. Jules Michelet did not write his *History of the French Revolution* without referring to Klopstock, Goethe, and Kant, that "rock," as he said, "formed by adamant in the granite of the Baltic." In the 1970s, André Glucksmann, one of the spokesmen of the *nouveaux philosophes*, quoted Heine to make his point against the "master thinkers" (Fichte, Hegel, Marx, Nietzsche) who, in his opinion, had provided the tools to implement twentieth-century totalitarianism (*Les Maîtres penseurs*, 1977).

Karl Marx and Friedrich Engels would not have agreed with Heine's equation of philosophical ideas and political action. For them, ideas as such cannot change the world. It takes the masses to execute the ideas with practical force. According to Marx and Engels, the German philosophers of the eighteenth century misunderstood the demands of the French Revolution as the demands of "Practical Reason" in general: "The utterance of the will of the revolutionary French bourgeoisie signified in [the philosophers'] eyes the laws of pure Will, of Will as it was bound to be, of true human Will generally" (*Communist Manifesto*, 1848). This critical analysis of the German response shows a profound understanding of the political forces of the French Revolution, which Marx and Engels considered the greatest revolution in history. It was the revolution "which founded the modern world" (Marx, "First Draft of *Civil War in France*," 1871).

Christoph Martin Wieland was one of the first to compare the events in France with drama in his essays in *The German Mercury* (*Der Teutsche Merkur*) between 1789–1793, but it was Karl Marx who firmly established drama as metaphor for the French Revolution in his famous 1852 essay, "The Eighteenth Brumaire of Louis Bonaparte":

> Camille Desmoulins, Danton, Robespierre, Saint-Just, Napoleon, the heroes as well as the parties and the masses of the old French Revolution, performed the task of their time in Roman costume and with Roman phrases.... In the classically austere traditions of the Roman republic [the gladiators of the bourgeois society] found the ideals and the art forms, the self-deceptions that they needed in order to conceal from themselves the bourgeois limitations of the content of their struggles and to keep their enthusiasm on the high plane of the great historical tragedy.... The awakening of the dead in those revolutions served the purpose of . . . magnifying the given task in imagination, . . . of finding once more the spirit of revolution.

During the later nineteenth and the twentieth century, however, the repeated attempts of German writers to claim the French Revolution as part of their own tradition were often met with opposition and repression. The failure of the revolution of 1848 had caused a change in the ideological climate. While most writers shared the prevailing anti-revolutionary mood, a few resorted to satire or chose other models of revolution, such as the Peasant Revolt of 1525 (Ferdinand von Lassalle), or the weavers' revolt of 1844 (Gerhart Hauptmann). Whereas the French Revolution was rarely a topic for the writers of the opposition, it frequently served conservative writers as a negative lesson in history. There were a great number of anti-revolutionary dramas dealing with Robespierre or Napoleon Bonaparte between 1850 and 1908.[1] The changes in the direction of conservatism are best exemplified by Robert Griepenkerl (1810–1868) and his dramas *Maximilian Robespierre* (1849) and *Girondisten* (1851). While the former drama ends with the Thermidorian triumph, foreshadowing Napoleon's ultimate defeat of the revolution, the latter idealizes Charlotte Corday and her assassination of Jean-Paul Marat.

In the twentieth century, this attitude changed. In 1902, Büchner's *Danton's Death* (*Dantons Tod*) was performed for the first time, although it took another eight years (until Leopold Jeßner's 1910 production) for it to become widely recognized and generally accepted on the German stage. While German Expressionism affected a revolutionary posture, references to the French Revolution in Expressionist literature are comparatively rare. (They are more frequent in Expressionist art, for example in works by Käte Kollwitz and Ludwig Meidner.) Heinrich Mann's drama *Madame Legros* of 1913 is an exception. Yet, there is one important source to document the internalization of the revolution. On 15 September 1911, the Expressionist poet Georg Heym writes in his diary:

> In my dreams, I always see myself as a Danton, or a man on the barricades. I cannot think of myself without the Jacobin cap of liberty. . . . My God, if I had only been born during the French Revolution, then I would have known where to lay down my life with dignity, at Hohenlinden or Jemappes.

This shows not only an intimate knowledge of the history of the French Revolution, but also of its function in providing role models and symbols. At his early death in 1912, Heym left behind a number of novelistic and dramatic fragments dealing with the French Revolution.[2]

Most surprising is Gertrud Kolmar's cycle of poems on Robespierre during the 1930s. The Jewish poet (who was later murdered in a concentration camp) chose the maligned Jacobin as a central figure for her poetry. Written after Hitler came to power, Kolmar's Robespierre poems were intended to restore the good name of a revolutionary leader before the tribunal of history. Defamation of Robespierre may have served the cause of anti-Semitism, but Kolmar's boldness is manifest also in comparison with Max Horkheimer's claim only a few years later that the members of the Committee of Public Safety of 1793 were to be identified with the Nazis, declaring that "the so-called progressive order established in 1789 had an inherent tendency towards National Socialism" ("The Jews and Europe," 1939).

The Nazis, however, hated the French Revolution. For Adolf Hitler, France and the French Republic were "by far the most terrible enemy," as he wrote in *Mein Kampf*.[3] He considered the French Revolution a betrayal of the "white race." "We want to eradicate the *Weltanschauung* of liberalism and the freedom of the individual and replace it by a new sense of community which comprises the whole nation and subordinates the individual to the common interest of the state," proclaimed Joseph Goebbels on April 1, 1933. "The year 1789 has been expunged from the records of history."[4]

On the other hand, German exile literature, with the exception of Lion Feuchtwanger's novels *Waffen für Amerika* (*Proud Destiny*) and *Narrenweisheit* (*Death and Transfiguration of Jean-Jacques Rousseau*) and Friedrich Wolf's drama on Beaumarchais, *Beaumarchais oder die Geburt des Figaro* (Beaumarchais, or the Birth of Figaro), did not draw heavily on the French Revolution as a theme. Napoleon as dictator was far more analogous to Hitler than the representatives of the French Revolution were analogous to those who resisted the Nazi regime. There is a large number of Napoleon plays in German exile literature between 1934 and 1942. Noteworthy in this context is Arnold Schoenberg's composition "Ode to Napoleon," opus 41, based on a satirical poem by Lord Byron, which gave the exiled composer an opportunity to express his contempt for the contemporary dictatorship of Hitler. The fact that the final stanza referred to George Washington as a counter-paradigm served Schoenberg as a way of thanking the country that had offered him a refuge in 1934.

After World War II, Peter Weiss wrote his *Marat/Sade* drama of 1964 to remind his German audience that they had never had a revolution. The drama contains numerous references to restoration ideology in post-war Germany, which is implicitly equated with the Napoleonic era after 1804, the time period of the play within the play of *Marat/Sade*. Jürgen Habermas pointed out in a review of the first production in West Berlin in 1964 that the drama uncovers a process of repression, excluding a painful period of German history from the conscious mind by blaming the French Revolution for the rise of the Nazis and exposing Robespierre as a forerunner of

Introduction 7

Hitler.[5] In retrospect, Habermas's 1964 review appears to anticipate the infamous "historians' controversy" (*Historikerstreit*) of the years 1986–1988.

The papers of the public colloquium "The Internalized Revolution: German Reactions to the French Revolution, 1789–1989," which took place on February 9–11, 1989, under the co-sponsorship of the Department of Germanic Languages at the University of California, Los Angeles, dealt with some of these problems. This book contains the proceedings of that colloquium. The intention of its organizers was to trace this discourse on the French Revolution in Germany and to reinterpret its documents in terms of their internalization. The individual contributors were invited to investigate the processes and results of adopting or rejecting the values of the French Revolution and making them part of or excluding them from the German tradition. One of the questions to be raised was whether the French Revolution is part of Germany's progressive tradition, that is, whether it has been repressed or whether it constitutes a viable counter-discourse within the political culture. Scholars from various disciplines and countries came to Los Angeles to present and discuss their papers with the other participants and the members of the audience. With one exception, the conference papers were presented in English (the one paper that was presented in German has been translated for this volume). Two participants had to cancel their appearance, but their papers were available to the participants at the conference. The last paper in the volume was not presented at the conference.

It is impossible to exhaust the topic of German reactions to the French Revolution in the course of a two-day conference. There are obvious gaps. We mention but a few of the authors who could not be treated at the UCLA colloquium: Fichte, Hegel, Friedrich and A.W. Schlegel, Kleist, Eichendorff, Karl Marx and Friedrich Engels, Lion Feuchtwanger, and Heinrich Mann, among others. However, the numerous conferences and publications on the topic of Germany and the French Revolution in 1989 provide a rather comprehensive treatment, and so we have added a selective bibliography to this volume.

The volume begins with Gonthier-Louis Fink's magisterial survey of reflections of the French Revolution in German literature and journalism between 1789–1800. W. Daniel Wilson assesses Wieland's problems with the widespread suspicion that the Illuminati had conspired to spread the French Revolution into Germany, showing that, in the end, Wieland's opinions follow "the vacillation of repression in Germany." Zwi Batscha shows that Kant reoriented his thought from the problems of a philosophy of Enlightenment to those of early political Liberalism, eventually becoming one of its major proponents. Analyzing post-revolutionary aesthetic discourse in Germany, Bernd Witte traces the anti-revolutionary tendencies of German Classicism, arguing that Goethe's "beautiful society" was intended as an antidote to the French Revolution. Klaus L. Berghahn emphasizes the centrality of aesthetic theory in Schiller's coming to terms with the political and social changes of his times. Thomas P. Saine offers a critical assessment of the Mainz revolution of 1792–1793. Jens Kruse reinterprets Klingsohr's fairy tale (*Märchen*) in Friedrich von Hardenberg's novel *Heinrich von Ofterdingen* as a "romanticist re-writing" of Goethe's most significant poetic reaction to the French Revolution, namely his own "Fairy Tale" (*Märchen*) at the end of *Unterhaltungen deutscher Ausgewanderten* (Conversations of German Emigrants) of 1795. Günter Mieth deals with the changes in history which Friedrich Hölderlin expected to be brought about by the French Revolution and his subsequent disappointments and never-ending utopian yearnings. Concentrating on Heinrich Heine's relationship to the French Revolution as represented by its Napoleonic phase, Jeffrey L. Sammons argues that for Heine "Napoleon was incomparably the most important figure of the international epoch . . . from 1776 to 1848." Herbert S. Lindenberger stresses the textuality of history in interpreting Georg Büchner's drama *Danton's Death* as "literature . . . already present in the history that literature purports to portray." Wolfgang Nehring's paper dealing with Arthur Schnitzler's one-act play *Der grüne Kakadu* (The Green Cockatoo) and his novella (*Die Frau des Richters* (The Judge's Wife) will be published elsewhere. The author argued that for the Viennese author the French Revolution was but "an example of the universal theatricality of human existence." Arlene A. Teraoka takes on the literary treatment of the independence movement in the slave colonies of the Caribbean, ending with the defeat of the revolutionary forces by expeditionary troops sent by Napoleon in 1802. Rereading Anna Seghers's Caribbean stories, which resume a tradition started by Heinrich von Kleist in his novella *Die Verlobung in St. Domingo* (The Engagement in Saint Domingo) of 1811, Teraoka uncovers the Eurocentric and sexist attitudes underlying these texts, concluding that Seghers's writing "reasserts the superiority of the white world despite its own intention." Ehrhard Bahr provides a conclusion by surveying the models and paradigm changes of the French Revolution in contemporary German drama (Peter Weiss and Heiner Müller) and by analyzing the new model of Third World revolution as a substitute for bourgeois and socialist revolutions in Heiner Müller's play *Der Auftrag* (The Task) of 1979.

In February, 1989, none of the participants could have expected or predicted the "Velvet Revolution" of October/November 1989 in Germany. The first successful revolution in Germany—and a peaceful one at that—surprised everyone, whether or not they were directly involved. There has been much discussion whether the "Velvet Revolution" fits the definition of

Introduction 9

"classic revolutions."⁶ The demonstrations in Leipzig which began on October 2, 1989, marked the beginning of a democratic revolution. By November 27, 1989, this democratic revolution had turned into a national revolution, demanding the unification of the two German states created in 1949 by the victorious Allies. The revolution ended in a change of power. The GDR elections of March 18 and May 6, 1990, made the results of the revolution irreversible.⁷ In this respect, this book is an anatomy of German political consciousness before 1989.

The February, 1989 public colloquium, "German Reactions to the French Revolution, 1789–1989" provided the forum for these contributions and discussions. Robert M. Maniquis, the director of the UCLA Bicentennial Program on the French Revolution 1789–1989, gave his enthusiastic support to the Department's project. He participated in the planning discussions and graciously provided the Department with the Program's services. Thomas P. Saine served as co-editor of this volume and generously took on the task of final editing and production. Michael Frank McAnear provided draft translations of the papers by Gonthier-Louis Fink and Günter Mieth and the first version of the index. Christa Johnson translated the paper by Bernd Witte.

The colloquium could not have taken place without the financial support of the UCLA Bicentennial Program on the French Revolution 1789/1989. Additional funding was provided by the French Cultural Services, Los Angeles, and Alexander Tolstoi, the French cultural attaché. Research for this volume was supported in part by a grant from the International Research and Exchanges Board (IREX), and by funds provided by the National Endowment for the Humanities, the Andrew W. Mellon Foundation, and the United States Department of State. None of these organizations is responsible for the views expressed in this volume, but we gratefully acknowledge their generosity.

NOTES

1. See Elisabeth Frenzel, *Stoffe der Weltliteratur: Ein Lexikon dichtungsgeschichtlicher Längsschnitte*. 2nd rev. ed. (Stuttgart: Kröner, 1963) 542–44.

2. See Hans-Wolf Jäger, "Zwischen Décadence und Expressionismus: 'Revolution' bei Schnitzler, Heym, Heinrich Mann und Klabund," in *Schreckensmythen—Hoffnungsbilder. Die Französische Revolution in der deutschen Literatur: Essays*, ed. Harro Zimmermann (Frankfurt/Main: Athenäum, 1989) 228–37.

3. Adolf Hitler, *Mein Kampf*, transl. Ralph Manheim (Boston: Houghton Mifflin, 1971) 624.

4. See *Freiheit, Gleichheit, Brüderlichkeit? Die Französische Revolution im deutschen Urteil*, ed. by Wolfgang von Hippel (Munich: Deutscher Taschenbuchverlag, 1989) 344.

5. Jürgen Habermas, "Ein Verdrängungsprozeß wird enthüllt," *Materialien zu Peter Weiss Marat/Sade*, ed. by Karlheinz Braun (Frankfurt/Main: Suhrkamp, 1967) 120–24.

6. See Hans Joachim Warbeck, *Die deutsche Revolution 1989–1990: Die Herstellung der staatlichen Einheit* (Berlin: Arno Spitz, 1991) 8–22.

7. See Hartmut Zwahr, "Die Revolution in der DDR," *Revolution in Deutschland? 1789–1989*, ed. Manfred Hettling (Göttingen: Vandenhoeck & Ruprecht, 1991) 122–43.

GONTHIER-LOUIS FINK

The French Revolution as Reflected in German Literature and Political Journals from 1789 to 1800

IN 1897 GEORGES CLEMENCEAU STATED THAT the French Revolution could only be understood in terms of the whole picture, that one had to accept this perspective or dismiss it. But this simplification, which arose from a desire to justify the terror that attended the historical situation and which conformed to the schism between aristocrats and democrats during the Reign of Terror, does not take into account the complex process of the Revolution or the often contradictory statements of contemporary observers—especially since many of them changed their minds repeatedly during the course of the Revolution. Apart from a few reactionaries who were strongly opposed to the French Revolution from the very beginning, most writers adopted differing attitudes with respect to its successive phases: The first, from 1789 to 1792, saw the striving for a constitutional monarchy, and it was marked by the liberation propaganda of the Girondists which led to the war of the European powers against revolutionary France; the second was the Jacobin dictatorship of 1793–1794; and the final phase saw the bourgeois Directory of 1795 to 1799. Thus it seems advisable, when considering contemporary German reception of the French Revolution in political journals and literature, to maintain a historical perspective—while bearing in mind that we can only hint at the complexity of the problem.

1. The German Deficit in Political Information 1788–1789

The newspapers, which had gained in importance since the American Revolution (albeit mostly on a local level), delivered news of the French Revolution to all regions and classes in Germany, news which was received by the common people "with the greatest curiosity." In his unfinished novel *Die Reise der Söhne Megaprazons* (The Journey of the Sons of Megaprazon) Goethe mocked "the fever of the times," or "the newspaper fever, a bad case of an infectious disease." The information conveyed to the German public was indeed full of gaps. Yet the German newspaper reader was sufficiently informed about revolutionary events (at least until 1792), even though journalists were restricted to publishing only what had been confirmed by official sources or letters written by well known figures. (They also had to refrain from inserting their own opinions.) The German public was, however, insufficiently informed with respect to the events leading up to the Revolution. While the *Cahiers de doleánces* and political pamphlets like those by Condorcet and Sieyès had contributed significantly toward the formation of French public opinion, they had not made a great impression on the German mind, and in the 1770s the German public had more or less missed its chance to gain the political education offered by the spectacle of the American Revolution.

Moreover, the information available to the German public varied according to education and social class. For example, the text of the Declaration of the Rights of Man and of the Citizen was published in August Ludwig Schlözer's *Staatsanzeigen* (Papers of State) in 1791 only in the original French version; in 1792 the liberal historian Ernst Ludwig Posselt published his *Krieg der Franken gegen die wider sie verbündeten Mächte* (War of the Franks Against the Allied Powers) in Latin so that, as H.A.O. Reichard noted in his *Revolutionsalmanach* for 1795, "no principles [might] be circulated among the common people that could kindle the flame of revolution."

Such a precautionary measure is understandable in light of the local German revolts which erupted chiefly in the border regions. While the farmers demanded above all the abrogation of *villeinage*, the townspeople were concerned for the most part with preserving their "traditional rights." The bourgeois were conservative-minded, because for generations the cities had maintained traditions that circumscribed all economic competition and promoted class consciousness. Since unrest was consistently confined to the local level, governments were always able to restore order quickly because demands arose sporadically and only from one social group, evoking little response among the rest of the populace. This is also why very little about popular unrest appeared in the German press.

Even in the first phase of the Revolution, censorship played a significant (but regionally varying) role in Germany. In 1791 Emperor Leopold II decreed that "the distribution of all publications inciting to unrest and revolt" should be prohibited. Many German governments conformed as fully as possible—for example Bavaria and Prussia—while certain imperial cities like Hamburg were more lax in their practice of censorship; and Altona, which belonged to the Danish Crown, enjoyed general freedom of the press.

2. Triumph of the Philosophy of "Them and not Us"

Louis XVI believed in 1788–1789 that summoning the *Etats Généraux* would initiate a reform and thus resolve the kingdom's financial troubles. But the limited reform that Louis XVI and his advisors had in mind proved futile. Since the representatives of the Estates considered themselves representatives of the nation and presumed that they had the right to draw up a national constitution, even "reform" constituted a revolution. But since this process was directed towards establishing a constitutional monarchy in France, it also corresponded to reforms desired by the liberal middle class in Germany.

Klopstock, one of the first German poets to note the historical import of the summons to the Estates, described it in his 1788 ode "Die Etats Généraux" as "the most important act of this century." He did not, however, regard it primarily as the cooperative gesture of a king who, by summoning the Estates, meant to usher in a revolution from above; rather, he regarded it as the outcome of demands voiced by the whole nation. In his ode, Klopstock did not direct a plea for reforms to the German princes. Instead he went over their heads and appealed to the Germans, challenging them to emulate their brothers, the "Franks." The ode resembles a call to revolt, but it was apparently not understood in that way. At this time Klopstock in fact desired a peaceful revolution for his fatherland, because the French Revolution itself still seemed to him to be a peaceable affair. Thus Klopstock, the prince of poets who contributed the most to the notion that the "intellectual nobility" could dare to take its place alongside the hereditary nobility, initiated the German enthusiasm for the French Revolution.

With this enthusiasm there came a significant reevaluation of the image of France. For many German writers the Revolution signified a regeneration, or palingenesis, of the French nation. While Klopstock and his followers had until now compared French vanity, frivolity, irresoluteness, and cowardice unfavorably with German loyalty, honesty, and valor, now they regarded the French as the new Greeks and Romans, or as "Franks" and brothers. Klopstock's 1790 ode "Sie und nicht Wir!" (Them and not Us) indicates clearly just how much it pained Germans to see that it was these same French, whom they had always considered a servile nation, who now proclaimed freedom to the entire world. Klopstock was not the only one concerned with salvaging the honor of Germany, as is shown by the comparison drawn by many contemporary writers between the French Revolution and the German Reformation, a comparison to which Klopstock added his observation that the French would not have been able to shake off the yoke of royal despotism had it not been for the Reformation.

The German image of the French Revolution in 1789 was formed largely from the travel reports which appeared in the newspapers. These reports were sent in by German "pilgrims of the Revolution" who noted the events in Paris from the vantage point of eyewitnesses caught up in the enthusiasm. A distinct echo of the events was found above all in the pedagogue Joachim Heinrich Campe's *Briefe aus Paris zur Zeit der Revolution* (Letters from Paris at the Time of the Revolution, published in book form in 1790 after having been serialized in the *Braunschweigisches Journal* in 1789). Campe arrived in Paris in the summer of 1789, convinced that the French Revolution was "the greatest and most far-reaching benefit" Providence had bestowed upon humanity since Luther's times. Not insignificantly, he was especially inspired by brotherhood (*fraternité*), the least obviously political of the three great principles of the Revolution. Campe thought the French were now overcoming their national, religious, and class differences; he felt that he was no longer observing mere Frenchmen, but rather whole human beings in their essential humanity. Responding to this aspect of humanity, Campe felt himself no longer a mere German, and wished that "this message of general human brotherhood might serve as a model for all states." France was to be henceforth a land "where . . . there will be no other aristocracy but that of talents and virtue. . . , no hierarchy nor despotism, but where all human beings will be equal." He dreamed of a monarchy in which middle-class values prevailed. He marveled at the perfect harmony he thought he perceived between the three main actors in the great historical drama that France was putting on for the world, namely between the king, the National Assembly, and the people; despite certain reservations he transmitted an idyllic picture of the French Revolution.

Much had already changed when Johann Friedrich Reichardt went to Paris in 1792. Yet on the whole he was amazed at "how little such a total revolution had cost the French," especially when one considered how for centuries the aristocratic classes had accustomed the people to all sorts of murder and theft. In his widely read *Vertraute Briefe aus Paris* (Intimate Letters from Paris) of 1792, he did not lambaste the Parisian people for the riots that had occurred; instead he took on the aristocrats, "these totally corrupt human beings," who were attempting "to reestablish their rule by all kinds of conspiracies." By showing that the nation was divided into factions, that aristocrats and democrats were in conflict with each other, and that the king and the court had conspired against the Revolution, he countered the idyllic picture painted by Campe and others. Despite his vigorous criticism of the nobility and the court, Reichardt was not in favor of founding a republic. Like other German liberals he regarded a moderate constitutional monarchy as the best form of government.

The enthusiasm of the "pilgrims of the Revolution" captured the imagination of numerous poets. Poetry played the most conspicuous role of all literary genres in reception of the principles of the French Revolution, especially since it had an advantage over the drama and the novel in being able to respond quickly to the course of events. Nevertheless, political themes occupied only a relatively modest space in poetry collections of the time, even in the poetry of avowed republicans. Arguing the cause of the French Revolution in the idealistic terms of liberty and the brotherhood of mankind was apparently not very fruitful from the poetic point of view. But since the principles of the Revolution exerted a magical fascination on the minds of the Germans as well as the French, many poets mixed slogans into their verse once Klopstock had shown the way.

The celebratory, allusive style of the ode was hardly suited to political discussion. This is attested by odes to liberty written by numerous poets. While they indeed captured comprehensively in the catchword of "freedom" what the Revolution meant to them and what they hoped would be its result, namely, that it would topple each and every despotism, the concept of liberty itself generally remained vague and nonpolitical. It seemed especially important to consecrate the concept by means of high-flown poetic language and suitable meter, as in Hölderlin's hymns, "An die Freiheit" (To Freedom) and "An die Menschheit" (To Humanity). The same goes for Christian Friedrich Daniel Schubart, who, in his own ode "An die Freiheit" of 1789, extolled freedom and depicted it as a "daughter" of the gods who descends from heaven to return to humanity its divine dignity. The poet asks for nothing more than to serve Freedom in her temple. In seven stanzas he glorifies this daughter of Heaven whose altar was already to be found "in Germany's forests" in the time of Hermann; now, having erected for herself "an easily accessible tent" in the new world, she reveals herself to all nations, beginning with France. Without a doubt exalted style and idealization mirrored well the enthusiasm of the poets, a poetic enthusiasm inspired above all by the enthusiasm for freedom. Yet on the whole the poets say little about the importance of the principles of 1789. In contrast to the inspired rhetoric of his poems, Schubart was much more down to earth in the political articles of his journal, the *Vaterländische Chronik*. But the allegorical treatment of freedom in odes demonstrates more than the mere limitations of the genre and the classical tradition to which the poets remained bound; such odes often enough also give the impression that it was only a simple slogan that was being glorified.

If one compares with these the poems of freedom that Gottlieb Conrad Pfeffel wrote, it is apparent that the epistle, the song, and the fable were far more suited to political poetry than the ode or the hymn. For Pfeffel, too, the destruction of the Bastille signified the destruction of despotism—not only the destruction of kings, but of the whole system along with courtiers and clergy. Henceforth, freedom of religion would be guaranteed, and the administration of the law would be freed from the influence of the wealthy and the powerful. Pfeffel was pleased that the nobility had to forfeit their privileges, that the peasant was freed from compulsory labor, and that the merit of the citizen was recognized. He sketched the image of a felicitous constitutional monarchy guaranteed by the Trinity of the Revolution: liberty, equality, and brotherhood.

To Pfeffel, as to others, liberty was the most important of the three principles of the Revolution. But in accordance with the popular character of the Revolution, he dispensed with the ingredients of genteel poetry and avoided complex poetic metaphors, allegorical forms, and allusions to Greek mythology. To take freedom and equality in the nation seriously also implied broadening the audience for poetry. In Pfeffel's fable "Die drei Stände" (The Three Estates) of 1790, which provided the commentary for a copperplate engraving, freedom means above all the emancipation of the Third Estate, which hitherto had been exploited by the nobility and the clergy. Thanks to the encouraging example of American freedom, the Third Estate now rises up and shows that it is far greater than either of the other two estates. Morally speaking, citizens and farmers were the only productive estate, and, towering above the clergy and the nobility—according to Sieyès—constituted the real nation.

In the first years of the Revolution the political demands of the poets were still relatively moderate. They lampooned despotism and sang the praises of liberty. Even such a later radical as Eulogius Schneider satisfied himself with demanding limits on the power of the despots. The Berlin pastor Daniel Jenisch was content to exhort the tyrants to found their thrones on "rectitude and kindness." Like Klopstock, Karl Philipp Conz attempted, in "Das Konstitutionsfest der Franken" (The Franks Celebrate the Constitution) of 1791, to rouse the Germans to emulate the "New Gaul," where "nature and law" now ruled. As idealists the poets believed in the power of the poetic word. They regarded constitutional monarchy as the ideal and hoped that with their poems they could prepare the way for such monarchies of their own in Germany.

After doing his part to extol the power of the writer, Adolph Freiherr von Knigge nevertheless stood up to the writer colleagues who proudly put on airs and fancied that the outbreak of revolution in the modern world was their own doing. Perhaps out of fear that by making such grand claims writers were only playing into the hands of opponents of the Revolution,

Knigge emphasized that "writers had never caused any events of world importance": at best they were the mouthpiece of the people.

While eyewitnesses wrote enthusiastically about events, and the praise of freedom often remained abstract in the numerous poems about it, serious discussion of the French Revolution began in the narrative genre with relatively little delay. Knigge's satirical novels are distinguished not so much by their literary as by their political significance. In *Benjamin Noldmanns Geschichte der Aufklärung in Abyssinien* (Benjamin Noldmann's History of Enlightenment in Abyssinia) of 1791, Knigge hoped that he might be able to discuss the Revolution and the probable consequences of a war between the European powers and revolutionary France more freely by transposing his story to an African setting. In Abyssinia an enlightened despotism is displaced by a constitutional monarchy as a result of the unsuccessful war with a revolutionary neighboring country. This allowed Knigge to express his views on the ideal of a constitution based on Reason, by which he aimed to enlighten both peoples and monarchs about their respective duties. He dreamed of a country where the greatest possible amount of freedom and equality would be guaranteed by dividing the land equally and placing strict limits on people's ability to consolidate and inherit wealth. In this manner the easily aroused masses would be integrated into society. Thus Knigge did not regard revolution as necessarily entailing bloody upheaval but rather as a fundamental change of government, which, thanks to Enlightenment, would supposedly come about without bloodshed.

In the journals directed chiefly to the well-educated, which, by virtue of their sheer numbers in the early years of the Revolution, can be considered a forum for a moderate political Enlightenment, all literary genres found their place: travel reports, letters from France, poems, essays, and commentaries. Politics, which at first remained on the periphery, was pushed more and more into the foreground. During the first phase of the Revolution, Wieland, in his *Neuer Teutscher Merkur* (New German Mercury), parceled out praise and blame impartially to both sides, battling extremists of all persuasions. He resorted frequently to dialogues in which the friends of the Revolution and the friends of the aristocracy pursued their respective arguments under various guises. Wieland indeed believed that he was being impartial, but in reality he was very seldom able to remain neutral; over and over he encouraged the reader to share his moderate views. The *Berlinische Monatsschrift* (Berlin Monthly) also allowed representatives of different generations and viewpoints to have their say. Thus the journals attempted, especially during 1790, to elucidate the rights of humanity from various perspectives.

Until 1791 representatives of all moderate positions had their say in numerous journals, but democrats did not—chiefly because there were as yet no genuinely revolutionary journals. Nevertheless, in 1792–1793, and again from 1795 on, numerous new and often short-lived journals appeared, so that the full spectrum of political thought, from the Jacobins to the counter-revolutionaries, was finally represented. The liberal journals asserted their impartiality over and over again, but they also acknowledged their commitment to the principles of the Revolution and condemned the abuses which marred it in practice. This can be seen, for example, in Paul Usteri's *Klio* of 1794–95 or in Ludwig Ferdinand Huber's *Friedenspräliminarien* (Preliminaries to Peace) of 1793–1796, which printed translations of French documents, letters from Paris, and essays on many of the problems aired in the National Assembly debates.

In the first phase of the Revolution, the writers mostly emphasized liberty. Yet even Schubart wanted to see "criminals" and "rabble rousers" excluded; by this he indirectly acknowledged that he viewed the Revolution as simply an important reform movement, not a radical upheaval. As for the constitution of 1791, the writers were committed to equality only as long as it realized the dream of the bourgeoisie, a dream which allowed only an aristocracy based on talent and virtue. At the same time, they were eager to reject all social leveling. Out of fear of the common people, the "rabble," they rejected democracy and along with it any notion of the sovereignty of the people.

Thus the larger number of Enlightenment authors acknowledged the principles of human and citizen rights; they defended an idea of the state which protected the rights of the Third Estate, while warning vigorously against anarchy. Schlözer voiced the widespread hope that "God might protect us Germans from such a revolution as occurred in France." Grievances were to be remedied "without revolution, without the people mixing in"; this was to be accomplished with the assistance of writers whose task was to denounce oppression and thereby prompt the "enlightened government" to put things to rights. Numerous writers demonstrated their conservative bent by their reluctance to speak out for sweeping reform. In the final analysis, enlightened despotism still conformed to their expectations.

In the beginning the French Revolution appeared to be the product of Reason. Liberal authors like Lichtenberg, Wieland and Graf Hertzberg, Georg Forster, Friedrich Gentz and Hölderlin proclaimed the Revolution a triumph of Enlightenment philosophy. Since the National Assembly deferred not to tradition but to Reason, and since it advocated not only the rights of the French but also those of all human beings and citizens everywhere, the idealism of the Enlightenment seemed to have overcome reality, and even history.

In the awareness that improvement of the world usually proceeds very slowly, as Herder noted, and that the collective consciousness develops only at a slow pace, the Enlightenment reckoned that it would still take centuries to effect substantial changes in society and human relations—as is shown in Louis-Sébastien Mercier's utopia *L'An 2440* (The Year 2440). Still, the French Revolution seemed to have brought about a metamorphosis of the nation practically in the course of a single day. This acceleration of the rhythm of history forced itself on the consciousness of the educated all the more as it contradicted all their previous ideas about history. By thus breaking with the past, the Revolution threatened radical historical disorientation. The only surety remaining was Reason itself. Whereas some greeted this acceleration of the historical process as the fulfillment of their dreams, others feared that the French Revolution meant the radicalization of the Enlightenment.

Without a doubt the French Revolution elicited considerable sympathy in Germany at first, and among members of all social classes. In 1791, Freiherr von Stein asserted with considerable conviction that among any twenty noblemen there would be no more than four who were not "democrats." In reality, however, German citizens (even Catholics) were still too much influenced by the traditional Lutheran idea of state authority, which firmly supported absolutism. While the reports from Paris were idyllic, they found a great resonance in Germany. The German elites, however, applauded only as long as they thought they saw Reason at work or at least believed it to be essentially present.

German writers drew differing conclusions from the Revolution. The universal appeal of the principles embodied in the Declaration of the Rights of Man and of the Citizen gave liberal writers reason to believe that the French example applied to Germans as well; it was an example that would introduce Germans to a lengthy process of development that would transform enlightened despotism into constitutional monarchy. For their part, conservatives feared that a constitution would too closely resemble the "republican form of government." They also claimed, the universal pretensions of the National Assembly notwithstanding, that the events in France ought to be regarded as purely an internal French affair, for the abuses of monarchy in France were much more evident than in Germany, where the princes were already much more enlightened than French monarchs had ever been. In 1790 Klopstock, eyeing the French, had envied their revolution in his ode "Sie und nicht Wir"; in 1791 the Austrian Johann Baptist von

Alxinger, in a poem about Leopold II, already called out to the French: "We have long been where you want to go."

3. Military Conflict and the War of the Quills: "La force des choses"

Although many believed that Louis XVI's acceptance of the constitution would mean the end of the Revolution and the return to a settled political and public life, after the proclamation of the Republic in September, 1792, talk turned to a "new Revolution." With that the dream of constitutional monarchy came to an end. The execution of the king in January, 1793, caused more German sympathizers to change their position, and the Terror finally alienated even the Revolution's most devoted liberal friends.

Isolated dissenting voices had already surfaced in 1789–1790. For Johann Wilhelm Gleim, even a poorly governed monarchy had at least the advantage that "the rage of the One [the king] was not hereditary," whereas the "twelve hundred despots" of the National Assembly were potentially immortal (as he wrote in a 1790 poem, "Auch Les Etats Généraux"). In a fable about "The Philosopher and his Tailor" (1790) Gottlieb Conrad Pfeffel complained that the "philosophers" of the National Assembly were only following their ideology and their abstract principles in tailoring a constitution for France. In this Pfeffel resembled Edmund Burke, whose *Reflections on the Revolution in France* (1790) was to become the Bible of the traditionalists. Pfeffel feared the further extension of the principle of equality, because that seemed no less dangerous than what the "philosophers" were doing.

While the educated friends of the Revolution often appeared intoxicated by their own enthusiasm, the conservatives understood very early on—often more effectively than the liberals—how to address a wide audience with a simplistic vocabulary, a style that drew on the manner of folk songs, and generalizations to the effect that in France the "poor sextons" were being robbed by the Jacobins. Rejecting the revolutionary model, the conservatives implicitly and explicitly defended the existing order, namely the hierarchical feudal state.

In his *Venetian Epigrams* of 1790, Goethe repeatedly attacked the "apostles of freedom" for confusing "arbitrary actions" and anarchy with freedom; he pilloried not only the revolutionary radicals, but also the princes, who betrayed the people, talking about the general good while only looking out for themselves. Because of that they bore the chief responsibility for the Revolution. In his view, both sides, the princes and the apostles of freedom, deserved the invectives he aimed at them. Goethe did not, however, believe in radical change: he did not attack the monarchical principle, only its abuses.

The emigration of anti-revolutionary conservatives from France reached its peak in 1792, and with the emigration the counter-revolution spread throughout Europe. The French émigrés preached a crusade against the usurpers, and in the Declaration of Pillnitz (August 27, 1791) they received the public support of the Emperor and the King of Prussia. Because the German princes had threatened to interfere in French internal affairs in order to "secure the foundations of a monarchical form of government," tension increased in France—where the revolutionaries feared for the gains of the Revolution—as well as in Germany.

The ideas of the counter-revolutionaries were received favorably above all in the Electorate of Hanover. Here August Wilhelm Rehberg and Johann Christian Brandes defended the traditions and privileges of the nobility. They did not summarily dismiss all possibility of social advancement for groups and individuals, but that could only be a gradual process and might take generations to be completed.

Whereas earlier the outmoded constitution of the Empire had been blamed for Germany's political and military weakness, it now came to be held up as a model in contrast to the new constitution of the French. In this critical situation, where the Revolution threatened the Empire, only the imperial constitution could save the "common fatherland" (although Schlözer admitted to Wieland that the constitution needed to be modified and brought up to date). This is another sign that the war and the radicalization of the French Revolution had strengthened conservative tendencies in Germany.

Counter-revolutionary ideas also found an echo in the conservative journals. In the *Historische Nachrichten* (Historical News), Christoph Girtanner observed, following Senac de Meilhan, that French finances were the decisive factor because "whoever has the money runs the government." According to Girtanner the middle class had the money, and consequently the political power. From this perspective he denounced both the propaganda of the democrats and the work of the National Assembly, which had caused great harm with its self-contradictory abstractions. In particular, he denounced the damage the National Assembly had done on the night of August 4, 1789, when it had "destroyed in five hours the work of ten centuries" by abolishing most feudal privileges. From his conservative bastion Girtanner commented polemically on the various actions of the revolutionaries and denounced the destructive influence of the masses. The *Journal von und für Deutschland* (Journal of and for Germany), which saw in the French Revolution the work of "vice," feared above all that German subjects would be infected by the "French epidemic of revolution"; and so the journal railed against liberty, equality, and anarchy, the dangerous ideas of the American and French Revolutions which threatened to seduce the masses in Germany as well. The journal called on the princes to destroy the Jacobins, who, under the pretext of fighting against despotism, sought to overthrow all thrones.

An historically influential conspiracy theory arose as well, first evoked in Leopold Alois Hoffmann's *Wiener Zeitschrift* (Vienna Journal) of 1792–1793, which saw in the "present frenzy of freedom" the fruits of an "unrestrained Enlightenment"—a harvest that had undermined both throne and altar. Advocates of the conspiracy theory put forward the notion that the Revolution was not simply the spontaneous work of poor, oppressed peasants, but had been meticulously planned in advance. They denounced the aristocratic despotism of the revolutionary clubs as well as the democratic despotism of the street, while unmasking the "dangerous omnipotence" of the Illuminati and other secret societies and condemning any and all writers who so much as made positive remarks about the Revolution, accusing them of being closet Jacobins preparing for a German revolution. Scarcely had the *Wiener Zeitschrift* ceased publication when the *Revolutionsalmanach* (1793ff.) took up the conspiracy theory, and from 1795 on the journal *Eudämonia* (1795–1798) joined the cause. These journals sought to exorcise the "German democratic demon," calling on the governments to enforce strict measures against the so-called Jacobins, including the strictest possible censorship.

While only a few of those who were denounced deserved to be labeled "Jacobins," the same goes for many who were denounced by the other side as "aristocrats." The German public was indeed divided into opponents and sympathizers of the Revolution. But within the two camps there were significant differences which obscured the meaning of the often used words "aristocrat," "democrat," and "Jacobin."

While the émigrés and the German counter-revolutionaries preached the crusade against revolutionary France, equally strident propaganda came from the republican quarter in response. The Revolution and the war propaganda of the Girondists gained momentum in the autumn of 1791. With the slogan "peace with the cottages, war on the palaces" the French called on the peoples of the world to liberate themselves from the yoke of despots. From Paris and especially from Strasbourg, where many German republicans had taken up residence, they disseminated newspapers and numerous pamphlets, among which must be mentioned Carl Clauer's *Der Kreuzzug gegen die Franken* (The Crusade Against the Franks) of 1791. Clauer depicted skillfully the advantages of a constitutional monarchy, which he contrasted to the despotic caprice and petticoat government of the Bourbons, a government that had exploited its citizens unmercifully. At the same time he unmasked the egotistic arguments of the émigrés. He reasoned that there was nothing to gain by armed intervention, even if the Allies won, because the Bourbons had always proven themselves the enemies of their neighbors; whereas the new French constitution embraced the notion of abolishing wars and establishing a perpetual peace between France and its neighbors. Meanwhile he warned against the dangerous illusion that German armies could manage to subjugate twenty-four million free citizens. The situation would become even worse if the French succeeded in counter-attacking and invading Germany, because then their revolutionary propaganda would be in a position to achieve even greater conquests. It would be far better to extinguish the fire in timely fashion than to allow the turbulence of war to "pour oil onto the fire."

In Germany itself numerous writers raised their voices against the crusade: Herder, Knigge, Klopstock, and Schubart warned their compatriots against a German war of aggression. Since the French had sworn to live free or die, then even the best-thought-out military tactics alone would not be able to conquer them. Such a war in defense of their Revolution would be a holy war for the French, truly the first just war they had ever fought. At the same time German writers were unmasking the war ideology of the French aristocratic émigrés who spoke of fighting for the "fatherland," but really had only their own advantage in mind. Some writers sought to enlighten the people about their own power, maintaining all the while that the people's interests were incompatible with those of the privileged classes. Since it was the counter-revolutionaries who preached the crusade against the revolution and thus defended the *ancien régime*, and it was the German republicans who defended the constitutional monarchy, this war became an ideological struggle, not unlike earlier wars over religion.

When the National Convention declared war on April 20, 1792 against the future Emperor Francis II, King of Hungary and Bohemia, who was also the nephew of Queen Marie Antoinette, many German publicists complained that France had gone back on the solemn renunciation of war which it had announced to the world on May 22, 1790. To argue in this way, however, they had to disregard the provocations of the émigrés and the electors of Trier and Mainz, who had avidly supported them. The Duke of Brunswick's pre-invasion manifesto of late July, 1792 certainly took a one-sided view of things. It threatened the people of Paris with direct reprisals; if the king was harmed, then the Allies would "take a revenge the likes of which had never been seen before and which would be remembered for all eternity." In the end the manifesto led to the downfall of Louis XVI and thus produced the opposite of the effect intended by the Allies.

The Allies had believed that the revolutionary government would collapse like a house of cards as soon as they crossed the border on their march to Paris. The invasion of France revealed their illusions because, as Christian Friedrich Laukhard, Karl Friedrich von Knesebeck and others reported, the lot of the French middle classes and the peasants had improved as a result of the Revolution, and thus they had no desire to reinstate the old régime. There were numerous examples of the true republican spirit, a fact that Goethe noted with admiration and some amazement in his *Campagne in Frankreich 1792* (1822). In view of all this, it became nearly impossible to conduct a successful war against the Revolution. As Goethe asserted *post festum* in *Campagne in Frankreich*, the battle of Valmy (September 20, 1792) denoted an important turning point in European and world history. It was not the beginning of the Revolution that signified the transition from the *ancien régime* to the modern age, but rather the defeat of the Allies, who now could no longer hope to put an end to the Revolution. This transition marked the restructuring of one of the oldest European kingdoms into a republic. While the Allies were retreating from Valmy the revolutionary army of General Adam-Philippe de Custine fulfilled the promise of the Girondists to go on the offensive to liberate other nations, and the people of Mainz founded the first modern republic on German territory. There was widespread fear that the Revolution would spread to other parts of the Holy Roman Empire.

Whereas earlier the Germans had not been much interested in politics, which they had left to their rulers, Schiller complained in 1795 in the introduction to his journal *Die Horen* that the battle of political opinions was now raging in every quarter. Politics had become the favorite topic of the day. Many demanded political and social peace, or (like Kant, Joseph Görres, and Friedrich Schlegel) dreamed out loud of eternal peace. But the call for peace came too late. In his *Friedenspräliminarien*, Ludwig Ferdinand Huber lamented that no one was impartial anymore, and he feared that things would never be the same again. Wieland, who characterized both democratic and aristocratic partisanship as "insanity," provoked the reply from Georg Forster that "impartiality at the present time and under present conditions . . . was neither possible nor permissible." While the terms "Jacobin" and "democrat" became terms of opprobrium for conservatives, democrats castigated their opponents as lackeys-of-despots, slaves, mercenaries, and robbers. As in France, the arguments on both sides were replaced by epithets; polemics displaced discussion, and the intellectual atmosphere was poisoned by such controversies.

In the first phase, revolution and thoroughgoing reform were synonymous, but it became clear soon enough that the French Revolution was not the product of the theories of philosophers, nor was history bound to obey Reason, as German idealists had at first believed. Forster saw the dynamic moment of political progress in "la force des choses," as Saint-Just was to call it, that is to say, in the blind force of the Revolution, the "brute force of the masses." He came to regard this force, the "public opinion," as the dynamic force of progress, because Reason alone was not in a position to defend the Revolution against its opponents. This radicalization of the French Revolution was noted in conservative quarters with great alarm. Gentz now described what was happening as a "total revolution"; the French had decided to cut "all the ties of bourgeois society, in order to bring about a totally new order of things."

The rule of Jacobin terror invited comparisons between the French and American Revolutions, because certain pressing questions confronted all liberals and republicans: how much blood could a total revolution justifiably cost? To what degree must Revolution and Terror necessarily be linked? Whereas in America lawful order and civic peace held sway, it appeared that in France freedom was confused with "bloodthirstiness and rapacity." Over in America, the "rights of humanity" were willingly observed, whereas in France they were continually and systematically violated. Whereas the French Revolution was criticized and denigrated, the example of the American Revolution helped to sustain belief in liberty, equality, and brotherhood in times of political uncertainty, namely during the Terror (at least for the republicans—conservatives took pains to cast the American republic in a negative light, so as to combat the menace posed by the republican spirit).

As the image of the Revolution darkened between 1792 and 1794, the "Franks" became the "Huns of the West" or "Hottentots." In its earliest phase the Germans had compared the French Revolution to a spectacular drama which they thought of as being played out in the neighboring country. Since the advent of the war, however, they had no longer enjoyed the luxury of being mere spectators; the drama had turned to tragedy because in Germany too the social order appeared threatened. Thus writers who had earlier greeted the Revolution as a new "dawn" compared it now to a natural catastrophe, a torrential river, a volcanic eruption, like Goethe in his *Reise der Söhne Megaprazons*.

Under such circumstances it is not surprising that most writers rejected the idea of a revolution for Germany. Even Georg Forster declared that reform suited the German national character far better than revolution. Germany should "learn from the mistakes and suffering of its neighbors." Freedom could be introduced in Germany gradually "from above," the kind of freedom for which France was now struggling "by force, from below and all at once." On this point Wieland agreed with him.

The change of mood was also noticeable in lyric poetry, as in Klopstock's recantation of his former enthusiasm for the Revolution in "Mein Irrtum" (My Error) in 1793. Writing in the same lofty style as before, he now declared that his illusion had been ended when the Jacobins unleashed anarchy and a war of conquest in Europe instead of transforming humanity by bringing it freedom. In 1791 Johann Caspar Lavater, in his "Lied eines Schweizers über die französische Revolution" (Song of a Swiss about the French Revolution), had still proclaimed joyfully that the Revolution had made the dream become reality; in 1792 he cursed the "Jacobin rabble" and the "tyranny of the democrats" in a parody of his own earlier song. Now he sang of the tyranny by which the "proclaimers of equality" had subjugated their fellows. Gleim also cried out against the "inhumanity" of the "hungry" Franks, who oppress the peoples or murder them and destroy their religion instead of treating them as brothers. Numerous poets took the Jacobins to task after Louis XVI's execution, accusing them of merciless cruelty. With the execution of Charlotte Corday in the summer of 1793, an event which, as Wieland declared, presented the problem of justifying political murder, the conservatives and liberals found a popular saint—especially since Marat, who had scorned the legal order, found no admirers in Germany.

After a certain time the Revolution also had an impact on the stage, although it did not inspire any masterpieces until Büchner's *Dantons Tod* of 1835. The theme of revolt was dealt with often in partly fictional historical dramas or tragedies, as in C.H. Ayrenhoff's *Virginia oder das abgeschaffte Decemvirat* (Virginia, or the Abolished Decemvirate) of 1790, in G. Edinhard's *Verschwörung der Pazzi zu Florenz* (Conspiracy of the Pazzi in Florence, 1791), and above all in *Die Kokarden* (The Cockades, 1791), where August Wilhelm Iffland created the stereotype of the Jacobin as a fellow who demands that his accomplices sacrifice all sensitivity and familial ties in the name of "cold Reason" to prove that they are true republicans. Iffland's Jacobin uses his intelligence chiefly to incite the good peasants against traditional authority. After plundering the city in pursuit of their dream of social equality, the peasants finally come to their senses. The play ends with the peasants' submission to the legitimate authority of a prince who forgives them, but not the conspirators. Like Wieland, Iffland derived the principle of paternalistic absolutism from the authority of the father-principle and thereby sanctified princely authority as the best bulwark against the threat of anarchy.

Isenburg von Buri dramatized spectacular moments in the history of the Revolution. In his 1793 play *Ludwig Capet oder der Königsmord* (Louis Capet or the Murder of the King) he portrayed Louis, in the manner of bourgeois tragedy, as the "loyal husband" and "tender father" who preferred "domestic bliss" to the throne and its dazzling vices. Such a drama focused on the human aspect, letting political features recede behind the private facade, but its effect was nonetheless political, since the murder of such a king had to cast those who sentenced him to death in a bad light.

Comedy was put to the purpose of satire, as in August Kotzebue's *Weiblicher Jakobinerklub* (Female Jacobin Club) of 1791 and Goethe's *Bürgergeneral* (The Citizen General) of 1793: Kotzebue's play brings out the discrepancy between the theory and the practice of equality; in Goethe's play, which was staged as a revolution-play with certain make-shift props of the Revolution, a traitor and a betrayed simpleton play out a farce which makes German sympathizers of the Revolution appear ridiculous by depicting them as either egotistical have-nots or simpletons.

Meanwhile the principles of the Revolution were also ridiculed in narrative, as for example in Kotzebue's 1793 *Der lange Hans und die Rechte des Menschen* (Tall Hans and the Rights of Man). In this story a naive apostle of equality is healed of his insanity in the end. Victims of the Revolution who had had to emigrate from France were the heroes and heroines of many a story or novel, or the radical but somewhat naive intellectual could be depicted seeing the light in sentimental or tragic conversion scenes—such was the stuff of works like August Heinrich J. Lafontaine's *Klara du Plessis und Klairant* of 1795, Therese Huber's *Die Familie Seeldorf* of 1795, and Pfeffel's *Louise* of 1796.

Thus after 1791 conservative views were expressed in all genres. On the stage and in lyric poetry there were satirical attacks on both the mistaken notion of freedom and on the revolutionaries' chimerical notion of equality, which necessarily implied anarchy. But the pictures drawn by the fiction writers seem to have been less one-sided than those of the poets and dramatists.

Yet the reactionaries were not the only ones who defamed their opponents in the struggle to shape public opinion. Making use of all the media resources at their disposal, the Mainz Jacobins attempted to "educate" the public through a political learning process and thereby win over their fellow citizens to a republican constitution. They extolled revolutionary principles while satirizing the regime of prerevolutionary electoral Mainz. Recognizing that they could exert a far-reaching influence only if they gained the confidence of their public, their talks became "folk speeches" and their songs became "folk songs." While they made much of their closeness to the folk, much of their production remained indebted to Schiller's philosophical poetry ("Gedankenlyrik"). The poets were more inspired, however, when they took the *Marseillaise* and the *Ça ira* for their models. Such militant songs inspired many in Germany, especially young students, and demonstrated the potential of the political song as a propaganda vehicle and as the common property of all republicans.

While the North German republicans Friedrich Wilhelm von Schütz, Heinrich Würzer, and Georg Friedrich Rebmann helped spread the ideals of the Revolution with their pamphlets and journals at a time when the censorship strove to smother all revolutionary propaganda, the Viennese Jacobins, who disseminated their proclamations and songs in hand-written copy, were more radical in their ideas. They took a stand for social equality and demanded a thoroughgoing revolution, by which they meant a bloody reckoning of accounts with all the "bigwigs" who exploited the people; this is demonstrated, for example, in the famous "Eipeldauerlied."

Thus the war of the quill raged on both sides, especially between 1792 and 1795. But while the counter-revolutionaries could broadcast their attacks in books and journals, or put them on the stage with few constraints, pro-revolutionary writers often encountered major difficulties. Only on the left bank of the Rhine did they have a stage at their disposal; only in the Danish city of Altona could they count on publishing relatively free of censorship. Even then there was no guarantee for the dissemination of their writings. After 1791 it also became very difficult to import revolutionary printed matter into Germany. The republican writers were practically muzzled, disheartened in any case, as is demonstrated by Gottfried August Bürger's little 1794 poem entitled "Goodbye to Politics" ("Entsagung der Politik"):

Ade Frau Politik! Sie mag sich fürbaß trollen:
Die Schrift-Zensur ist heut zu Tage scharf.
Was mancher Edle will, scheint er oft nicht zu sollen;
Dagegen, was er schreiben soll und darf,
Kann doch ein Edler oft nicht wollen.

(Adieu Lady Politics! Just keep lurching along: these days the censorship is strict. Many a noble soul wants what is not allowed; and what he is encouraged and allowed to write is not at all what he can want.)

4. Political Freedom or Moral Education?

In Germany, too, the Ninth of Thermidor (July 27, 1794) was considered the turning point of the French Revolution. Republicans and conservatives alike appeared to rejoice at the downfall of Robespierre, the "worst of the tyrants," the horrible one, or whatever other ugly names they gave him when celebrating his posthumous fame in prose and verse. This joyful reaction of the Germans gave the impression of a certain unanimity of opinion, reminiscent of the early period of the Revolution. In the German periodicals there began a campaign to downsize the dictator. Whereas Ludwig Ferdinand Huber sought to explain Robespierre's tyranny psychologically, Andreas Riem approached the problem from a political point of view, arguing that Robespierre and his cohorts had embraced the Terror as their only alternative under the circumstances, as the only means of reaching their goals for the Revolution.

The Directory, which came to power in 1795, was viewed very critically by Rebmann because it persecuted the "patriots" and because corruption was everywhere. In general, however, the Directory aroused hope that the nightmare of spreading revolution had been ended, since it had concluded the Peace of Basel, a treaty that (for a time) brought Northern Germany a deceptive easing of tensions. Since France adopted a new liberal constitution, the intellectuals calmed down somewhat in print. Still, it was not long before reactionary publicists, in order to combat enthusiasm for the new constitution of 1795, began to claim again that democracy would necessarily lead to anarchy and despotism. Thus the bourgeois government in France also strengthened the hand of the reactionaries in Germany, whose intentions Huber revealed: they hoped that freedom of the press would disappear again with the Revolution. Even Riem acknowledged that "any revolution is an evil," because revolution always leads to anarchy, and he concluded that "the masses should never have the vote." With regard to the excesses of the Jacobin Terror, even republicans believed that political equality and democracy were suited only for a divine people, as Rousseau had claimed in his *Contrat Social*; but they were not suited for ordinary mortals, as Wieland too had stated repeatedly. Kant considered democracy a "despotism" because it did not respect the "constitutional principle" of the separation of executive and legislative powers, a principle that the Germans took to be the essential characteristic of republicanism.

At the same time, the dilemma as to whether political freedom should take precedence over moral education attracted new attention. On the one hand, Forster, Kant, and Görres maintained along with Laukhard that "freedom from material need and political oppression" was an indispensable prerequisite for moral education. On the basis of this insight, the German Jacobins had reached the conclusion that one first had to educate people about the social and political requirements of moral freedom so that they could eventually gain this freedom. In the same spirit, the Romantics in Jena concurred with Würzer that "civil and moral liberty" could only be achieved together; but they also believed that "without wisdom and virtue no free constitution can exist." Herder, however, noted that the higher development of mankind could not be expected to result from revolution; rather, it could only be achieved by better education. Wieland, Schiller, and Adam Weishaupt reached the same conclusion, namely that moral education (in Schiller's case, aesthetic education) must take precedence over political emancipation. Thus, in the words of Matthias Claudius, the person must be improved first—not the constitution.

Since Northern Germany was removed from the battle against the Revolution by the line of demarcation determined at the Peace of Basel, and since the Directory fought against the Jacobins and the Sansculottes in France and thus distanced itself from the Jacobins in Southern Germany, the dream of a German revolution and a German republic faded in the 1790s. Whereas the French consuls proclaimed in 1799 that the Revolution was completed, Görres, Hölderlin, and the Romantics in Jena maintained that the work of the Revolution had only just begun; since the French Revolution had foundered, the work of raising mankind now fell to the Germans. In Germany, which slowly but surely would take the lead from other nations, the traces of a new world could already be seen, as Novalis announced, in agreement with Herder and Schiller, in his *Die Christenheit oder Europa* (Christianity or Europe). Thus admiration for the French, who (as Klopstock had noted with envy) had introduced the political revolution, ended with an apologia affirming the moral and cultural mission of the Germans. The people of poets and thinkers now seemed destined to prepare the true Revolution, the Revolution of the Mind.

Since the French Revolution did not provoke a revolution in Germany, numerous scholars have believed themselves justified in maintaining that the Germans were incapable of carrying out a revolution. Without a doubt the German habit of submissiveness to higher authority still played a noticeable role in the eighteenth century, as can be concluded from the exceptionally moderate character of the German Enlightenment. Nevertheless, such a generalization overlooks the fact that a revolution is also always the result of a breakdown, signaling that the society is at a developmental impasse. This is not to say that the absence of a revolution is be taken as a sign of virtue in a society or nation, as some conservatives would gladly believe. It can with equal justice be taken as a sign of lacking enlightenment or rigidity, because, as Tocqueville has taught us, revolutions do not begin just because the people are oppressed; rather, they break out whenever the reins are loosened a bit after first having been held too tightly. This was surely the case with the French Revolution.

In light of the division into rival camps, the German reception of the French Revolution cannot be taken to mirror the mentality of the Germans; the written record allows us at best to grasp the mentality of the class responsible for intellectual culture at the end of the eighteenth century. And, for all that, we must not overlook the differences between the south of Germany, where the tensions between tradition and revolution (and even democracy) were greater, and the Protestant north, which was more strongly marked by the Enlightenment and more inclined to republicanism. Aside from the extremists among the counter-revolutionaries on the one side and those among the revolutionary democrats on the other, most writers seem to have been liberal-minded, placing more stock in evolution than in revolution. They could see either truly enlightened monarchy or constitutional monarchy as the form of government that corresponded to the spirit of the times; Kant himself expressed his preference for the latter.

The French Revolution was without a doubt a challenge to the German princes to reform their states in the spirit of the times. Moreover, the reception of the Revolution in general contributed greatly to the political education of the Germans. In the final analysis, however, the war and the attendant radicalization of the Revolution, and especially the final displacement of the Revolution by a dictatorship, dashed hopes for reforms and political education in Germany, since the French example could only be attractive to the hotheads. In Germany the reactionaries triumphed in the end. Not until the critical period between 1806 and 1813 did the Prussian reformers demonstrate that they did not just abhor the French Revolution, but that they had learned from it as well. Many of the promises made by the rulers in order to enlist the support of their subjects in the struggle were nullified by the Congress of Vienna in 1815; nevertheless, the dream of the revolution lived on in the minds of many members of the German liberal student movement and survived into the so-called *Vormärz*, the prerevolutionary period between 1815 and 1848.

W. DANIEL WILSON

Internalizing the Counter-Revolution: Wieland and the Illuminati Scare[1]

TIMES OF POLITICAL UPHEAVAL OFTEN produce far-fetched theories to explain confusing events, and at the beginning of modern political turmoil during the French Revolution one of the most bizarre such theories arose, one that is still operative even today: the notion that the Germans were responsible for the cataclysm in France. In the words of one of the most extreme adherents of this theory, Leopold Alois Hoffmann, in 1793:

> It is not the French who are ... the real inventors of this grand project of turning the world upside down; that honor goes to the Germans. ... The French only have the distinction of having been the ones who began carrying it out. ... The political committees that gave rise to the Jacobin Club had their origin in Illuminatism, which started in Germany, and—far from having been snuffed out—is operating underground and has become all the more dangerous.[2]

While this conspiracy theory evokes little more than bemusement among most of us today, it played a major role in nineteenth-century politics; and as Johannes Rogalla von Bieberstein has shown, the Nazis were guided by this idea in their persecution of Freemasons. In fact, it can even be found haunting the pages of reputable modern scholarship.[3] More important for our purposes, it was one of the most important conservative discourses of the revolutionary period.

Adam Weishaupt and his followers certainly frightened many people in the 1780s and after. He founded the secret society of the Illuminati at Ingolstadt in 1776; within a few years it had grown to over two thousand members, not only in Bavaria but in Northern Germany and the Rhineland. While generally the goals of the Illuminati were of a broadly enlightened and moral-pedagogic nature, some of their writings pointed the way toward abolition of the state: In a speech meant only for the highest ranks of the order, Weishaupt wrote: "Monarchs and nations will disappear from the earth without recourse to violence."[4] Such statements were less radical than they seemed to outsiders, since their tactics involved a very long-term process of moral improvement—their goals were not revolutionary, but rather an expression of the ideal of enlightened absolutism. Still, the Illuminati operated by infiltrating the government, recruiting as members the highest civil servants and even princes, and this process seemed very conspiratorial. When the Illuminati were suppressed by the Bavarian and other governments in 1784–1785, and when some confiscated documents were published in 1786 and 1787, Germans were generally stunned at this apparent plot against the political and social order. Consider the book by a Privy Councillor in the Duchy of Weimar, Ernst August von Göchhausen of Eisenach: *Enthüllung des Systems der Weltbürger-Republik* (The System of the Cosmopolitan Republic Revealed, 1786): this important conspiracy theorist warns already in 1786 of "inevitable revolutions that I expect and predict with certainty," which would be the results of Illuminati activity.[5] When the French Revolution broke out in 1789, it did not take long for conservatives and even moderates to associate the Illuminati with it. As Jochen Hoffmann has written, faced with the shock of 1789 people remembered all too well the scandal that had been caused by the publication of the Illuminati papers.[6] Two of the German conspiracy theorists later claimed that when they heard the news of the storming of the Bastille, they had looked at each other and said simultaneously: "That is the work of the Illuminati,"[7] and such conclusions hardly seemed wild even to reasonable intellectuals. By 1793 the conservatives had found what seemed to them to be a smoking gun: one of the leading Illuminati, Johann Christoph Bode, and a companion had visited Parisian Freemasons—among them many future leading revolutionaries—just two years before the outbreak of the Revolution. Leopold Alois Hoffmann and others quickly spun out a tale that had these Illuminati organizing cells that formed the basis of the Jacobin Clubs and therefore directly instigating the Revolution.[8] The flip side of the conspiracy theory was the notion that the French Revolutionary government fomented insurrection in the rest of Europe through Masonic fronts.

Surprisingly, scholars have hardly touched on the significance of the Illuminati for German literature. Their interest has largely been limited to Schiller's *Don Carlos* or to Goethe's membership in the order.[9] Part of this neglect stems from ignorance of the facts: Most literary scholars—in fact, most historians—rely for information about the Illuminati on the work first published by Richard van Dülmen in 1975.[10] Van Dülmen, however, generally underemphasizes the significance and the membership of the order, as especially Ernst-Otto Fehn has pointed out.[11] The significance of the order for the literary elite lay not in any political radicalism, but rather in their attitudes toward the conspiracy theory. After the political program of the Illuminati was made public in the late 1780s and especially after these implications seemed to have been realized in the Revolution, some of the most important literary figures were concerned that their real or imagined associations with the order might taint them politically, and I wish to suggest that their political conservatism might partly be explained in this light. Since I have already treated Goethe and other Weimar Illuminati in another study,[12] I will limit myself in this paper to Wieland.

First, some preliminary facts that have been overlooked. Van Dülmen reports that Bode, the Illuminati who was supposed to have instigated the French Revolution on his 1787 journey to Paris, and who had been living in Weimar since 1778, recruited members of the Masonic lodge "Anna Amalia" in Weimar as Illuminati. Van Dülmen goes on to say that "supposedly" even Carl August, Goethe, and Herder signed on, "but nothing is known of any particular society activity in Weimar" (66), and most literary scholars let it rest with this ambiguous statement. As Fehn has pointed out, van Dülmen was unaware that Goethe and others were *definitely* Illuminati; there were at least fifteen members of the Illuminati lodge at Weimar. Among them were three of the four members of the Privy Council: Duke Carl August himself, Goethe, and Jakob Friedrich von Fritsch, as well as a future member of the Council, Christian Gottlob Voigt. The other Illuminati besides Bode included Herder.[13] We also know that Karl Leonhard Reinhold, the noted Kantian professor of philosophy in Jena and Wieland's son-in-law, was an Illuminati (though van Dülmen does not include him on his list of Illuminati).[14] One need only add that Weishaupt was harbored by the duke of nearby Saxe-Gotha, and that Bode—whom the conspiracy theorist Hoffmann called "the greatest lever of the French Revolution"[15]—was happily ensconced in Weimar, eating regularly at the duke's table, to understand why reactionaries felt sure that "the whole Weimar School," in the words of one scholar, was a "nest of Illuminatism."[16] It turns out that the Weimar Illuminati, who were indeed an important center of the organization, did not share any of the radical political goals put forth in some of the secret Illuminati documents, but the important factor here is the *perception* of political subversiveness. Duke Carl August was already suspect among reactionaries for his liberal rule, and since these reactionaries believed that "almost all of our rulers are surrounded by Illuminati"[17] the duchy that harbored such a dangerous Illuminati as Bode was automatically at the top of the watch list. After the suppression of the Illuminati the members of the Weimar lodge must have lived with a certain fear that the information about their associations with the society would become public. They had not only a public relations disaster to fear, but the disapproval of their powerful neighbors, Electoral Saxony and Prussia, that would result from such accusations. Saxony's reactionary politics are well known; for example, Karl-Heinz Fallbacher has established beyond doubt that it was Saxon pressure and the threat to recall all of its students from the University of Jena that forced Carl August to dismiss Fichte in 1799 (Fichte had been tarred as an Illuminati as early as 1796, and this attack probably partly motivated the Saxon campaign against him).[18] And in Prussia, where Frederick II's death in 1786 had led to the obscurantist reign of Frederick William II, the new king had hatched a crude conspiracy theory within months of the outbreak of the Revolution, warning the Elector of Saxony about the Illuminati and the danger of a recurrence of the French cataclysm in Germany.[19] Small territories were anything but sovereign and independent of the larger powers; for example, when a new repression of former Illuminati seemed to be brewing in 1793, Weishaupt felt that even his own duke would not be able to protect him—and the prince of Schleswig-Holstein-Augustenburg was willing to promise him sanctuary only if he lived *incognito*.[20] Weimar, too, had felt pressure from its larger neighbors in the past, and for economic reasons it had to be careful not to provoke them again. Thus the former Illuminati in the government itself had to fear direct economic consequences for Weimar because of their past affiliations; but even former Illuminati who were not themselves government officials had to realize that the Weimar government might give in to pressure from abroad and persecute them; a writer in 1792 asked rhetorically about this sort of reactionary pressure: "Will even princes like —* dare to resist manfully the insinuations and presumptions of powerful courts with whom they disagree?"[21] It is doubtless because of such fears that we do not know much about the (former) Illuminati in Northern Germany; they had to hide their discussions of the organization, sometimes even writing letters in code.[22]

However, the conspiracy theorists were not very careful about whom they branded as Illuminati; evidence was for them a minor point. Consequently, non-Illuminati intellectuals often had to defend themselves against their accusations; as Rogalla von Bieberstein points out, "even in the Protestant part of Germany enlightened intellectuals were put on the defensive because of the Illuminati scandals" (85). Wieland falls into this category: he had never been an Illuminati, but he was widely suspected of it.

Wieland's problems were twofold. First, a list of books that the Illuminati leaders recommended to their novices was included among the confiscated Illuminati papers published in 1787, and three of Wieland's writings were among the twenty works on the list.[23] The next year, two of those titles were on a similar list recommended to members of the Deutsche Union,[24] which was—and often still is—widely viewed as a successor organization to the Illuminati.[25] Second, Wieland's novel *Die Abderiten* (1774–1780) contained references to a metaphorical "Orden der Kosmopoliten" (Order of Cosmopolitans), and some took the reference literally, identifying this 'order' with the Illuminati. The Illuminati had in fact made extensive use of cosmopolitan sentiments in the writings and documents that were made public in 1787.[26] And these "cosmopolitan" ideas had provided the basis for conservative attacks on the Illuminati, as in the book by Göchhausen mentioned above, where we read: "The feeling of being a world citizen. What does that mean? . . . You are a citizen of the state, or you are a rebel. There's no other possibility" (177). In these ways, Wieland had unwittingly led others to see Illuminati principles in his writings.

The reaction to Göchhausen's remarkable book is the first evidence of Wieland's rapprochement with the conspiracy theory.[27] In 1786 Wieland had asked his son-in-law Reinhold to praise it in a review in the *Teutscher Merkur*, but Reinhold wrote a critical review instead.[28] Wieland's approval probably is to be attributed to one of Göchhausen's most insistent theses, the assertion that none other than the Jesuits (who had been banned in 1773) secretly controlled an important secret society (by which Göchhausen rather transparently meant the Illuminati). The notion that the Illuminati were controlled by the Jesuits, whom they had originally been formed to combat, certainly seems bizarre to us today, but it had gained a certain credence in the confusing atmosphere of the 1780s. It had been championed by none other than Biester in the *Berlinische Monatsschrift*, and Wieland himself made clear his agreement with Biester.[29] One must remember that Wieland had for many years been an outspoken enemy of the Jesuits and their machinations at European courts, and I think it is in this context that we must see his consistent and often-repeated aversion to all secret societies.[30] He seems to have tolerated the Illuminati around him silently; as we saw, his son-in-law Reinhold was an active one; in fact, documents recently brought to light show that at this time Reinhold, together with Bode, was one of the leaders of the North German Illuminati.[31] Reinhold not only participated in the reinvigoration of the order after its suppression in Bavaria, but even conferred with Bode on the document Bode had prepared for his infamous trip to Paris in 1787[32] and participated in discussions on reviving the order as late as the mid-1790s.[33] One can imagine that Wieland was very uncomfortable with Reinhold's Illuminati connections, if he knew about them; in any case, he knew that Reinhold had not praised Göchhausen's conspiracy theories, as Wieland had expected, but had ridiculed them. It is perhaps not far-fetched to speculate that the cool relations between Wieland and Reinhold may have been caused by such differences over the Illuminati, and even that Reinhold's removal from Weimar to Jena—at the height of the persecution of Illuminati, in 1787!—may have been due to these differences. After all, Schiller reports, after speaking to Reinhold: "Although he loves Reinhold more than anyone else on earth, Wieland is the one who really drove him from Weimar with his bad moods and his alternating affection for and rejection of him. Today he calls him a great mind and tomorrow he calls him an ass."[34] Wieland's hatred for the Jesuits led him to reject *all* secret societies; Reinhold's hatred for the Jesuits led him to join the Illuminati. What initially seemed to unite the two men may have led to tension between them.

Aside from this personal connection to Illuminati, the appearance of Wieland's works on Illuminati reading lists and their Wielandian "cosmopolitan" aspirations forced him to respond. In August and October of 1788, Wieland published in the *Merkur* an essay entitled *Das Geheimnis des Kosmopolitenordens* (The Secret of the Society of Cosmopolitans).[35] Here he clearly pronounces his intent to distance himself from associations with the Illuminati; the word "Secret" in his title is used ironically to indicate that true cosmopolitans do not need secrecy, because, as he declares with disarming optimism, "The time has finally come when nothing that is good needs to shun the light; at least this time has come for Germany" (552). According to him, the "Kosmopoliten" can tell the world without shame who they are and what their program is (553). It turns out, in fact, that the cosmopolitans have *no* "secret" at all (556). In short, "true cosmopolitans can't and won't stand by idly any longer while secret societies . . . give the impression that they use the same means and have the same goals as cosmopolitans . . . and are capable of working with them in a common cause" (552). In fact, here as elsewhere Wieland calls for banning secret societies:[36] "[The cosmopolitans] say it is quite clear that any independent organization whose members have sworn oaths and whose existence is not authorized by the highest authorities, with full knowledge of their undertaking, is a kind of conspiracy that leads to establishing a state within the state which can become dangerous and harmful to society" (555). Other remarks make clear that he is speaking of the Illuminati.[37] Wieland's intimation that any secret society is *eo ipso* "a kind of conspiracy" leads him close to the camp that prepared the way for the conspiracy theory, by way of distancing himself in no uncertain terms from an association that he thought was dangerous and that he probably thought would ruin his reputation. Though Wieland was honestly scandalized by the Illuminati, he muddles the debate somewhat by indicating that the Cosmopolitans, who are contrasted with the Illuminati throughout the essay, would never take part in a violent revolution (563), thus suggesting a revolutionary Illuminati program; the Illuminati, in fact, explicitly opposed violent insurrection. Thus we find Wieland among that group of conservatives who paved the way for the conspiracy theory's identification of "Illuminati" and "Jacobins." There are, to be sure, certain inconsistencies in the essay, as when Wieland suggests that a cosmopolitan would not hesitate an instant to support the "future representatives" of the French nation, if these would only embrace the idea of putting reasonable and appropriate limits on the arbitrary power of the king and his ministers (566); but of course Wieland had no idea that the convening of the Estates General in 1788 would be followed by revolutionary violence in the following years. Still, this passage, as well as Wieland's vigorous support for a free and critical press, gives this essay a flavor of liberality that clashes with its polemic against the Illuminati.[38] We thus begin to see a political split in Wieland, for which we may perhaps modify Foucault's concept of 'dividing practices' that the imperatives of power dictate to the individual. At heart a liberal, Wieland's nervousness over public identifications of him with Illuminati forced him to take a position that drove him closer to a reactionary camp with which he would not consciously wish to be associated.

Something of Wieland's private opinions on the Illuminati can be gleaned from a conversation—hitherto entirely overlooked in Wieland research[39]— with a young Bavarian Illuminati, Clemens Neumayr, very shortly before the storming of the Bastille in 1789.[40] Though Wieland said that the Illuminati's progress demonstrated the "energy" of the Bavarians and showed that great things could be expected of them, and though he disapproved of the harsh repression of the Illuminati, he still felt that on the whole the demise of the order was a good thing. Then he repeated his disapproval of all secret societies. Wieland's assessment here is remarkably more balanced than his public pronouncements. This contrast indicates again that his harsh *public* condemnation of the order was an attitude forced on him partly by the dictates of power. This thesis is supported by the hardening of his attitudes toward the Illuminati and the conspiracy theory in the following years, as the Revolution put pressure on liberals.

The first evidence of this attitude can be found in 1791, in Wieland's postscript to a long account of the life of the so-called Count Cagliostro (Joseph Balsamo) in the *Teutscher Merkur*.[41] The report consists mainly of evidence from Cagliostro's interrogation by the Roman Inquisition in 1790, in which this confidence man told of his supposed connection, before the Revolution, with leading Illuminati, who allegedly had planned to "eradicate" all the "despotic" rulers, and who had decided that France was to be the first target, and after that, Rome.[42] The conspiracy theorists quickly seized on this confession and painted Cagliostro as the secret chief of the Illuminati and the main instigator of the French Revolution.[43] Though Wieland has some questions about the reliability of the report itself, he believes that Cagliostro's interrogation shows clearly

> that the European states are nourishing *secret societies* at their breast, and that these will ... form a *state within the state*, and what is even worse, an *invisible* state within the *visible* one; and, whatever they want us to believe about their means and ends, their goals are almost certainly not entirely *pure*. (377)

This dark warning echoes what Wieland had written in the 'Kosmopoliten'-essay of 1788, and clearly refers to the same organization he had attacked then, the Illuminati.[44] But after the beginning of the Revolution and the full-blown conspiracy theory that accompanied it, such a statement is now laden with much more serious political implications. To be sure, Wieland criticizes the harsh persecution of former Illuminati, just as he had done in his conversation with Neumayr. And he goes on to suggest that if princes were to reform their realms and allow complete freedom of expression, the *raison d'être* for such politically dangerous secret societies would disappear (378–79)—such were the persistent illusions of Enlightenment belief in absolutism. But when he denies that Cagliostro's sect of "pyramidal Masonry" could have caused the French Revolution (378), Wieland leaves open the question as to whether the *Illuminati* could have done so—a question that had been raised in the Cagliostro report that he published. And his assertion of the existence of such dangerous organizations furnished ammunition to the conspiracy theorists in their crusade against liberals. Furthermore, Wieland supported this notion of the continued existence of seditious Illuminati at a time when, as far as he later claimed to have known (from his friend Bode), they had definitively disbanded (see below). In addition, Bode had published in the previous year a book in which he had exploded the myth that Cagliostro was "Chief of the Illuminati" and shown that the myth had arisen not in Italy, but among German counter-revolutionary journalists.[45] In fact, some of the most absurdly irrational conspiracy theorists avoided using Cagliostro as a source of information, since he was obviously so unreliable,[46] so that Wieland finds himself here in very bad company indeed. While pleading for reform and for freedom of the press in the style of the liberalism and reform conservatism of the day, Wieland, a highly respected publicist, delivered to the conspiracy theorists and other reactionaries ready-made excuses for repression.

The result of Wieland's tactics was that in early 1792 friends of the Revolution still felt they could count him as a supporter, whereas by later in the same year the conspiracy theorists could with a great deal of justification claim him as their own. In January, 1792, the Parisian *Moniteur Universel* attacked the foremost proponent of the conspiracy theory, Leopold Alois Hoffmann, in the same article in which it lavishly praised Wieland.[47] Hoffmann himself mentioned Wieland several times in his infamous *Wiener Zeitschrift* (Viennese Journal); in the very first issue (Jan. 1792) Hoffmann charges that Wieland, after years of deftly obscuring his position, had finally taken the part of the liberals in a *Teutscher Merkur* note directed against Göchhausen.[48] Hoffmann also attacks another *Teutscher Merkur* article in this issue[49] (just before an article in which he identifies the Illuminati as the cause of revolutions[50]). Thus, in early 1792 the *Moniteur Universel* in Paris and its polar opposite, the *Wiener Zeitschrift*, agree that Wieland fosters a liberal attitude toward the Revolution—each side apparently saw in pieces like Wieland's comments on Cagliostro exactly what it wanted to see. But by September of the same year, Hoffmann was heaping praise on Wieland; he quotes ten full pages from an article Wieland had published in July, and concludes, "the agreement of a *Wieland* with the principles I have adhered to for so long (which are contested only by short-sighted people or by revolutionary sympathizers) cannot but afford me right honorable satisfaction."[51] Martin Ehlers, a professor in Kiel, had attacked Hoffmann in a pro-revolutionary article for the *Teutscher Merkur*. Wieland had responded by criticizing Ehlers's views, and it is Wieland's response which Hoffmann approvingly quotes at length. What had happened to Wieland in the intervening months that allowed Hoffmann to make this claim?. Of course, the radicalization of the Revolution itself by July, 1792 in itself had led Wieland to a less liberal standpoint. But I think there were more compelling reasons why Wieland slowly worked himself into a position where the conspiracy theorists could claim him as one of their own. Wieland knew which way the wind was blowing. Hoffmann had become a powerful figure. He was very close to his patron, Emperor Leopold II, before the latter's death in March, 1792,[52] and initially he also enjoyed the favor of Leopold's successor, Francis II.[53] Hoffmann paraded his influence for all to see: in two letters he published in the *Wiener Zeitschrift*, the reactionary Prussian king Frederick William II praised Hoffmann's efforts and pledged to support them; in an obvious reference to the conspiracy theory, the king urged Hoffmann to continue his efforts to unmask "the *secret* machinations of a *hidden* band" of shady and malevolent people who would sooner or later be chastened by the "avenging sword of divine and human justice."[54] It was becoming very clear that power was decidedly on the side of counter-revolution and the conspiracy theory. Hoffmann never tired of reminding his readers of this fact; for example, just before criticizing Ehlers and praising Wieland he published the text of the manifestos issued by the Prussian king and the Duke of Brunswick at the opening of hostilities in July, 1792, and he invoked the manifestos repeatedly in the article praising Wieland.[55]

In Weimar, too, power was on the side of repression. Student disturbances in Jena fed the fears of conspiratorial secret societies, and at almost exactly the same time as Hoffmann was gleefully approving Wieland's political position, Carl August, who was at the front fighting the French revolutionary armies, sharply criticized Wieland's supposed interventions in politics. In a letter that I published in my recent book, the duke demands that scholars and intellectuals should not, "as Wieland had often claimed they had a right to do, look upon themselves in the future as the teachers of rulers and peoples."[56] The addressee of this letter, the Weimar minister of state Christian Gottlob Voigt, relayed other warnings in the duke's message to Professor Gottlieb Hufeland, and it is entirely plausible that he (or Hufeland) might have passed on the duke's warning to Wieland, too. In any case, Wieland now behaved entirely as if he had, indeed, been warned by the duke to avoid publishing politically suspect remarks.

Like Hoffmann, Wieland's readers now began to notice his leanings toward the conspiracy theorists; a letter from a hostile reader late in 1792 pointed out that the "aristocratic principles" espoused in Wieland's essays in the *Teutscher Merkur* had even gained him the approval and support of an Alois Hoffmann.[57] In his reply, Wieland represses the recognition of the company into which he has put himself and the betrayal of his native liberality that the former associations with the Illuminati have put him. His dishonesty is evident when he denies ever having heard of Hoffmann—a denial disproved by the mentions of Hoffmann in Ehlers's essay,[58] and by Wieland's earlier apparent interest in Alxinger's attack on Hoffmann.[59] The false denial of ever knowing about Hoffmann corresponds to the false denial—the repression—of being allied with him.[60]

This alliance reached its zenith when Wieland opened the October, 1793, issue of the *Teutscher Merkur* with an essay entitled "Neuer merkwürdiger Beweis des Daseyns und der gefährlichen Thätigkeit einer französisch-teutschen Aufrührer-Propaganda"; the anonymous author rehashes one of the favorite themes of the conspiracy theory: the myth, invented by a French emigré in Germany, that a French "Club de Propagande," with enormous sums of money at its disposal, was operating through Masonic lodges to prepare a revolution in Germany.[61] It is very significant that the conspiracy theorist submits this article to Wieland's journal, since he claims in a letter that Wieland shares his political views, and he bases this claim on Wieland's writings (113 n.). To his credit, Wieland's general political position in his annotations to this article is less conservative than that of the article's author; and in his introductory note Wieland hedges on the question of the existence of such a conspiracy. In a succeeding note, however, he speaks of this "secret society" as a given fact.[62] The gap between Wieland's mild liberal criticism of this article and his affirmation of the existence of the conspiracy that it asserts is a good indicator of the division forced on him by the Illuminati who had associated his ideas with their political program. In any case, the publication of the article was certainly a blow in favor of the conspiracy theory. Now, more than ever, it became clear to contemporaries that Wieland was toeing the line of the conspiracy theorists. The article provoked a stinging reply in the liberal *Schleswigsches Journal*, which begins by ascertaining that in the *Teutscher Merkur* over the last year Wieland, contrary to his usual principles, had "raised the banner of an unliberated way of thinking," and that he is now propagating an idiotic fairy tale about—and here the author quotes Wieland himself—a supposed secret society which has as its goal the "violent overthrow of all civil society and all the presently existing forms of government in Europe." He points out that not even an arch-conservative like Gentz believes in this legend.[63] The author points out all the obvious signs that this article in the *Teutscher Merkur* is a fabrication, and chastises Wieland for printing it: "What terrible nonsense! How unworthy of being published in a journal which up to now has circulated so many fine ideas in Germany!" Regarding Wieland's footnote asserting the existence of the "Club de Propagande," the writer asks how Wieland could possibly have been so taken in by such an old wives' tale.[64] Fortunately, this episode marks both the extreme and the end of Wieland's collusion with the conspiracy theorists.

After Bode, the prime suspect in the conspiracy theory, died at the end of 1793, Wieland's co-editor at the *Teutscher Merkur*, Carl August Böttiger, wrote a necrology defending Bode against the charges of Hoffmann, whom he calls a "worthless Viennese scribbler." He claims that Bode had worked as an Illuminati to further the noblest causes of mankind, but had criticized the organization when Weishaupt and Knigge's human foibles began to dominate.[65] One of Wieland's closest associates had thus openly attacked the conspiracy theorists and identified himself with their enemies. In turn, Hoffmann gleefully pounced on Böttiger; fully a third of his infamous "biography" of Bode—one of the central documents of the conspiracy theory—is directed against Böttiger's short piece.[66] Hoffmann gloats triumphantly that the necrology shows that Böttiger himself is an Illuminati, since he had disclosed that Bode was the traveller to Paris whom Hoffmann had never actually identified. Hoffmann even insinuates that Bode's still anonymous companion "B" may have been Böttiger himself.[67]

In 1795 Wieland burned his bridges, finally joining the fray against Hoffmann and consorts. He published a letter from a correspondent in Hamburg defending Bode's reputation, and wrote a postscript himself forcefully attacking the "despicable slanders" directed against the man who had been his friend for fourteen years, claiming categorically that Bode would never have supported violent insurrection.[68] Even here, Wieland takes the opportunity to repeat that he himself has never belonged to such secret organizations (217). He still seems somewhat frightened of the conspiracy theory, but he has the courage to attack it when it concerns his deceased friend Bode and his living colleague Böttiger—perhaps because it also concerns the reputation of Weimar in general. After this episode, criticism of the conspiracy theory surfaces sporadically in the *Teutscher Merkur* for years, especially from Böttiger's pen; not only is Hoffmann's book on Bode in one instance called a "despicable squib,"[69] but Abbé Augustin de Barruel's monster compilation on the conspiracy theory, which appeared in 1797,[70] comes in for criticism by a contributor from London. Ironically, he calls Barruel's thesis an "old wives' tale,"[71] the same epithet applied to Wieland's ideas about the "Propaganda" by his critic in 1793. Böttiger writes a supportive footnote to the critique of Barruel, claiming that it is well known that as of the year 1790 *all* Illuminati organizations had ceased to exist (267 n.).

The final chapter in Wieland's relations to the Illuminati and the conspiracy theory can be summarized briefly, since Fritz Martini has told most of it in more detail.[72] The old suspicion that Wieland had been an Illuminati finally came home to haunt him. Wieland had suggested in 1798 that the French should anoint Bonaparte as dictator to save themselves from anarchy. After this suggestion became reality the next year, a journal close to the British court, relying on information from a (probably German[73]) "foreign Minister," attacked the "German author Wieland" as an accomplice, claiming that Wieland's suggestion had in fact been a surreptitious effort to alert fellow Illuminati to the fact that Napoleon would be an acceptable leader. Wieland was forced to defend himself, and in his defense he comes out against the conspiracy theory, although not quite straightforwardly, by means of his favorite vehicle, irony; he ridicules the British notion that the Illuminati are a "horrible and accursed sect" which, according to Barruel and Robison, has "declared war on God and man and works toward no lesser goal than the complete destruction of all civil, religious, and moral order."[74] In a footnote Wieland opines that it is highly unlikely that such a "sect or secret society" actually exists (273). Though his colleague Böttiger had for years ridiculed Barruel and Robison at every opportunity,[75] this is the only point at which Wieland definitively reversed himself and rejected the conspiracy theory. He did so only after it had touched him personally, and only after the Revolution had settled into a less threatening phase after 1795; in these years the conspiracy theorists rapidly lost power and influence (not least of all because of the advancing French armies), which is shown clearly by the fate of the *Eudämonia*, the successor to Hoffmann's journal, which had to move from Leipzig to Frankfurt to Nürnberg in the few years of its existence (1795–1798). It was much safer to attack the conspiracy theory during the years of French dominance in Germany, and Wieland's attitude in this period contrasts sharply to his pandering to the conspiracy theorists during their heyday in 1793.

***

It is only fair to add here that the conspiracy theory perhaps represents the only way many people could really understand the Revolution. Class-based social movements were alien to Germany, which had no masses comparable to the politicized urban Parisian proletariat. Many Germans thus looked for other causes of the Revolution, and they felt compelled to overlay the events of class discontent with a dynamic that had the *individual subject*, the conspirator, at its center. This impulse has always fed conspiracy theories; as Epstein points out, "This type of theory has often proved very attractive to beneficiaries of a threatened *status quo* because of its optimistic implications: if the danger of revolution arises from the merely subjective will of a few conspirators—rather than the inexorable, objective development of social forces—then this danger can be removed simply by efficient police work, and there is no need for far-reaching reforms to remove genuine grievances" (503). In addition, any revolutionary movement contains conspiratorial elements. The French Revolution was no exception,[76] so that events (such as Bode's journey to Paris) seemed to offer confirmation of the theory. By the same token, secret societies were clearly the only oppositional political (or quasi-political) institution to which eighteenth-century intellectuals had recourse, and they have been rightly seen as forerunners of the political parties of the modern era,[77] so that when Wieland suggested banning all secret societies, he was effectively insisting on an end to all oppositional political activity (ridiculously ineffective though it might have been), which would have helped to cement the dominance of the feudal order. Thus there are two sides to the conspiracy theories. I would like to stress both the difficulties of intellectuals struggling to comprehend a novel and baffling phenomenon and to impose order on it, and their own socio-political interests, their inextricable participation in the structures of power, which prejudice the outcome of their struggle to comprehend. So an inevitable aporia arises in the interplay of these two forces. The essentially active work of imposing order, of creating a comprehensible narrative with a conspiratorial individual will at its center, is a process that tends to reinforce the subject's desire to confirm his own discrete individuality, the freedom of his will and his own integrity. But the opposite force of class interest and fear of repression robs the individual of this integrity at the same time as he asserts it, since the formation of the conspiracy theory is ultimately a function of power and class (as Epstein's statement suggests).

In Wieland's case, the rupture in individual autonomy is clear. Even Wieland once described himself as a 'chameleon.'[78] Wieland scholars have always shown some embarrassment at this and similar statements; they have generally conceived of it in connection with Wieland's fictional works and successfully argued that his extreme virtuosity with respect to themes and styles, his perspectivism, should not be interpreted as a weakness of character. His vacillation in political matters is more difficult to explain away. Though here, too, scholars have gone to great lengths to explain Wieland's changing political views (for example, on the French Revolution) in terms of his perspectivism, i.e. his penchant for empathizing with various points of view,[79] Wieland's own contemporaries saw the political consequences of his waffling quite clearly. One reader wrote in, pointedly criticizing one of Wieland's conservative pieces: "Your works are read far and wide in Germany, particularly by the powerful. Your correct manner of thinking and your . . . good style must perforce have a strong effect on those who are naturally inclined to oppose good state constitutions, and rulers won't so readily dare to resort to despotic measures if you speak steadfastly for human rights."[80] Though Wieland disputed the influence of his own writings, there is every reason for us to believe today that this correspondent was right; more than one project was advanced to engage leading German writers—in one case Goethe, Wieland, Meiners, Rehberg, and others[81]—in support of counterrevolutionary repression in Germany; such a project would not even have been considered had it not been for Wieland's considerable influence in public affairs. My ultimate point is not to mount a new attack on the 'chameleon' Wieland for his possibly legitimizing influence on reactionary politics in Germany, but rather to insist that we move beyond the usual analyses of writers' opinions on political matters which assume the writers were autonomous subjects writing with complete freedom of judgment and from the vantage of pure rationality. The short-sighted rejection of a supposedly "neo-positivistic" pursuit of "biographical trivia" begins to look like a vestige of idealism, a denial of the web of social, political, and economic forces that crushed the individual seeking to maintain a semblance of autonomy in a very turbulent period. We saw clearly in Wieland's relation to the conspiracy theory that his opinions followed the ebb and flow of repression in Germany. His own contemporaries speculated on the pressures that led Wieland to adapt his views to changing circumstances: one of them wrote in 1791, after a conversation with Wieland about Louis XVI's flight to Varennes:

> In this matter, as in all others, Wieland keeps changing his mind and is dependent on external impressions. At first he was all in favor of the National Assembly, later he thought it had gone too far, or he allowed the court—the duke and duchess, whose brother, the Landgrave of Hesse-Darmstadt, is suffering because of the Revolution—to change his mind. Now, however, since the court is attending the Diet in Eisenach and Duchess Anna Amalia, with whom he spends a lot of time, is enthusiastically for the National Assembly, he has changed his tone for her sake.[82]

The irony of this passage, of course, is that the visitor thinks he would act quite differently if he were in Wieland's position; the experience of others at the Weimar court is grounds for skepticism in this regard. Only rarely does the recognition that one is subject to political pressures penetrate the consciousness of many Weimar intellectuals; it is perhaps symptomatic of Wieland's political contradictions that in one of those rare instances, Karl Ludwig von Knebel asks Böttiger to persuade Wieland that his readers see through the pretense of individual autonomy in the face of political interests: "Just between you and me, I wish that you would get him to leave off his politicking completely. All of us who eat the bread of Germany's minor princes would be better off not talking about political matters at all."[83]

NOTES

1. After giving this paper in 1989 I was able to undertake the first comprehensive study of the previously unpublished papers of the Weimar Illuminati group, which numbered Goethe and Carl August among its members; in a recent book resulting from this study I treat other aspects of the conspiracy theory that I had treated in this paper. W. Daniel Wilson, *Geheimbünde gegen Geheimräte: Ein unbekanntes Kapitel der klassisch-romantischen Geschichte Weimars* (Stuttgart: Metzler, 1991).

2. "Ein wichtiger Aufschluß über eine noch wenig bekannte Veranlassung der französischen Revolution (Mitgetheilt von zuverlässiger Hand)," *Wiener Zeitschrift* 1793.2:145–58, here 156, quoted by [Leopold Alois Hoffmann], *Fragmente zur Biographie des verstorbenen Geheimen Raths Bode in Weimar. Mit zuverlässigen Urkunden*. Rom [= Wien], auf Kosten der Propaganda, 1795, 30–32. This article was reprinted in various forms; see the standard work on the conspiracy theory, Johannes Rogalla von Bieberstein, *Die These von der Verschwörung 1776–1945: Philosophen, Freimaurer, Juden, Liberale und Sozialisten als Verschwörer gegen die Sozialordnung*, Europäische Hochschulschriften III/63 (Frankfurt/Main: Lang, 1976) 104–05. See also Woldemar Wenck, *Deutschland vor hundert Jahren*, Vol. 2: *Politische Meinungen und Stimmungen in der Revolutionszeit* (Leipzig: Grunow, 1890) 38–43, 136–50; Leopold Engel, *Geschichte des Illuminaten-Ordens: Ein Beitrag zur Geschichte Bayerns* (Berlin: Bermühler, 1906) 402–25; R[ené] Le Forestier, *Les illuminés de Bavière et la Franc-Maçonnerie allemande* (Paris 1914, rpt. Geneva: Slatkine-Megariotis, 1974) 613–717; Fritz Valjavec, *Die Entstehung der politischen Strömungen in Deutschland 1770–1815*, (Munich: Oldenbourg, 1951) 302–27; Klaus Epstein, *The Genesis of German Conservatism* (Princeton: Princeton University Press, 1966) 503–46; Gustav Krüger, "Die Eudämonisten: Ein Beitrag zur Publizistik des ausgehenden 18. Jahrhunderts," *Historische Zeitschrift* 143 (1931): 467–500; and Richard van Dülmen, *Der Geheimbund der Illuminaten*, 2nd ed., Neuzeit im Aufbau, 1 (Stuttgart, Bad Cannstatt: Frommann-Holzboog, 1977) 93–98. Max Braubach ("Die 'Eudämonia' [1795–1798]: Ein Beitrag zur deutschen Publizistik der Aufklärung und der Revolution," *Historisches Jahrbuch der Görres-Gesellschaft* 47 [1927]: 309–39, here 313) and most other scholars find no basis for the conspiracy theory.

3. Rogalla von Bieberstein gives numerous examples from before the early 1970s; the most troublesome more recent examples are an otherwise fine piece of scholarship by Reinhard Lauth, "Nouvelles recherches sur Reinhold et l'Aufklaerung," *Archives de Philosophie* 42 (1979): 593–629 (repeated in the Austrian Academy of Sciences edn. of Reinhold's *Korres-*

pondenz [note 14] 229 n.); and an article whose title and numerous remarks betray an ideology from which the author tries to distance himself: Hans Graßl, "Tragende Ideen der illuminatistisch-jakobinischen Propaganda und ihre Nachwirkungen in der deutschen Literatur," in Ludz (note 11) 335–66. Lauth (617–21), in particular, bolsters his arguments with conspiracy theorists like Barruel, Starcke, Göchhausen, and Reichard who have long been known as unreliable fanatics. See my article, "Shades of the Illuminati Conspiracy: Koselleck on Enlightenment and Revolution," *The Enlightenment and its Legacy: Studies in Honor of Helga Slessarev*, ed. Sara Friedrichsmeyer and Barbara Becker-Cantarino (Bonn: Bouvier, 1990) 15–25.

4. Van Dülmen 179.

5. [Göchhausen, Ernst August Anton von,] *Enthüllung des Systems der Weltbürger-Republik. In Briefen aus der Verlassenschaft eines Freymaurers. Wahrscheinlich manchem Leser um zwantzig Jahre zu spät publizirt.* Rom [=Leipzig], 1786, vii.

6. Jochen Hoffmann, "Bedeutung und Funktion des Illuminatenordens in Norddeutschland," *Zeitschrift für bayerische Landesgeschichte* 45 (1982): 363–79, here 377. Rogalla von Bieberstein concurs in the view that in the light of the heated controversies and debates that had been going on even before the storming of the Bastille "it is hardly surprising that only a short time later Freemasonry was blamed for the French Revolution" (88).

7. Qtd. Rogalla von Bieberstein 88. The two men were Ludwig Adolf Christian von Grolmann and Johann August Starck, later editors of *Eudämonia* (see below).

8. On the Bode link, see Epstein 513; Le Forestier 664–70; Engel 406–09; Rogalla von Bieberstein 103–04; the most complete modern account is Claus Werner, "Le Voyage de Bode à Paris en 1787 et le 'complot maçonnique,'" *Annales historiques de la Révolution française* 55 (1983): 432–45, which should be supplemented by Lauth, in his article (note 3) and in Reinhold, *Korrespondenz* (note 14) 228–30; Lauth, however, leans toward the conspiracy theory (see note 3). Ironically—in view of the Nazi propaganda of the conspiracy theory—it was a Nazi author, hostile to the Illuminati, who was able to use Bode's diary (which he found among Masonic documents confiscated by the regime), which clearly showed, against Rossberg's interpretation, that Bode spoke about Illuminati matters with Parisian Masons, but did not agitate politically: Adolf Rossberg, *Freimaurerei und Politik im Zeitalter der Französischen Revolution*, Quellen und Darstellungen zur Freimaurerfrage, 2 (Berlin: Nordland, 1942) 82–83; see Werner 439. Engel had also published a letter of Bode's from Paris with a view to proving that Bode's mission was non-political (410–15).

9. Hans Graßl's various writings have treated certain connections between Illuminatism and German literature, but they must be read with the greatest skepticism, since his work contains gross distortions and errors. For example, he discusses several supposed writings of Wieland that all turn out to be by other authors (*Aufbruch zur Romantik: Bayerns Beitrag zur deutschen Geistesgeschichte 1765–1785*, Munich: Beck, 1968, 257–58). He makes the absurd claim that Goethe, Herder, Bode and Carl August joined the French Philalèthes (221; he gives no sources).

10. See note 2.

11. Ernst-Otto Fehn, "Zur Wiederentdeckung des Illuminatenordens: Ergänzende Bemerkungen zu Richard van Dülmens Buch," in *Geheime Gesellschaften*, ed. Peter Christian Ludz, Wolfenbütteler Studien zur Aufklärung, 5/1 (Heidelberg: Lambert Schneider, 1979) 231–64.

12. After the suppression of the Illuminati Goethe was motivated by his past Illuminati membership and by his fear of secret societies to participate in the suppression of Masons and of free speech generally in Weimar and Jena. See my book cited in note 1, and (in English) my article, "Weimar Politics in the Age of the French Revolution: Goethe and the Spectre of Illuminati Conspiracy," *Goethe Yearbook* 5 (1989): 163–86.

13. Compiled from Le Forestier and Arthur Ott, "Goethe und der Illuminatenorden," *Stunden mit Goethe: Für die Freunde seiner Kunst und Weisheit*, ed. Wilhelm Bode, vol. 6 (Berlin: Mittler, 1910) 85–91; Hugo Wernekke, *Goethe und die königliche Kunst* (Leipzig: Poeschel & Kippenberg, 1905) 24–25; and Gotthold Deile, *Goethe als Freimaurer* (Berlin: Mittler, 1908) 35–36.

14. See Karl Leonhard Reinhold, *Korrespondenz 1773–1788*, ed. Reinhard Lauth, Eberhard Heller, Kurt Hiller, Vol. 1 of *Korrespondenzausgabe der Österreichischen Akademie der Wissenschaften*, ed. Reinhard Lauth et al. (Stuttgart, Bad Cannstatt: Frommann-Holzboog, 1983) 115, 341; Lauth (note 3). The information had been available since 1883 in Keil (note 53) 60.

15. Friedrich Sommer, *Die Wiener Zeitschrift (1792–1793): Die Geschichte eines antirevolutionären Journals*, Diss. Bonn (Zeulenroda: Sporn, 1923) 47.

16. Engel 425.

17. Robert Plersch, *Was war eigentlich die Hauptursache der Französischen Revolution? Zur ernsten Warnung für die Fürsten und Regenten Deutschlands, vorgestellt von einem Patrioten in der Schweiz* (n.p., n.d. [1796]) 140, qtd. by Rogalla von Bieberstein 108.

18. Karl-Heinz Fallbacher, "Fichtes Entlassung. Ein Beitrag zur Weimar-Jenaischen Institutionengeschichte," *Archiv für Kulturgeschichte* 67 (1985): 111–35. On the attack on Fichte and its effects on Schlegel in Jena, see W. Daniel Wilson, " 'Philosophen- und Schriftstellerkabale': The Conspiracy Theory of the French Revolution and the Origins of German Romanticism

(Fichte, F. Schlegel, Novalis)," *Euphorion* 83 (1989): 131–59, and Wilson (note 1), ch. 5.3.

19. The text is in Engel 246–47. Frederick William II was not the only Prussian leader to adhere to the conspiracy theory; his ambassador in Paris, Graf von der Goltz, wrote to the king in January, 1790 about the supposed Masonic plot of the so-called "Club de Propagande" (on which see below); see Rossberg 145–46.

20. Letter of Weishaupt to Friedrich Christian, Aug. 1793, and response, *Aus dem Briefwechsel des Herzogs Friedrich Christian zu Schleswig-Holstein: Briefanhang zur Biographie 1910*, ed. Hans Schulz (Stuttgart: Deutsche Verlags-Anstalt, 1913) 117, 119.

21. [Martin] E[hlers], "An den Herausgeber des T[eutschen] M[erkurs]. Antwort auf das Sendschreiben desselben, im 1sten Stück des T. Merkur 1792," *Neuer teutscher Merkur*, 1792.2 (July): 217–77, here 228. The asterisk refers to a note by Wieland, the editor: "Here my friend names some people whom I consider it unnecessary to name publicly."

22. As in Baggesen's and Weishaupt's correspondence with Friedrich Christian; see note 20 and *Timoleon und Immanuel: Dokumente einer Freundschaft: Briefwechsel zwischen Friedrich Christian zu Schleswig-Holstein und Jens Baggesen*, ed. Hans Schulz (Leipzig: Hirzel, 1910).

23. The novels *Geschichte des Agathon* (1766–1767, 2nd ed. 1773) and *Der goldne Spiegel* (1772), and the semi-fictional essay on Rousseau, *Beyträge zur Geheimen Geschichte des menschlichen Verstandes und Herzens* (1770). See *Einige Originalschriften des Illuminatenordens, welche bey [Franz Xaver von] Zwackh durch vorgenommene Hausvisitation zu Landshut den 11. und 12. Oct. 1786 vorgefunden worden. Auf höchsten Befehl Seiner Churfürstlichen Durchlaucht zum Druck befördert* (Munich, 1787) 33; rpt. in van Dülmen 150; cf. Le Forestier 500. I find Graßl's attempt to find Illuminati ideas in *Agathon* very unconvincing (192–95).

24. *X.Y.Z. oder neue Aufschlüsse über die deutsche Union* (Berlin 1788); see Le Forestier, 628 n. Though the list of writings recommended for the Illuminati is known to Wieland research (see below), the Deutsche Union list is not, to my knowledge.

25. Even scholars who argue that the Deutsche Union was not a successor to the Illuminati identify many similarities; the important point, again, is that contemporaries saw a strong connection. Agatha Kobuch claims that the Deutsche Union can be categorized as a "progressive further development" of Illuminatism ("Die Deutsche Union: Radikale Spätaufklärung, Freimaurerei und Illuminatismus am Vorabend der Französischen Revolution," *Beiträge zur Archivwissenschaft und Geschichtsforschung*, ed. Reiner Groß and Manfred Kobuch, Schriftenreihe des Staatsarchivs Dresden, 10 [Weimar:

Hermann Böhlau, 1977] 277–91, here 290); similarly, Fehn 235; against this view: Hoffmann 370–71, van Dülmen 97.

26. E.g. in Weishaupt's seminal "Anrede an die neu aufzunehmenden Illuminatos dirigentes" (Address to Those who are about to become *Illuminatos dirigentes*): "The union of men in states is the cradle and the grave of despotism. . . ."; "With the arising of nations and peoples the world ceased to be one great family, one single commonwealth: the strong bonds of Nature were broken" (van Dülmen 172–73).

27. Epstein treats Göchhausen under the heading "The Birth of the 'Conspiracy Theory' " (96–100).

28. *TM* 1786.2 (May): 176–90; Reinhold claims in a letter to Nicolai that Wieland gave him the book "to be praised in the *Merkur*" (*Korrespondenz* [note 14] 184). It is possible, judging from indications in this letter, that Wieland had not actually read the book, but had merely taken Bertuch's recommendation at face value. Wieland later read part of the book as scrappaper without knowing (or remembering) what book it was (note 48). But he must have known of the content of the book, since it created a stir in intellectual circles, and since he would hardly have asked that it be praised without some knowledge of it.

29. In his "Vorbericht" and notes to "Briefe eines Maurers an seinen Freund bey Gelegenheit der Berliner Monats-Schrift vom Jahre 1785," *TM* 1786.1 (Mar.): 244–85; see *Wielands Gesammelte Schriften*, hrsg. v. der Deutschen Kommission der Preußischen Akademie der Wissenschaften, 1. Abt.: *Werke*, Berlin: Weidmann, 1909ff. (abbreviated in the following as AA), vol. 23: *Kleine Schriften III: 1783–1791*, ed. William Clark (1969) 105–12.

30. Fritz Martini (note 35) suggests that Wieland may have been an Illuminati (92–93), but if this were so, he would surely have been in the lodge in Weimar, and there is no mention of him in the available lists from Weimar. Wieland became a Mason only many years later.

31. Lauth 622 (on Reinhold's relations to Bode: 615). In a letter of 20 Aug. 1787, Reinhold writes that because of the revelations afforded by the published documents, especially regarding Weishaupt's personal character and the political goals of the Illuminati, most units of the order have been dissolved, but not in Northern Germany: "The districts and churches under Bode's supervision regarded that as a good opportunity to reform the order and to continue it under the leadership of no other than the superior who was already known to the brothers in the higher ranks [= Bode or Duke Ernst II of Gotha], whose honesty and magnificent character we all know and honor," and Reinhold expects "a total recasting," not a dissolution of the order (*Korrespondenz* [n. 14] 252). Thus Reinhold felt that the order could be reformed, eliminating some of Weishaupt's abuses. Like Reinhold,

Bode had remarked in 1787, after reading all the Illuminati secrets in *Einige Originalschriften* (note 23), that because of these revelations a total reform of the order would be necessary (Rossberg 82). The plans appeared to have been laid already in March, 1788, when Reinhold writes that there would soon be new, revised rules "because the old ones are *antiquated*." Weishaupt was to be excluded from the new Illuminati: "He and his followers will not be part of it; they won't even know about the new organization" (341).

32. Reinhold, *Korrespondenz* (note 14) 249.
33. Lauth 623–25.
34. *Schillers Briefe*, ed. Fritz Jonas, 7 vols. (Stuttgart: Deutsche Verlags-Anstalt, 1892–1896) 1:399 (to Körner, 29 Aug. 1787). In a letter of 10 Sept. Schiller speaks of the Illuminati: "Right now everybody in the world is talking about Weishaupt" (1:409).
35. Quoted from Christoph Martin Wieland, *Werke*, 5 vols., ed. Fritz Martini and Hans Werner Seiffert, vol. 3 (Munich: Hanser, 1967) 550–75. In his commentary (esp. 913), Martini takes up the references to the Illuminati from Wilhelm Kurrelmeyer: AA 15: *Prosaische Schriften II, 1783–1794*, ed. Wilhelm Kurrelmeyer (1930), with *Bericht des Herausgebers* (1930), 68A–69A ("A" after page no. indicates the *Bericht*). See also Martini's excellent article, "Wieland, Napoleon und die Illuminaten: Zu einem bisher unbekannten Briefe," *Un Dialogue des Nations: A. Fuchs zum 70. Geburtstag* (Paris: Klincksieck, 1967) 65–95, here 87–90. One point on which I disagree with Martini's analysis of Wieland's essay is his suggestion that it may have been intended as a defense of the Illuminati against the accusations of Göchhausen and other early conspiracy theorists (88 n.); Wieland is clearly defending the true "cosmopolites" *against* the Illuminati.
36. E.g., in *TM* April 1789: AA 23:274.
37. E.g.: "The reassurance offered by such a conspiratorial secret society that neither its by-laws nor its activities will harm the state, religion, or morals. . . ." (555) refers almost word-for-word to the declaration that Illuminati had to sign when they joined the order, affirming that they had been reassured by the persons who inducted them that "nothing would be undertaken in this society that is directed against the state, religion, or morals"; one such declaration had been published in *Einige Originalschriften* (note 23), rpt. in van Dülmen, 158.
38. Martini (note 35) 89 points out the contradictions this essay; see also Reinhart Koselleck, *Kritik und Krise: Eine Studie zur Pathogenese der bürgerlichen Welt*, 3rd ed. (Frankfurt/Main: Suhrkamp, 1979) 80–81.
39. In particular, it is not contained in Thomas C. Starnes's pioneering work, *Christoph Martin Wieland: Leben und Werk: Aus zeitgenössischen Quellen chronologisch dargestellt*, 3 vols. (Sigmaringen: Thorbecke, 1987).

40. "Ein bayerisches Beamtenleben zwischen Aufklärung und Romantik: Die Autobiographie des Staatsrats Clemens von Neumayr," ed. Hans Schmidt, *Zeitschrift für bayerische Landesgeschichte* 35 (1972): 591–690, here 651. Neumayr and his companion had visited Weishaupt in Gotha and Bode near Weimar, before Herder's return to Weimar (9 July 1789), and at a time when Goethe was out of Weimar and spent much of his time at Belvedere (651), which might point to early June; however, it could not have been long before the beginning of July, since Neumayr heard Schiller's Jena lecture on the Flood (653) soon after visiting Weimar; this refers to Schiller's series of lectures "Etwas über die erste Menschengesellschaft" from the summer semester, 1789; this series began in late June, but the section on the Flood is near the end of what seem to have been five lectures. Late June thus seems a plausible dating for the conversation with Wieland.

41. "Leben und Thaten Josephs Balsamo, des so genannten Grafen Cagliostro, gezogen aus dem wider ihn zu Rom im Jahr 1790 angestellten Prozeß; worin zugleich auch Nachrichten von der Freymäurerey gegeben werden. Aus dem Italiänischen übersetzt von C[hristian] J[oseph] J[agemann]," *NTM* 1791.2:181–219 (June), 225–317 (July), 337–77 (Aug.); "Zusatz des Herausgebers des T. M.," 377–85 (Aug.); AA 23:374–79 (I quote Wieland from AA, the report itself from *NTM*); the translator, Jagemann, was Duchess Anna Amalia's librarian. For a 1786 Wieland remark on Cagliostro see AA 23:120–23.

42. *NTM* 1791.2 (July): 290.

43. Rogalla von Bieberstein 89–95 (the theory was fully developed in 1790).

44. The Illuminati are mentioned in the Cagliostro report, not only in the passage cited above (289–91), but also on 283.

45. *Ist Cagliostro der Chef der Illuminaten? Oder, das Buch: Sur la secte des illuminés. In Deutsch. Mit erklärenden Worten des deutschen Translators* (Gotha, 1790); see Rogalla von Bieberstein 91.

46. Rogalla von Bieberstein, 93–94.

47. W[ilhelm] Kurrelmeyer, "Wieland und die *Wiener Zeitschrift*," *MLN* 44 (1929): 96–101, referring to the *Moniteur* of 12 and 16 Feb. 1792. Kurrelmeyer provides only a chronicle of the events in this exchange, without analysis, and he misses some of the references to Wieland in the *Wiener Zeitschrift* and elsewhere that I cite below.

48. *Wiener Zeitschrift* 1792.1 (Jan.): 68 n. (Kurrelmeyer overlooks this exchange between Hoffmann and Wieland). For the context of this note, see AA 23:382–384; in 1791 Wieland had printed a lengthy exchange between Göchhausen and an unnamed critic; the accusations against the Illuminati are mentioned at *NTM* 1791.2 (July): 324, 1791.3 (Sept.): 58. Wieland says

that if he had known that the book he was criticizing was by Göchhausen (it got into his hands as scrap-paper!), he would have written nothing, or something in a tone more appropriate to "our relationship" (383); this is probably because Göchhausen was an active Weimar official in Eisenach (on a 1789 official task that he undertook with Goethe in the presence of Carl August, see Grumach 3:300–03, 310), but it might also refer to a personal acquaintance with Göchhausen or to Wieland's approval of Göchhausen's work.

49. *Wiener Zeitschrift* 1792.1 (Jan.): 97–100.

50. *Wiener Zeitschrift* 1792.1 (Jan.): 100–01.

51. *Wiener Zeitschrift* 1792.3 (Sept.): 301; cf. Kurrelmeyer 99; Sommer 84–87.

52. See Epstein 523–24.

53. A letter from Alxinger to Reinhold attests to this: "Huber ... was turned away from the Emperor's audience, just because he had written against Hoffmann, and the explanation was that the Emperor doesn't waste words talking with hired inkslingers," 6 May 1792, in Robert Keil, *Wiener Freunde 1784–1808: Beiträge zur Jugendgeschichte der deutsch-österreichischen Literatur* (Wien: Konegen, 1883) 54.

54. *Wiener Zeitschrift* 1792.1 (March): 273–75 (my emphasis). On Frederick William's support of Hoffmann see Epstein 524.

55. *Wiener Zeitschrift* 1792.3 (Sept.): 257–74; the article attacking Ehlers and praising Wieland is entitled: "Nacherinnerungen über die Manifeste der Höfe gegen Frankreich; nebst einer abgenöthigten Apologie gegen Herrn Professor Ehlers in Kiel," and Hoffmann begins by claiming that the monarchs have finally realized what he has been saying all along.

56. Carl August to Christian Gottlob Voigt, near Verdun, 4 Sept. 1792, Staatsarchiv Weimar, J 288, fol. 47v (Voigt noted the receipt of the letter on 14 Sept.); cf. Wilson (note 1) 179, 228. A letter from Voigt to Gottlieb Hufeland, in which Voigt quotes this letter from the duke, was published in the nineteenth century, but the editor (or Voigt?) excised Wieland's name (August Diezmann, ed., *Aus Weimars Glanzzeit: Ungedruckte Briefe von und über Goethe und Schiller, nebst einer Auswahl ungedruckter vertraulicher Schreiben von Goethe's Collegen, Geh. Rath v. Voigt* [Leipzig, 1855] 59).

57. AA 15:771; both in his commentary (AA 15:166A) and in his article (99), Kurrelmeyer speculates that Wieland himself wrote the letter; it is signed "C.M.," which Kurrelmeyer interprets as "Christoph Martin." There is no evidence at all for this assumption; Wieland could have cleared the air about his association with Hoffmann without a fictive missive, and the invective in the letter against Wieland's "aristocratic principles" rings too true to suggest that Wieland could have written it. In any case, Wieland

notes with exasperation that he has recently been plagued with similar letters (778).

58. Cf. Kurrelmeyer 100; again, I cannot agree with Kurrelmeyer that Wieland's statement, "This is the latest thing I've heard, since neither Herr Alois Hoffmann, nor what he writes or does, is anything that would interest me [innerhalb meines Gesichtskreises liegt]," could mean that Wieland wants nothing to do with Hoffmann, rather than that he knows nothing of him.

59. Alxinger wrote to Reinhold on 6 May 1792: "I didn't think that my Anti-Hoffmann would interest you ["euch," here clearly plural], otherwise I would have sent Wieland a copy" (53). Alxinger, a former Illuminati, published his *Anti-Hoffmann* in 2 vols., Vienna 1792–1793 (see Epstein 531). Kurrelmeyer missed this letter.

60. Reinhold gave voice to this denial when he claimed in the *Teutscher Merkur* that Wieland's name came up neither in the Parisian democratic clubs nor in the *Wiener Zeitschrift* as a combatant "for either of their respective good causes" (1793.1 [Apr.]: 387–88); Hoffmann's lengthy quotation of Wieland months earlier refutes this claim.

61. *NTM* 1793.3 (Oct.): 113–51; on the myth: Rogalla von Bieberstein 96–97.

62. Ibid. 128. In Wieland's own earlier pronouncements on the "Club de Propagande," he had seemed to discount its danger (AA 15:499, 655 [Jan. 1791 and Aug. 1792]; cf. AA 15:116A).

63. "Einige Bemerkungen und Fragen eines Mannes, der an keine Propaganda als an die in Rom glaubt, über einen sogenannten *neuen merkwürdigen Beweis des Daseyns und der gefährlichen Thätigkeit einer französisch-deutschen Aufrührer-Propagande.* (im 10ten Stück des deutschen Merkurs von 1793. S. 113 u. f." *Schleswigsches Journal* 1793.3 (Dec.): 479–89; the quotation from Wieland is from *NTM* 1793.3 (Oct.): 115 n. Cf. Kurrelmeyer 100–02; the editor of the *Schleswigsches Journal* was August von Hennings; see Paul Hocks and Peter Schmidt, *Literarische und politische Zeitschriften 1789–1805*, Sammlung Metzler 121 (Stuttgart: Metzler, 1975) 58–60; Sommer 60–64.

64. Ibid., 485–86. Wieland dropped a few words of sarcasm against this critic: AA 15:816; cf. Kurrelmeyer 101.

65. Qtd. by Hoffmann in *Fragmente zur Biographie . . . Bode* (note 2) 48–50, from *Archiv für die neueste Kirchengeschichte*, 1794, 1. Stück. Böttiger seems to have authored a separate necrology, possibly in response to Hoffmann: *Denkschrift auf Bode in Weimar* (Weimar 1796) (apparently identical to the one in *Michael Montaigne's Gedanken und Meinungen über allerley Gegenstände. Ins Deutsche übersetzt* von Johann Joachim Christoph Bode, Berlin

1793–1799, vol. 6 [1795]). Interestingly, Wieland himself apparently wrote a necrology for Bode (Starnes 2:329), but it was never published!
66. Hoffmann, *Fragmente* (note 2) 38–90, 105, 135.
67. Ibid., 53–54; 84–85.
68. "Auszug aus einem Briefe," *NTM* 1795.1 (Feb.): 213–17; "Zusatz des Herausgebers," signed "Wieland," 217–18.
69. *NTM* 1795.1 (Feb.): 174 n.
70. *Mémoires pour servir à l'histoire du Jacobinisme*, 4 vols. (London, 1797–1798); for a bibliography of the editions in French, English, German, and seven other languages, see Rogalla von Bieberstein 234; cf. Epstein 504–05. Barruel's work became the Bible of conspiracy theorists the world over.
71. "Auswärtige Korrespondenz," *NTM* 1797.3 (Nov.): 265–69, here 266; on 268 the writer also criticizes the other important compilation published in 1797, John Robison's *Proofs of a Conspiracy against all the Religions and Governments of Europe, Carried on in Secret Meetings of Free Masons, Illuminati and Reading Societies* (Edinburgh, 1797), which Böttiger also attacks in the next issue (*NTM* 1797.3 [Dec.]: [334]); on Robison see Rogalla von Bieberstein 234, Epstein 505–06.
72. Martini, "Wieland, Napoleon und die Illuminaten" (note 35). Martini does not treat some of the *Teutscher Merkur* pieces that I examine here.
73. Böttiger writes in a letter: "Herr von Lenthe in Hanover has been named" (Ernst Ludwig Julius von Lenthe, a Hanoverian diplomat [Starnes 3:8, 577]).
74. "Meine Erklärung über einen im St. James Chronicle, January 25, 1800 abgedruckten Artikel, der zur Ueberschrift hat: Prediction concerning Buonaparte, mit dem Beysatz: the following Dialogue is now circulating in *the higher Circles*; the observations are of the pen of a *foreign Minister*," *NTM* 1800.1 (Apr.): 243–76, esp. 250; cf. Martini 79.
75. *NTM* 1798.3 (Dec.): 387, 1799.2 (May): 93–94, 1800.1 (Apr.): 280–93 (cf. Martini 81–82, 95), 1800.2 (May): 70–71, 89–91, 1800.2 (July): 238 n., 240–41. Böttiger published a moderate defense of Robison's character, though Böttiger still indicated in a footnote that Robison's ideas were false: *NTM* 1800.2 (July): 249–54. It is interesting to note that in his repeated denial of the existence of the Illuminati order after the beginning of the Revolution, and particularly in his denial that he himself had been an Illuminati, Böttiger may have been less than frank about his own past. See Böttiger's intriguing letter to Campe, dated 7 Oct. 1793, in which he expresses fear that the sitting Imperial Diet will take repressive measures: "Increasingly one fears an explosion against Enlightenment and freedom of conscience in the Diet itself. . . . But in every city, even the smallest ones, there is a small group of the elect who—in the case of such an event—can close ranks

and transform themselves into a fearsome phalanx within a month. I hate and ridicule all secret societies, which murdered the most beautiful days of my youth. But here it would still be a good thing to agree on passwords and signs for such an event" (qtd. Rossberg 212–13). Böttiger had been a Mason, and Hermann Schüttler has recently cited archival evidence that he was an Illuminati (*Die Mitglieder des Illuminatenordens 1776–1787/93*, Deutsche Hochschuledition, 18 [Munich: ars una, 1991] 27; however, see my forthcoming review of Schüttler's book in *Internationales Archiv für Sozialgeschichte der deutschen Literatur*. See also Ernst Friedrich Sondermann, *Karl August Böttiger: Literarischer Journalist der Goethezeit in Weimar*, Mitteilungen zur Theatergeschichte der Goethezeit, 7 (Bonn: Bouvier, 1983) 34–37.

76. Eberhard Schmitt points out minor conspiratorial elements leading to the Revolution: "Elemente einer Theorie der politischen Konspiration im 18. Jahrhundert: Einige typologische Bemerkungen," in Ludz (note 11) 65–88.

77. Johannes Rogalla von Bieberstein, "Geheime Gesellschaften als Vorläufer politischer Parteien," in Ludz (note 11) 429–60.

78. In the 1750s Wieland wrote: "Je ressemble pour mon malheur au Cameleon; je parois vert aupres des Objets verts, et jaune aupres des jaunes; mais je ne suis ni jaune ni vert; Je suis transparent, ou blanc comme veut Mr. de la Motte"; *Wielands Briefwechsel*, hrsg. von der Deutschen Akademie der Wissenschaften zu Berlin, Institut für deutsche Sprache und Literatur [durch Hans Werner Seiffert] (Berlin: Akademie-Verlag, 1963-) 1:415. On the context of this passage: John A. McCarthy, "Wielands Metamorphose," *DVjs*. 49, Sonderbd. (1975): 149*–67*, here 152*–53*.

79. On Wieland and the French Revolution see especially: Bernd Weyergraf, *Der skeptische Bürger: Wielands Schriften zur Französischen Revolution* (Stuttgart: Metzler, 1972); Gonthier-Louis Fink, "Wieland und die Französische Revolution," in *Deutsche Literatur und Französische Revolution: Sieben Studien* by Richard Brinkmann et al. (Göttingen: Vandenhoeck & Ruprecht, 1974) 5–38; Lieselotte Kurth-Voigt, "Wieland and the French Revolution: The Writings of the First Year," *Studies in Eighteenth-Century Culture* 7 (1978): 79–103; Fritz Martini, "Nachwort," in Christoph Martin Wieland, *Meine Antworten: Aufsätze über die Französische Revolution 1789–1793. Nach den Erstdrucken im 'Teutschen Merkur,'* ed. Fritz Martini (Marbach: Deutsche Schillergesellschaft, 1983) 132–44.

80. AA 15:411; the writer is Ehlers.

81. Hans Christoph Ernst von Gagern, *Ein deutscher Edelmann an seine Landsleute* (1794), qtd. in a letter by Georg Ludwig von Edelsheim, the leading statesman in Baden; the letter was part of the preparations for the meeting of princes that led to the founding of *Eudämonia*. It is significant that both Goethe (see my article cited in note 12) and Wieland are listed

along with leading contemporary conservatives as possible candidates for inclusion in this propaganda project of the conspiracy theorists. *Politische Korrespondenz Karl Friedrichs von Baden 1783–1806*, ed. B. Erdmannsdörffer (Heidelberg: Winter, 1892) 2:174–75.

82. Friedrich Münter (a Dane and former Illuminati!), in a diary entry, 5 July 1791, Starnes 2:237.

83. 4 Apr. 1794, qtd. Starnes 2:343–44.

ZWI BATSCHA

Kant and the French Revolution

KARL POPPER DEDICATED THE GERMAN EDITION of his classic study *The Open Society and Its Enemies* to Immanuel Kant with the epigraph: "To the memory of the philosopher of liberty and humanity" ("Dem Andenken des Philosophen der Freiheit und Menschlichkeit"). For the preface to this edition Popper chose the text of his commemorative radio address, broadcast from London on 12 February 1954, in honor of the hundred and fiftieth anniversary of the philosopher's death. In it he asserted that the bells that tolled at the passing of this great thinker reverberated with the echoes of the ideas of 1776 and 1789. He then went on to observe: "To his compatriots Kant had become a symbol of these ideas, and they came to his funeral in order to give thanks to the teacher and herald of the rights of man, equality before the law, internationalism, enduring peace in the world and—perhaps most important of all—self-liberation through knowledge and thought."[1] Now if Popper is right in his evaluation (as I am inclined to think he is), then in postulating the inalienable rights of man, constitutionalism, the dominion of peace in the world, and the self-emancipation of mankind, Kant had achieved a triumph of theory over the wretchedness of the German past, and set new goals for humanity at large that were totally opposed to the political and socioeconomic reality that prevailed in the German territories. The distinctive features of that reality were absolutism, a feudal system of which serfdom was still a part, and the exclusion of the ordinary subjects of the German territorial states from the processes by which they might become a politically enlightened public. In this respect Marx was correct in claiming that Kant's thought represented a real French Revolution for German theory. For the doctrines of this philosopher overcame the past and furnished new elements for a theory of politics from which they in fact became inseparable—just as, in the domain of practical reason, it is the inner human conflict between two causalities that is the dominant element in the realization of freedom, so that only with the emergence of a strong German bourgeoisie in the nineteenth century did it become possible to begin the struggle for the political participation of citizens in the process of public enlightenment.

In undertaking to demonstrate Kant's progressive and liberal position in the political debate at the close of the eighteenth century, as well as his efforts to come to grips with the political traditions of the past, I should like to begin with a consideration of two issues. The first of these is, quite simply, the question of how Kant should be categorized in the context of the theories of politics prevalent in his day. The second concerns the influences at work in the formation of Kant's later political theory. Thus we need first to show how the French Revolution influenced Kant's thinking—in other words, the manner in which he incorporated its consequences in his fundamental philosophical positions, thereby reorienting his ideas from the problems of a philosophy of the Enlightenment to the problems of early political liberalism, one of whose major proponents he eventually became.

This occurred toward the end of the eighteenth century as a postulate consequent upon the participation of citizens in the life of the state, and was the final stage of a development that took place on multiple levels with fluid transitions from one stage to the next. Concepts such as the rights of man, the social contract, liberty, and equality could have been formulated in the theoretical domain only as the result of a constitutional tendency at work over a prolonged period.[2] It should be remembered, however, that the doctrines of Christian Wolff—who conceived of natural law in absolute and hierarchical feudal terms, in the same way that his demonstrative deductions followed the example of mathematics in being derived from the system to which they pertain[3]—in some measure guarantee justice through the social contract. The state oversees the actions of the individual and reduces its "subjects"—by means of a paternalism concerned with the well-being of the state—to the status of objects of the activity of a sovereign authority that originated in the "patriarchal contract." As different aspects of Western European Enlightenment philosophy gradually made their way into the older concept of natural law, a variant began to emerge under the guise of the "machine state," wherein the class structure of society assumes the character of a functional association in which a person's status as a citizen is concretely realized in the fulfillment of his vocational duties. A number of Wolff's disciples joined with the exponents of Prussian bureaucracy in order to establish this particular variant in the theoretical complex of an enlightened absolutism that comprised the components of natural law and state corporatism, and from which the constitutional postulates of the Prussian state law of 1794 were excluded.[4] Thus the members of the corporate estates would assume the status of subordinate subjects so as eventually to evolve into citizens; and legal rights would be guaranteed not universally, but under the patronage of the several corporations.

Another group of Wolff disciples, wishing to free themselves of their mentor's systematic mathematical mode of thinking, felt that they might fill the void created by setting aside the deductive formulations of the master, if these were replaced by the empirical approach of the Anglo-Scottish philosophers. Their principal aspiration was to be of use to society and to work in its behalf, an ambition that resulted in their theoretical preference for practical philosophy. Happiness became the *telos* of their moral philosophy, and its spokesmen took part in all aspects of the debate over the French Revolution. Among the diverse popular philosophical approaches were a number of efforts to combine concepts of public order and natural rights, but none surpassed the model of enlightened absolutism in this respect.[5]

But later eighteenth-century thought was not distinguished merely by differences in approach to the idea of natural law.[6] One of the distinctive characteristics of other varieties of theory was the shift in stress from a function based on sovereign authority to one based on law; positivistic and historical legal conceptions were especially prominent features of these—whether based on the model of the imperial state or the territorial state. The first influential justification of the latter was furnished by Justus Möser of Osnabrück, whereas A.W. Rehberg of Hannover had offered a historical criticism of natural law from the standpoint of a modernized version of the rule of the nobility and privilege, condemning the concept for its abstractness in relation to concrete reality. In addition, there were various historical theories of cultural progress as well as a cyclical theory.

With the onset of the French Revolution, the Enlightenment—then already engaged in a process of self-examination—became involved in an intensive political debate. Absolutism, orthodoxy, and the older corporate-state ideology joined forces in their own defense against the inroads of constitutional and liberal theories, which they regarded as a threat to the further continuance of their privileges, the intellectual foundation of which was to be found in the existing ideologies of government. They made common cause against every particular variety of association, whether clandestine or open, indiscriminately denouncing them all as Jacobin, and sought to repress the spirit of reform in all its manifestations. In opposition to these dyed-in-the-wool forces of conservatism, there emerged an extreme republican wing which, albeit weak in numbers, was uncompromising in its attitude, whose adherents sought to introduce the most radical aspects of the French developments into the German territorial states. Their one-sided doctrine failed to distinguish between socioeconomic developments in France and in Germany, aiming to transplant the humane ideals of the French Revolution in their entirety, without first attempting to determine specifically local characteristics of the realities in France. In the period from the beginning of the French Revolution to the end of 1792 the majority of German intellectuals committed themselves to revolutionary ideals, which they regarded as the concrete realization of the ideals of the Enlightenment and the rights of man, and no longer merely stratagems for use against the state—as had in fact been the case up until 1789.[7] Their advocacy of these ideals proceeded from a perspective that was internal to the state and from a constitutional point of view. Political discussions inspired by the pamphlets published in 1789–1790 superseded the intellectual preoccupations of the Enlightenment centered around philosophical, theological, and moral issues. Concepts such as freedom, equality, and constitutionality were now introduced into the political debate. Thus the principle of natural law struck an increasingly responsive chord—no longer in conjunction with the establishment of human happiness through the agency of the state, but as the equivalent of the rule of the law of reason. This development culminated in Kant's philosophy, according to which freedom could only be based on the rational activity of the mind.

Immanuel Kant was one of the most significant representatives of this variety of political liberalism, in whose ideals he found an expression for his own philosophical-political theory. Was it mere chance, then, that Kant should have ended his critical decade in 1789 with his *Critique of Judgment*, and that this should have been followed by a political decade lasting until 1798? In any event, in his three *Critiques*, Kant attempted to answer the question of how philosophy in its three principal branches was at all possible after popular philosophy, preoccupied as it was with utilitarian aspirations, had failed to address the issue.[8] If, in Kant's Copernican Revolution, the understanding imposed its laws on the world of experience, and, in the domain of practical philosophy, it determined moral imperatives without being subject to natural cause, submitting solely to the *noumenon*—now the new, unfettered individuality in its diverse forms, with its new possibilities, duties, and rights, was made manifest in his political doctrine. In the political sphere, vigorous demands were put forward on behalf of liberty, equality, the preservation of rights, the guarantee of the property of the bourgeoisie, and aspirations for legitimate government. According to Kant, the outcome of all this had to be a republican form of government which rejected collective guardianship in the international sphere as well as in the economic, political, and intellectual processes.

Mention should be made, too, of Kant's native city of Königsberg,[9] which the philosopher never left during his lifetime. Until the establishment of the Continental System this port and capital city, in its dual capacity as a political and economic center, had continuously extended its connections toward the East and West. It had also opened its doors to the influences of Western Enlightenment, a circumstance that allowed Kant to surmount the constraints of narrow provincialism. In my opinion it was by way of the philosophy of Thomas Hobbes that Kant came under the influence of the positivistic ideas that rejected the right of rebellion[10] and denied the legitimacy of any demand by the representatives of the *ancien régime* for the restoration of the French monarchy after their flight from the country.[11] We can also assume that it was under Montesquieu's influence that Kant condemned absolute despotism and gave his approval to the principle of representation and the idea of forced exile,[12] these being required by the establishment of limited monarchy. The idea of guaranteeing property (which in its natural condition is merely temporary property) by compulsory measures proceeding from the state, as well as obliging the latter to assist in bringing about the full realization of natural rights, may have been influenced by John Locke, just as the notion of the rule of objective and universal law was mediated through Jean Jacques Rousseau. In the philosophies of these last two thinkers the social contract assumed a significance which transcended the empirical.

Of the four thinkers mentioned above, only Montesquieu was the founder of a historico-sociological school of thought. The others represented three varieties of the tradition of natural law,[13] which reached its zenith on the eve of the French Revolution, only to fade in the period of the Restoration. This tradition asserted a norm-giving authority for judging the legitimacy of positive law, which helped Kant to accommodate past and present in his own philosophy. For it was on the basis of the rational norm of natural law that Kant denounced serfdom,[14] colonialism,[15] aristocratic privilege,[16] and state-ordained church dogma. In Kant, this nature-mediated concept had neither a descriptive meaning, in the broader sense of the term, nor a teleological one—rather it had a moral significance rooted in reason which was stressed by Kant with particular methodological clarity. This pure metaphysics of right, together with the critique of practical reason, constituted the cutting edge of the attack against every variety of theoretical empiricism and aesthetic skepticism regarding the issue of natural law.

Kant had taught the theory of natural law since 1767, at the foundations of which he placed the compendium of nature by the Göttingen thinker Gottfried Achenwall, in which philosophical and historical erudition were uniquely combined with juridical argumentation.[17] By means of this norm of reason Kant sought to submit refractory religion and legislation to rational critique. Through it he also banished all empirical elements, and within this rational framework he set out the formal principles of a pure theory of law that was alone capable of coming to grips with the task of realizing the goals of authentic politics—unencumbered by any admixture of the content of practical knowledge—by intervening in nature and history, so that the preeminent human right of liberty might, indeed should, be put into practice. Thus the state was conceived neither anthropologically nor historically and sociologically, but in terms of a metaphysics which derived from the *a priori* necessity of law, and which determined the ultimate goal of mankind's social existence.

This rational doctrine of law took root in Kant in the mid-1760s, after he had managed, with the help of Rousseau, to free himself from the sensualist moral philosophy of thinkers like Shaftesbury and Hutcheson, and had adopted the methodology and systematology of Christian Wolff. But it was the Scottish moral philosophers (whose thinking had in some aspects been influenced by Montesquieu) who on a number of occasions helped Kant to overcome the past in the theoretical domain—that is to say, to surmount the philosophical schooling and doctrine of Wolff. So, for example, the skepticism of David Hume undermined Kant's faith in the theoretical philosophy originating in the systems of Leibniz and Wolff[18]; and (this being a thesis I should like to demonstrate) an element of Adam Smith, to whose writings Kant was particularly partial, entered into his reception of the French Revolution. It was, after all, Kant who greeted this event with such enthusiasm in his *Streit der Fakultäten* (Controversy Among the Faculties) of 1798. He, the "spectator," recognized the moral significance of the Revolution. Thus the German onlooker (the "spectator") judged the French "actor" neutrally and impartially. However, considering the issue from a universal perspective, it was a case of the observing part of humanity judging the active part. In the first chapter of Part Three of *The Theory of Moral Sentiment*, Smith makes a distinction between the part of a person that undertakes an activity and the part that observes and judges the activity.[19] Smith's contemporary, Adam Ferguson, rejected this differentiation and placed political activity alone at the center of political morality.[20] At any rate, this judgment of the "spectator"—which motivated Kant to accept the realization of Enlightenment philosophy in France into his own theory as a political issue, and to see in it an omen of human progress—needs to be examined in regard to the relationship, and the changes in the relationship, between the Enlightenment and revolution.

The introduction of elements of western European Enlightenment into Germany brought about a change in some of the intellectual presuppositions associated with the Wolffian system. In this new climate there arose voluntary associations devoted to intellectual and political issues; in the period between 1780 and 1790 alone, as many as 120 periodicals became available to the reading public. The middle class, having previously concerned itself primarily with general issues of human existence, now developed a curiosity about political questions. The effect of the events in France (and of the American Revolution in the preceding decade) on the intellectual and socio-political climate was to shift people's concern away from cosmopolitan and humanitarian ideals and to focus it on the political sphere.

The differing relationships between enlightenment and revolution are represented in two pieces of writing by Kant dating from 1784 and 1798; these give us an insight into the way in which the French Revolution transformed this relationship, thereby allowing Kant to become the protagonist of political liberalism. According to my thesis, the French Revolution must be regarded as having exerted a major influence on Kant's political theory, affecting its development and definitive formulation.

Kant's 1784 essay, "What is Enlightenment?," was written against the background of a transitional situation; there he is concerned in particular with the *period* of the Enlightenment, the time in which the process of enlightenment unfolds, as represented by the age of Frederick II of Prussia. Enlightenment had need of the security furnished by an absolute state if it was to develop; and although this enlightenment-promoting sovereign had put himself at the disposal of the rational ends of the state so as to achieve the progress of civilization, his military-based power persisted as the factor that determined the limits to which enlightenment might be taken.[21] In this conception, Kant had not yet managed fully to surmount the past, in that he placed society and its intellectual elite in a relation of dependency on political power. And even if Kant did provide Enlightenment with an intellectual and moral task (as well as enough room to pursue it freely) in defining it as "man's leaving his self-caused immaturity,"[22] he nevertheless qualified even this demand for intellectual autonomy. The dichotomy between "public" and "private" use prohibits the holders of public office—who are responsible to the state rather than to reason and to the community of mature rational beings—from putting forward their private enlightened and independent opinions. Thus opportunity for communication and intellectual exchange is ruled out in the domain of public affairs. Hope for the unfolding of a peaceful and gradual development fostered by the state depends on this division between those who are free to express their enlightened views on all subjects and those who are enjoined from doing so. Political changes can only be effected from above and may not entail the loss of state control, even over the Enlightenment. Regarded in this light, the effect of a revolution may be evaluated negatively, since it can produce no "true reform of the state of mind," and instead "new prejudices, just like the old ones, will serve as the guiding reins of the great, unthinking mass."[23] At this historical stage enlightenment is possible only for the intellectual elite under the aegis of absolutism. Revolution, which would interrupt this process, could only confirm the unenlightened in their prejudices. It acts as a negative catalyst in the enlightenment process by eliminating the role of the state as patron. By distinguishing between the public and private use of reason, Kant's postulate of enlightenment is already qualified and put into question. And if, moreover, Kant assumes that the individual is barely capable of surmounting the obstacles of immaturity on his own, and then only within the public realm, so that in the end the path to enlightenment is eased for the public at large—then the thrust of Kant's thinking in this regard must inevitably lead to the conclusion that the possibility of spontaneous activity in the intellectual domain by society as a whole is reduced to a bare minimum. Revolution would thus be a phenomenon confined to the practice of statecraft that cannot exert a positive influence on the shaping of opinion in the public realm. The state and the intellectual representatives of society can find no means of mediating between and among themselves, so that in this sense the Enlightenment fails to fulfill its social function.

A change is already discernible in 1793. In the second part of "Theory and Practice Concerning the Common Saying: This May Be True in Theory but Does not Apply to Practice," the relationship between enlightenment and the right of resistance is loosened: If the latter is negated on the grounds of the positive existence of the state and of the governing authority, the erring head of state is shown the true direction by which human rights may be realized through the enlightenment of his policy. "As a result, the freedom of the pen is the sole shield of the rights of people."[24] In this connection, oral and written expression are no longer bound by constraints, but are rather in some measure desirable, in order to encourage the type of reforms that would head off revolution. Although, by functioning politically in this manner, the Enlightenment would help to uphold the existing order and reinforce the existence of positive governance, it would also guide these toward implementing the rule of law. The demand for written expression that would preserve or enlarge the scope of human rights within the existing order is no longer taboo and there would be no impediment to Absolutism becoming enlightened.

The arguments Kant put forward in 1793 occupy a middle ground between those of 1784 and 1798. It seems to me that in the end, in 1798, Kant evaluated the Revolution positively in its relation to the Enlightenment, because the changes brought about by the Revolution represented the realization of important political postulates of European Enlightenment. In this regard—in the matter of surmounting the past in his political thought—Kant stood in the forefront of his age. For what was it that caused this "spectator"—this evaluating observer—to abandon his purely objective stance? First of all, in order to avoid judging the Revolution *per se*, he designated it as a "great transformation," or (for example) in his Reflection No. 8077, as "a febrile inner movement," so that, without having to endorse the political and social upheaval itself, he could nevertheless enthusiastically welcome its consequences. In assessing these, one can discern universal and altruistic features that reveal a "moral character," in consequence of which one must conclude that humanity is progressing, at least with regard to its ultimate direction, toward a higher level of morality. This progress—or perhaps better, the belief in progress—is of the very essence of Enlightenment, and now, for the first time, the Revolution had provided empirical proof of its existence. Thus a postulate which might otherwise never have been fulfilled was transformed into enlightened, actual, historical reality. Accordingly, we read in the Cracow Fragment that this was "the moment that must finally come, and be unerringly laid hold of by the people in order . . . to attain a condition from which a permanent progress toward the betterment of humanity, one that was no longer subject to backsliding, could be set on its course."[25] From the standpoint of the belief in progress the consequences of this "transformation" were considered irreversible in nature, since the Enlightenment discovered in the Revolution the transition from theory to practice. The spectator inferred the emergence of a moral tendency in mankind on two grounds. The first of these was that a nation, without any external intervention, was capable of submitting itself to a bourgeois constitution based on what it regarded as suitable principles of law. The second factor that excited the enthusiasm of the spectator was his approval of the republican constitution, which had existed since 1795 in a form that was acceptable to Kant, and whose quintessential feature was the renunciation of all wars of conquest. In this regard the revolution had effected a "true reform of the [spectator's] state of mind"; and despite Kant's having disassociated himself from the events of 1793–1794 and their advocates, the Revolution had put a new and decisive stamp on the times.

In Kant's theory of the Enlightenment, the Revolution was legitimate because it was a politically formative agent: "The enlightenment of the people is the public instruction of the people in their duties and rights as regards the state of which they are a part."[26] If the views of philosophers and cultural enlighteners are to be put into practice on a qualitatively high level, the leader has to heed those views and encourage their public dissemination. The Enlightenment must be qualitatively extended to new strata among the populace, and qualitatively deepened so that it will take root in more and more spheres of existence. What this means for politics is that the natural rights of liberty, equality, and independence must be realized to the fullest possible extent—the first two as the watchwords of Enlightenment, and the last as enacted through the census in the French constitutions of 1791 and 1795. Judging by the manner in which the Revolution was being conducted in France, Kant found it proper to describe it (albeit relying erroneously in this on Johann Benjamin Erhard) as the "evolution of a constitution of natural right."[27] In so doing, he attached to the Revolution the significance of having made manifest the possibility of a true reform of intention in respect of natural law by means of a radical upheaval—thus establishing a point of no return for realizing the postulates of the Enlightenment. It was not metaphysics that furnished the basis of revolutions, as was assumed by A.W. Rehberg and other adversaries of political enlightenment. Rather, the revolution had overcome the impediments of the past, and had created the basis for the ultimate consummation of a constitution based on the metaphysics of right. Hence we witness in this particular revolution an event "which alone united nature and liberty in humankind, in accordance with the inner principles of right,"[28] which is to say that "the causes of this event [were] in fact prepared by nature."[29] The teleological explication therefore makes it possible to establish the objective temporal stage at which the natural prehistory of mankind comes to an end, and the known history of the human race, through the agency of rational liberty, sets in motion the process by which the postulate of natural law is finally realized.

Kant's response to the implementation of the republican constitution in France was to assume that he had found a mediating path between a practical ideal and reality. In this regard his thinking had not only overcome the past, but pointed to the future. Thus in his *Critique of Pure Reason*, the philosopher had asserted that the idea of a "constitution of the greatest possible human freedom according to laws, by which the liberty of every individual can consist with the liberty of each other,"[30] is a necessary norm. This idea had to be held up to every possible experience as a practical example. The position taken by Kant in 1781 was as yet wholly abstract; and it was not until 1798 that Kant's thinking, under the impact of the French Revolution, could take a concrete turn. The principle that those who obey the laws should also be the ones who make the laws was now elevated to the status of an absolute norm, and designated as a *respublica noumenon*. The intermediate stage, concerned with "an organized society in conformity with this as a representation based on laws of freedom by way of an example in experience (*respublica phaenomenon*),"[31] is capable of being established only after numerous conflicts. For the present it is unattainable, and has to be conceived of as a possibility that cannot be put into effect outside the scope of experience in the future. In any event, this concept derived from reason is thereby brought nearer its realization, rather than being consigned to languish eternally; and real conditions are presupposed that make it possible for that concept to assume a concrete form. Additionally, in order to ensure future progress toward a republican constitution, Kant demanded of the sovereign that, notwithstanding the autocratic nature of his government, he should nevertheless rule in a republican manner. This meant that the sovereign had to institute a division of powers, and that a constitution should be drawn up that would be in conformity with the original social contract, so as to preserve the inalienable rights of man. As a result of such a qualitative transformation in the conduct of government, from arbitrary rule to the rule of law, the third stage in this development can be concretized, in order that a *respublica phaenomenon* may emerge in the succeeding stage as a realizable possibility.

In the mid-1780s Kant noted an important turning point in the development of his thinking. His elitist tendency to see in his studies the essence of everything human, and the only standard for judging the world around him, was disturbed by an emergent sensitivity to the dignity of man. Thus he observed in this regard that "Rousseau has put me right."[32] Henceforth we note a growing tendency to affirm the elements of a constitution based on natural law. However, with all the emphasis he now laid on the rights of man—and perhaps even because of his emphasis on them—Kant remained deeply attached to the intellectual world of the Enlightenment. He could therefore contemplate political development, and even the revolutions of 1776 and 1789, without taking national and social factors into account.[33] In this respect he had not gone far enough beyond the theoretical development of the past, which exerted too powerful a hold over him. Thus, apropos of the American Revolution, he noted: "In the history of contemporary England, her subjugation of America went a long way toward reviving the cosmopolitan memory of the same."[34] But even his satisfaction at the success of the revolution in the New World, which he considered to represent a "complete transformation," was expressed in legalistic moral categories: "For in a whole of this kind certainly no member should be a mere means, and should also be an end."[35] A form of social organization had been attained in which the individual was not an object—in other words, not merely the means of another's will—but rather, in his capacity as a participating subject, himself an end, thereby helping to determine the whole, as he too could now claim. Here was a reassertion of Kant's maxim that any social organization in which the individual functioned only as a means was to be regarded as illegal. Legalistic criteria were not adequate to all of the phenomena of the revolution in France, but rather limited their focus and scope. Thus the convening of the Estates was conceived of by Kant as the very quintessence of this "transformation," which had been consummated on the foundations of legality: "In France the National Assembly could change the constitution, even were it convoked only to put the credit standing of the nation in order. For they were the representatives of all the people, since the king had permitted decrees to be issued on the basis of unspecified powers."[36] For it was Kant's view that although the king was the representative of a sovereign people, this role was abolished once he had summoned the Estates since he had dispensed with it himself and had relinquished the dignity and duties of that function. This was therefore a voluntary and legal surrender of his power. In this same regard, it was also the greatest sin of the Revolution that it should have formally convicted and executed Louis XVI, since this represented a "complete subversion of the principles governing the relationship between the sovereign and his people."[37] That the people should decide the fate of the king and permit his execution is to be regarded as a monstrous illegality which can never be put right, since the life of the true representative of sovereignty had been taken.

It was in fact the social aspect of the revolution which Kant was criticizing by condemning the execution of the king. Legitimate rule had been destroyed by this illegal action of an unorganized people, behaving in violation of the principles of law. In taking this action the people were behaving as a group apart which did not represent the interests of the nation at large, but rather the opposite: they were acting in behalf of special interests which were opposed to the *bonum commune* of legal governance, and thereby only furthering the cause of anarchy and preparing the way for it. It was therefore Kant's opinion that "everything that happens by means of the mob (*per turbas*) is in contravention of constitutional law."[38] Since the eruptions of the impassioned and impetuous revolutionary multitudes occurred under the color of that very same legal unity, the individual participants were relieved of their responsibility as citizens and required to resume the status of obedient and subservient subjects. Accordingly, only the self-sufficient, the owners of the means of production, could qualify as citizens of the state. Kant was thus pointing toward the Aristotelian theory of revolution, according to which the existence of a strong middle class prevented revolution by ensuring a social stability in which rich and poor would not be at loggerheads (a theory which would appear to have been confirmed by the contemporary situation of western industrialized states). The rule of the proprietors was restored in revolutionary France in 1795, following the period of radicalization; and Kant for his part approved of many of the Thermidorean institutional and economic arrangements.[39] In his social views the philosopher had identified with the needs of the Third Estate, but he took no account of the rights of man in respect of the Fourth Estate. Although Kant had in large measure overcome the theory and practice of the past, he had also insulated himself from the future course of events, in keeping with the interests of the bourgeoisie in that period.

NOTES

Since no comprehensive English edition of Kant's works is available, I follow the practice of adding to those works which I have cited in English translation a reference to the original German version in Wilhelm Weischedel, ed., *Werke in 12 Bänden*, Werkausgabe (Frankfurt/Main: Suhrkamp, 1977). Kant's "Reflections" are not included in Weischedel's edition, and for these I shall refer to my own *Materialien zu Kants Rechtsphilosophie* (Frankfurt/Main: Suhrkamp, 1976)—hereafter cited as *Materialien*. The passage quoted from Kant's *Streit der Fakultäten* (The Conflict of the Faculties) and the so-called "Cracow Fragment" which pertains to it, as well as passages from the "Reflections," have been translated by me. For further secondary literature, I refer to the bibliography contained in the work by Howard Williams cited in note 12 below.

1. Karl R. Popper, *Die offene Gesellschaft und ihre Feinde*, 6th ed. (Bern/Munich: Francke, 1980), vol. 1, *Der Zauber Platons* 9.

2. What follows in the next pages is a brief account of some of the ideas treated at length in my introduction to Zwi Batscha and Jörn Garber, eds., *Von der ständischen zur bürgerlichen Gesellschaft: Politisch-soziale Theorien im Deutschland der zweiten Hälfte des 18. Jahrhunderts* (Frankfurt/Main: Suhrkamp, 1981).

3. For Christian Wolff's political theory, see Hanns-Martin Bachmann, *Die naturrechtliche Staatslehre Christian Wolffs* (Berlin: Duncker & Humblot, 1977), which contributes significantly to our understanding of the subject.

4. For an account of this group of thinkers, who were associated with the representatives of the Prussian bureaucracy and promoted their interests, see Eckhard Hellmuth, *Naturrechtsphilosophie und bürokratischer Welthorizont*, Studien zur preußischen Geistes- und Sozialgeschichte des 18. Jahrhunderts (Göttingen: Vandenhoeck & Ruprecht, 1985).

5. On popular philosophy, see *inter alia* two of my articles in the *Jahrbuch des Instituts für deutsche Geschichte* (Tel Aviv): "Christian Garves politische Philosophie," in 14 (1985): 113–55; and "Die politische Theorie des Göttinger Philosophen J.G.H. Feder im Revolutionszeitalter," in 15 (1986): 139–64. See also Bernhard Fabian, ed., *Friedrich Nicolai 1733–1811: Essays zum 250. Geburtstag* (Berlin: Nicolaische Verlagsbuchhandlung, 1983).

6. A highly informative discussion of this theme is offered in Diethelm Klippel, *Politische Freiheit und Freiheitsrechte im deutschen Naturrecht des 18. Jahrhunderts* (Paderborn: Schoeningh, 1976).

7. The literature on the German response to the French Revolution is being augmented constantly, especially since 1989. The following are only

some representative earlier studies in the field: Fritz Valjavec, *Die Entstehung der politischen Strömungen in Deutschland 1770–1815* (Munich: Oldenbourg, 1951); Alfred Stern, *Der Einfluß der französischen Revolution auf das deutsche Geistesleben* (Stuttgart and Berlin: Cotta, 1928); Jacques Droz, *Deutschland und die französische Revolution* (Wiesbaden: Steiner, 1955; originally Paris, 1949); George Peabody Gooch, *Germany and the French Revolution* (London: Longmans, Green, and Co., 1920); Reinhold Aris, *History of Political Thought in Germany from 1789 to 1815*, 2nd ed. (New York: Russell & Russell, 1965); Zwi Batscha, *Studien zur politischen Theorie des deutschen Frühliberalismus* (Frankfurt/Main: Suhrkamp, 1981).

8. See Wilhelm Schmidt-Biggemann, "Nicolai oder vom Altern der Wahrheit," in *Friedrich Nicolai 1733–1811* (note 5): "And so within the realm of eclectic philosophy there was still an area that escaped historical and empirical determination: that was what legitimized one's own position" (243).

9. Regarding the influence of Königsberg on Kant see Christian Ritter, "Immanuel Kant," in *Staatsdenker im 17. und 18. Jahrhundert: Reichspublizistik, Politik, Naturrecht*, ed. Michael Stolleis (Frankfurt/Main: Metzner, 1977) 272ff.

10. On Kant's theory of rebellion, see *inter alia* H.S. Reiss, "Kant and the Right to Rebellion," *Journal of the History of Ideas* 17 (1956): 179–92; Werner Haensel, *Kants Lehre vom Widerstandsrecht: Ein Beitrag zur Systematik der Kantschen Rechtsphilosophie* (Berlin: Heise, 1926); Hella Mandt, *Tyrannislehre und Widerstandsrecht: Studien zur deutschen politischen Theorie des 19. Jahrhunderts* (Darmstadt/Neuwied: Luchterhand, 1974) 106–56.

11. Iring Fetscher, "Immanuel Kant und die französische Revolution," in *Immanuel Kant 1724–1974: Kant als politischer Denker*, ed. Eduard Gerresheim (Bonn/Bad Godesberg: Inter Nationes, 1974) 33.

12. Howard Williams, *Kant's Political Philosophy* (Oxford: Oxford University Press, 1983) 16.

13. There is considerable literature devoted as well to Kant's treatment of natural law. In this regard see most recently Ottfried Höffe, *Politische Gerechtigkeit: Grundlegung einer kritischen Philosophie von Recht und Staat* (Frankfurt/Main: Suhrkamp, 1987) 93ff.

14. Immanuel Kant, "Die Metaphysik der Sitten," Weischedel 8:397, para. 30.

15. Ibid. 475. Although para. 30 is omitted from John Ladd's abridged transl., para. 58 has been included in *The Metaphysical Elements of Justice*, trans. John Ladd (Indianapolis/New York: Bobbs-Merrill, 1965) 122.

16. "Metaphysik der Sitten," 8:96; and *Metaphysical Elements of Justice*, 450.

17. Ritter (note 9) 273.

18. Immanuel Kant, "Prolegomena to Every Future Metaphysics that May be Presented as Science (1783)," in *The Philosophy of Kant: Immanuel Kant's Moral and Political Writings*, ed. with an introduction by Carl J. Friedrich (New York: Modern Library, 1949): "I readily confess that the reminder (challenge) of David Hume was what first interrupted my dogmatic slumber many years ago and gave my research in the field of speculative philosophy quite a different direction" (45). For the German see "Prolegomena zu einer jeden künftigen Metaphysik, die als Wissenschaft wird auftreten können," Weischedel 5:118.

19. Adam Smith, *The Theory of Moral Sentiments*, ed. D.D. Raphael and A.L. Macfie (Oxford: Liberty Classics, 1976): "We endeavour to examine our own conduct as we imagine any other fair and impartial spectator would examine it" (110).

20. For the difference between Ferguson and Smith on these issues see " 'Of the Principles of Moral Estimation: A Discourse between Robert Clerc and Adam Smith.' An Unpublished Ms. by Adam Ferguson, with a preface by E.C. Mossner," in *Journal of the History of Ideas* 21 (1960): 222-32.

21. See in this regard the remarks of Hans Carl Finsen, *Das Werden des deutschen Staatsbürgers: Studien zur bürgerlichen Ideologie unter dem Absolutismus in der zweiten Hälfte des 18. und zu Beginn des 19. Jahrhunderts* (Copenhagen/Munich: Fink, 1983) 60ff.

22. Immanuel Kant, "What is Enlightenment?," in *The Philosophy of Kant*, 132; "Beantwortung der Frage: Was ist Aufklärung?," Weischedel 8:53.

23. Kant, "What is Enlightenment?" 134; "Was ist Aufklärung?" 8:55.

24. Immanuel Kant, "Theory and Practice concerning the Common Saying: This May Be True in Theory but Does not Apply to Practice (1793)," *The Philosophy of Kant*, 427; "Über den Gemeinspruch: Das mag in der Theorie richtig sein, taugt aber nicht für die Praxis," Weischedel 11:161.

25. Immanuel Kant, "Krakauer Fragment zum Streit der Fakultäten. Erneuerte Frage: Ob das menschliche Geschlecht im beständigen Fortschreiten zum Bessern begriffen sei?," *Immanuel Kant: Politische Schriften*, Klassiker der Politik n.s. 1, ed. Otto Heinrich von der Gablenz (Cologne, Opladen: Westdeutscher Verlag, 1965) 170.

26. Immanuel Kant, "Der Streit der Fakultäten (1798)," Weischedel 11:362.

27. Ibid. 360. Also of importance to the problem of natural law and the French Revolution is Peter Burg, *Kant und die französische Revolution* (Berlin: Duncker & Humblot, 1974) 126ff.

28. Kant, "Der Streit der Fakultäten," 361.

29. Kant, "Krakauer Fragment," 137.

30. Immanuel Kant, *Critique of Pure Reason* (1781), trans. J.M. Meikeljohn (New York: Willey, 1934); *Kritik der reinen Vernunft*, Weischedel 3:323–24.
31. Kant, "Der Streit der Fakultäten," 364.
32. Zwi Batscha, *Materialien* 55.
33. Aris (note 7): "He had but little understanding for national and social problems, which seemed to be beyond the scope of a man, who had never left his small home province and hardly even his home town" (75).
34. Batscha, *Materialien* 39, s.v. "Reflexion No. 1444."
35. Immanuel Kant, *Critique of Judgment*, in *The Philosophy of Kant* 316–17, para. 65, note; *Kritik der Urteilskraft* (1790), Weischedel 10:323.
36. Batscha, *Materialien* 54, s.v. "Reflexion No. 8055."
37. Kant, *The Metaphysical Elements of Justice*: "The reason why the thought of a formal execution of a monarch by his people is so horrible is that, whereas murder must be conceived of only as an exception to the rule, a formal execution must be conceived as a complete subversion of the principles governing the relationship between the sovereign and his people" (88). For the German see *Metaphysik der Sitten*, Weischedel 8:441.
38. Batscha, *Materialien* 53, s.v. "Reflexion No. 8043."
39. See *inter alia* Johann Friedrich Abegg, *Reisetagebuch von 1798*, ed. by Walter and Jolanda Abegg in collaboration with Zwi Batscha (Frankfurt/Main: Insel, 1976): "Things will go well now. The Directory consists of superior people—that much must be admitted. One cannot expect right to come before *might*. That is how it *ought* to be, but *is* not so" (180).

BERND WITTE

The Beautiful Society and the Symbolic Work of Art: The Anti-Revolutionary Origin of the Bildungsroman

I

THE FRENCH REVOLUTION AND ITS EFFECTS profoundly changed the historical awareness of German authors of the late eighteenth and early nineteenth centuries. It would, however, be too simple to deduce these changes solely from the compromises these writers offer in their works as responses to social upheaval in the neighboring country.[1] Only an analysis of the transformations that aesthetic discourse underwent as a result of the political situation can begin to elucidate the influence of the French Revolution in Germany.

The theory of the symbolic work of art as a self-contained, harmonious entity, whose formal structures capture the totality of the cosmos, had been fully articulated before 1789. The canonical formulation of this aesthetic theory had been presented by Karl Philip Moritz in his treatise *Über die bildende Nachahmung des Schönen* (On the Creative Imitation of the Beautiful), published in 1788.[2] If the essence of this new aesthetic discourse had already been formulated by the Storm and Stress generation, what is it that is added to it at the end of the century so as to constitute what regarded itself as the epoch of Classicism and has been canonized as such by subsequent generations? As far as content is concerned, nothing. However, the function of aesthetics changes in the period after 1794. It is not until the concluding phase of the French Revolution, the *terreur* experienced in Germany as a world crisis, that literature is assigned a new mission within the historical process. Literature becomes the custodian of the existing social order and the guarantor of the perfectibility of humanity.

The indictment and execution of King Louis XVI, the invasion of Germany by the revolutionary armies, and the Jacobin Reign of Terror deeply disturbed both Goethe and Schiller. At the end of 1791, the honorary French citizen Schiller began to write an open letter in defense of the king. Even thirty years later, Goethe remarks in the *Tag- und Jahreshefte* (Annals) for 1793:

> One has to give credit to an active and productive mind, to a man inspired by a truly patriotic feeling and championing his national literature, if the upheaval of everything that exists frightens him, while he has not the faintest idea that something better, or even that something different might be the result of it all.

And for 1794 he added: "Yet how was one to recover, when the monstrous movements in France threatened and frightened us every day? In the previous year, we had very much regretted the deaths of the King and the Queen..., the atrocities of Robespierre had shocked the world."[3] Goethe and Schiller turned the previously established aesthetic model into a defense against the personal danger represented by this crisis. The connection posited by this model between the world, interpreted as a natural, harmonious cosmos, and the symbolic work of art was thus used to advocate the same structural harmony for contemporary society. In the transfer of this aesthetic notion, harmony became a utopian goal, its purpose being to make society immune to the violent conflicts through which social progress was being achieved in France.

In 1795, Schiller had made this transference of the aesthetic model to the social level explicit in his letters *Über die ästhetische Erziehung des Menschen* (On the Aesthetic Education of Man). Here the historical crisis is reflected in the fact that nature and reason have been separated from each other, and both are considered to be negative principles of political reality. A self-contained, perfected society, patterned on the Greek model, is now proposed, and, in analogy to the unity and wholeness of the symbolic work of art, it is called the "aesthetic state":

> Everybody in the aesthetic state—even the most subservient—is a free citizen, and has the same rights as the most noble.... It is here, then, in the realm of aesthetic appearance, that the ideal of equality is fulfilled, which the dreamer would so much like to see realized in its essence.[4]

In these closing lines of the twenty-seventh letter Schiller cites the central political principles of the Revolution, *liberté* and *égalité*, only to eliminate their application to politics. Instead he transfers the realm of their realization to the contemplation of the autonomous work of art. According to Schiller only the disinterested, apolitical reception of art can form man into a harmonious whole, enabling him to join with other such individuals to form the "beautiful society." Schiller's model, which still greatly influences the understanding of the effects of art today, is doubly limited by its elitism. It presupposes the artist as the sole teacher of a liberated humanity, and it addresses itself only to the small minority of those individuals who, free of social obligations, are fortunate enough to have sufficient leisure to be able to devote themselves to the arts. Schiller's transformation, functioning on the basis of structural homologies, thus reverses the original intention of the Storm and Stress aesthetics of genius to free the individual through productive aesthetic work. Seen from a historical perspective, this transformation can be termed a refusal to acknowledge the existence of the historical crisis of 1794 by transferring it to the realm of aesthetics.

Goethe gave expression to the historical significance of classical aesthetics in his *Märchen* (Fairy Tale). Published in 1795 in Schiller's journal *Die Horen* at the same time as the letters *Über die ästhetische Erziehung des Menschen*, the *Märchen* was a continuation to Goethe's *Unterhaltungen deutscher Ausgewanderten* (Conversations of German Emigrants).[5] After having demonstrated the inadequacy of the literature of the marvelous, as well as that of the sentimental and moral novels of the Enlightenment in his *Unterhaltungen*, Goethe describes the origins of the classical work of art in his *Märchen*. Like Schiller, he substitutes art for politics. The central motif of the *Märchen*, the marriage of the young man and the beautiful lily, i.e., the union of art and nature, assigns to the appearance of the perfect work of art its place in history. On the young man's wedding day, the golden, silver, and bronze kings appoint him as their successor. Through their forms and the symbols that he attributes to them, Goethe identifies the three old kings as representatives of the three ages of world history: antiquity, the medieval era, and absolutism. Their kingdom has now come to an end, as is indicated by the collapse of the fourth, the "compound" king, a clear reference to the death of Louis XVI.[6] Their place is taken by the young man, who himself is called king at this very moment. Goethe thus reinterprets the ancient myth of the three ages, giving it a happy ending. In his version, the declining succession of the three kings is not, as in Hesiod, followed by the iron age of war, but by the paradisiacal age of youth. In a scene of investiture, the three kings give the new ruler the tokens of their power. The bronze king, the "mighty prince," hands him "a sword in a bronze sheath," the silver king commands him to "shepherd the sheep" and the golden king tells him to "recognize the highest!"[7] We can interpret this to mean that during the present crisis situation caused by the revolution, art should fulfill the functions which were performed by political powers in the most recent past, by the Church during the Middle Ages, and by philosophy in antiquity.

The *Märchen* thus proves to be a poetological as well as a historico-philosophical text. Through its mythical resonances, Goethe represents the crisis of the old order in the French Revolution as the culmination of an era to which he opposes the new era of art. Revolutionary France appears in the guise of a giant whose shadow causes extensive damage on the other side of the river, that is, east of the Rhein. This allegorical image makes the very same statement that appears in political form in the *Tag- und Jahreshefte* for

1793, namely that "these influences have reached Germany, and crazy, even unworthy people are seizing power."[8] With the event that renders the giant harmless, Goethe returns again to the notion he had already formulated in the reinterpretation of Hesiod's myth:

> Meanwhile the giant was drawing nearer and nearer, and in astonishment at what he saw, his eyes now wide open, he dropped his hands, and did no further harm as, gaping, he stepped into the vestibule. He was just heading for the portal of the temple when suddenly, in the middle of the court, he was rooted to the ground. There he stood, a colossal and powerful pillar of gleaming reddish stone; and his shadow pointed to the hours set into the pavement, not in numbers, but in noble and significant images.[9]

By changing the giant into the stylus of a sundial, Goethe's narrative presents the aesthetic dream of the Weimar Classicists in a single vision. In it, every word is of the utmost significance: it is the beauty of the temple, representing the perfect work of art, which paralyzes the giant and brings the revolutionary movement to a standstill. At the same time the perfect work of art, transcending history, incorporates historical experience, thus becoming an indicator for what is historically timely. It is this idea that Goethe intends to express by giving the allegorical figure of revolution its place in petrified form in the vestibule of the temple. The progression of time is rendered powerless and replaced by an endless circular movement through "noble and significant images." Within this single allegory, the historico-philosophical index contained in every modern work of art can be traced back to its historical origin.

Schiller formulated a similar metaphor for the standstill of historical time and the eternal return of aesthetic time in the prologue to his journal *Die Horen*. In the earlier *Ankündigung* (Advertisement), Schiller explains the name of *Die Horen*:

> In these divine figures, the Greeks worshipped the order that held the world together. All excellence flows from this order, the most appropriate symbol for which is the uniform rhythm of the sun's movement. Mythology makes them the daughters of Themis and Zeus, of law and power.[10]

The anti-revolutionary origin of German classical aesthetics is clearly stated in this mythical genealogy, where order is conceived simultaneously as an aesthetic, a natural, and a political value. In obedience to the laws governing the revolution of the sun and the seasons, this order stands at the very apex of the scale of values. As in Goethe's *Märchen*, time is no longer seen as a goal-oriented process, but rather as the return of the eternally same, and is thus largely anti-historical. The concept of "epoch" here returns to its etymological origin: the *Kunstepoche* (Period of Art) of German Classicism, bringing time to a standstill in an aesthetic paradise, reveals itself as the attempted mythical exorcism of the danger of the historical moment. In the political sphere, this translates into a defense of the *status quo*. The new aesthetics, represented by Schiller in the image of the "newborn Venus," is specifically placed under the protection of the ruling powers, insofar as Schiller appoints Themis and Zeus, law and power, her guardians. The enormity of this gesture cannot be fully understood unless we recall Goethe's Storm and Stress hymn "Prometheus," written twenty years earlier. There creative mankind speaks out rebelliously in a self-confident and defiant tone against all religious and worldly powers as represented in the figure of the most powerful of all Gods: "Cover your heavens with clouds, Zeus. . . ." This revolutionary gesture is retracted by Schiller in *Die Horen*. In the face of the terror prevailing in France and threatening to cross over into Germany, Weimar Classicism, in its founding manifesto, embraces the existing order and constitutes itself as an "inner world protected by power."

II

Goethe's most significant and powerful reflection on the French Revolution is found neither in his comedies, nor in his tragedy *Die natürliche Tochter* (The Natural Daughter), but in the "bourgeois" genre of the novel.[11] During the years 1794–1795, in which the *Unterhaltungen* and the *Märchen* appeared in Schiller's *Horen*, Goethe was working on the final version and the publication of *Wilhelm Meisters Lehrjahre* (Wilhelm Meister's Apprenticeship), the fourth volume of which, containing books seven and eight, appeared in the autumn of 1796. These works show remarkable structural similarities. The novellas in the *Unterhaltungen* demonstrate the impotence of bourgeois Enlightenment literature in the face of the chaos and war resulting from the French Revolution. This disrupted order is directly juxtaposed to the peaceful era guaranteed by the perfect symbolic work of art and developed as a utopian program in the *Märchen*. Similarly, *Wilhelm Meisters Lehrjahre* is divided into two contrasting parts: The first five books (a revised version of the unfinished theater novel Goethe worked on between 1777 and 1785) lead up to Wilhelm's failure to realize his original plan of educating himself through the theater. The seventh and eighth books, on the other hand, separated formally from the first part of the novel by the insertion of the *Bekenntnisse einer schönen Seele* (Confessions of a Beautiful Soul), provide Wilhelm, within the Tower Society, with a practical and socially effective new goal for his life.

Goethe's ideas about the French Revolution have become far more radical in *Wilhelm Meisters Lehrjahre* than they were in the *Märchen*. The historical significance of this radicalization can be seen from the bipartite structure of the novel, in which even the symbolic work of art, still praised a year earlier as the epitome of a postrevolutionary era, becomes one of the objects of his critique. The crisis and turning-point of the novel comes in the fifth book, when a production of Shakespeare's *Hamlet* and its aftermath demonstrate the total failure of the theater as an educational institution. This leads to the disappointment of the idealistic Wilhelm and the abandonment of his theatrical mission.[12] Many references in the text indicate that the discussions of Shakespeare's masterpiece and of the most appropriate way to produce it are meant to address the issue of how to deal with a classical, symbolic work of art. In contrast to the production practices of the times, Wilhelm demands of Serlo and his troupe that *Hamlet* be staged "completely and not all cut up."[13] Wilhelm reworks the play and creates an "aesthetic whole,"[14] as he himself calls it, from the wild growth of the Renaissance tragedy. The metaphysical basis for this notion, which is central to the new understanding of art, is indicated by Wilhelm in a single metaphor which has been used time and again since Herder's Storm and Stress writings. In Wilhelm's eyes, the tragedy is "one tree trunk, with branches, leaves, buds, blossoms, and fruits."[15] Thus, *Hamlet* is understood as an organic entity, in which all the parts are connected to each other and each single part reflects the whole.

Wilhelm attaches his hope for the educational effect of theater to the production of the play conceived as a whole, perfect work of art. "No pleasure is temporary, for it leaves a lasting effect; and our own work and effort conveys some sense of a hidden energy to the audience, and one never knows what effect that may have."[16] With these words, Goethe's protagonist formulates the very same position that Schiller developed in his understanding of aesthetic education through the contemplation of the symbolic work of art. Nevertheless, in the fifth book of the novel, the attempt to carry this idealistic plan through fails miserably. As in the *Unterhaltungen*, the political reasons for this inadequacy of literature are indicated only allegorically; the aesthetic crisis is accompanied by a nocturnal fire. From then on, the actors attach only entertainment value to their activities and lose themselves in the routine of everyday theater life. Moreover, it turns out that the play has no didactic effect on the audience whatsoever. Wilhelm's high aspirations "to educate the taste of the nation" must be disappointed by the tasteless reactions of the audience at the *Hamlet* performance. Thus, the inadequacies of the theater as institution undermine the idealistic goal of social education through art.

Theater is finally unmasked for what it is, a bourgeois cultural institution, which—like any other commodity—is subject to the laws of supply, demand, and profit-making. During Wilhelm's absence, Melina and Serlo, the two leaders of the group, plan a theater reform of their own. In order to realize their financial aspirations they wish to lower the performance niveau to the level of popular comedy:

> Melina referred rather crudely to Wilhelm's "pedantic" ideals, his presumptuous claims of educating the public, instead of being educated by them; and both he and Serlo vehemently asserted that all they wanted was to make money, get rich, and enjoy life, and to rid themselves of anyone who stood in the way of such plans.[17]

It cannot escape the reader's attention that this is identical to the principle of "get rich and have a good time" to which the businessman Werner subscribes.[18] Wilhelm's lofty educational ideal could hardly be betrayed more cynically than by reducing theater to a bourgeois institution that knows only two goals: to make a profit for the producer and to provide the public with entertainment.

III

What is doomed in the world of aesthetic appearance is renewed and transformed into a social ideal in the second part of the novel. The structure of the society around Lothario and Natalie that Wilhelm enters in the last two books of the novel reproduces the formal qualities of the symbolic work of art. Moreover, in its unmistakable echoes of the language of the French Revolution, it incorporates as a positive, redemptive element those middle class values ("Verbürgerlichung") responsible for the failure of Wilhelm's theatrical project. With this transformation, Goethe made the dubious attempt to synthesize the political upheaval that he feared and the classical work of art, of whose social inefficiencies he had become aware, in order to preserve the achievements of both without having to accept the negative consequences of the Reign of Terror.

In the second part of the novel, in place of the quickly disintegrating group of actors, Goethe introduces an extensive bourgeois-aristocratic family as the ideal form of society. It is united by the relationship that binds Lothario, Natalie, Friedrich, and the countess as brothers and sisters. In this group—in contrast to the reality of the times—class barriers are not considered obstacles to marriage, so that the bourgeois protagonists Therese, Wilhelm, and Philine can be assimilated into the existing family through marriage.

Goethe's concept of a group held together through fraternal and marital love and serving as the model for the organisation of a future better world is the social equivalent of the organic unity that characterizes the symbolic work of art in classical aesthetics. This transference is much more relevant for the historical evaluation of the novel than Wilhelm's and Natalie's marriage of renunciation ("Entsagungsehe"), in which most commentators find Goethe's answer to the French Revolution.[19] Such marriages between partners of unequal social status had already been proposed as a social corrective in the German Enlightenment novel, long before the Revolution. It is evident to anyone familiar with the eighteenth-century novel that it is not Goethe's voice which speaks in the comic finale of *Wilhelm Meisters Lehrjahre*, but rather that of his long-ago Leipzig teacher, Christian Fürchtegott Gellert. In his 1747 novel, *Leben der schwedischen Gräfin von G.* (Life of the Swedish Countess G.), Gellert had already built a society of rational individuals through a marriage that transcended the barriers between bourgeoisie and nobility.[20]

This similarity is underlined by the fact that both novels exclude marriage between partners of the same social class; intermarriage between the nobility and the bourgeoisie proves to be an ideological aim of the Enlightenment as well as the Classical model of society. However, this class compromise, represented in Gellert's novel only by the one relationship between the countess and Herr R., occurs three times in *Wilhelm Meisters Lehrjahre*. This heightened emphasis seems necessary because, after the execution of the French king and the establishment of the equality of all the people of France as *citoyens*, such a compromise appears to be less persuasive than in prerevolutionary times.

Passionate love has no place in this exemplary society. As in Gellert's novel, where marriage between a sister and brother leads to death, the couple Sperata and Augustin are punished for their incest with insanity and death. By giving passionate love a catastrophic ending, Goethe alludes to the conditions under which the desired society—a society based on compromise—can be realized. As Wilhelm's renunciation of Therese makes clear, the beautiful society can be realized only through renunciation, in the sacrifice of personal desires. Goethe reaches above and beyond Gellert's model by letting all of the characters who possess any kind of passionate, individual private life, like Mariane, Mignon and Aurelie, die without admitting them to the beautiful society. This motif, too, contains in its transformations the traces of a later time. Those who refuse to compromise their individuality, and who have to die because of their rich emotional life, are no longer morally condemned as in Gellert's novel, but transfigured into saints. Although doomed during their lifetime, they are justified in the realm of the ideal. After the discovery of spiritual and emotional love in *Die Leiden des jungen Werthers* (The Sorrows of Young Werther), Goethe depicts these uncompromising individuals—like Werther—as the tragic, but also the humanely beautiful figures of the novel.

While in the poetic texts of the time marriage appears as a metaphor for the harmonious whole of the symbolic work of art, Goethe here brings it back to the level of fictional reality. In the *Lehrjahre* the union of two people is not an image for the bonding of two opposite elements in the classical work of art, as in Schiller's *Briefe* or in Goethe's own *Märchen*. Rather, Goethe reforms social reality by organizing it as a community of small families related by marriage. This is, of course, the exact opposite of contemporary French society, torn by political strife, and is meant to be understood as the fulfillment of *fraternité*, of brotherliness in the true sense of the word.

The "beautiful society" in which Goethe's utopian vision of society finds its fulfillment at the end of the novel is not the one that Schiller had envisioned in his letters *Über die ästhetische Erziehung des Menschen*. It is not given to leisurely contemplation of the work of art, but is part of active life. It is, however, a beautiful society, because it is constructed according to the proportions of the symbolic work of art as an organic totality. The harmonious structure, which had demonstrated its impotence in its apparent realization in the work of art, is thus rescued by becoming objective and socially concrete, and is considered as working actively toward harmonizing and reconciling society.[21]

IV

The aesthetization of society outlined here functions as the transformation of the formal structures of an aesthetic discourse into the conceptual categories of a political discourse. It is provoked by what German intellectuals regarded as the crisis of the Enlightenment represented by the social conflict in France. They rejected less the economic and social goals of the Revolution than the violent means by which these were achieved in France. According to their interpretation, reason had unveiled its violent face in the body politic of "freedom and equality" fashioned by Robespierre and his followers. Thus the Goethean model of society can be read as a counter-project to the rational state in France. In the Goethean model, the central goals of the revolutionary state should be achieved in a peaceful manner, with the tools of the prerevolutionary Enlightenment. In the Tower Society, instead of the direct use of power in social struggles, Goethe advocates the "unfolding of indirect power" as the central vehicle of social change. In his analysis of the Masonic secret societies of the eighteenth century Reinhart Koselleck has established the importance of this indirect power for the realization of bourgeois interests vis à vis the absolutist state.[22]

This basic trend is confirmed by the very concrete, programmatic advice offered by Lothario, the embodiment of the new social order. His praise of Therese's virtues as a housewife extends to a description of the bourgeois environment itself:

> The sensible housewife really governs, rules over all that is in the home and makes possible every kind of satisfying activity for the whole family. What is the greatest joy of mankind but pursuing what we perceive to be good and right, really mastering the means to our ends? And where should these ends be if not inside the home? (277)

Here the house, the private domain, is described as the realm of social influence par excellence. At the same time it is claimed—as in the literature of the Enlightenment—that the social structure of the private domain should be expanded to include virtually the entire society. The nobleman Lothario, who had fought under Lafayette for the independence of the United States, proves to be a good family man, actively taking care of his big household and farms. "Here or nowhere is America" is one of his sayings. It is he too who allows all members of his household, and, by extension, the entire society, to take part in his fortune—"Here or nowhere is Herrnhut" (a tightly-knit religious community) is another of his maxims.

Lothario also makes a plea for the economic equality of all citizens. He joins forces with Werner, the archetypical bourgeois merchant, to practice agriculture according to capitalist principles. Before this can happen, however, the country estates have to be freed from their feudal restrictions. For the property of the nobility Lothario demands "equality with all other possessions," which implies the abolition of the nobility's exemptions from taxes and other civil obligations. Lothario is willing to pay taxes, "if the state would abolish the hocus-pocus of feudal tenure in exchange for an equitable regular tax payment and allow us to do as we please with our estates."[23] Such statements, especially the key word equality (égalité), cannot be made in 1796 without referring directly to revolutionary events in France.[24] Goethe, a member of the cabinet of the Duke of Weimar, demands nothing less than equality of economic opportunity in the most important economic sector of his time, in agriculture. This equality—as Goethe himself points out—presupposes the total disposability of one's possessions. Estates should become freely circulating commodities, no longer subject to traditional restrictions. Goethe is advocating a free market in a sector of the German economy which was—at least to a certain extent—still governed by special privilege until the twentieth century.[25]

To be sure, these progressive economic ideas remain subordinated to the novel's basic anti-revolutionary goal. When talking about his future plans Lothario articulates clearly an awareness of historical crisis inspired by the experience of property owners during the revolutionary years:

> From our ancient Tower a Society shall emerge, which will extend into every corner of the globe, and people from all over the world will be allowed to join it. We will cooperate in safeguarding our means of existence, in case some political revolution should displace one of our members from the land he owns. (345)

The future society to which Wilhelm will belong functions as a "mutual insurance company" against the risks of expropriation through revolutionary upheavals. It appears to be nothing less than a defense of the economic status quo, and it has objectively restorative qualities.[26]

Thus the Janus-face of the Tower Society is revealed. On the one hand, it inscribes the bourgeois domain, the bourgeois economic morality, founded on the principles of the free market, into the future society. On the other hand, it refuses its members the individual freedom which is the prerequisite for all social emancipation. Natalie, who takes the place of the loving female characters Mariane and Aurelie at the end of the novel, embodies the essence of the beautiful society. This shining symbolic figure represents the principles of social balance which, in the economic sphere, regulate the powers of the market according to the doctrines of Adam Smith and his followers. Natalie says of herself: "My greatest delight was, and still is, to be presented with some deficiency, some need in others, and be able to think of some way of repairing or alleviating it" (322). These maxims should not be misunderstood simply as expressions of Christian love of one's fellow man. That Goethe's novel insists on a rigorous secularization of all religious ideas is reflected by the fact that the chapel of the castle is stripped of all Christian symbols and, decorated with a few allegorical images, becomes the secret society's initiation room. In this secular context, Natalie embodies the principle of balance. She is the active remedy for what is lacking in society. In her character the worldly expectation of salvation, inherent in the "beautiful society," is celebrated.

By marrying Natalie, Wilhelm binds himself to the social ideal she embodies. Lothario says as much when he promises Wilhelm his sister's hand:

> Since we encountered each other in such an extraordinary way, let us not live ordinary lives, let us work together in a worthy enterprise. It is beyond belief what a cultivated man can achieve for himself and others, if, without trying to lord it over others, he has the temperament to be the guardian of many, helping them to find the right occasion to do what they would all like to do, and guiding them toward the goals they have clearly in mind without knowing how to reach them. Let us then join

together in a common purpose—that is not mere enthusiasm, but an idea which can quite well be put into practice, and is indeed often implemented, though not always consciously. My sister Natalie is a living example of this. (372)

With these statements, in which the ideal content of the beautiful society is depicted as the fulfillment of Wilhelm's striving for educational experience, Goethe specifically denies the very essence of that Enlightenment which Kant had defined in 1784 in the famous maxim as "man's release from his self-incurred tutelage." In marked contrast to the Kantian view, Lothario requires the establishment of a "bourgeois" private sphere under the tutelage of aristocratic "legal guardians," a system that has been in effect from the very beginning of the novel in the plot's direction of Wilhelm's educational development.

Wilhelm's original plan to "educate himself completely and totally" presupposes the freedom of the individual.[27] Seen from the perspective of the end of the novel, however, such freedom is questionable. The analytical structure of the novel, which obscures until the very end the relationship that has existed between Wilhelm and the Tower Society from the start, not only shows the society as the educational institution that guides the individual, but also makes it appear to be the text's objective horizon of reason. Goethe attempts to justify his holistic world view, which in Modernity has authority and plausibility only as the *Weltanschauung* of the individual, by means of a society which, as the embodiment of objective reason, seems to guarantee the orderly progress of world history. One could also say that, in place of the metaphysical realm of a God, Goethe regards a society of rational men and women as the highest authority, by which the fate of the individual is guided and justified. The closed form of the symbolic novel thus implies the model of a closed society in which basic openness, the acceptance of the opposing interests of the individual members, is suppressed.

The freedom of the individual does not manifest itself in *Wilhelm Meisters Lehrjahre* as political freedom, but paradoxically as liberation from the recently established bourgeois sexual morality. Goethe underlines this reinterpretation of *liberté*, the other key word of the Revolution, by means of a highly ironic contrast. The bourgeois hero, Wilhelm, whose development is driven by guilt towards Mariane, his first lover, and who promised Aurelie he would fall in love only with the woman whom he would later marry, comes to the castle solely to reprimand Lothario for his behavior towards Aurelie. Instead of carrying out his plan, however, Wilhelm is caught up in the nobleman's social projects and made an accomplice in his carefree love-affairs.

As his name suggests, Lothario's *liberté* is that of the *libertin*, who, in the eighteenth-century English novel, is synonymous with the aristocratic seducer.[28] Wounded in a duel because of "a little adventure" over a lady, Lothario asks Wilhelm to lure away his present lover, Lydie. Wilhelm brings her to Therese, who tells him about her love for Lothario. Therese's reasons for her separation from him have to do with the fact that she has found out about his earlier love affair with her mother, Lady St. Alban. When Wilhelm returns from his mission, Lothario has recovered and has renewed an earlier acquaintance with the daughter of a tenant farmer. Thus each of the six chapters of the seventh book tells the story of one of Lothario's liaisons. This proliferation of its leader's romantic adventures suggests that the projected society is as independent of traditional moral values as of religious or artistic objectives.

Living with Lothario, Wilhelm is introduced to this "free" way of life. The anthropological model according to which Wilhelm educates himself defines, through the character of Lothario, the economic and the erotic emancipation of man as interrelated and equally valuable goals. A similar notion is expressed in the maxims of the *Lehrbrief* that Wilhelm receives from the Tower Society. One of them reads: "No one is ever happy until his unlimited striving has set itself a limitation" (339). Here, too, an aristocratic elitist model of emancipation is proposed as the ideal, an ideal whose extreme form can be found in the novels of the Marquis de Sade. This is what Wilhelm is led into. In other words, his education implies, among other things, that he is finally freed from his bourgeois moral scruples, his Wertherian fixation on marriage based on love. Thus, Goethe's "most incommensurable production," as he himself called it, ends in total ambivalence.[29] The opposition of the economic freedom of the market and the moral freedom of the "great personality," on the one hand, and the social bonding of the individual in the "beautiful society" of the extended "family" on the other, remains unresolved.

V

And art—what is its function in all of this? In the last two books of the novel, art is a matter of only minor importance. In the ideal society that has constituted itself according to the symbolic work of art, it is excluded—as is passionate love and religion. Goethe shows this through the description of the Hall of the Past, located in Natalie's castle. This hall is, in essence, the aesthetic realm, in which each detail manifests certain characteristics of symbolic art: its artificiality, its harmony, its enigmatic character in the sphinxes guarding the entrance; its memorial function that preserves the dead under the appearance of life. This is the reason why Goethe can ascribe to this hall the same educational function that has been ascribed to symbolic art: "And so everyone who entered [here] seemed to be elevated above himself." The Hall of the Past represents the aesthetic realm itself. It is the symbol of the artistic symbol. However, it presents itself as the art of the past preserved as in a museum, which also means that it has become a commodity. The art works that decorate the hall come from the collection of Wilhelm's grandfather or have been purchased by the Marchese for Natalie's uncle.[30] The name, then, "Hall of the Past," not only indicates that the past, the dead, are preserved in it, but also that art, being the appearance of beauty, no longer has any active function in a society which has defined itself as the absolute work of art. That is why the Hall of the Past is the place where the embalmed body of Mignon, the symbolic figure for art itself, will be kept. The contemplation of the work of art in the Schillerian sense is expressly negated here in this context, as summarized by Wilhelm: "Nothing perishes except him who observes and enjoys" (331). The exhortation "Flee, young man, flee," which the Abbé in the guise of Hamlet's father's ghost leaves behind for Wilhelm, is paralleled by the inscription on the statue in the Hall of the Past: "Turn to life." The rejection of symbolic art that the plot reveals in the failure of Wilhelm's theater project is once more symbolically present. That scarcely anyone has recognized these associations since the publication of the novel almost 200 years ago, even though the author underlined them twice, is rooted in the total ambiguity of the venture. The rejection of symbolic art has been formulated within a text that itself has legitimately been seen as a classical model of a symbolic work.

At the end of *Wilhelm Meisters Lehrjahre*, however, we find another, a non-symbolic form of art. The Tower Society maintains an archive in which the life stories of its members are stored on scrolls. "Wilhelm walked up to them and looked at the names on the scrolls. To his amazement he found there Lothario's apprenticeship, Jarno's apprenticeship, and his own, in amongst many others with names unknown to him" (304). By citing its own title, the novel mirrors itself at the end in the library of the Tower Society. The book the reader is reading is *Wilhelm Meisters Lehrjahre*, the same *Lehrjahre* that Wilhelm finds in the castle after having completed his apprenticeship.

The library of the Tower Society, to which this book belongs, is, in essence, infinite. Underlying the Tower Society's project is the utopian idea that only the amassing of the biographies of all educated people will make possible both an objective insight into the world and its final salvation. "All men make up mankind and all forces together make up the world," as Jarno reads in Wilhelm's *Lehrbrief* (338). This is why the Tower Society initiates this enormous writing project. "We wanted to make our own observations, and establish our own archive of knowledge. That is how the various confessions arose, written sometimes by ourselves and sometimes by others, from which the records of apprenticeship were subsequently put together" (336). Thus the Tower Society is finally revealed as an infinite writing project run by the Abbé, through which social, objective reason is to be collected into an archive of world knowledge.

Here the anti-speculative, worldly Goethe has reached a point where he touches upon the mystic dimensions of literature. The transformation of all individual histories—which in their totality constitute world history—into Scripture is conceived as the final and most extreme counter-project to a revolutionary transformation of society. This translation into writing can rightfully be called an archive, a collective memory of mankind. Bound to the utopian, never to be completed mission of the writing of all lives is the hope for a different revolution, a peaceful renewal of the world, an end to all domination. It is this hope that drives the eternal human striving that lies at the heart of what could be called, to use a term coined by Goethe himself, *Weltliteratur*.

NOTES

A German version of this paper was published in *Juni: Magazin für Kultur und Politik* 3, 2–3 (1989): *Dossier: Die große Französische Revolution*, 116–32.

1. Walter Müller-Seidel, "Deutsche Klassik und Französische Revolution," in *Die Geschichtlichkeit der deutschen Klassik* (Stuttgart: Metzler, 1983) 35. Müller-Seidel cites within this context a dictum of the early Lukács: "The truly social in literature, however, is the form." To be sure, this methodological stance is too undialectically direct. It is possible to discern the historical placement value of each change in this system only if one understands literature as a system of discourse that is continuously undergoing transformation.
2. See Bernd Witte, "Genie, Revolution, Totalität: Mythische Tendenzen der Kunstepoche," in *Zerstörung, Rettung des Mythos durch Licht*, ed. Christa Bürger (Frankfurt/Main: Suhrkamp, 1986) 19ff.
3. *Goethes Werke* (Hamburger Ausgabe), vol. 10, 8th ed. (Munich: Beck, 1982) 438ff. Subsequent references to this edition will be cited simply as HA with volume and page number.
4. *Schillers Werke* (Nationalausgabe), vol. 20 (Weimar: Böhlau, 1962) 412. Further citations from this edition will appear simply as NA with volume and page number.
5. See Bernd Witte, "Das Opfer der Schlange: Zur Auseinandersetzung Goethes mit Schiller in den *Unterhaltungen deutscher Ausgewanderten* und im *Märchen*," in *Unser Commercium: Goethes und Schillers Literaturpolitik*, ed. Wilfried Barner et al. (Stuttgart: Metzler, 1984) 461–84.
6. In the figure of the "compound king," who is especially vulnerable because of his constitution, Goethe alludes to a biblical motif, namely the idol with the feet of clay.
7. HA 6:237.
8. HA 10:439.
9. HA 6:240.
10. NA 22:107.
11. Regarding the comedies about revolution see Herbert Kraft, ". . . alle Jahre einmal als ein Wahrzeichen: Goethes Lustspiel *Der Groß-Cophta*," in *Unser Commercium* (note 5) 275–88. On Goethe's *Die natürliche Tochter*, see Ehrhard Bahr, "Goethes 'Natürliche Tochter': Weimarer Hofklassik und Französische Revolution," in *Deutsche Literatur zur Zeit der Klassik*, ed. Karl Otto Conrady (Stuttgart: Reclam, 1977) 226ff.
12. The structural importance of the fifth book has been pointed out, particularly by Helmut Koopmann, "Wilhelm Meisters Lehrjahre," in *Goe-*

thes Erzählwerk: Interpretationen, ed. Paul Michael Lützeler and James E. McLeod (Stuttgart: Reclam, 1985) 168–91.

13. HA 7:293.
14. HA 7:295.
15. HA 7:294.
16. Quoted according to the translation by Eric A. Blackall, *Wilhelm Meister's Apprenticeship*, in Victor Lange et al., eds, Goethe's Collected Works, vol. 9 (New York: Suhrkamp Publishers New York, 1989) 191. Further references to this volume will appear in parentheses in the text.
17. (213). To some extent Jane Brown is right when she states that "Wilhelm represents the limitations of the neo-classical point of view." Jane Brown, "The Theatrical Mission of the *Lehrjahre*," in *Goethe's Narrative Fiction: The Irvine Goethe Symposium*, ed. William J. Lillyman (Berlin, New York: De Gruyter, 1983) 81. However, her analysis becomes completely ahistorical when she concludes from this that "the theatrical mission of the *Lehrjahre* is to return the drama from Aristotelian neo-classical forms to the indigenous tradition of allegorical and festival drama." Goethe is not concerned with reversing Gottsched's theater reform. Rather, he is concerned with depicting precisely this most advanced form of art, the drama understood as the symbolic work of art, in its inadequacy for the education of the individual as well as the society.
18. HA 7:287.
19. For an example of the kind of research referred to here, see Ehrhard Bahr, "Goethe's 'Natürliche Tochter,' " 236: "It is the marriage of renunciation that Goethe makes the symbol of the ethical and political regeneration that he hopes for in the future from the alliance between aristocracy and bourgeoisie."
20. See Bernd Witte, "Der Roman als moralische Anstalt: Gellerts *Leben der schwedischen Gräfin von G.* und der Roman des 18. Jahrhunderts," in *Germanisch-Romanische Monatsschrift* 30 (1980): 150–68.
21. In this settling of the poetic principle into the heart of the new society, the final—although unfortunate—victory of "poetry over prose" is much more evident than in the "Diaphanie" of isolated "mythical images" with which Hannelore Schlaffer attempts to rescue the novel for poetry. Schlaffer, *Wilhelm Meister: Das Ende der Kunst und die Wiederkehr des Mythos* (Stuttgart: Metzler, 1980). Wilfried Barner's attempt to defend the Tower Society against the reproach that it is utterly "prosaic" and "economical" also falls short of an accurate analysis. Barner, "Geheime Lenkung: Zur Turmgesellschaft in Goethes *Wilhelm Meister*," in *Goethe's Narrative Fiction* (note 17) 85ff. Barner convincingly points to the fact that with the quasi-divine "secret" guidance of Wilhelm's path, a naive, epic element on the

model of the *Odyssey* is included in the novel. However, this alone does not suffice to guarantee the "aesthetic" quality of the Tower Society. This aesthetic quality can only be found in its structure.

22. Reinhart Koselleck, *Kritik und Krise: Eine Studie zur Pathogenese der bürgerlichen Welt* (Frankfurt/Main: Suhrkamp, 1973).

23. HA 7:507.

24. Rolf-Peter Janz, "Zum sozialen Gehalt der 'Lehrjahre,' " in *Literaturwissenschaft und Geschichtsphilosophie: Festschrift Wilhelm Emrich* (Berlin, New York: De Gruyter, 1975) 320ff. Janz rightly emphasizes the propinquity of Lothario's demands to those of the French Revolution.

25. The connection of these ideas to the theories of Adam Smith was first pointed out by Stefan Blessin, *Die Romane Goethes* (Königstein/Ts.: Athenäum, 1979) 29–38.

26. Guiliano Baioni, " 'Märchen'—'Wilhelm Meisters Lehrjahre'— 'Hermann und Dorothea': Zur Gesellschaftsidee der deutschen Klassik,"in *Goethe Jahrbuch* 92 (1975): 73–127. Baioni interprets the Tower Society as a return to the *ancien régime* and thus as the height of Goethe's "Restoration project." In this way he mistakes the obvious adoption of revolutionary principles in Goethe's text. Stefan Blessin (note 27) 32 characterizes the social contents of the *Lehrjahre* pertinently as a "social change without revolutionary violence." Dieter Borchmeyer, *Höfische Gesellschaft und französische Revolution bei Goethe* (Kronberg/Ts.: Athenäum, 1977) 164–84 comes to a similar conclusion when he compares the goals of the Tower Society to the contemporary reform ideas of A.W. Rehberg and Adam Müller. Borchmeyer concludes from this that Goethe anticipated important aspects of Stein's reform project. In order to assess properly the placement value of the two final books of the *Lehrjahre*, it is not enough simply to analyse the contents of the suggested solutions to social problems and then, according to one's political beliefs, to praise them as a far-sighted reform or condemn them as a step backward. Only by realizing that Goethe's societal model is based on the structures of the symbolic work of art, as developed in aesthetic discourse, can the questionable nature of the political aspects of Goethe's text as well as its tremendous literary and social effectiveness be elucidated.

27. The "historical incompatibility of the Tower Society with the concept of the bourgeois individual Wilhelm" is already established by Barner (note 21) 109. However, Barner does not draw any consequences from this for the historical assessment of the genre of the *Bildungsroman*.

28. Jane Brown (note 17) 69ff. refers to the figure of Lothario in Nicholas Rowe's *The Fair Peasant* (1703) as the origin of this association. Lothario's name "had already become synonymous with 'seducer' in English by the end of the eighteenth century."

29. *Tag- und Jahreshefte* 1796. HA 10:446.

30. This aspect is emphasized by Hannelore Schlaffer (note 21) 67: "The object of the connoisseur is changed into an object to be bought, its inner value is transformed into its monetary value."

KLAUS L. BERGHAHN

Gedankenfreiheit: From Political Reform to Aesthetic Revolution in Schiller's Works

Commonplaces

EVER SINCE FRIEDRICH SCHLEGEL'S FAMOUS claim that "the French Revolution, Fichte's Theory of Knowledge and Goethe's Wilhelm Meister are the greatest trends of our age,"[1] it has become a commonplace of intellectual history to speculate about the influence the French Revolution had on German philosophers and poets. There seems to be a general consensus by now that German Idealism as well as Weimar Classicism are responses to this monumental political event of the eighteenth century[2]; and it is equally common to note, what many contemporaries already knew, that in contrast to the French who instigated a political revolution, the Germans compensated for their lack of political action with a spiritual revolution.[3] They contemplated philosophically and/or aesthetically what the French had undertaken politically. Consequently, the Germans were either praised for their spiritual culture as a "nation of poets and philosophers" (Madame de Staël), or blamed for their lack of a political culture, "the German misery" (Marx/Engels). Whereas Engels sees Goethe merely as a victim of German circumstances, he scolds Schiller for exchanging the insipid German misery for an effusive one.[4] The tacit assumption here is that somehow Schiller's works reflect the "German misery," in order to transcend it through an aesthetic education. But Engels is only one of a few mildly critical voices in the nineteenth century, and despite his criticism Schiller became the most popular German poet.[5] His *epitheta ornantia* were innumerable: Poet of rebellion, poet of freedom, poet of national unification, even poet of the proletariat, and of course classical author for pupils. Every generation and political party seemed to have admired him and liked to quote him; especially his famous one-liners which became proverbs for any occasion and embellished Büchmann's collection of quotations.

There was only one political issue that could divide the ecclesia of his admirers: Schiller and the French Revolution. The treatment of this topic became a political litmus test, especially after 1945. Indeed, German scholarship on this subject "all too often reminds us of a battle between the two Germanies over Schiller's legacy."[6] Was he for or against it? Did the ideals of the French Revolution influence Schiller's political thinking and his aesthetics or even his works? In the West, the answer for over two decades was an unequivocal "No." As in the period of Weimar Classicism, scholars in the West separated art from life, aesthetics from politics, and works from their times, as if the classical concept of autonomous art were also the yardstick of literary criticism.[7] It is certainly easy to ferret out two or three quotations from his letters as evidence of his lack of enthusiasm for the French Revolution and to place him squarely, together with Goethe, in the conservative camp. Once having contended with this biographical question, one could then concentrate on the universal and timeless form of Schiller's works. In the East, Marxists assumed a more dialectical approach to this topic, which politicized it as much as the West depoliticized it.[8] Based on Marx's and Engels's criticism of Schiller's idealism and on Mehring's interpretation of Schiller for the proletariat,[9] Lukács, in 1935, was the first to interpret Schiller's aesthetics as a response to the French Revolution.[10] In so doing, he not only politicized the purely ontological interpretation of Schiller's philosophy of beauty, he also rediscovered Schiller's social criticism. Although he praises Schiller for his political and social awareness, he faults him for the aesthetic solution and utopian vision by which he seeks to render a revolution in Germany superfluous. This reading in turn became a commonplace of Marxist interpretation.

I realize that this overview of Schiller's reception in the West and East is oversimplified even in terms of the commonplaces which govern the discourse on this topic. But sifting through the innumerable books and articles on my subject, I see only a well-trodden path which is tedious to pursue and which I am reluctant to follow. I could, of course, simply admit that there is nothing new to say. Since I am unwilling to rehash old battles and still hold fast to the ethos of originality, I am tempted to assume the arrogant stance of Friedrich Schlegel in his Lessing-essay. Confronted with the traditionalist perspective that everything had already been said, Schlegel countered that not much had been said yet; which implies that it is necessary to say more, and that it is possible to say something better.[11]

The great historical moment and everyday experience

The French Revolution was greeted with great enthusiasm by many German intellectuals. This revolution without a civil war, the idyllic image of a new harmony between the king, his subjects and the National Assembly, as it was reported by the first travellers to Paris, made a deep impression on German readers.[12] The political ideals of freedom, equality and above all the cosmopolitan message of brotherly love were, so it seemed, practiced in Paris, and the German audience admired the French for it. Many German intellectuals projected their political hopes onto this utopian experiment in France, and they demonstrated their enthusiasm for the great revolution by celebrating its anniversaries. In Hamburg even the patrician Sieveking and his friends (among them Klopstock) celebrated the first anniversary in their reading circle, and in Tübingen Hegel, Hölderlin and Schelling were considered Jacobins when they erected a freedom-tree on July 14, 1791. But in Weimar and Jena it was quiet, and so, strangely enough, was Friedrich Schiller. Reading through his correspondence between 1789 and 1794, one can hardly find a remark about the French Revolution, let alone a substantial analysis of it; and the same holds true if we examine his life in that period. These were perhaps the most difficult years of Schiller's life, and it seems that he was so preoccupied by the problems of everyday life that he lost sight of the most important event of his time. When he finally did take note of it—after the revolution had almost run its course—his critical response in the form of an aesthetic theory was more significant than his silence during the revolution.

Skimming through the Schiller-Körner correspondence between 1789 and 1794, one cannot but feel that this dialogue occurs in a historical vacuum, rather than in the center of Europe during the French Revolution. A historian, expecting to learn what impression the political events in France made on two intellectuals in Germany, would be wasting his time reading the correspondence. There is virtually no reflection on the French Revolution, the Mainz Republic or the counter-revolutionary wars. Schiller makes only two or three marginal remarks on contemporary history worth mentioning. On December 21, 1792, he criticizes "Forster's conduct" during the founding of the Mainz Republic, an event for which he lacks any understanding: "I cannot become interested in the people of Mainz at all; their actions show much more evidence of a ridiculous desire for making a grandstand play than for sane principles. Moreover, they do not tolerate dissenters."[13] In the same letter, he feels compelled to tell the French "a few important truths" by composing a pamphlet for the king. After the execution of Louis XVI, on January 21, 1793, Schiller turns away in disgust from the contemporary scene: "For the past two weeks I have not been able to read a French newspaper; I am simply nauseated by the mindless brutality of those scoundrels."[14] For Schiller as for many German intellectuals the enthusiasm for the French Revolution had already collapsed a year before the Ninth Thermidor. Readers of this correspondence are probably justified in concluding that private and aesthetic problems were more important for the two friends than politics.

When we look at the chronicle of Schiller's life between 1789 and 1794, a similar picture emerges. Schiller, who has just been appointed "professor of philosophy" at the University of Jena—an appointment for which he did not even receive a regular salary—is completely absorbed by his new duties. He has to lecture on history (later also aesthetics) up to five times a week. As an autodidact, he is hard put just to stay ahead of his students. Meanwhile, his prolonged courtship of Charlotte von Lengefeld has become an emotionally draining and time-consuming affair. He needs a patent of nobility to marry her as her equal, and he lacks the financial resources to establish a household. If he is not asking Duke Carl August—in vain—for a fixed salary, he is begging his publishers for money. To support his family, he becomes a freelance writer, working simultaneously on many projects: writing a serialized Gothic novel and a history of the Thirty Years War, publishing historical memoirs, editing a journal and his prose works. These various odd jobs—on top of his duties as a professor of history—even prevent him from returning to poetry. In 1791 he collapses, his friends fear for his life, and he never fully recovers from his lung ailment. Then a miracle happens: A generous stipend from Duke Friedrich Christian of Augustenburg relieves him of his depressing circumstances and guarantees some financial independence for the next three years. By 1792 he starts studying Kant in earnest, mainly the third Critique—a time-consuming task indeed. This sketch of his life during a time of revolution may help explain his political abstinence. Indeed his remark to J.F. Reichardt, who pressed him to declare publicly what he thought of the French Revolution, might even be true. "It is literally true that I do not really live in my century," he replied, "although I have been told that a revolution has occurred in France, that fact is about all I know of it."[15] At that time he was already working closely with Goethe, and together they developed those timeless and universal tendencies which characterize Weimar Classicism. But even if Schiller by 1795 would largely have agreed with Goethe's political philosophy, his relationship to the French Revolution is nevertheless more complex and his aesthetic solution for the political and cultural crisis after 1789 is more interesting.

The poet of revolt

On August 26, 1792, the French National Assembly awarded Schiller, *publiciste allemand*, an honorary French citizenship. Together with sixteen other outstanding personalities, among them the Germans Klopstock and Campe, and the Americans Washington, Hamilton, Madison and Paine, Schiller was even invited to become a candidate for the upcoming election of the national assembly. The poet of the *Robbers* was viewed in France as a sympathizer of the French Revolution, if not as a revolutionary. This may have been a productive misunderstanding, but Schiller's "robber phantasies" (Scherpe) certainly provided a text that could be staged as a revolutionary drama—and as such it was performed in Paris in 1792. Since Schiller was not concerned with a specific political situation, only a few changes were necessary to transform Karl Moor's total rebellion against society into an action play for any revolution. Although Karl Moor appears to be a rebel without a cause, his actions as robber are directed against all those who abuse their position of privilege in order to satisfy their lust for wealth and power. What Schiller depicts in his play is the anarchic struggle of one righteous individual against an "ink-splashing age," and it is indicative of Karl's revolt that personal injury leads to frustration and only then to battle against social injustice. And yet, there are those famous lines which transform a band of robbers into virtuous republicans: "Put me in front of an army of guys like this and I will make a republic out of Germany." It was this rebellious gesture and the moral pathos of his play that earned Schiller his French citizenship. Ironically, the diploma reached Schiller only years later, when he had long since changed his view on the French Revolution.

Schiller's next three plays, a bourgeois tragedy, a republican tragedy and a historical drama, firmly established him as the "poet of freedom," if not of revolution. His audience in Mannheim's National Theater certainly understood them as contemporary plays and as an indictment of the existing social and political order. As Schiller correctly observed, they are all books that should be burned by the authorities.

The conditions of bourgeois life under enlightened despotism, as Schiller depicts them in *Intrigue and Love*, were only too familiar to him from his own experiences in Württemberg: The patriarchal figure of Duke Karl Eugen who controlled everything in his oppressed state, the lavish imitation of Versailles at the expense of his subjects, the selling of his subjects as mercenaries to foreign powers in order to fill his empty coffers. Abuse of power, oppression and injustice were daily experiences in this petty German state. What Schiller experienced at Karl Eugen's cadet school and as a medical officer in Stuttgart is all condensed into his criticism of courtly life, which is amplified in the play by the fact that the despotic ruler is absent from its action and that his president and his creatures are doing all the dirty work for him—and for themselves. Here the theater truly becomes a moral institution which passes judgment on crimes that escape the law.[16] The class conflict between aristocracy and bourgeoisie is triggered by Ferdinand von Walter's love for Luise Miller. He believes that God's design of the universe invalidates class distinctions, and as an active idealist and fierce lover he demands their removal: "I am a nobleman. Let us see whether my patent is older than the pattern of the universe, or my coat of arms more valid than the signature of heaven in Luise's eyes."[17] Ferdinand is the only revolutionary in the play; all the other characters, bourgeois as well as noble, are thoroughly conservative and against this marriage which would shake the foundations of the existing social order. He is the only one who wants to tear down the class barriers by marrying Luise. But to blame the failure of absolute love exclusively on the success of intrigue and outside force would be a misreading of this love-tragedy. Their love is also destroyed from within, since Ferdinand speaks and acts as a child of his class and therefore misunderstands or misjudges the language and the silence of pious Luise. Nevertheless, this would merely be a simple love story if the social conditions of the time had not perverted it into a tragedy of love.

"Republican freedom in this country is a concept without meaning, an empty phrase," Schiller observed already in 1784, when he was about to stage his "republican tragedy," *Fiesco*.[18] How difficult it was for Schiller to present his idea of republican freedom on stage, or more precisely, how ambivalent he feels about it becomes obvious when one examines the different versions of the ending. It is clear that he is against any form of despotism, and Fiesco is the hero of a justifiable rebellion up to the moment when he succeeds. But at the end of the first version, Verrina, the true republican, dumps him into the sea and goes back to the old order of Andreas Doria rather than subjugate himself to Duke Fiesco. From the perspective of this ending, Fiesco's rebellion becomes merely a putsch, and instead of exchanging one tyranny for another, Verrina returns to the old benevolent ruler. In the last version, when the real and the potential tyrant are both overthrown, Verrina surrenders himself to the court of the people. Here the sovereignty of the people appears to be the guarantee of freedom. But this is more a *bon mot* than the result of a dramatic development.[19]

Common to these early tendentious plays are idealistic noblemen who rebel against an established order. Their revolutionary activism and their pathos of freedom shake the foundations of absolutism; but in the end they are either defeated or forced to bow to the old order. These endings, more than the fact that all these rebels are noblemen, should warn us to read these plays already as an anticipation of the French Revolution. Schiller's early political dramas are—upon a closer look—still entangled in his contradictory views of enlightened despotism. This is most obvious in *Don Carlos*.

The drama is famous for its centerpiece, the tenth scene of the third act, in which Posa, the political idealist, pleads with King Philipp to allow "freedom of thought." Posa's famous line, "Give back mankind's lost dignity, sire, allow freedom of thought," seemed to encapsulate the meaning of the play and became a topos independent of it. But as is often the case with reductions like this, it neither renders the meaning of the play nor of the scene. Freedom of thought would be too modest an ideal for Posa, who has far more in mind, namely the political freedom of the Netherlands. He has to argue prudently before the despot: Freedom of thought seems harmless in comparison to the republican freedom to which he aspires, but which would be unspeakable under these circumstances. For Philipp even Posa's cautious utterances are unheard of and constitute already a dangerous practice of freedom of thought. But it is doubtful whether Philipp really listens or understands what Posa is talking about, since he is preoccupied with other problems. As the preceding scene already made clear, Philipp desperately needs someone whom he can trust, a confidant who will put his jealous mind to rest. The outcome of this central scene stands in sharp contrast to its beginning: Posa's ideas of political reform are no longer the issue but rather the unhappy state of the king's mind. Posa becomes Philipp's privy counselor whose task it is to spy on the queen and on Carlos. The private has superseded the political.

Posa now has the power to advance his own political agenda, and with every step he takes it becomes clearer what he is up to. He is part of a conspiracy against the Spanish crown, and his aim is freedom for the Netherlands—and for Spain itself, "the most possible freedom for the individual under a flourishing state." Carlos, the crown prince, is his hope and the instrument of his political will. In the end, when their dreams are shattered, the audience recognizes what they were up against. The triumph of the Inquisition sheds a new light on the tragedy as a whole. In his "Letters on Don Carlos," Schiller claims that he had wanted to avenge prostituted humanity by exposing the power and infamy of the Inquisition: "The drama shows the confrontation between an absolute despot who is controlled by the Inquisition, and the ideal of a cosmopolitan republic in which tolerance and religious freedom rule."[20]

How Posa establishes a connection between the rebellion in the Netherlands and his ideal of a "new state of freedom" seems at times revolutionary, but he is no Robespierre *ad portas*.[21] What Schiller historicized in his play are the best ideals of Enlightenment, provocative in his time and in Germany, yet still prerevolutionary. The play holds up a mirror to kings and princes who consider themselves enlightened, without living up to the universal ideas of human freedom and dignity. What Schiller advocates is nothing less, but also not more, than political reform: Religious tolerance even under a state church, freedom of thought as a precondition of a bourgeois public sphere, and the pursuit of happiness under enlightened absolutism. This is Schiller's utopia of a bourgeois age, of "our decade," as he calls it. His "new state" would be a constitutional monarchy that guarantees freedom, justice and happiness for its subjects.

One year later, in his introduction to *The History of the Secession of the United Netherlands from the Spanish Government*, Schiller goes a step further by praising the "new republic" as an example of "what people dare to do for a just cause and what they can accomplish through unity." The insurrection is seen here as a model for oppressed people under similar circumstances, and he concludes that the happy success of this daring rebellion "will not be denied to us, if time is on our side and similar circumstances require such action from us."[22] That was the closest Schiller ever came to legitimating a revolution.

Beauty is freedom in appearance

Schiller, the idealistic reformer, was surprised by the events of 1789 and dissatisfied with the direction the revolution had taken after 1793. Like many German intellectuals, he shared the ideals and hopes of the French Revolution, but shrank from the harshness of revolutionary measures and was horrified by its bloody logic. How much the French Revolution shattered his optimistic view of history and how it changed his teleological belief in the perfectibility of humankind becomes obvious when one compares the praise of "our enlightened age" in his inaugural address of 1789 with his cultural criticism at the beginning of the *Aesthetic Education of Man* of 1795. Seven weeks before the French Revolution he confronts his students with an idealized image of "our humanitarian age" which culminates in the praise of the "productive middle class, the creator of our whole culture which anticipates a lasting happiness for mankind."[23] By overlooking (or concealing) the miserable political reality in Germany and by stressing the cultural importance of the bourgeoisie for progress, he indirectly makes his audience aware of the social antagonism which has yet to be overcome. When the same bourgeoisie, however, took the first step in France to free itself from the oppressive old order and to extend its cultural influence into the political sphere, Schiller insisted on his enlightened ideal of a "monarchy of reason" in which the happiness of its subjects could still be reconciled with absolutism. It would have been possible for Schiller, the historian he had become, to familiarize himself with the causes and results of the French Revolution and to apply his teleological view of history to the current events in France. Protest, rebellion and the idea of a "new state" are the themes of his early dramas, and the historian, who was mainly interested in the progress of freedom throughout history, could have explained the French Revolution as he had interpreted the secession of the Netherlands. Turning away from history, however, he substituted aesthetic theory to come to terms with the political and social situation of his times.

This decisive turn toward aesthetics occurred at the end of 1792. It is surely no coincidence that the often quoted letters of December 21, 1792, and of February 8, 1793, in which Schiller contemplated writing a memoir for the French king and in which he reacted with disgust to his execution, are the same letters in which he first speaks of his aesthetic project, later known as the *Kallias*-letters. In the letter of December 21, Schiller only alludes to his new ideas about beauty; in his letter of February 8, he develops his argument for the first time, summing it up with the famous definition: "Beauty is nothing else but freedom in appearance."[24] What is so surprising about this original definition, despite its controversial deduction, is the fact that Schiller uses the moral and political concept of freedom to make it a part of the aesthetic experience. Since beauty is a subjective experience, based on autonomy, and since freedom is only projected onto the appearance of the beautiful object, freedom can only be an inner experience which is anticipated through art. This, *in nuce*, is Schiller's program of an aesthetic education of mankind: "All improvement in the political sphere is to proceed from the ennobling of character," and the instrument to achieve this "is art."[25] This is Schiller's aesthetic response to the French revolution.

If this is too aphoristic or sounds too speculative, and if this relationship between aesthetics and politics seems only accidental in the two letters mentioned above, let us turn to another document which establishes this relationship more conclusively. Only one day after Schiller conveyed his extraordinary definition of beauty to Körner, he promised the Prince of Augustenburg, his Danish benefactor, a "philosophy of beauty," which is actually the blueprint for his later *Aesthetic Education of Man*.[26] In a programmatic letter to the Prince of July 13, 1793, Schiller clearly draws the connection between politics and aesthetics, between his hopes for the French Revolution and the need for an aesthetic education. In his lengthy letter he confronts the question whether it would not be a sign of backwardness "to worry about the needs of aesthetics when present political matters are really closer to our interests." Although he understands the French Revolution as an attempt to institute a government of reason, he doubts whether it has succeeded:

> If it were true, that this extraordinary change really had happened, that political legislation had been assigned to reason, that man was respected and treated as an end in himself, that law had been enthroned and true freedom made the keystone of the state, then I would say farewell to the Muses forever and devote all my activities to the most glorious of all works of art, to the monarchy of reason. But it is precisely this fact that I dare to doubt. I am very far from believing that a political regeneration has begun; indeed, present events rob me of all hope that this will ever come to pass for centuries.[27]

Schiller already assumes by 1793 that the French Revolution has failed. Based on this premature assessment he develops his cultural criticism and his aesthetic theory, imbuing contemporary history with a utopian perspective. Since he rejects a violent overthrow of the present form of government and since he has also no intention of nursing feudal despotism back to health, he advocates the following solution to the dilemma: By means of an aesthetic education, humanity should attain such high ethical standards that a gradual transition from absolutism to a state of reason would become possible. This peculiar interdependence of aesthetics and politics, of cultural and social Utopia, henceforth determines Schiller's aesthetic philosophy of history. It is formulated most succinctly in the letters *On the Aesthetic Education of Man.*

Through beauty to freedom

Schiller's epistolary essay is more than just an ontology of beauty, as it is usually interpreted; it can also be read as the first political aesthetic, since it tries to find a long-term aesthetic solution to a threatening political situation. In light of the French Revolution and of Schiller's princely benefactor, the letters have reformist as well as utopian tendencies. The idealistic reformer here becomes the prince's educator, his text is a mirror for princes, a literary genre through which intellectuals seek to influence and encourage future rulers to transform their government in accordance with enlightened and humanitarian principles. Under the threat of the French Revolution, this pedagogical tendency gains in urgency. The prince, addressed as "a liberal citizen of the world," is admonished to reform his state to avoid a revolution. Despite this reformist tendency and regardless of the aesthetic importance of the letters, they also have a utopian dimension, namely to inquire about "a merely hypothetical (even though morally necessary) ideal of society" (13).

Disenchanted with the course of the French Revolution, and unable in good conscience to defend the existing form of government, Schiller must contend with the problem of how to transform a "state of need" into a "state of freedom." The revolution in France suggests that the time is ripe to leave behind the natural state and strive for a moral state, but society is unprepared for such a change. Since Schiller objects to a revolutionary overthrow of the old order, only a gradual transition appears possible. Using a rather problematic image, Schiller maintains that the state machinery must be repaired while it is still in motion. This means that he must accept the actual state as a necessity until a smooth transition to a state of reason is possible. "For this reason a support must be looked for which will ensure the continuance of society, and make it independent of the natural state which is to be abolished" (30). Where can an institution be found that is firmly grounded in society and at the same time independent of the state? An indication of how this problem might be solved can already be found in the second letter, in which Schiller rather cryptically states, "if man is ever to solve that problem of politics in practice he will have to approach it through the problem of aesthetics, because it is only through Beauty that man makes his way to Freedom" (9). This is a highly unusual route that must be justified. To prove that there is no other alternative for the renovation of the political and social system, Schiller has to criticize existing culture.

Schiller begins his cultural critique in a rather general anthropological fashion by juxtaposing savage and barbarian: The savage despises civilization and only recognizes nature, "his feelings rule his principles." The barbarian derides nature, "his principles destroy his feelings." Both are unfit to establish a new culture. Only the man of culture "makes a friend of nature, and honors her freedom whilst curbing only her caprice" (21). In the following letter, Schiller can easily project this antagonism onto a class society. The crude and lawless impulses of the "lower and more numerous classes" threaten the bonds of civil order, while "the enervation of the cultivated classes presents an even more repugnant spectacle of lethargy and of a depravity which is all the more offensive because culture itself is its source" (25–27). The condemnation of the lawless sansculottes comes as no surprise after the Ninth Thermidor, but with his criticism of the cultivated classes he comes dangerously close to the Jacobins' position. But rather than carrying this criticism to its extreme, Schiller changes course once again by using Rousseau's argument that culture is the apostasy from nature through reason: "It was civilization itself which inflicted this wound upon modern man" (33). This, for Schiller, is the heart of the matter: Alienation from nature, division of labor, and specialization have reduced mankind to a productive army of dwarves: The state has become "an ingenious clockwork, in which, out of the piecing together of innumerable but lifeless parts, a mechanical kind of collective life ensued. . . . Enjoyment was divorced from labor, the means from the end, the effort from the reward. Chained forever to a single little fragment of the whole, man himself develops into nothing but a fragment; everlasting in his ear the monotonous sound of the wheel that he turns, he never develops the harmony of his being, and instead of putting the stamp of humanity upon his own nature, he becomes nothing more than the imprint of his occupation or of his specialized knowledge" (35). With this often quoted sixth letter, Schiller becomes the prophet of young Marx. The important difference between the two cultural critics is that Schiller does not blame capitalism, which is still in its infancy in Germany, but rather the "barbaric state" whose abstractness frustrates its subjects. The state remains alien to its citizens, "since at no point does it ever make contact with their feelings" (37). The state watches jealously over the exclusive possession of its servants, it enforces class antagonism and specialization in order to classify and functionalize its subjects.

In the larger context of human history this development is also necessary. "Onesidedness in the exercise of his powers must, it is true, inevitably lead the individual into error, but the species as a whole to truth" (41). Division of labor, specialization and the antagonism of faculties are "the great instruments of civilization." But the price of progress is high. Wherever one looks, one sees only victims of civilization, crippled creatures who cannot develop their manifold potential. Although Schiller does not denounce this development on moral grounds, he suffers from "the curse of this universal goal," which makes the individual a victim of this historical necessity. "It must be wrong that the cultivation of individual powers necessitates the sacrifice of their totality" (43). Schiller, therefore, searches for means to retrieve the lost totality even under the antagonistic conditions of present-day culture. Since this is not possible under the auspices of the state or contemporary society, which have brought about this unhappy state of affairs, he has to find a sphere that lies outside the influence of the state and beyond the necessity of labor. For Schiller, this autonomous institution can only be the fine arts, which gain a truly universal and utopian function in modern society.

At this point Schiller has to prove that art is independent of all external influences, and that the aesthetic condition allows the individual to experience his or her totality. The groundwork is laid in the ninth letter, where Schiller states: "Art, like science, is absolved from all positive constraint and from all conventions introduced by man; both enjoy absolute immunity from human arbitrariness" (55). Schiller distances himself from both, the "barbaric constitution of the state," which does not allow for a political renewal, and from the dominant culture, which threatens the totality of human nature. Autonomy of art means first of all freedom from any control of art by the state or the church; it also requires independence from all audience expectations which demand entertainment and/or useful/moral instruction. "Poetry never carries out a specific task," reads another programmatic statement, "its sphere of effect is the totality of human nature."[28] This declaration of art's autonomy is Schiller's answer to the historical crisis of the state and it stands in opposition to the dominant culture of Enlightenment. In practical terms, this meant that Schiller consciously turned away from political and social reality. According to the prospectus of Schiller's *Horen*, in which his Aesthetic Letters were first published in 1795, the journal intended to remain apolitical and far removed from contemporary events: "The more the limited interest of present-day events tenses, narrows and subjugates our minds, the more pressing becomes our need to return our mind to freedom and to reunite the politically divided world under the flag of truth and beauty through a universal and higher interest in what is purely human and above all temporal influences."[29] This aestheticization of political reality, which henceforth would be Schiller's "confession of political belief," corresponds to the aesthetic principles of Weimar Classicism: It demands that the artist distance himself both from his subjective experiences and from contemporary reality, in order to create works of universal and timeless validity.

The concept of autonomous art as "the pure product of separation" is opposed to reality, political interests, and social concerns. This renders it vulnerable to accusations of ideology, a reproach which repeatedly has been levied against it. The argument runs as follows: The concept of autonomy justifies the withdrawal of art from reality, it separates art from life, and it compensates for an unbearable reality through a beautiful illusion. The negative dialectic of autonomous art is worth mentioning, because it not only offers resistance to the reality principle but also becomes abstract through the renunciation of social practice. Art compensates for what is lacking in society (freedom, equality, justice), without being able to change it. According to this interpretation, autonomous art can lead to an affirmative culture that internalizes human suffering and accepts the existing order.[30]

All this was well known to Schiller, although in more specific terms: He knew Rousseau's letter to d'Alambert,[31] Herder's protest against the separation of art from life,[32] and the resistance of many late Enlightenment writers to the new concept.[33] It is certainly true that Schiller's aesthetic theory legitimates art as a compensation for the miserable political and social situation in Germany of the late eighteenth century; and yet he compensates with a good conscience. He is aware that art is an illusion and therefore radically different from life, but in artistic illusion he finds a truth that is not corrupted in life. "The truth lives on in the midst of deception," he states, "and from the copy the original will once again be restored" (57). The positive dialectic of autonomy admits that art is an illusion and therefore devoid of social practice, but at the same time it recognizes art's critical potential in relation to reality and its utopian function for society. Autonomy of art establishes freedom from external restraints and projects onto the future what does not yet exist.

Now Schiller has to prove that beauty is also a "necessary condition of humanity" which sets the individual free in reality. The aesthetic experience confronts the audience with the possibility of human wholeness and anticipates what a new culture and state would look like. Since the process of civilization is responsible for the deplorable cultural crisis, Schiller has to search for its causes and for the means to overcome it. Anthropologically, the crisis is the result of antagonistic forces within man. In typical Kantian fashion, Schiller establishes a dualism between nature and freedom, sensuousness and reason, or in his own terms: material impulse and form impulse. Schiller defines the third impulse that mediates between the two as the play impulse. If the play impulse were only a matter of aesthetics, as benevolent traditional interpretation would have us believe, it would only be of marginal interest for our topic, but in the larger context of Schiller's cultural criticism, the aesthetic experience becomes the central issue of human existence. The crisis of modern civilization came about through the alienation of reason from nature. The dominant form impulse is responsible for a condition in which repressive reason subjugates sensuousness in order to increase cultural productivity. The result is a rational culture in which instrumentalized reason has dominated nature—by exploiting outside nature and repressing inner nature. Alienated labor, specialization and loss of totality are the consequences of the renunciation of sensuousness. Since the harmonious interaction of the two basic impulses has been lost in the process of civilization, a third force has to reconcile them "by making sensuousness rational and reason sensuous."[34] For Schiller, this can only be the function of the play impulse, "whose objective is beauty, and whose goal is freedom."[35] Schiller even promises that the play impulse will not only support the whole fabric of aesthetic art but also "the still more difficult art of living" (109). At this point, the revolutionary quality of Schiller's aesthetic education comes into focus, because life under the auspices of the play impulse "loses its seriousness" and is freed "from the bonds of every purpose, every duty, every care" (109). Life would become a carefree existence without the constraint of want or the coercion of labor; it would be a blissful state of mind, since the Greeks had "transferred to Olympus what was meant to be realized on earth." Then human beings could play with all their possibilities and playfully develop all their potential. Then they would be human beings in the fullest sense of the word.

Schiller is, however, aware of the necessary prerequisites of such a blissful human condition: "For as long as necessity dictates and need impels, imagination remains tied to reality with powerful bonds; only when wants are stilled does it develop its unlimited potential" (193). When reality loses its seriousness, when want and need are satisfied, a new culture can emerge in which individuals can develop their capacities without restraint. On this point, the idealistic and materialistic critiques of culture agree. Marx states at the end of *Das Kapital*: "The sphere of freedom begins indeed only at a point where labor, which is determined by want and necessity, ends." Freedom lies outside the sphere of material production and beyond the struggle for existence.[36] The highest maturity of culture becomes possible only "when all basic needs can be satisfied with a minimum expenditure of physical and mental energy in a minimum of time."[37] The necessities of life have to be taken care of and a new order of abundance has to be created before a new higher culture can emerge.

Under the dominant conditions of a barbaric state and of alienated labor individuals can never be in harmony with themselves, and the play impulse cannot overcome the reality principle. Only in an aesthetic culture can human beings be free to be what they ought to be. As long as culture has not reached this stage of maturity, art and the aesthetic experience uphold this ideal of humanity and anticipate the self-perfection of the individual. It is the function of art to give humanity its most complete expression, and through the aesthetic experience a sense of its future liberation. Since art is indifferent to reality and since the aesthetic condition allows the individual to experience what totality would feel like, it is a "true enlargement of humanity."

If art sets the individual free momentarily and if the play impulse is to be the liberating force for a new civilization, the question arises what an "Aesthetic State" would look like. Schiller's answer, at the end of his lengthy essay, is rather short and a bit cryptic: "In the Aesthetic State everybody is a free citizen, having equal rights with the noblest. . . . As a need, it exists in every finely tuned soul; as a realized fact, we are likely to find it, like the pure church and the pure republic, only in some few chosen circles" (219). This is certainly less than we expected as a response to the French Revolution and it seems to corroborate the argument of those who criticize the abstract and esoteric nature of the essay. But even here, there is more to discover than meets the untrained eye.

The allusion to the "finely tuned soul" corresponds to the individualization and internalization of the aesthetic education; for Schiller makes it clear from the beginning that "all improvement in the political sphere must proceed from the ennobling of character" (55). If one can speak of any revolution at all, it would be "a complete revolution of the whole mode of sensuous perception," (205) which is to say, an aesthetic revolution. It would involve "the abolition of the repressive controls that civilization has imposed on sensuousness,"[38] and art would be the tool to accomplish the change of consciousness which precedes political change. This seems to be the main idea of the Aesthetic Education.

As to the "few chosen circles" which have already achieved the conditions of the Aesthetic State in Schiller's times, one could think of the Weimar court, the Romantic circles or the Jewish salons in Berlin. There a fine public, whose members are already free from want/need and beyond the struggle for existence, anticipates that "a future generation might experience in blissful indolence . . . and develop the free growth of its humanity" (43). These circles are the nucleus of a future Aesthetic State in which the individual will be led through beauty to freedom. Schiller's Aesthetic State is no social Utopia, but a utopian model of harmonious humanity, where the antagonistic forces of nature and freedom, sensuousness and reason, individual and state would be in balance. "The Aesthetic State alone can make it real because it consummates the will of the whole through the nature of the individual," and its universal law is "to bestow freedom by means of freedom" (215).

But let us not forget that we are only talking about a "State of Aesthetic Semblance" and that we are still in the aesthetic sphere, which only anticipates freedom in reality. What the Aesthetic State and the State of Reason have in common is freedom, i.e. the correspondence of the law with the nature of the individual; the symbol of this harmony is beauty, because it is "beauty alone [that] we enjoy at once as individual and as species, i.e. as representatives of the human race" (217). This is the universal nature of beauty: It unites society in the aesthetic mode of communication, "because it relates to that which is common to all" (215). Indeed, it is this idea of an aesthetic sense of commonality which anticipates a political civic sense in a future Republic of Reason.

Poor in action, rich in thought

Schiller's aesthetic theory is an idealistic and peculiarly German answer to the French Revolution. It replaces political education with an aesthetic one, which changes nothing but our perception of beauty—this change, however, is radical. Art becomes autonomous and its function is to transform humanity in order to make freedom possible. Schiller's radical criticism of the existing political order leads him to demand "freedom of thought," which aims at a bourgeois public sphere and ultimately at an enlightened constitutional monarchy. His cultural criticism is far more radical and his aesthetic solution truly utopian: Schiller's aesthetic Utopia aims at a liberation of humanity from want and need and toward a state of freedom beyond necessity. His ideal of humanity is something infinite, "which in the course of time we can approximate ever more closely, without ever being able to reach it" (95). It is a regulative principle that demands, what is not yet, but is to come. Art keeps this ideal alive, points out humanity's potential and strengthens the utopian impulse. The aesthetic illusion becomes pre-appearance (*Vorschein*) which anticipates human freedom in the aesthetic sphere, where it becomes unassailable. The aesthetic experience allows, at least momentarily and through contemplation, for a feeling of totality, it strengthens and motivates the individual. Artistic illusion precedes political practice, anticipates future possibilities and opens new perspectives. This is far more than was ever expected of art: It becomes universal and utopian.

The contradictions of Schiller's aesthetic theory were already apparent in his own time. Favoring the development of a spiritual over a political culture, the reception of Schiller's Aesthetic Education became a German tradition. The Germans are, as Hölderlin mockingly noted, rich in thought, but destitute in action. And Forster complained that free and public criticism was so poorly developed in Germany that even the concept of "public opinion" was "so new, so strange that everyone demands an explanation."[39] Like many politically minded thinkers, Forster encouraged the formation of a new political culture out of which a new aesthetic culture could emerge. Like Schiller, he was fully aware of the objective barriers that prevented political criticism and reform in Germany. There was certainly enough oppression and injustice under Germany's despotic absolutism to justify a revolution, but, in contrast to France, geographical, political and economic conditions worked against a political uprising. Confronted with the political and social reality of Germany, the ideals of the French Revolution became the illusions of an intellectual elite. While Forster and other Jacobins prepared themselves for a long political struggle, most intellectuals compensated for the impossible political revolution with a spiritual one.

What, at first glance, seems to be merely a matter of priority or opportunity, emerged in the German context as a tradition, a way of thinking: Inner, spiritual culture was valued higher than any form of practical civilization. The belief in the superiority of this world of ideas and art was so strong that instead of using the power of ideas to challenge the old order and its institutions, these inner values were put on a pedestal, cultivated and kept pure. In practical terms, this also meant that freedom became merely a philosophical and aesthetic concept instead of an energy with which to establish a free society. Freedom of thought, praised as inner freedom that cannot be subjugated by outside force, must also take into account the prison, where the longing for freedom is most authentic. In the German context a strange transformation occurred: Since the subject is unable to overcome the oppression of the state or authoritarian structures of society, the prison is interpreted as merely an external restriction and freedom as the true inner value. The longing for freedom was clearly expressed in the arts and aesthetics of the times, but it was so internalized that it could only break open the doors of the prison metaphorically by projecting freedom onto the beautiful object or by anticipating it in an Aesthetic State of Semblance. Posa's speech and the trumpet signal in Beethoven's *Fidelio* are signs of hope and of political impotence at the same time. To be sure, the autonomy of art and its utopian vision keeps the ideals of humanity alive, but in the context of German history, i.e. of failed revolutions, they were increasingly relegated to the aesthetic sphere where art could be celebrated without having practical consequences. This criticism of the German tradition of spiritual culture does not detract from Schiller's aesthetic Utopia, but the reception of his Aesthetic Education as a substitute for political criticism should warn us about adhering to it as if it were a cultural axiom. The German tradition of freedom of thought and of an aesthetic revolution has imprisoned freedom: it has become an internalized aesthetic experience. It is time to correct this German misconception and the other one which is so closely linked to it, that somehow a spiritual culture is more important than a political one. To put it bluntly in an American context: Culture is as important as *Kultur*.[40]

NOTES

1. Friedrich Schlegel, *Kritische Schriften*, ed. Wolfdietrich Rasch (Munich: Hanser, 1956) 46.
2. See Gerhard Schulz, *Die deutsche Literatur zwischen Französischer Revolution und Restauration (1789–1806)* (Munich: Beck, 1983).
3. This "revolution in ways of thinking" (Kant) was already a commonplace among German intellectuals of the time, and it was used by Fr. Schlegel, Hölderlin, Hegel, and Marx.
4. Karl Marx/Friedrich Engels, *Über Kunst und Literatur* (Frankfurt/Main: Europäische Verlagsanstalt, 1968) 1:468.
5. *Schiller—Zeitgenosse aller Epochen: Dokumente zur Wirkungsgeschichte Schillers in Deutschland*, ed. Norbert Oellers, 2 vols. (Frankfurt/Main: Athenäum, 1970).
6. David Pugh, "Schiller and Revolution." Unpublished lecture at the University of California, Santa Barbara (May 1988).
7. It would be as easy as it is tedious to quote from the standard biographies by B. von Wiese, G. Storz and E. Staiger.
8. The French Revolution became a model for the later bourgeois and proletarian revolutions, which were sublated into the new socialist state in 1949. See Claus Träger, ed., *Die Französische Revolution im Spiegel der deutschen Literatur* (Leipzig: Reclam, 1975) 7f.
9. Franz Mehring, *Schiller—Ein Lebensbild für deutsche Arbeiter* (Leipzig: Leipziger Buchdruckerei, 1905).
10. Georg Lukács, "Zur Ästhetik Schillers" (1935), in *Probleme der Ästhetik* (Neuwied: Luchterhand, 1969), 17–106.
11. Friedrich Schlegel 226.
12. See Joachim Heinrich Campe, *Briefe aus Paris, zur Zeit der Revolution geschrieben* (Braunschweig: Schulbuchhandlung, 1790).
13. *Schillers Briefe*, ed. Fritz Jonas (Stuttgart: Deutsche Verlagsanstalt, 1893) 3:233.
14. Ibid. 3:246.
15. Ibid. 4:218.
16. Friedrich Schiller, "Was kann eine gute stehende Schaubühne eigentlich wirken?" Schiller, *Sämtliche Werke*, ed. G. Fricke and Herbert G. Göpfert (Munich: Hanser, 1960) 5:823.
17. Schiller, *Sämtliche Werke* 1:766.
18. *Schillers Briefe* 1:185.
19. See Paul Michael Lützeler, " 'Die große Linie zu einem Brutuskopfe.' Republikanismus und Cäsarismus in Schillers *Fiesco*," *Monatshefte* 70 (1978): 15–28.

20. Friedrich Schiller, "Briefe über Don Carlos," *Sämtliche Werke* 2:229.
21. Wilfried Malsch, "Robespierre ad portas?," *Houston German Studies* 9, ed. Edward Haymes (Munich/Paderborn: Fink, 1989).
22. Friedrich Schiller, *Über den Abfall der vereinigten Niederlande von der spanischen Krone* (1788), *Sämtliche Werke* 4:1020. In the second edition of 1801, Schiller was careful enough to omit these sentences.
23. Friedrich Schiller, "Was heißt und zu welchem Ende studiert man Universalgeschichte?," *Sämtliche Werke* 4:759.
24. *Schillers Briefe* 3:246.
25. Friedrich Schiller, *On the Aesthetic Education of Man*, translated and edited by E.M. Wilkinson and L.A. Willoughby (Oxford: Clarendon Press, 1967) 55. All the following quotations are from this edition and page numbers will be cited in my text.
26. *Schillers Briefe* 3:247–51. It is not astonishing to find Schiller's original definition of beauty again in a footnote to the twenty-third aesthetic letter: "Beauty is the only possible expression of freedom in appearance."
27. *Schillers Briefe* 3:332.
28. Schiller, "Über das Pathetische," *Sämtliche Werke* 5:535.
29. Ibid. 5:870.
30. See Herbert Marcuse, "Über den affirmativen Charakter der Kultur" (1937), in *Kultur und Gesellschaft I* (Frankfurt/Main: Suhrkamp, 1965) 56ff.
31. See Schiller's response in the 10th letter. See also Bernd Bräutigam, "Rousseaus Kritik ästhetischer Versöhnung. Eine Problemvorgabe der Bildungsästhetik Schillers," *Jahrbuch der deutschen Schillergesellschaft* 31 (1987): 137–55.
32. Schiller's letter to Herder, Nov. 4, 1795. *Schillers Briefe* 4:313f.
33. See Klaus L. Berghahn, "Maßlose Kritik. Friedrich Nicolai als Kritiker und Opfer der Weimarer Klassiker," *Zeitschrift für Germanistik* 8 (1987): 58ff.
34. Herbert Marcuse, *Eros and Civilization* (New York: Vintage Books, 1962) 170. Marcuse must be credited with having rediscovered the existential and utopian function of Schiller's play impulse.
35. Ibid. 170.
36. Marx/Engels, *Werke* 25:828.
37. Marcuse 177.
38. Ibid. 174.
39. Georg Forster, "Über die öffentliche Meinung." Forster, *Sämtliche Schriften, Tagebücher, Briefe*, vol. 8, ed. S. Scheibe (Berlin: Akademie-Verlag, 1974) 364.
40. Theodor W. Adorno, "Auf die Frage: Was ist deutsch?" *Stichworte* (Frankfurt/Main: Suhrkamp, 1969) 102ff.

THOMAS P. SAINE

Georg Forster and the Mainz Revolution

OF ALL THE GERMAN INTELLECTUALS WHO became caught up in the revolutionary upheavals of the 1790s and for whom the Revolution became a destiny, none is better known than Georg Forster. His fate has attained exemplary status. While, as was only to be expected, Forster was cursed by the conservatives and royalists of his day, his revolutionary activity was rejected and bemoaned even by the liberals who had admired him and had been his friends before the French occupied Mainz. This is one more piece of evidence that very few Germans of the time thought the country really needed a revolution or was ready for one. To the twentieth century, in the meantime—above all to Marxists and to others who believe in revolutions—he has become a German hero and an ideological forebear. Those who look for ideological forebears often overlook the physical and psychological suffering and the anxieties caused (both to themselves and to others) by revolutionaries defending their positions, as though the good cause were so obviously just that one should embrace it without hesitation or afterthought. A fervent advocate of revolutionizing Mainz and the rest of the French-occupied territory on the Left Bank of the Rhine in 1792–1793, Forster came face to face with the Revolution in Paris during the Terror that began in the spring of 1793. In many of his letters from Paris he despaired of the French revolutionaries and their Revolution, and yet in one of his last fragments, the *Parisische Umrisse* (Parisian Sketches), he seems to have regained his belief in the rightness of the Revolution and his faith in its ultimate legacy, even as it devoured its own contemporaries and its children. No respectable symposium or collection of essays on the topic of Germany and the French Revolution can do without a paper on Georg Forster.

It is tempting to want to write about Forster and the French Revolution, about the big picture, so to speak. Unfortunately, a lot has already been written on the subject of Forster and the French Revolution, and it is not easy to come up with anything dramatically new. Misstatements and misinformation abound in the literature.[1] There is a twofold problem: we have to get the correct information to begin with, and then we have to try to set it in the proper context while making up our minds whom to believe. It is not helpful that most of those who have written on the subject have one or the other ideological or methodological axe to grind, probably including myself.[2] The primary evidence with which we have to deal in discussing the topic of Forster and the French Revolution are his letters from October, 1792, to his death in January, 1794, the speeches he delivered at the Mainz Club and the Rhenish-German National Convention, his contributions to Mainz newspapers during 1792–1793, and three works undertaken just before his death: *Darstellung der Revolution in Mainz* (History of the Revolution in Mainz), *Über die Beziehung der Staatskunst auf das Glück der Menschheit* (On the Relationship between the Art of Governing and the Happiness of Mankind), and *Parisische Umrisse*. In general, the state of Forster philology has improved considerably since the early 1970s, when I wrote my own monograph, as the Akademie-Ausgabe finally nears completion.[3] Since the 1989 UCLA Symposium two important volumes have appeared: the last volume of his letters (vol. 17), covering the period from the beginning of 1792 to his death,[4] and the volume containing his revolutionary writings (vol. 10,1).[5] Unfortunately the notes and apparatus to go along with the material in volume 10,1 have not yet appeared, so one uses it at one's own risk or relies heavily on other sources of information. Volume 17 is disappointing to those who had hoped that the Akademie editors might succeed in discovering and publishing significant new material: there is very little in the volume that was not known previously, and what is completely lost still remains lost.[6]

The new volumes of the Akademie-Ausgabe, while certainly welcome, will not provide the basis for a wide-ranging reevaluation of Forster's relationship to the French Revolution until the apparatus to volume 10,1 becomes available. Too much is still not known about Forster's last months in France and about his associates and acquaintances. On a narrower front, however, the Mainz revolution in which Forster was involved and which first catapulted him into the maelstrom, there has been a significant increase in information since the early 1970s. In 1975 Heinrich Scheel published the first volume of his documentation of *Die Mainzer Republik*, more than 800 pages of text dealing with the history and activities of the Mainz Jacobin Club, and in 1981 a somewhat smaller but still quite substantial second volume dealing with the elections of 1793 and the Rhenish-German National Convention that proclaimed the independence of the French-occupied Rhenish territories and petitioned the National Convention in Paris for annexation.[7] Scheel's commentary to these volumes is rather less than totally objective, since he maintains a committed Marxist viewpoint; some of it, in fact, is downright strange. One also inevitably suspects that the Marxist viewpoint has influenced the selection of the supporting evidence printed in the apparatus and notes of the two volumes, but that is something that cannot be checked without going back and repeating the archival research that led to the publication of the volumes in the first place. One of Scheel's most irritating traits is that he labels everyone who opposed the French-sponsored revolution in Mainz a "counterrevolutionary," no matter what the reason for the opposition, and he dismisses most previous "bourgeois" scholarship on the Mainz revolution out of hand. Still, Scheel's two volumes of documents allow us to take a giant step in understanding the context of the Mainz revolution, and it is this more limited topic that I wish to address here: not "Forster and the French Revolution," but rather "Forster and the Mainz Revolution."

Up until October, 1792, Forster had definitely viewed the French Revolution sympathetically, hoping that it would be good for the French people, and perhaps for Europe as a whole. He had not refrained from expressing his sympathies in works like the *Ansichten vom Niederrhein* (Views of the Lower Rhine) and the *Erinnerungen aus dem Jahr 1790* (Recollections of the Year 1790)—but most German intellectuals approved of the French Revolution in the beginning, to one extent or another. He had not engaged himself on behalf of the Revolution in any way. He was just a spectator, like so many other German writers and intellectuals of his day, and he had not yet done anything to set himself apart. His business as a writer and an intellectual was to keep track of what was going on in the world and work to inform and educate his public about it. For purposes of getting reliable news of important events, Mainz was a good place to be. The city was connected to reliable French sources (notably Strasbourg). In a number of his letters between August and November, 1792, Forster supplies a more "authentic" version of events to correspondents (especially his father-in-law Christian Gottlob Heyne) who were otherwise dependent on biased sources like the Brussels papers for their news, for example the news they got about the disastrous allied campaign in France.[8] It is not clear whether Forster had any inkling of the momentous events that were soon to transpire as a result of the failed invasion—while the Prussians and Austrians were evacuating France farther north, the French army in Alsace was to counterattack opportunistically and invade the Rhineland—but he had been skeptical of the Austro-Prussian campaign from the very beginning.

In spite of his sympathies for the French, Forster was far from eager to see their Revolution transplanted to Germany. In an October 2 letter to his publisher, Christian Friedrich Voß, he took a position on this issue to which he adhered throughout, even at the height of his career as a Mainz revolutionary: "I have sought to stress *one* idea in particular in these revolutionary times: namely, that we in Germany should take the French as an example of what *not* to do, and that we are not yet *ripe* for a revolution."[9] On this very same day, October 2, Forster begins reporting news of events transpiring very close to Mainz: he has received the first reports of the French capture of Speyer on September 29. By October 6 he is reporting to his friend Samuel Thomas Sömmerring that the French have attacked Worms and are threatening Mainz. Mainz aristocrats were beginning to flee, the French émigrés—who had been the principal agitators for the allied invasion of France—had cleared out, and even the elector of Mainz had left hurriedly on the night of October 4 in a coach from which the electoral coat-of-arms had been removed. Mainz was exposed, abandoned, and defenseless, because a large part of its small military forces, which had been fulfilling their assigned role in the allied war effort guarding military stores near the front lines, had been captured by the French at Speyer. "Everyone has lost his head, no one had any really good information about how strong the French are and *where* they are." The French forces under Adam-Philippe de Custine did not rush to conquer Mainz—they did not arrive at the city gates until two weeks after the elector had left—but on October 19 they were demanding the surrender of the fortress. Seeing no hope of a successful defense against such a force, the military leaders and electoral officials in charge of Mainz capitulated on October 21 without having put up any resistance at all, which quickly gave rise to rumors and charges that the city had been delivered over to the French by treason. Before occupying Mainz on October 22, as agreed in the capitulation, Custine sent a detachment on farther to threaten Frankfurt. Frankfurt was occupied on October 23, and Custine advanced briefly into Hessia, where he issued a ringing denunciation of the Landgrave of Hesse-Kassel before ending his offensive. There were rumors—fears or expectations, depending on one's point of view—that Custine's army, or other French armies, would soon also occupy Koblenz, cutting off the Prussian line of retreat from France. Meanwhile, Mainz became Custine's headquarters for defending and administering the occupied German Left Bank territories, and French military authority superseded or sought to subordinate all local civilian authorities.

Custine's army had occupied, after a fashion, a bewilderingly complex piece of the Holy Roman Empire. This area—referred to collectively in French occupation proclamations and revolutionary propaganda as "the territory from Bingen to Landau"—included two imperial free cities, Worms and Speyer, the prince-bishoprics of Worms and Speyer and parts of the prince-archbishopric of Mainz, territories belonging to, administered by, or owing tithes and rents to the cathedral chapters of the three bishoprics and various cloisters and orders, as well as a large number of pieces of real estate owned, co-owned, or administered by diverse secular princes (including Holy Roman Emperor Francis II in his capacity as Count of Falkenstein). I cannot even try to describe this situation and will simply point out the fact that on March 18, 1793, the first decree of the Rhenish-German National Convention deposed, banned, and expropriated more than twenty different rulers and corporations.[10] The administrative, propaganda, and military difficulties were exacerbated by the fact that the territories occupied by Custine's army did not make up a solid bloc of contiguous entities. They were widely scattered and separated by substantial pieces of Electoral Palatine and Palatine-Zweibrücken territory. Up to this point the Palatinate had remained neutral in the war of the German powers against revolutionary France. Palatine neutrality was bothersome to both sides, but certainly more useful to the French than open hostility would have been, and therefore the French made a show of respecting it. Consequently, while French troops were stationed all around the borders of the Left-Bank Palatine territories and even marched through them from time to time, the revolutionizing efforts directed from Mainz excluded the Palatinate and Zweibrücken.[11] When the National Convention in Paris, on March 30, 1793, annexed the territories that had sent delegates to the Rhenish-German National Convention, it by no means annexed a solid strip of German land extending from the French borders to the Rhine, but rather a series of enclaves.[12]

Upon occupying the Left Bank territories Custine immediately issued a proclamation addressed to the Germans in general, stressing that the French had come as brothers to liberate peoples who had until now been living under the oppression of feudal despots. At the moment, pending the arrival of representatives of the French National Convention who would announce and implement the definitive policy toward the occupied areas, Custine could offer no specifics, but he promised the Germans that they would eventually be allowed to choose their own form of government: "*Your own free will* shall decide your fate. Even if you should decide to prefer *slavery* over the benefits with which *liberty* beckons, it remains up to you to decide which despot shall be the one to give you back your chains."[13] In the meantime, pending the promised elections, it was necessary to collect taxes as usual and keep the old administrative apparatus in place in the occupied territories. In a second proclamation a few days later, addressed specifically to the inhabitants of Mainz, Worms, and Speyer, Custine recounted the oppressions that had been visited upon them by their despots in the past, promising that they would be freed from all oppression in the near future. He stressed, however, that it would be necessary for the "liberated" Germans to prove themselves worthy of the gift of liberty by scrupulously obeying their old governments (under French control, of course) until they could be replaced by freely elected ones:

> The beautiful day that will abolish so much injustice is about to dawn. The French *National Assembly* is in the process of abolishing those onerous burdens once and for all. When I, the Assembly's representative here on the banks of the Rhine, demanded that you respect your *governments*, it was because you will prove yourselves worthy of liberty by respecting even your old laws. Citizens! True liberty consists in *being subject to no one but the law that one has chosen for oneself*; and until you have new laws it is necessary to obey even the laws of your oppressors, so as to show that you are people worthy of having new and more equitable laws.[14]

I quote this at length to show that, for all their liberation propaganda, the French were determined to maintain control of the German territories by all means at their disposal, and because Custine's definition of liberty, "being subject to no one but the law that one has chosen for oneself," is repeated over and over again in the speeches by members of the Mainz Club when explicating the features of the French constitution they urged their fellow citizens to adopt in place of their old "despotic" forms of government.

Undoubtedly neither Custine, the general at the front, nor the National Convention in Paris at first had any clear notion as to the proper policy toward the "liberated" Germans in the occupied territories. The shift from having to defend France at all costs against the German invaders to going on the offensive themselves had been so swift that it is not at all surprising that the French were not prepared to deal with the new situation and exploit it immediately in the most expedient fashion. Furthermore, the fact that French armies were scoring other successes in these days, occupying Nice, Savoy, and much of Belgium in addition to much of the German Rhineland, meant that it was desirable to debate and adopt a comprehensive national policy rather than settling for purely *ad hoc* solutions to local situations. For the moment Custine was acting more or less on his own, although in accordance with the thinking of a strong faction of the National Convention. It was practically unavoidable that some of his policies and actions would later be revoked by higher authorities. Official French policy was settled in the course of November and December by a series of decrees applying to all the "liberated" territories, and ready for implementation in the Rhineland at the beginning of 1793.

The French were in something of an ideological quandary. They had loudly renounced the intention of ever again waging wars of conquest. It would have been the easiest, the most efficient, and probably also the most acceptable course of action for all concerned—including the Germans and their erstwhile rulers—if the French *had* simply acted as conquerors, imposing their will on the occupied territories. There was certainly every reason why they should do everything in their power to maintain their forces on the Rhine, at least for the duration of the war, and there were ample historical and legal precedents for doing so, as well as a body of international law governing acceptable practices in this regard. Since, however, it was against their stated constitutional principles to act baldly as conquerors, the French had to act as though they were "liberators" instead, bringing the Germans the precious gift of freedom. It quickly became clear, however, that Custine had not really been serious when he told the Germans that the main thing was for them to elect their own governments, and that they were even free to choose their old despotism if they wanted. What he really had in mind was that the Germans should elect to embrace the principles of liberty and equality, that is, adopt an approximate version of the French constitution tailored to local conditions, depose their former rulers, declare their independence of the Holy Roman Empire, and seek the protection of the French Republic, meaning, ideally, that they should petition to be annexed by France. Here, in rudimentary and hastily improvised form, is the earliest version of the French revolutionary objective of extending French borders to the Rhine, and this is basically what was accomplished by the Rhenish-German National Convention (in conformity with the National Convention decrees of December, 1792) in March, 1793.

Custine had hardly set up shop in Mainz when the Jacobin Club, which Heinrich Scheel calls "the soul of the Mainz Republic" (*MR* I:12), was established. It began meeting on October 24, at first daily, later only four days a week, with Custine's support and encouragement. It is obvious that, whatever else one thinks about the Club, it was encouraged by the French and perceived by the citizens of Mainz as a vehicle for furthering French policy. This is already apparent, in programmatic fashion, in the official name of the Club, which called itself the "Society of the Friends of Liberty and Equality," which was a kind of shorthand reference to the French constitution which the Club members eagerly urged their compatriots to embrace for themselves. Upon occasion the Club and its members referred to themselves as "Friends of the Constitution," again a reference to themselves as friends of the French constitution and advocates of adopting the same or a similar constitution for the occupied German territories.[15]

Members of the Mainz Club swore an oath to uphold liberty and equality, to live free or die, and to denounce all enemies of liberty, equality, and the constitution. The Club had a president, elected to a one-month term of office, several secretaries, and a number of committees: originally there seem to have been only a correspondence committee and a surveillance or safety committee (the "Wachhabender Ausschuß"), but later there were also committees for instruction, welfare or charity, and finances. During its last two months the Club elected a vice-president as well. Because the Club had French members and visitors—members of the French military and administration—it was necessary that the officers and committee chairs speak and write both French and German, thus considerably limiting the number of members qualified to fill leadership positions. It would appear that considerable time was taken up during Club meetings with translating back and forth. For a while in January, while Forster was president, separate meetings were held for the French and the German members, but this innovation did not catch on, and after only a few meetings the two groups were combined again.[16]

In accordance with Custine's objectives, members of the Club saw their mission in enlightening the populace, educating the citizens of Mainz and the occupied Left Bank territories to exercise responsibly the freedom of choice they were to enjoy in the promised elections. The task of enlightenment was carried out mainly in the form of speeches delivered at the Club meetings and then printed, either in the newspapers and journals, or as pamphlets, for the widest possible distribution. Whenever someone reported at the Club that inhabitants of some village or other had expressed an interest in liberty and equality, it was usually resolved to send a supply of pamphlets there immediately. Most of the speechifying and pamphlet-writing was done by a handful of members, the intellectuals.[17] Georg Wedekind, professor of medicine at the Mainz university, was by far the most prominent speaker. He apparently was ready to talk at the drop of a hat and also published a journal, *Der Patriot*. Other frequent speakers included Georg Wilhelm Böhmer, from the university of Göttingen by way of the Worms higher school, who had attached himself to Custine, translated many of the general's speeches, proclamations, and other government documents into German, and published the *Mainzer National-Zeitung*.[18] Matthias Metternich, a Mainz professor of mathematics, published his own journal, *Der Bürgerfreund*. Friedrich Cotta, a Strasbourg journalist who had moved to Mainz after the capitulation, was a frequent speaker, pamphleteer, and leader of the Club, although he did not publish a journal of his own in Mainz.[19] In comparison with these others, Forster spoke rarely at the Club, and he only started his own newspaper, *Die neue Mainzer Zeitung oder der Volksfreund*, in competition with the *Mainzer National-Zeitung* after Böhmer's positions on issues began to deviate from the line pursued by the Club leaders and the government. It must be noted that the speakers, propagandists, and leaders were largely the same people: most of the Club's officers came from the group I have just described.

The members insisted from beginning to end (in accordance with French law and practice) that the Club was not a legal entity entitled to lobby or act officially on anyone's behalf. In fact, the Club does not seem to have acted, as a body, on behalf of the French military, the occupation administration, or the civilian government, except in the general sense of supporting them enthusiastically (although a number of Club members participated, in a quasi-governmental status, in the propaganda and election activities in the countryside from late November, 1792, through February, 1793). From the very beginning speakers at the Club concerned themselves with defining and explicating "liberty" and "equality," differentiating the three traditional forms of government (monarchy, oligarchy, and democracy), characterizing both monarchy and oligarchy as brands of despotism, and urging their compatriots to embrace the French constitution and apply for French protection from the revenge of their banished German despots, always referring to them as their "former" ("ci-devant") rulers. Since the occupied territories were predominantly Catholic, and the Mainz, Worms, and Speyer territories were ecclesiastical states, it was especially necessary to convince the inhabitants that the French constitution was compatible with the Roman Church, indeed that democratic-republican government represented the highest form of enlightened Christianity imaginable (which does not mean that there was not a prominent anti-clerical element in their propaganda[20]). Since it was the merchants of the city (the "Handelsstand") and the guilds who put up the strongest opposition to the French agenda, Club speakers expatiated often on how the revolution would be good for business and trade and enable Mainz soon to overtake and surpass Frankfurt, the arch-rival.[21] The Club proceedings for October 25, as reported in the *Aachener Zuschauer* (Aachen Observer), gave a foretaste of what was to come:

> [Böhmer from Göttingen took the podium and talked] about the necessity of making common cause [Verbrüderung] with the French and about the excellence of their constitution, in the course of which he bitterly attacked the previous conduct of the elector, whom he called a despot. . . . It was agreed that from now on the hall would always be open until 8:00 in the evening, as a meeting place for those citizens who were interested in fully achieving their liberty and setting up the laws. (*MR* I:57).

It was of course important that the Mainz Club appear to be the cutting edge of a mass movement for liberty and equality. It is difficult to establish (conclusively) its true size and strength, but it is possible to say that the Club flourished during the first weeks of the French presence and declined dramatically from January, 1793, on. Neither of the two membership lists published by Scheel (*MR* I:819ff.) is exhaustive, but the longer of them still contains less than 500 names, and so it is reasonable to assume that at its high point the Club did not have more than 500 real members. Some of the members were French military, others were not citizens of Mainz but came from the surrounding countryside (for example Adam Lux, one of the two other delegates who accompanied Forster to Paris in March), or lived in Worms or Speyer, so the number of genuine citizens of Mainz supporting the Club was probably significantly less than 500. It is rare to encounter numbers in the minutes published by Scheel, but what numbers there are are rather revealing. The Club had constant financial difficulties because of the failure of members to pay their dues. The minutes of January 6, 1793, record the finance committee's report that only 121 of 449 members had paid up. From mid-January until the effective end of the Club in mid-March the minutes record a steady stream of members announcing their desire to be stricken from the lists, largely because of an infantile challenge to the King of Prussia published in December by Friedrich Georg Pape, one of the Club's lesser lights.[22] Citizens were required to swear an oath to liberty and equality before they were allowed to vote in the elections held on February 24 (in Mainz—the voting in the countryside went on longer). Those who refused to swear the oath were threatened with expulsion from the territory and loss of their property. A total of 372 Mainz citizens, 8% of those eligible to vote, swore the oath by February 26, two days *after* the elections.[23] It turned out that even many Club members had not sworn the oath or voted, and this was the last straw. The membership rolls were purged and a new president elected on March 13 by the 45 members present, thus putting an end to the original club. The new club did not survive the month of March— at least there are no trustworthy records of its continued activity—largely because it was quickly cast into the shade by the Rhenish-German National Convention that convened on March 17, 1793.

Unfortunately, it is not possible here to go more deeply into the substance of the speeches delivered at the Club and printed for the benefit of the public. It is necessary to conclude, however, that on the whole there is no remarkable development in the thinking and the level of sophistication represented in the Club speeches. The positions propagated by adherents of the French solution at the beginning of the Club's activities were still the ones being propagated at the end, but with increasing shrillness and bitterness because of the stubbornness of the Mainz citizenry in refusing to embrace the French constitution voluntarily. On the whole, the Mainz Club members were not of the intellectual caliber of other leading proponents of Enlightenment who could be mentioned here, like Adolph Freiherr Knigge and Andreas Georg Friedrich Rebmann, both of whom wrote extensively on Germany and the Revolution. This is partly to be explained by the fact that before October 21, 1792, only a few of them, notably Forster and Cotta, had had any extensive experience as writers and publicists, and none of them had had any practical political or government experience before the arrival of the French.

It appeared at first that the citizens of Mainz were eager to embrace the French gospel of liberty and equality. Probably both Custine and the organizers of the Club mistook the clear antipathy of the Mainz citizens for the now-departed French émigrés and their anger at their elector, who had supported the émigrés so wholeheartedly, for a genuine readiness to revolutionize their way of life.[24] They were soon to be disabused of this optimistic belief, which Forster clearly shared at first.[25] From the very outset Forster was pressured to join in the revolutionizing and lend his prestige to the Club. By all accounts his wife Therese was (at least originally) an ardent republican, and it has often been claimed that she was the one who talked him into joining the revolution. He held out, however, prudently assessing the situation before taking a step that would forever alter his life. After all, what would happen to friends of the French if the Germans should eventually retake Mainz? He did not want to have to emigrate or flee from Mainz unless his future was assured elsewhere. It seems that in late October and early November Forster still had hope of receiving an appointment with a stipend at the Academy of Sciences in Berlin. This would have been quite attractive, but of course he would have had to keep from alienating the people who had the power to appoint him. He was also in acute financial difficulty and was negotiating with Voß for a loan or an advance on future royalties so he could keep his head above water if, as he feared with good reason, the university should no longer be able to pay his salary.[26]

In addition to these good reasons for not rushing into anything, Forster seems to have been skeptical of the quality of the would-be revolutionaries and the wisdom of founding the Club in the first place. On October 24 he wrote to his friend Ludwig Ferdinand Huber that the day before he had sought to dissuade Böhmer and others from taking any hasty action. On October 25 he wrote to Heyne that "the day before yesterday the general founded a Jacobin Club, which I, along with some other moderate people, have not yet joined, and won't join until we have sufficient reason for doing so. But people are watching to see what we do." On October 26 he wrote Huber: "The people in the Club are incompetent, they feel their impotence and have no confidence; but nevertheless the general sentiment is decidedly for the revolution. But people are demanding that we should also join in, they want me in particular. But this won't happen until some things are cleared up." There is no clue as to what Forster means about needing a "sufficient reason" to join the revolutionaries or what things needed to be "cleared up" first. Still, it is apparent that Forster enjoyed being wanted. In fact, one may surmise that he was also approaching the matter in his own way, trying to establish his value to the French before committing himself to anything. In the October 24 letter to Huber he had also announced that he was to see Custine the next day as the spokesman for a university delegation: "Perhaps he and I will get to know each other better, in case that means anything to him." After seeing Custine, he reported to Huber (on October 25) in apparent disappointment: "Unfortunately, it doesn't look as though this visit brought us any closer. He asked for a copy of my remarks [on the situation of the university]; I will send it to him and perhaps add something to it."

Forster persevered. Although there is not a lot of evidence for the period from the capitulation on October 21 to November 5, when Forster is reported to have joined the Club,[27] it would seem that he paved the way by making the acquaintance of a number of high officers and the war commissioners and making himself useful to them. The fact that he spoke perfect French and was a well-known writer was of course an advantage and gave Forster a higher value in French eyes than the run-of-the-mill Club member. By November 4 Custine was convinced that he had made a prime acquisition in Forster,[28] and when he had made up his mind to abolish the old administrations and replace them with a provisional government of his own choosing, he probably very quickly concluded that Forster would be very valuable. By November 10, Forster could announce to Voß (without saying anything about having joined the Club) that he had made a good impression on the French and would probably be a member of the provisional government:

> The university delegated me to talk to the general on its behalf and ask him to protect it. Since my speech was at least successful enough that he could see some difference between my French and what normally passes for French in Mainz, I gained a certain amount of respect from then on. Since it is not in my nature to be pushy, that respect has grown since then. ... I have reason to believe that they intend to make use of me in the provisional government they are about to appoint, and I consider it my duty not to refuse to take on any task, whatever it may be, if it puts me in a position to do something for my fellow citizens at a time like this.[29]

When Custine announced the formation of the provisional government for the Worms, Speyer, and Mainz territories on November 19, Forster was one of those appointed.[30] He functioned from then until his departure for Paris on March 25, 1793 as its vice-president. It would appear that Forster gradually came to overshadow the president, Anton Joseph Dorsch, an ex-priest and ex-Mainz philosophy professor who apparently did not command the respect to go with his status. In any case Forster seems to have been the member of the provisional government in whom the French military and the political commissioners ultimately had the most confidence. He eventually handled most of the relations between the provisional government and the French military and political authorities and drafted reports and decrees in French.

Toward the beginning of the November 10 letter, before telling Voß about the role he expected to play in Mainz under the French, Forster reassured him that he had no intention of acting like a wild man. Later, toward the end of the letter, Forster *does* seem to allude to membership in the Club as something that one simply has to put up with, without taking one's own role in it terribly seriously: "There is no lack of people here from all walks of life, craftsmen, guild members, merchants, scholars, clerics, who are working with full apostolic devotion to convert the people of Mainz to French republicanism, and they are being very successful at it, without people like me being in a position to do anything more than just go along with them—but we can't do any less than that, either, if we want to effect the good that I spoke of above." I believe that this in fact more or less truthfully represents Forster's attitude toward the Club, at least initially. Forster had his hands full with his work in the provisional government and did not have the time, or apparently the inclination, to shine at the Club as well. It is not clear how often he may have spoken *at* the Club in the course of its meetings, as the Club minutes do not systematically note the names of the speakers. He seems, however, to have spoken *to* the Club, formally, only twice, one of these occasions being his New Year's speech as the incoming president for January, 1793. His only really important address to the Club was the speech "Über das Verhältnis der Mainzer gegen die Franken" (On the Behavior of the Citizens of Mainz toward the French), delivered on November 15, 1792. This address, printed as a pamphlet and distributed far and wide, made Forster notorious among opponents of the Mainz revolution, but it did not really go much beyond what others—Wedekind, Böhmer, Metternich, and Andreas Josef Hofmann, for example—had been saying ever since the founding of the Club. Forster is more readable than others whose Club speeches were printed about the same time, but otherwise the only notable things about this speech are his insistence on the Rhine as the natural boundary of France[31] and his readiness to urge the citizens of Mainz to actually *become* French rather than simply vote for a constitution *like* the French constitution: "Doubt not, fellow citizens, that the French Republic is only waiting for you to declare yourselves so that it can offer you its protection and take you into the family. Once the inhabitants of Mainz and the surrounding territory have expressed their desire, *the desire* to become free and French citizens—then you will be incorporated into the indestructible republic" (*MR* I:226). In exhorting the citizens of Mainz to cooperate with the French Forster appealed to the authority of Johannes von Müller, a high Electoral Mainz official who had recently been in the city to wind up his personal affairs and had counseled cooperation with the occupying forces in the interest of saving lives and property.[32] At the close of the speech Forster made his own bow to a silly propaganda device initiated by the Club, urging his listeners to hasten to sign their names in the red book of liberty:

"So hurry, stream forward, press around and inscribe your names in the book that contains the wishes of free men; let the French finally see how Germans too can be inspired by liberty."[33]

Forster's maiden speech shows him in total agreement with the French line as laid down by Custine and reinforced by the National Convention decree of November 19, 1792, which proclaimed that the French republic would aid all peoples who sought to liberate themselves from despotism. This was the line followed by the occupation forces through November and December while the National Convention was debating policy towards the so quickly acquired territories, and Forster, as a member of the provisional government, was one of those responsible for organizing plebiscites in the countryside to ascertain that the people did in fact want to embrace liberty and equality. To judge by the results in a relatively small number of villages polled during this undertaking, the inhabitants of the countryside did in fact seem to be open to accepting the gospel.[34] The cities, however, were another matter altogether. Influential groups in Worms and Speyer, the two imperial free cities occupied by the French, insisted (like other imperial free cities the French occupied during this period, notably Aachen) that they had always had a republican form of government and thus did not need to adopt the French constitution, while in Mainz the merchants and the guilds resisted the idea of radically changing the form of their government, pleading that it would be sufficient simply to reform the old system under a new, perhaps elected, ruler. They didn't want Friedrich Karl von Erthal back any more than anyone else, but they held out hope that the coadjutor, the well-liked Karl Theodor von Dalberg, could be installed at the head of a reformed government.

Forster's initial belief that it would be relatively easy to revolutionize Mainz soon gave way to disillusionment with the unwillingness of the Mainz citizens to embrace change. There were good reasons for this unwillingness. The Mainz economy was depressed under French occupation. The vanished elector, the needs of the electoral government bureaucracy, and the aristocrats who had left the city had accounted for a large share of total employment and spending, and the French occupation forces, instead of spending and circulating money, which would have kept the economy going, requisitioned large amounts of goods and services either without payment or against the promise of payment in the future. The French also disrupted trade and transportation by requisitioning ships on the Rhine and draft animals both in the country and in the city.[35] One of the more obvious results was that garbage piled up in the streets because the peasants could not haul it away. Because the French controlled or had first call on all significant resources, the provisional government was continually strapped for money.

When the Rhenish-German National Convention met in March, 1793, one of the first items on the agenda was to borrow money from the French in order to pay the expenses of the delegates! The greatest and most obvious deterrent to embracing the revolution, however, was the fact that the Prussians, who had retaken Frankfurt on December 2, were nearby and could be expected to move against Mainz and the Left Bank as soon as the 1793 campaigning season started.[36]

Under the circumstances it was rather unreasonable to expect the citizens of Mainz to become wholehearted republicans. Forster reacted to his disappointment by looking down on them for their apathy and identifying ever more closely with the French occupiers. Writing to Huber on December 4, he complains:

> To sacrifice oneself for a people that has no use for that sacrifice is manifest stupidity. One cannot, may not conceal from oneself the fact that the Mainz citizens—although they are not about to fall upon the French treacherously [like the citizens of Frankfurt] because they lack the energy . . .—don't want to be free at all without being most graciously commanded by the general to do so, and they can't and won't take a single step in that direction. As far as I am concerned I consider myself only a French official on temporary assignment, whose presence here will end with the departure of the French army.

He threw himself into his work with the provisional government, feeling like the only honest man in Mainz, finding himself increasingly isolated but wanting to do a creditable job so as perhaps eventually to find employment in France if Mainz reverted to German rule. On January 28 he writes to Therese, who had left Mainz for Strasbourg early in December and gone on from there to Switzerland:

> Where everything is motivated by mistrust—toward the ministers, . . . toward the generals, toward the officers and soldiers, toward the municipal government and the provisional administration, toward the merchants, toward the priests, toward the women, toward individual citizens—that's no place for true, unselfish virtue; and I am prepared to believe that especially in Mainz morality is too little valued for one to hope to find any higher motive than pure selfishness. [Except for a handful of people] I have, up to now, nowhere seen any patriotism or spirit of sacrifice, and certainly nowhere the faintest acknowledgment of what the few high-minded people are doing for the good cause.

No matter what one thinks of Forster's revolutionary activity *per se*, and even though he clearly had ambitions to advance in the service of the French,[37] he took up the cause with the outlook and the unconditional commitment of a highly moral person. Unfortunately, as one revolution after the other has demonstrated over the last two hundred years, the right morality alone was not enough to guarantee a satisfactory result.

January, 1793, had not been a good month for Forster, the Club, or the provisional government. The provisional government had a difficult time of it, anyway, since it had no power to speak of, and could not do anything against the will of the French. It did not have the opportunity to effect much change during the time it was in existence (up to the end of March, 1793),[38] since it could not radically change the bureaucracy it had inherited from the predecessor governments. Mainz was declared to be on a war footing on December 6, and in a state of siege on January 26, thus giving the military even more authority and still more drastically limiting the provisional government's room for initiative. At the beginning of January the long-awaited deputies of the National Convention arrived from Paris, headed by Antoine-Christophe Merlin de Thionville.[39] They promptly undermined the authority of the provisional government by refusing to recognize it, on the grounds that it had not been elected by the people! The most pressing project—the campaign to hold elections for municipal officers in the cities and towns and for delegates to the Rhenish-German National Convention—had to be delayed until late January pending the arrival of yet another set of French representatives, Johann Friedrich Simon and Gabriel Grégoire, sent by the government (the "pouvoir executif") to oversee the elections in accordance with the guidelines laid down in the National Convention decrees of December 15, 17, and 22. After this second set of commissioners arrived the provisional government had three French masters to please: the occupation military, the National Convention, and the executive authority. Because of delays the elections had to be postponed to late February, by which time the military situation in the occupied territories was rapidly deteriorating.

Forster was president of the Club in January, and he might have been able to do something to consolidate the revolution by bringing the Club, the French, and the provisional government closer together. Instead, however, there was a dramatic blowup in the Club on January 10 and 11: Andreas Josef Hofmann, professor of natural law and the history of philosophy at the university, who appears to have been the most incorruptible of the hard-line Mainz revolutionaries and the idol of the younger generation,[40] rose to denounce the Club, the French military commissioners, the provisional government, and practically everyone associated with them. The military commissioners were corrupt, the Club had taken in disreputable members and scared away the honest people, its members had wasted everyone's time and corrupted the public with their propagandizing instead of educating it, they had defamed the citizens of Mainz (here he seems to have referred specifically to Forster and several of his actions), the Club insiders had plotted to hold on to their power (here he accused Forster of ambition), and so on. Hofmann then attacked Dorsch, the president of the provisional government:

> He accused him of angling for the highest office in the land without having the requisite qualifications, of deceiving the General, of passing out the other jobs arbitrarily, of miserably failing to do his duty, of not putting an end to the robbery of the army supply commissioners, of even sharing the booty with them.... (MR I:507)

Forster was of course greatly embarrassed by the attacks on himself and on the administration.[41] Eventually peace was restored in the Club and it was agreed to expunge the record of the January 10 and 11 meetings from the minutes, but Hofmann's—probably on the whole—well-founded attack had done considerable damage to the revolutionaries and their prestige.

The last act of the Mainz revolution—its goal from the very beginning— was the elections that began on February 24 and the Rhenish-German National Convention that constituted itself on March 17. For the elections the French invented a set of new rules which, on the whole, turned out to be counterproductive. The efforts of the revolutionaries to ascertain the will of the populace during November and December of 1792 had assumed—under the impression given by the National Convention decree of November 19— that it was more or less sufficient for the people to express their opinion for or against the French constitution and then to form a new government. A decree of December 15/17 directed French generals in occupied territories to proclaim the end of feudalism, abolish all feudal levies and privileges, and call on the people to hold elections and allow the French to protect them from their former rulers. Article 11 was particularly ominous: "The French Republic declares that it will treat as its enemy any people that does not accept or renounces the liberty and equality we offer it and wants to keep, recall, or negotiate with its old rulers and privileged classes."[42]

A December 22 supplement to the December 15/17 decree prescribed that no citizen could vote or hold office without first swearing an oath to liberty and equality and renouncing all feudal rights and privileges. In practice it was not just those "peoples" who refused to accept liberty and equality that were treated as the enemy, but also all individuals who refused to swear the oath. The National Convention representatives and government commissioners soon demanded the expulsion of the large number of citizens who refused to swear the oath and the expropriation or sequestration of their property, as well as the sequestration of the property of citizens who had emigrated before the start of the election campaign.[43] The required oath, as formulated in the election regulations, seems innocuous enough: each voter was to declare, before casting the first of a series of prescribed ballots, "I swear to be true to the people and to the principles of liberty and equality." The Germans balked, however, at the oath, agitating in vain for the substitution of a simple oath of submission (a "Huldigungseid"), a promise not to resist the conquering French and to obey their commands— the kind of oath, as they pointed out, that had been extracted from conquered peoples in the past and to which they, the conquered, could have no serious objection. The oath requirement led directly to the exceptionally low turnout in the cities (although citizens of Worms and Speyer voted in proportionately larger numbers than the inhabitants of Mainz, which is possibly further evidence that the Mainz Club itself had hurt the cause more than it had helped). In the countryside the provisional government and its commissars, under the direction of the French commissioners, taught the people how to exercise their new rights, by force if necessary. Forster took part in these efforts and was proud of one such encounter at Grünstadt, where he had called in troops to arrest the Counts of Leiningen for inciting the inhabitants to resist taking the oath and voting, and to transport them to Landau as hostages. Forster reported these events in a letter to Therese written from Grünstadt on February 27. In conclusion he exults: "Thus everything that opposes the cause must yield to us."[44] When the citizens of Worms voiced objections to voting on the appointed day, on the grounds that they had never been properly informed of the December 15/17 decree, the three National Convention deputies told the German election commissar in Worms in no uncertain terms: "True patriots have long been accustomed not to worry about numbers, no matter how large or how small; they are certain of their victory and of foiling all the attacks and machinations of the aristocratic party." The commissar was to proceed with the elections forthwith.[45] Under the circumstances it is not surprising if, of all the cities, towns, and villages in the occupied territories, only 126 elected delegates to the Rhenish-German National Convention, not all of whom actually showed up to participate.[46] The most important act of the Convention, the annexation petition addressed to the French National Convention, was signed on March 25, 1793 by the (only) ninety deputies present at the time.

Those who were willing to swear the prescribed oath first elected municipal officials, then a delegate to represent them at the Rhenish-German National Convention. It was not necessary to reside in a locality to be elected to the Convention. Thus most of the leading Club members found a place that would elect them and were among the delegates. They starred in the debates of the Convention as they had previously starred at the Club. Hofmann was elected president, Forster was the runner-up in the balloting and became vice-president. On March 21 Forster boasted to his wife that he was one of the leading actors in the Convention: "[I made it a point] to take an active part in all the debates up to now, and with great success. The peasants love me and let me know it in their naive fashion [about half the delegates were peasants], and the so-called educated members of the Convention say I'm the soul of the whole thing." Forster drafted the major decrees of the Convention and delivered an impassioned speech in favor of unification with France on March 21, the day the delegates voted to petition for annexation. He was one of the three delegates selected to go to Paris to present the petition to the National Convention and left Mainz on March 25, intending, as he wrote Therese, to remain away only two to three weeks. He seems to have intended to return to Mainz and stand for election as a deputy to the National Convention. He presented the Mainz petition on March 30, and by acclamation the National Convention annexed, not the whole occupied Left Bank, but only and specifically the towns and villages represented by the ninety delegates who had signed the petition.[47] Forster of course never returned to Mainz, because by the end of March the Prussians had driven the French out of most of the Left Bank and were moving to encircle the city. The area of the Rhenish republic was reduced to the one city, Mainz, which was besieged by Prussian, Austrian, and imperial troops and finally capitulated on July 23, 1793, thus effectively ending the first German experiment in representative democracy under the tutelage of the French. The French were more successful at retaining some of the other territories they had "liberated" and annexed in 1792-1793.

Both the German revolutionaries and the French were responsible for what happened in Mainz, of course, but it is impossible not to cast the greater part of the blame for the overall fiasco of the Mainz republic on the French. Their rigid enforcement of the December 15/17 decrees, forcing the conquered to declare themselves unequivocally as friend or foe, totally poisoned the atmosphere in the occupied Rhineland and contributed substantially to German resistance and apathy in the elections of February, 1793. As I have already noted, the attempt to revolutionize, democratize, and annex the occupied territories was a substitute for outright conquest, which on the whole might have been a more profitable method of approaching the problem of securing the Rhine border against Prussian and Austrian forces. In the last analysis, however—aside from the question whether it would have been better to conquer or to revolutionize—the French in 1792-1793 were still acting out of military and political weakness and lacked the firm resolve that was finally supplied under the Jacobin dictatorship from the fall of 1793 on. Contemporaries were greatly puzzled by the early French capitulation at Mainz—by all accounts the French forces were well provisioned and could have continued to hold the fortress for months. They might also have mounted a much more determined effort to break the siege and relieve the city, but they did not. Custine, whose military talents were rather dubious anyway, became the scapegoat for the loss of Mainz and was executed in the summer of 1793, but that did nothing to change the fact that the German revolutionaries had been betrayed by their faith in the power of republican France and its willingness to defend them at the Rhine boundary. One of the strongest arguments the Club propagandists had had at their disposal was that the French were there to stay, and that it was therefore safe to embrace French liberty and equality. It was, they argued, obviously in the French interest to hold the occupied Left-Bank territories, and even if the French were to withdraw from the Left Bank honor would demand that they insist in any peace negotiations with the German powers that the inhabitants be allowed to retain their new republican form of government. Having disappointed the expectations of their German sympathizers that they would hold the Left Bank and the fortress of Mainz at all costs, the surrendering French betrayed their allies yet again, by failing to insist in the capitulation agreement on any stipulation about the political future of Mainz, or even about the fate of the Club members who were forced to remain behind.[48]

In conclusion, I would certainly not wish to argue that Forster was any worse than other Mainz revolutionaries; in some respects he was probably better. In fact, I believe or am willing to concede that they mostly were quite honorable and well-intentioned people. Forster became a revolutionary for complex personal and political reasons which are impossible to sort out neatly. At the outset he maintained (in letters to friends) that a major reason for his participation was to do what he could to preserve Mainz and his fellow-citizens from harm. He considered that the duty of any right-minded citizen, and the record of his dealings with the French as a member of the provisional government (at least in the pre-electioneering period) shows that he interceded on behalf of a number of citizens who were being harassed by the occupiers.[49] The imperial edict of December 19, 1792, made clear that he had burned his bridges to Germany and that his commitment to the revolution was irreversible. From that point on he seems to have identified more and more with the occupiers and viewed himself ever more exclusively in his capacity as a French official. If the citizens of Mainz would not voluntarily choose liberty and equality, he was prepared to help the French force it upon them. He worked closely with Simon, the election commissioner, and impressed him so favorably that he recommended Forster to Paris as a replacement for Grégoire, who was ill when he arrived in Mainz and incapable of performing much useful work. In one letter Simon praises Forster as one of the "matadors" of the revolution in Mainz.[50]

If nothing else, publication of the two document volumes of *Die Mainzer Republik* and volume 10,1 of the Akademie-Ausgabe makes it clear without a shadow of a doubt that the Mainz revolution was a totally French-inspired and -directed undertaking and that Forster played a prominent role in it. No amount of Marxist wishful thinking about the "first bourgeois democratic revolution in Germany" or praise for the "altruism" of the Mainz revolutionaries can change this fact. The French may have acted reprehensibly in Mainz and the occupied Left Bank territories in 1792–1793, and on every later occasion when they had driven out the German forces, but at least they had the excuse that they were only reacting to the exigencies of the situation, protecting the "natural boundaries" of France and waging war on the enemies who had sworn to extinguish their Revolution and bring all the leading revolutionaries to "justice." No such defense can be mounted for the Mainz revolutionaries, and it seems to me to be somewhat obtuse to insist on admiring them for attempting to overthrow the old order so precipitously. Attempts to plant a revolution against the wishes of a large part of the population being revolutionized always lead to the need for moral judgments. Who was right and who was wrong? Is it morally justified to force the majority to do what the minority, the true religion, the pure ideology, etc., postulate to be the only correct thing? The Mainz revolutionaries, a tiny minority in the occupied territories who could prevail only by collaborating with the French occupiers, clearly trampled on the rights, the economic and social interests, and the sensibilities of their fellow citizens in the course of propagating change. Mainz citizens who had had to leave the city because of the revolution returned in the summer of 1793 and quite understandably vented their anger on those revolutionaries who had had the misfortune not to be able to escape the besieged city. A number of captured Club members were beaten black and blue before being delivered to their jailers. On the other hand, no one was hanged in Germany for participating in the Mainz revolution, a welcome contrast to the revolutionary justice that prevailed in Paris in 1793–1794. In the end, one is forced to conclude that the Mainz revolutionaries were totally inexperienced in politics, and they were naive to believe in the altruism of the French who were offering to help them establish liberty and equality.

NOTES

The symposium version of this paper was published in German, in shortened form (with minimal documentation), as "Georg Forster und die Mainzer Revolution," in *Juni: Magazin für Kultur und Politik* 3, 2-3 (1989): *Dossier: Die große Französische Revolution*, 80-95. Much of the material relating to the Mainz Club and the elections of 1793 was published in "Mainz Revisited: Or, Was this Really a Revolution to be Admired? A Response to Wolfgang Albrecht," in *Lessing Yearbook* XXII (1990): 77-89 (for Albrecht see the Bibliography in this volume).

1. A good example is a recent attempt at a popular Forster biography, Klaus Harpprecht's *Georg Forster oder Die Liebe zur Welt: Eine Biographie* (Reinbek bei Hamburg: Rowohlt, 1987). Harpprecht's chapters dealing with Forster and the Revolution become incredibly jumbled and confusing.

2. When I wrote my own monograph, *Georg Forster* (New York: Twayne Publishers, 1972 [Twayne World Authors Series, 215]), I was considerably more sympathetic toward the Mainz Revolution than I have since become.

3. *Georg Forsters Werke: Sämtliche Schriften, Tagebücher, Briefe*, herausgegeben von der Deutschen Akademie der Wissenschaften, Zentralinstitut für deutsche Sprache und Literatur (Berlin: Akademie-Verlag, 1958ff.). Cited in the following as AA.

4. AA 17: *Briefe 1792 bis 1794 und Nachträge* (Berlin: Akademie-Verlag, 1989).

5. AA 10,1: *Revolutionsschriften 1792/93: Reden, administrative Schriftstücke, Zeitungsartikel, politische und diplomatische Korrespondenz, Aufsätze* (Berlin: Akademie-Verlag, 1990).

6. In particular one had perhaps hoped to recover more of Forster's original text from the scissors-and-paste editing technique of Therese Forster/Huber, through whose hands passed most of Forster's letters to herself, Ludwig Ferdinand Huber, and several other major correspondents. The editors of volume 17 had at their disposal transcriptions of many of the original letters which Therese had had made while working up her edition, and they used the transcriptions, where available, as the basis for their published text. While a certain amount of Forster text has thus been recovered, it is obvious that the transcriptions, being philologically unverifiable and perhaps still not containing the entire text, are not a perfect substitute for the originals. It is disappointing that Therese's edition still remains the basis text for so many of the letters in AA 17.

7. *Die Mainzer Republik I: Protokolle des Jakobinerklubs* and *Die Mainzer Republik II: Protokolle des Rheinisch-deutschen Nationalkonvents mit Quellen*

zu seiner Vorgeschichte (Berlin: Akademie-Verlag, 1975 & 1981). After the UCLA Symposium the third volume of Scheel's work appeared: *Die Mainzer Republik III: Die erste bürgerlich-demokratische Republik auf deutschem Boden. Eine Darstellung mit 54 Abbildungen, 10 Spezialstudien und einer Farbfaltkarte* (Berlin: Akademie-Verlag, 1989). In the volume, which purports to be a definitive history of the Mainz revolution and republic, Scheel drew the logical ideological consequences from the evidence he had presented with such diligence in the first two volumes, at precisely the same time as the GDR and the standard Marxist approach to German revolutionary history had reached the end of the line. I shall make grateful use of the two volumes of documents, which will generally be cited in parentheses in the text as *MR* I or II.

8. In a letter to Heyne of October 20, 1792 Forster gives a reasonably accurate account of the confrontation between the French and German armies at Valmy on September 20, the negotiations between the French and the Prussians, and the subsequent German retreat. See chapter three of my book, *Black Bread—White Bread: German Intellectuals and the French Revolution* (Columbia, S.C.: Camden House, 1988) for a detailed study of the 1792 Austro-Prussian campaign against the French.

9. Here and in the following, I simply quote Forster's letters by date, according to the text now available in AA 17.

10. The best succinct description of the geopolitical situation in the area occupied by Custine's forces is offered by Scheel in the introduction to *MR* II.

11. Which is not to say, however, that the French were not sorely tempted to go into the Palatine territories or that inhabitants of these territories were impervious to the appeal of French revolutionary propaganda. Some, in fact, seem to have been disappointed that they were not revolutionized.

12. See the map labeled "Die Wahlen zum Mainzer Konvent" in the catalogue of the 1981 Mainz exhibition: *Deutsche Jakobiner: Mainzer Republik und Cisrhenanen 1792–1798*, Band 3: *Katalog* (Mainz, 1981) 93.

13. *MR* I:56. The proclamation may have been the work of Georg Wilhelm Böhmer, who functioned as Custine's "secretary" and seems in general to have been in charge of Custine's German-language public relations operations. On October 25 Böhmer is reported to have read the proclamation at the Club the day before (*MR* I:55).

14. *MR* I:111. The proclamation was published in Böhmer's *Mainzer National-Zeitung* on November 5.

15. Marxist scholars are fond of referring to the members of the Mainz Club as "Jacobins," since for them "Jacobins" are the highest form of revolutionary existence, but this is misleading. Although the Mainz Club even-

tually became affiliated with (or was accredited by) the Paris Jacobin Club, the members hardly ever referred to themselves—and certainly not in general—as "Jacobins." If one insists on calling them "Jacobins," then it should at least be kept in mind that the Girondins too were still Jacobins in good standing at the time in question. There is little or nothing in the records of the Mainz Club to indicate that its members took sides in the developing debate between the Gironde and the Mountain factions in Paris, or that they were even very aware of it. In any case that struggle came to a head only in the spring of 1793, at a time when the outcome was of no significance whatsoever for the activities of the Mainz revolutionaries. In practice, the Mainz Club, which never finished drafting its own statutes, was close to the Strasbourg Club, took the Strasbourg Club's statutes as a guide for its own organization and operation, and benefitted from the experience of several members of the Strasbourg Club who moved to Mainz after October 21, 1792.

16. On January 28, 1793, Forster wrote to his wife about his activities in the Club that month, which had included presiding over both the French and the German meetings and having to speak constantly, because he had acted as the chief translator.

17. See Franz Dumont's interesting brief analysis of "Die Mainzer Republik von 1792/93" in the catalogue of the 1981 Mainz exhibition, *Deutsche Jakobiner: Mainzer Republik und Cisrhenanen 1792–1798*, Band 1: *Handbuch* (Mainz, 1981), 25–36. Dumont registers the rather obvious fact that it was the "officials and intellectuals" who played by far the greatest role in the Club, concluding—against the traditional doctrinaire Marxist position—that the Mainz Club had neither had a "mass basis" among the "working population" nor been greatly influenced by the lower classes (26). Dumont comes to similar conclusions regarding makeup of the Rhenish-German National Convention and participation in its debates (see Dumont's charts illustrating the composition of the Rhenish-German Convention in the exhibition catalogue, Band 3: *Katalog*, 98).

18. By all indications the *National-Zeitung* was the Mainz propaganda organ most loathed outside the occupied territories. See *Black Bread—White Bread* 253–58.

19. Before his move to Mainz Cotta had published the *Strasburgisches politisches Journal, eine Zeitschrift für Aufklärung und Freiheit* (Strasbourg, 1792, 2 volumes), and the last issues of the journal were edited from Mainz. For example, he published the two proclamations by Custine already cited above, a third proclamation by Custine establishing the new provisional government on November 19, 1792, and Forster's maiden speech in the Club "Ueber das Verhältnis der Mainzer gegen die Franken."

20. See for example Andreas Josef Hofmann, *Der Aristokratenkatechismus: Ein wunderschönes Büchlein, gar erbaulich zu lesen für Junge und Alte* (Mainz, 1792).

21. This was also one of the selling points that Forster stressed in his address to the Paris National Convention petitioning for annexation of the Rhenish republic in March, 1793. See AA 10,1:469, 471: Mainz, with its favored situation on the Rhine, would allow France to dominate trade in the area.

22. The minutes of January 29 record that Matthias Metternich had been elected president for February with twenty votes, Friedrich Cotta vice-president with twenty-five. The minutes of February 23 record a speech by Metternich expressing disdain for all the Mainz citizens who had done their best to belittle the Club and hinder its work: "He had heard that people wanted to break up the Club and drive away and murder its members. But such a project was ridiculous, since the members of the Club had their principles and people with principles couldn't be diverted from their undertaking.... The Club would continue in existence, even if there were only thirty-six members, and its decisions would endure. All of humanity had to be saved, so one mustn't look to spare the present generation" (*MR* I:728).

23. See *MR* I:769. This means, of course, that even fewer than 372 had actually voted. In actual fact, the deadline for swearing the oath was extended into March up to the deadline for turning over the list of election participants to the French commissioners. Scheel is proud to point out that in the end—doubtless because of the desire not to be expelled or lose their property—13% (610) of the Mainz citizens eligible to vote had sworn the oath (*MR* III:185).

24. For a discussion of the émigrés in Germany, see chapter two of *Black Bread—White Bread*.

25. On November 10 he writes to Voß: "A lot has changed in the three weeks since the capitulation. Public opinion against the previous order of things is overwhelming; the desire to become free in the new French manner is almost as loud. There's no doubt that that's good for the French, since the Rhine seems such a natural boundary for them that—in light of their present successes—they can consider such a rounding off of their territory an appropriate compensation for their war expenses. The false measures taken by the previous government, or rather its total apathy, have contributed incredibly towards accelerating the decision of the citizens."

26. Negotiations over the loan and the conditions attached to it (Forster wanted to be assured that taking the money would not obligate him to hew to the Prussian line in politics) occupied a large part of Forster's correspondence with Voß during this period. In the end Forster received the money

with no strings attached, but had to be careful that the *French* did not find out about it, or at least draw the wrong conclusion from the affair, namely that he had been bought by Prussia.

27. There seems to be no conclusive evidence that Forster joined on this date, as no minutes survive. See *MR* I:136. In his letters Forster does not mention being a member of the Club until well after November 5. There could, of course, have been very good reasons for this.

28. See Custine's November 4, 1792 letter to Paris: "Je dois faire part aux représentants du peuple français d'une conquête que nous venons de faire en liant aux intérets de la raison: M. Forster, un des compagnons de Cook, ce savant philosophe qui rendait hommage depuis longtemps à tous les principes de notre gouvernement, va devenir citoyen français. Bibliothécaire de Mayence et professeur de physique, je l'ai conservé provisoirement dans ces fonctions; il n'était pas possible de faire un meilleur choix" (*MR* I:136–37, also *MR* II:98).

29. Forster is probably not being completely forthright in this letter. According to Scheel (*MR* II:98), Custine had been planning to install a provisional government since November 4 at the latest (the day on which he wrote about Forster to Paris!) and had originally intended for it to begin operating on November 10, the day Forster wrote to Voß. Surely Forster knew quite well on November 10 that he would in fact be a member of the provisional government!

30. Custine's proclamation is printed in *MR* II:96–98.

31. See *MR* I:226. According to Forster, the Rhine was the "natural boundary" of a great republic "which demands to make no conquests and is only opening its arms to nations which want to unite with it on their own." The French republic was "justified in demanding from its enemies appropriate compensation" for the war they had capriciously loosed upon it, and it was only just that the French should keep the Rhine as their boundary at the conclusion of the war. On the history of French efforts to extend their borders to the Rhine during the revolutionary period, see Sydney Seymour Biro, *The German Policy of Revolutionary France: A Study in French Diplomacy during the War of the First Coalition 1792–1797.* 2 vols. (Cambridge, Mass.: Harvard University Press, 1957).

32. Appeal to Müller's authority was controversial under the circumstances. Müller himself was of course quite unhappy with the use to which Forster and other revolutionaries had put his advice.

33. *MR* I:232. Soon after the founding of the Club someone (apparently Böhmer) got the bright idea of inviting all those who were ready to embrace their French liberators to sign their names in the red book of liberty, while those who preferred to remain slaves were to sign in a black book decked

with chains. Those who did not sign in the red book of their own accord were to be treated as though they had signed in the black book. By mid-January, when the Club gave up the project, the red book contained some 1200 names, the black book only four. Needless to say, the propaganda surrounding the red and black books represented extreme psychological coercion, as Forster himself recognized by the time he began work on his *Darstellung der Revolution in Mainz*.

34. There is considerable material about the November-December plebiscites in *MR* II:143–85. Rural ardor for liberation cooled remarkably, however, when it became clear that the peasants would not enjoy a substantially lighter tax burden than before: what they had previously had to pay to their landlords or to the church was now to be paid to the provisional government and the French commissars.

35. Things had gotten so bad by January that the provisional government was forced to complain about the army and its requisitioning practices when the representatives of the French National Convention arrived on the scene. Forster authored a draft "Entwurf des Schreibens der Allgemeinen Administration (von Mainz) an die Kommissarien des National-convents." As no French version of the memo seems to exist, one must assume that it was never delivered in written form, although possibly Forster or Dorsch made oral representations based on the draft. The "Entwurf" is reprinted with commentary in *MR* I:517–23, and, for now without any commentary, in AA 10,1:123–32.

36. The recapture of Frankfurt was a severe blow to French prestige and to the Mainz revolutionists. To explain the loss it was necessary to hatch a conspiracy theory (the treacherous citizens of Frankfurt had conspired to aid the Prussians and Hessians and to attack unsuspecting French soldiers within the city itself!), although the French forces available to defend the city had hardly been strong enough to hold it against a large-scale threat. See *Black Bread—White Bread* 244ff. Forster was one of those who loudly vilified the Frankfurters for their "perfidy," which led among other things to a break with his long-time friend Johann Georg Schlosser, a native of that city.

37. Realistically speaking, Forster was in a very difficult situation, forced to hope for a future with the French. An imperial edict ("Mandatum Avocatorium") of December 19, 1792, had outlawed and proscribed all German officials who entered French service. For the text of the edict see *MR* I:663–65.

38. Although a civilian government continued after the end of the Rhenish German National Convention with Andreas Josef Hofmann at its head, the original provisional government was crippled by the end of March: Forster, the vice-president, had left for Paris, and Dorsch, the president, had

fled Mainz, as the German troops approached, before the end of the Convention.

39. The other "representatives on mission" were Jean-François Reubel and Nicolas Haussmann.

40. On Hofmann see the article by Helmut Mathy, "Andreas Josef Hofmann, der Präsident des rheinisch-deutschen Nationalkonvents von 1793," in the Mainz exhibition catalogue, Band 1: *Handbuch*, 235–38. See also the article on Hofmann in the *Neue deutsche Biographie*.

41. Forster described the affair in a letter to Therese on January 20/22 (see AA 17). See also *MR* I:513.

42. I quote according to the German version published in Böhmer's *Mainzer National-Zeitung*, *MR* I:429. Article 11 continues: "[The French nation] promises not to conclude a peace treaty or lay down its arms until the sovereignty and independence of the people upon whose territory its troops are stationed are secured, and until that people has accepted the principles of equality and established a free popular government." The French versions of the decrees of November 19, December 15/17, and December 22 are contained (in excerpt) in AA 10,1:647ff.

43. Here there was considerable controversy, since the capitulation agreement of October 21, 1792, had provided for any citizens who wanted to leave the city with all their property. The French policy of expelling non-juring citizens and taking their property, which seems excessively harsh, was predicated on the perceived necessity of ridding themselves of all internal enemies. It was basically an extension of policies already applied to French aristocratic émigrés and non-juring priests. While space does not allow for extended treatment of the subject here, it is clear that Forster strongly supported the French policy both as an official and in the pages of his *Neue Mainzer Zeitung* (see for example what are presumably his own editorial comments in issues 29 and 30, dated March 8 and 10, 1793, AA 10,1:375–77 and 382–84). In the issue of March 8 non-juring citizens are compared to gangrenous limbs that must be amputated in order to save the body politic from its otherwise mortal fever.

44. Forster's version of these events in the letter to Therese reads: "The counts of Leiningen had even remained in Grünstadt in order to hinder my operations. I had sixty men sent here and called on the counts, with all their officials, to become French citizens. They protested and plotted, they incited citizens and peasants and had one of my soldiers attacked and wounded. I called for another 130 men, and as soon as they arrived I placed myself at their head, took possession of both castles, and took the counts into custody. Today I sent them off to Landau as prisoners; tomorrow their women will be put across the Rhine." For some evidence as to how non-revolutionary con-

temporaries viewed this kind of electioneering in Mainz, see *Black Bread—White Bread* 248-59.

45. *MR* II:282. This particular communication, signed by all three of the representatives on mission, was even printed and distributed as a broadside.

46. The Mainz exhibition catalogue (Band 3: *Katalog* 94-95) lists the 126 municipalities. The Rhenish-German National Convention repeatedly debated measures to entice or force all the elected deputies to appear, and to get municipalities that had not yet elected deputies to do so.

47. This did not, of course, prevent the French from continuing to act as occupiers in the areas that had not sent representatives to the Convention.

48. The Prussians refused to grant remaining German revolutionaries safe passage out of the city with the departing French. Some of them escaped successfully, others were captured and imprisoned until they were finally exchanged for hostages the French had earlier taken from Mainz and sent to France.

49. See the section of AA 10,1 titled "Mainzer Allgemeine Administration." Most such activity on Forster's part (at least to the extent that it survives) seems to have been concentrated in the period from late November, 1792, to early January, 1793.

50. See the section of correspondence between the election commissioners and their ministry in Paris in AA 10,1.

JENS KRUSE

The French Revolution and the German Romanticists

"THE FRENCH REVOLUTION AND THE GERMAN Romanticists." The title has a nice ring to it. There is a pleasing balance: French, German; Revolution, Romanticists. There is the "and," the plus-sign connecting the two elements: it seems to promise something positive, a result, a sum, an increase, a profit; it says: these elements add up to something. But to what? What do we enter on the other side of the equation? The French Revolution and the German Romanticists equal *what*?

If we turn to the German Romanticists themselves for an answer to that question we encounter an impressive line-up of definitions and characterizations. The French Revolution is one of the "greatest tendencies of the age,"[1] it can be seen as "the greatest and most noteworthy phenomenon of the history of states," as an almost "universal earthquake, a measureless inundation of the political world," or it can be considered the "archetype of revolutions, the revolution pure and simple,"[2] and its "torches of revolution" are the comets which periodically revolutionize the "system of the intellectual world."[3] Alternatively, it can be seen as the "the most frightful grotesquerie of the age," as a "tragicomedy of humanity." The French Revolution can also be understood as the "center and ... high point of the French national character,"[4] because the French are "a chemical nation," the age is "a chemical age," and revolutions are "universal not organic but chemical movements."[5] But then again we read that "the best thing the French have gained through the revolution is a portion of Germanness."[6] Or would it be better to conceive of the French Revolution as a "life-threatening and contagious disease,"[7] a "feverish state,"[8] which might turn out to be nothing but the "crisis of the onset of puberty."[9]

This catalogue of attempted definitions is as impressive as it is confounding. The array of fields appealed to for explanatory power is astonishing: philosophy of history, political history, geology and astronomy, theory of stage and drama, national psychology, chemistry, medicine and human developmental biology. But any initial exhilaration at such astonishing diversity of attempted conceptualization soon gives way to confusion and dejection: how are we supposed to see a common thread in such a jumble, how is one supposed to discern order in such chaos? When confronted with such vastness and diversity, literary scholars and historians tend to employ two strategies: narrow the scope of the material and consult the scholarly literature. Unfortunately neither seems to help all that much in our case.

The first strategy will not help us much, because all of the pronouncements quoted above are drawn from the works of only two of the German Romanticists: Friedrich Schlegel (1772–1829) and Friedrich von Hardenberg (1772–1801), who called his poetic self Novalis. Even though or perhaps precisely because such a move offers very little help in the sense of conceptual simplification, I will restrict my remarks to these two German Romanticists, for a good case can be made that these two authors, in a very few years around the turn of the century, thought and wrote most of what might be helpful in our attempt to complete the equation of our title.[10]

If we turn to the scholarly literature on the question our confusion is not necessarily alleviated.[11] The fact that the history of *Germanistik* is very closely intertwined with the reception-history of German Romanticism has not helped its dispassionate analysis and evaluation.[12] The extreme judgments of Carl Schmitt and Georg Lukács may or may not prove that the history of the study of Romanticism is the history of its misinterpretations,[13] but it does sometimes make one think that many scholarly reactions say more about their own age than about the period they try to elucidate.[14] Even when one surveys the many excellent studies and collections of articles published in the last two decades,[15] the impression remains that the student revolutionaries see the Jacobin Romanticists, the neo-Marxists see the Frankfurtian Romanticists, the Gadamerians the first hermeneuticists, and the deconstructionists the pre-Derridean and proto-Lacanian Romanticists.

So the apparently neat and orderly formula of the title "The French Revolution and the German Romanticists" seems to have deconstructed itself into chaos and confusion. Not even the question whether French Revolution and German Romanticists add up to revolution or reaction, which would seem to require no more than a distinction between extremes, appears to be easily answerable. In view of such a discouraging state of affairs it seems to be prudent to set out relatively modest goals for my paper. Instead of attempting to come up with the total that completes the equation, it may be more promising to see how the problem might be solvable, if a solution could be approximated. Since we are attempting to assess the impact of a set of historical events on a segment of poetic production, what this more modest goal means for us, I think, is to ask the question: How did the historical forces of the French Revolution impact on the textual production of the Jena Romanticists, specifically Schlegel and Novalis? What consequences did these events, which unfolded during the formative years of their respective literary careers, have for the material of their production, for their language and its form?[16]

It is obvious that even this question presents difficult problems of mediation between historical event and literary production. It stands at the starting point of a project of which only the slimmest fragment can be presented within the limits of a single paper. In view of the fact, however, that Schlegel[17] and Novalis, more than any other German Romanticists, reacted to the French Revolution by giving fragments a position of centrality in their works, this should not hold us back, should instead encourage us to seek guidance and enlightenment in the fragmentary.

Accordingly, I would like to start by quoting two of Schlegel's fragments:

> The French Revolution, Fichtes Wissenschaftslehre, und Goethe's Meister are the greatest tendencies of the age. Whoever finds this combination objectionable, whoever cannot regard any revolution as important if it is not loud and material, has not yet attained the high and broad standpoint of the history of humankind. Even in our thin cultural histories—which mostly resemble a collection of variants accompanied by a running commentary, to which the classic text has been lost—many a little book, of which the noisy crowd of its time took little note, plays a larger role than anything done by that crowd.[18]

It is only one of the curiosities of this fragment's strange reception history that whereas the first sentence of the fragment is quoted in almost every paper on the French Revolution and German Romanticists, and the second frequently enough, the third is almost uniformly ignored. This is all the more to be regretted since it is precisely this sentence that might yet yield valuable clues for the solution of our problem. In the third sentence, Schlegel's analogy quickly moves the issue from political to cultural history. This is in accordance with the thrust of the fragment and the Romanticists' general tendency to see the events in France merely as the sign of a much more pervasive revolution. Furthermore, Schlegel makes it clear that this cultural history can and should be traced in apparently insignificant texts, that some "little book" such as Goethe's *Wilhelm Meister* or Fichte's *Wissenschaftslehre* can indeed play a great role as commentary upon a "classic text" such as the French Revolution. If we try to follow Schlegel's instruction nowadays, however, we have to deal with an ironic result of the fragment's reception history which, I think, Schlegel would have appreciated. Not least of all because of Schlegel's fragment, the "little books" highlighted by it have, in a curious transfer of terms, themselves become classic texts. If we want to follow Schlegel's instruction and find the little books that can provide novel commentary on the classic text of the French Revolution, we may have to look at new little books.

In order to find such texts we should take guidance from the second Schlegel fragment, which deals with critical method: "One has to drill the board where it is thickest."[19] Taken together, the two fragments instruct us to find the little text in which the "tendencies of the age," their vectors of force, have become bundled most densely, where history has most strikingly thickened into poetry, where "Geschichte" has become "Gedicht."

There may well be many such texts,[20] but to my mind very few could more perfectly meet our requirements than Klingsohr's "Märchen," which forms the end and culmination of the first and only completed part of Novalis's *Heinrich von Ofterdingen*. It promises to be "thick" with the "tendencies of the age" in numerous ways. The genre of *Märchen* has been identified as one of the literary forms in which the Romanticists tried to represent their revolutionary project[21]; the *Märchen*, together with the novel, was the form which the Romanticists themselves most often saw as the incarnation of their new poetics.[22] The fact that both Schlegel and Novalis devoted an almost obsessive amount of their aesthetic reflection to Goethe and his *Wilhelm Meister* gives the climactic text-segment of Novalis's counter-*Meister* a privileged position[23]; finally, the fact that Klingsohr's "Märchen" presents itself as Novalis's romanticist rewriting[24] of what is arguably Goethe's most significant poetic reaction to the French Revolution,[25] namely his "Märchen" at the end of *Unterhaltungen deutscher Ausgewanderten*, gives us the opportunity to use the latter as a contrastive foil to help us define more clearly in what specifically romanticist ways Novalis's little text is a commentary on the classic text of the French Revolution.

***

We cannot even hope to exhaust these texts' extraordinary complexity here, but even a cursory analysis of their common gross structural segments will prove illuminating. Like any self-respecting tale, these "Märchen" have a beginning, a middle, and an end: they begin in an old world on the threshold of change (1), in the middle they go through a period of transition (2) which culminates in redemption (3), and they end in a new world (4).

(1) The opening sentences of these two "Märchen" could hardly be more different. "The long night had just begun,"[26] the starkly simple beginning of Novalis's "Märchen," presents a striking contrast to Goethe's complex hypotactical structure: "By the great river, which had just been swelled by heavy rains and overflooded its banks, the old ferryman lay in his small hut and slept, tired from the exertions of the day."[27] Ironically, Novalis's simple sentence introduces the reader to a world which appears to refer not merely

to simple astronomical but to eschatological time. Goethe's complex sentence, on the other hand, appears to be saturated with particles of the natural and secular world.

This evolving opposition between a relatively normal everyday world in Goethe's "Märchen" and a mythic eschatological realm in Novalis's tale is furthered by the next few sentences and paragraphs of each tale. Whereas the first structure we encountered in Goethe was a "hut," it is a "palace" in Novalis; likewise the first character in Goethe is the mundane "old ferryman" who can hardly compare to Novalis's "old hero"; and while the ferryman's exhaustion is the unsurprising result of the day's labor, Freya's languid passivity seems more profoundly connected to the eschatological moment.

Similar observations can be made when we pursue the construction of these fictional worlds further. The world of Goethe's "Märchen" is largely a horizontal playing field, divided into two banks by the flowing river. Movement on these banks and across the river occurs according to severely constraining rules and is characterized by regularity and repetitiveness,[28] but it is fairly constant and ongoing. The horizontal playing field is supplemented by the underworld of the subterranean temple, but this underworld is not a categorically different realm. In Novalis's "Märchen," on the other hand, the playing field is an elaborate structure with three distinct levels. The palace in its heart is surrounded by an icy sea. Most of the movement occurs between these levels, not within them, and along a vertical, not a horizontal axis.

While the world of Novalis's "Märchen" is much larger and more complex than Goethe's, indeed seems to be of cosmological expanse, its hierarchical, circular, and concentric structure, reminiscent of the Ptolemaic model, also gives it an air of inwardness, even claustrophobia. It is symptomatic of this paradox that in Goethe's "Märchen" the connectors between the world and the subterranean temple are crevices and veins of ore which lend the world of the story a certain natural grandeur and sublimity, whereas in the grand cosmological design of Novalis "Märchen" the "at home" ("zu Hause") of the human realm is connected with the astral- und underworlds by means of stairs and ladders which lend this fictional world of cosmological sweep some of the cozy domesticity of a three-story house.

(2) In Novalis,[29] the transition starts with the flight of Fable down to the realm of the Fates and ends with her final arrival in the world of Arctur; in Goethe, the transition starts with the snake's first narrated visit to the subterranean temple and ends with the temple's subterranean transport of nearly all of the tale's cast of characters to the hut of the ferryman. While even this highly simplified summary of the events shows that the transitional pro-

cess is linear in Novalis and circular in Goethe, it is the detailed path of that linearity, the detailed trajectory of that circularity which is truly interesting.

In Novalis, it is essentially Fable alone who carries an action marked by antagonism through the transition. She does battle with the Fates, stills Eros's destructive restlessness, collects the mother's ashes and leads Eros to Freya. Her linear movement from Fates to Arctur is characterized by an ever more rapid oscillation between the two extremes and ever shorter sojourns in the middle realm of "zu Hause." In fact, at the end of this transitional process of linear oscillation between the two liminal realms the "human" world in the middle seems to have been squeezed into near-nonexistence.

In Goethe, on the other hand, the visits to the subterranean world merely mark the beginning and end point of a spiral motion around the center of the horizontal playing field on the surface in general, and the garden of the Lily in particular. The snake and the man with the lamp are important, but by no means the only players in an action marked by cooperation. At the end of this process, neither the underworld nor the surface world has been destroyed—rather they have been merged and synthesized.[30]

(3) In Novalis, the redemption of Freya is the culmination of a general rebirth of nature. The process of reawakening Freya is specifically anchored in this natural process. It is the result of the connection water-chain-Eros-sword-Freya through which the galvanic spark of nature's force is transmitted.[31] It is noteworthy that Freya is truly being awakened. She had been in a slumber throughout the complicated redemptive process that culminates in her awakening: even the spark from her to Eros, her only contribution to the process, is the result of the galvanic setup, not her active voluntary doing. Only after she is awakened and their union has been sealed by the long kiss are Freya and Eros invested as the new royal couple.

In Goethe, Lily does not have to be reawakened but redeemed of the curse of her deadly touch. She is an active participant in the complicated redemptive process. In contrast to Novalis, the redemptive acts are characterized by mutuality and exchange. Before the youth can redeem Lily she has to revive him. This act in itself is complex: she has to touch the snake and the youth, giving death to the snake and life to him. The twofold act is significant: the jewel-remains of the snake will metamorphose again into the prophesied bridge. The snake's death and sacrifice turn into the central socioeconomic accomplishment of the tale. The motif of erotic completion is therefore from the very beginning tied to the theme of social and political completion. This is further developed by the remarkable three-stage process of Lily's redemption: the youth is returned to life through the cooperation of

Lily and the snake; he receives spirit again through the investiture by the three kings, i.e. a political act of awakening; only now can he kiss Lily and free her of her curse.

(4) The endings of both fairy tales begin with the full arrival of daylight, but the scenes upon which these days shine display many interesting differences. In Novalis, a multitude of people streams into the royal hall of the palace. It witnesses the investiture of the new royal couple, which is not part of the transition, as it was in Goethe, but takes place after its completion. The new royal couple is adored by the multitude and greeted as their old rulers. In Goethe, the new royal couple is not joined by the populace within the temple and adored, rather it gazes through the open portals of the temple upon the multitude outside and admires them. Erotic completion is now explicitly connected with the sociopolitical and economic reawakening: "and the new king with his wife was as delighted by the activity and life of this great multitude as their reciprocal love made them happy."[32]

It is also fascinating that in the same structural spot of the end-narrative where Novalis celebrates the achieved transition to a redeemed world with the investiture of the new royal couple, Goethe introduces a potentially threatening disturbance into his new world. The giant, just awakened, stumbles across the unfamiliar bridge and his shadow causes some harm to the multitude. But once he reaches the courtyard of the temple he is charmed by its beauty and is transformed into a colossal statue whose shadow functions to mark time on a sundial. This opposition is illustrative of a significant difference between the two "Märchen": Goethe's new world is not beyond the shadow of the potentially destructive force of the French Revolution, but it is redeemed in the sense that potentially chaotic historical time can be transformed into the beauty and utility of socially regularized natural time; in Novalis's "Märchen," on the other hand, historical time is not tamed but transcended, the new and old rulers live in eternal spring, the realm they have founded is beyond time.

The transformation of the giant also raises the more general question how the remnants of the old world function in the new. In Novalis, the Fates and their realm of conflict are dispersed into a number of harmless petrifications: the Fates themselves, along with the Sphinx, are transformed into the supports of Eros's and Freya's marriage bed; the war and work of the underworld has been petrified, regularized, and miniaturized in the game of chess. In Goethe, the three kings are admired by the populace as monumental symbols of historical power rather than being reduced to supports and playthings of a transcendent world. Even the fourth king, who bears strong traits of the flawed *ancien régime*, is given a beneficial function in the new world. The gold licked out of his malformed body by the will-o'-the-wisps is not immobilized, but transformed into money, which shakes the crowd out of its passive curiosity.

In this context the final few sentences of both "Märchen" are also interesting. In Novalis, the quadruple repetition of the word "eternal" ("ewig") sets the tone for the song with which Fable completes the tale. The end is the beginning of the eternal realm, the future is mentioned but not addressed, because once transcendence and eternity have been reached there is nothing more to say. In Goethe, the last sentence starts with the word "finally" ("endlich"), and reports that between the moment so reached and the moment of narration a temporal future has occurred during which the beneficial hustle and bustle around bridge and temple have continued. This means that in this renewed world time is not transcended but continues, and that it does so not in the realm of eternity, but, as the last words state, "all over the world."

In sum, our comparative textual analysis seems to have yielded the following results: While Novalis starts with a simple sentence to describe a complex circular and mythical world characterized by stasis in eschatological time, Goethe starts with a complex sentence to describe a relatively simple linear everyday world characterized by movement within natural time. Although Goethe's world is local and circumscribed it has an air of openness; although Novalis's world is of cosmological expanse it has an air of closeness and domesticity.

During the transition the dominant structure is reversed in both texts. It is now circular, specifically spiral, in Goethe, while it is linear, specifically oscillating, in Novalis. The dominant mode of action is continuous, collective, and cooperative in Goethe, while it is spasmodic, individualistic and antagonistic in Novalis. In Goethe, the action accomplishes an integrative and preserving synthesis of under- and surface world, in Novalis it accomplishes the near-destruction of the under- and human worlds and the triumph of the astral world.

In Goethe, both the redemption of Lily and the construction of the new world are characterized by integration: of sexual and economic completion, old and new world, past and present time; in Novalis both the redemption of Freya and the construction of the new world are characterized by transcendence: redeemed nature transcends the old world, erotic bliss transcends social and economic relations, and eternity transcends historic time. In Novalis the new triumphs utterly over the old, transcendence most emphatically means disintegration of the old.

What, then are we to make of this? In what way are these texts "thick" with the "tendencies of the age?" What specifically romanticist commentary does Novalis's little text give us on the classic text of the French Revolution? Just as two fragments on revolution and critical method led us into this textual analysis, two other fragments on Romantic poetry in general and the poetics of the *Märchen* in particular might lead us out of it. The first is Schlegel's famous definition of Romantic poetry:

> Romantic poesy is a progressive universal poesy.... The romantic type of poetry is still in the process of becoming; in fact, that is its most essential characteristic, that it can only eternally become, never be completed.... It alone is infinite, just as it alone is free.[33]

The second is perhaps the most fascinating of Novalis's many theoretical reflections on the *Märchen*:

> The world of the fairy tale is the *utterly opposite* world to the world of truth (history)—and precisely because of that it is so *utterly similar* to it—as *chaos* resembles the *completed creation*....
>
> In the *future* world everything is as in the *former world*—and yet everything is *completely different*. The *future* world is the *rational* chaos—the chaos which permeated itself—which is inside and outside of itself—*chaos*^{2} or ∞.
>
> The *genuine Märchen* must be, at the same time, *prophetic representation*—ideal representation—absolutely necessary representation. The genuine writer of *Märchen* sees the future....
>
> (With time, history must become *Märchen*—it becomes again as it was when it began.)[34]

Goethe's "Märchen" provides commentary on the classic text of the French Revolution with a narrative which extols the virtues of collective and cooperative human *praxis* in a finite world; it presents the promise of such action in historical time as integrative, restorative and, in both senses of the word, conservative. Analyzed with this contrastive foil in mind, Klingsohr's "Märchen" in Novalis's *Heinrich von Ofterdingen* can clearly be seen as a commentary which emphasizes an antagonistic struggle, leading to the apocalyptic disintegration of the old and the rebirth of the new, a narrative that follows a trajectory in eschatological time pointing toward transcendence, infinity, and eternity.

With this, Novalis's text follows the prescription of Schlegel's fragment on Romantic poetry, and, more specifically, of his own fragment on the romanticists' poetics of the fairy tale. For as we had seen, Novalis's narrative confronts the reader with a number of paradoxically joined opposites: a fictional world of cosmological expanse but domestic closeness, a transcendent triumph built on tragedy, and new rulers who are recognized as the same as the old. With these paradoxes, Novalis follows his fragment which demands that the *Märchen* must be both congruent with and opposite to history, that chaos must be similar to creation, that the future world must be the same as the past, and yet utterly other, that history must become fairy tale.

When Novalis defines the "future world" as "rational chaos," as "Chaos^2 or ∞," he shows astonishing insight into the consequences implied in the kind of commentary his "Märchen" provides on the French Revolution. He says that the Romanticist looks at the French Revolution and pushes its tendencies beyond the human realm towards transcendence, until the result of the addition "French Revolution plus German Romanticists" is infinity. But the "Märchen" showed us that in the case of the German Romanticists ∞ is a Möbius-strip, a two-dimensional twisted space which reverses the orientation of anybody or anything that travels along it. As one travels along the Möbius-strip of infinity one comes to a point where left and right, plus and minus, up and down are about to reverse and are momentarily the same. It was the German Romanticists' intention to push the tendency of the French Revolution toward that spot, and in his "Märchen" Novalis succeeded—in this little text he reached the point on the Möbius-strip where opposites can coexist because for an instant they are one. For one short glorious moment in the spring of 1800 the French Revolution and the German Romanticists had produced a text in which chaos had become infinity, and all opposites were the same: revolution reaction, future past, history fairy tale: "Geschichte," that is, "Geschichte."

NOTES

1. Friedrich Schlegel is quoted according to Ernst Behler, ed., *Kritische Friedrich-Schlegel-Ausgabe*, 35 vols. (Munich: Schöningh, 1967ff.), cited as KA. Here KA 2:198–99 (Athenäums-Fragment 216). All translations are my own. They strive to be as literal as possible without doing undue violence to the English language.
2. KA 2:247–48 (Athenäums-Fragment 424).
3. Novalis is quoted according to Paul Kluckhohn and Richard Samuel, eds., Novalis, *Schriften*, 2nd ed. (Stuttgart: Kohlhammer, 1960ff.). Cited as Kl. Here Kl. 2:489–90 (Glauben und Liebe 21).
4. KA 2:248 (Athenäums-Fragment 424).
5. KA 2:248 (Athenäums-Fragment 426).
6. Kl. 2:436 (Blüthenstaub 63).
7. Kl. 2:464 (Blüthenstaub 116).
8. Kl. 2:490 (Glauben und Liebe 21).
9. Kl. 2:466 (Blüthenstaub 116).
10. See Richard Brinkmann, "Deutsche Frühromantik und Französische Revolution," in: R.B, *Wirklichkeiten: Essays zur Literatur* (Tübingen: Niemeyer, 1982) 189–220 (first published in: *Deutsche Literatur und Französische Revolution* (Göttingen: Vandenhoeck & Ruprecht, 1974) 172–91), here 195: "It is Friedrich Schlegel, and above all, Novalis, who treat the phenomenon of revolution within a conceptual framework which . . . simultaneously both represents something new, highly original and important, and . . . possesses the qualities of the typical and historically representative."
11. Together with Brinkmann's essay cited in the previous note, the following articles shed fascinating light on the topic, but they do not amount to any kind of consensus. Wilfried Malsch, *"Europa." Poetische Rede des Novalis: Deutung der französischen Revolution und Reflexion auf die Poesie in der Geschichte* (Stuttgart: Metzler, 1965); Richard Faber, *Novalis: Die Phantasie an die Macht* (Stuttgart: Metzler, 1970); Werner Weiland, *Der junge Friedrich Schlegel oder Die Revolution in der Frühromantik* (Stuttgart: Kohlhammer, 1968); Ernst Behler, "Die Auffassung der Revolution in der deutschen Frühromantik," in: *Essays in European Literature. In Honor of Lieselotte Dieckmann* (St. Louis, 1972) 191–215; Christa Krüger, *Georg Forsters und Friedrich Schlegels Beurteilung der Französischen Revolution als Ausdruck des Problems einer Einheit von Theorie und Praxis* (Göppingen, Kümmerle, 1974); Ingrid Oesterle, "Der 'glückliche Anstoß' ästhetischer Revolution und die Anstößigkeit politischer Revolution. Ein Denk- und Belegversuch zum Zusammenhang von politischer Formveränderung und kultureller Revolution im *Studium*-Aufsatz Friedrich Schlegels," in: Dieter Bänsch, ed., *Zur Modernität*

der Romantik (Literaturwissenschaft und Sozialwissenschaften 8) (Stuttgart: Metzler, 1977) 166–216; Werner Weiland, "Politische Romantikinterpretation," in: *Bänsch* 1977, 1–59; Harro Segeberg, "Deutsche Literatur und Französische Revolution. Zum Verhältnis von Weimarer Klassik, Frühromantik und Spätaufklärung," in Karl-Otto Conrady, ed., *Deutsche Literatur zur Zeit der Klassik* (Stuttgart: Metzler, 1977) 243–66; Susan L. Cocalis, "Prophete rechts, Prophete links, Ästhetik in der Mitten. Die amerikanische und die französische Revolution in ihrem Einfluß auf die Romanform der deutschen Klassik und Romantik," in: Wolfgang Paulsen, ed., *Der deutsche Roman und seine historischen und politischen Bedingungen* (Bern/Munich, 1977) 73–89; Klaus Peter, "Adel und Revolution als Thema der Romantik," in: Peter Uwe Hohendahl und Paul Michael Lützeler, eds., *Legitimationskrisen des deutschen Adels von 1200–1900* (Literaturwissenschaft und Sozialwissenschaften 11) (Stuttgart: Metzler, 1979) 197–217; Friedrich A. Kittler, *Aufschreibesysteme 1800/1900* (Munich: Fink, 1985); Raimar Zons, "Gepflegtes Chaos. Romantische Kulturrevolution: Ein Selbstgespräch," *KultuRRevolution* 12 (1986): 26–29.

12. For an excellent survey of the history of the scholarly reception of German Romanticism see Richard Brinkmann, "Romantik als Herausforderung. Zu ihrer wissenschaftsgeschichtlichen Rezeption," in: R.B., *Wirklichkeiten: Essays zur Literatur* (Tübingen: Niemeyer, 1982) 127–88.

13. See Klaus Doderer, "Das englische und französische Bild von der deutschen Romantik," *GRM* NF 36 (1955): 128–47, here 129.

14. In a way both involuntary and inverse, they thus bear witness to the truth of Walter Benjamin's prescription for literary history: "For it is not a matter of interpreting literary works in the context of their times, but rather of representing the time which recognizes them—our time—in the time in which they were created." ("Literaturgeschichte und Literaturwissenschaft," in: Walter Benjamin, *Gesammelte Schriften (werkausgabe edition suhrkamp)*, Rolf Tiedemann and Hermann Schweppenhäuser, eds. [Frankfurt/Main: Suhrkamp, 1974ff.], here 9:290.)

15. For excellent surveys of recent scholarly work on the German Romanticists see e.g. Dieter Bänsch (note 11); Richard Brinkmann, ed., *Romantik in Deutschland: Ein interdiziplinäres Symposion* (Sonderband der *Deutschen Vierteljahresschrift für Literaturwissenschaft und Geistesgeschichte*) (Stuttgart: Metzler, 1978); Klaus Peter, ed., *Romantikforschung seit 1945* (Königstein/Ts.: Athenäum, 1980); Silvio Vietta, ed., *Die literarische Frühromantik* (Göttingen: Vandenhoeck & Ruprecht, 1983); Ernst Behler and Jochen Hörisch,eds., *Die Aktualität der Frühromantik* (Munich: Schöningh, 1987).

16. For a longer explanation of the reasons for and consequences of such a question see Jens Kruse, "Flamme im Wasser, Schimmel im Kalk: Französische Revolution und Naturwissenschaft im Werk Goethes," *Goethe Yearbook* IV (1988) 209–34.

17. In this paper "Schlegel" always refers to Friedrich Schlegel.

18. KA 2:198–99 (Athenäums-Fragment 216).

19. KA 2:148 (Lyceums-Fragment 10).

20. On a slightly larger scale, it might be interesting to examine Schlegel's *Gespräch über die Poesie* in contrast with Goethe's *Unterhaltungen deutscher Ausgewanderten* or Novalis's *Die Christenheit oder Europa* in comparison with Schiller's *Über die Ästhetische Erziehung des Menschen*.

21. See Hans-Joachim Mähl, "Der poetische Staat. Utopie und Utopiereflexion bei den Frühromantikern," in: Wilhelm Voßkamp, ed., *Utopieforschung: Interdisziplinäre Studien zur neuzeitlichen Utopie*, vol. 3 (Stuttgart: Metzler, 1982) 273–302, especially 281.

22. See Novalis's numerous entries on this topic in his *Allgemeines Brouillon*: e.g. Kl. 3:280–81, 377, 389.

23. For an excellent discussion of Novalis's struggle with Goethe's *Wilhelm Meisters Lehrjahre* in preparation for his writing of *Heinrich von Ofterdingen*, see Hans-Joachim Beck, *Friedrich von Hardenberg's "Oeconomie des Styls"* (Bonn: Bouvier, 1976).

24. Beyond the fact that Klingsohr is generally seen as Goethe-representation in *Heinrich von Ofterdingen*, there is widespread agreement on the close relationship between the two *Märchen*. See e.g. Friedrich Hiebel, "Goethe's *Maerchen* in the Light of Novalis," *PMLA* 63 (1948): 918–34; Karl Justus Obenauer, *Das Märchen: Dichtung und Deutung* (Frankfurt/Main: Klostermann, 1959) 99–100; Max Diez, "Novalis und das allegorische Märchen," in: Gerhard Schulz, ed., *Novalis: Beiträge zu Werk und Persönlichkeit Friedrich von Hardenbergs* (Wege der Forschung 248) (Darmstadt: Wissenschaftliche Buchgesellschaft, 1970) 131–59, here 138–39; Waltraud Bartscht, *Goethe's "Das Märchen": Translation and Analysis* (Lexington: University Press of Kentucky, 1972) 68–69.

25. See Gonthier-Louis Fink, " 'Das Märchen.' Goethe's Auseinandersetzung mit seiner Zeit," *Goethe* 33 (1971): 96–122; Hans Mayer, *Goethe: Ein Versuch über den Erfolg* (Frankfurt/Main: Suhrkamp, 1973) 56; Bernd Witte, "Das Opfer der Schlange," in: Wilfried Barner et al., eds., *Unser Commercium: Goethes und Schillers Literaturpolitik* (Stuttgart: Cotta, 1984) 461–84, especially 477–84; Peter Morgan, "The Fairy-Tale as Radical Perspective: Enlightenment as Barrier and Bridge to Civic Values in Goethe's *Märchen*," *Orbis Litterarum* 40 (1985): 222–43.

26. Kl. 1:290.

27. Goethe's "Märchen" is quoted from Johann Wolfgang Goethe, *Werke*: Hamburger Ausgabe in 14 Bänden, vol. 6, ed. Erich Trunz. Henceforth quoted as HA 6. Here HA 6:209.

28. For an excellent analysis of this aspect of Goethe's "Märchen," see Ingrid Kreuzer, "Strukturprinzipien in Goethes Märchen," *Jahrbuch der deutschen Schillergesellschaft* XXI (1977): 216–46.

29. In the course of this textual analysis, "Novalis" and "Goethe" will, from now on, be used as shorthand for their respective "Märchen."

30. The transitional dynamics in Goethe thus closely resemble the movement of Hegelian dialectic and culminate in the—literal—"Aufhebung" of the temple; the transitional dynamics in Novalis, on the other hand, closely resemble the movement of the Fichtean "Ich." See e.g. Ernst Behler's description of the dynamic character of Friedrich Schlegel's thought: "Mediation between the opposites does not consist in a higher synthesis or a harmonious fulfillment, but rather in the movement itself . . ." (Behler 213).

31. For Novalis's use of recent discoveries in the field of galvanic electricity in his "Klingsohr-Märchen," see Walter D. Wetzels, "Klingsohrs Märchen als Science Fiction," *Monatshefte* 65 (1973): 167–75.

32. HA 6:238.

33. KA 2:182–83 (Athenäums-Fragment 116).

34. Kl. 3:281.

GÜNTER MIETH

Hölderlin and the French Revolution

IN TAKING THIS OPPORTUNITY OF THE two-hundredth anniversary of the event to reexamine Hölderlin's experience of the French Revolution, that is, his ideological-theoretical and poetic treatment of it, we must examine above all the presuppositions that determined his image and concept of the Revolution. First there is the political atmosphere and intellectual climate of his homeland to consider: the historically unique duchy of Württemberg, the peculiar strain of Pietism that flourished there, and the relatively pronounced politicizing of public life and the literary sphere. There is also his family background. Hölderlin came from the urban patriciate and went through the stages of training expected of a young man destined for the Lutheran ministry: to the Tübingen seminary by way of the top-flight cloister schools. In Tübingen the nineteen-year-old theology student, already ambitious to win the poetic laurel, experienced the year 1789 in miserable circumstances. Although no letters or records of conversations survive from the period, we can assume that Hölderlin greeted the beginning of the revolution with the same feelings that Hegel described much later: "Sublime emotions prevailed at that time, a spirit of enthusiasm gripped the world, as though it were only now truly to be reconciled with the Divine."[1] One can assume that this statement by Hölderlin's fellow seminarian describes the abstract model of Hölderlin's own Tübingen hymns, referring as it does to the juxtaposition of the political and religious realms. Unlike Christian Friedrich Schubart, Gotthold Friedrich Stäudlin, and Eulogius Schneider, Hölderlin wrote no political poems directly concerned with the French Revolution. Nevertheless, his enthusiasm for the Revolution was articulated from the very beginning in a hymnic style that embraced the whole universe and the total history of mankind. The poetic and aesthetic orientation for Hölderlin's hymns can be found in Schiller's major poems, in Schiller's inaugural lecture at Jena, and in Schiller's criticism of Gottfried August Bürger, while the political content was supplied by Jean-Jacques Rousseau's *Contrat social* and the French revolutionary Declaration of the Rights of Man and the Citizen. Perhaps we can also take the "Hymnen an die Ideale der Menschheit" (Hymns to the Ideals of Mankind) as a lyrical response to the program set forth in the Declaration for the emancipation of mankind. One should, however, note one reservation, namely that Hölderlin's ideal of human existence already culminates in 1790–1792 in the "Idea of Beauty," that idea which was later to occupy a central position in the so-called "Oldest Program for a System of German Idealism." Thus in Hölderlin's early hymns the expectation of human and political emancipation has an aesthetic overlay, not to mention being poetically overburdened. This should, however, by no means be confused with a flight into the realm of aesthetic appearance (*Schein*).

It is crucial to note the following literary-historical fact, which has been disregarded over and over again: Hölderlin's poetic individuality, that is, the uniqueness of his *Weltanschauung* and his poetry, was formed precisely in the years from 1792–1793 to 1796–1797. Historically speaking, these were the years of the War of the First Coalition against revolutionary France; this period brought a decisive process of differentiation in political thinking; in the history of philosophy, these years saw the development from Kant's critical philosophy, by way of Fichte's theory of "scientific philosophy" (*Wissenschaftslehre*), to Schelling's nature philosophy; and finally, in the history of German literature this period saw the first phase of early Romantic thinking and literary output, the decisive years of revolutionary democratic literature, and the formulation of Weimar classical aesthetics.[2]

This historical context is absolutely critical for any attempt even halfway to understand the complex ideological framework into which the developing poet was integrated. And he was in fact integrated into it through his high expectations of the revolutionary war, through his intellectual and personal involvement with philosophical developments of the period, and through his constant preoccupation and confrontation with contemporary literary works and the greats of his time: with Herder, with Schiller, with Goethe. And not least of all: these are precisely the years in which Hölderlin's *Hyperion* came into being, the novel in which—what a task he set himself here!—Hölderlin, advancing with the spirit of the times, sought to get a poetic grasp of his own experiences (both personal and public-political) and to gain a foothold in poetic *terra incognita*[3] in the process.

In the years 1792–1793 the Revolution began to manifest itself in the form of a War of the Revolution. In conjunction with the transition from constitutional monarchy to the Republic and then to the Jacobin Terror, this made it necessary, especially for revolutionary enthusiasts abroad, to rethink their ideological positions. The apparently unavoidable concomitance of revolution and war now made it impossible to overlook the European dimensions of what originally had largely been viewed as purely a French political event. Hölderlin's well-known plea to his sister, "pray for the French, the champions of human rights" (*Werke* 4:94), could easily be legitimated by looking to history, whether it be the Persian Wars that were the precondition for the greatness of Athens, the revolution in the Netherlands with which Hölderlin was familiar from Schiller's sympathetic history, or the American revolutionary war, which he had probably heard about from Major von Kalb, who had participated in it. But Hölderlin's confidence in the revolutionary army's mission of political liberation was severely shaken by the sometimes brutal behavior of the French soldiers in 1796. The contradictions inherent in the dilemma of political liberation vs. war of national conquest were bound in any case to remain problematic not only for Hölderlin, but for contemporary consciousness in general. We need mention only two poetic works which reflect this problematic very soon after the fact: Goethe's *Hermann und Dorothea* and Schiller's *Wallenstein*. With regard to content and structure, Hölderlin's *Hyperion oder Der Eremit in Griechenland* (Hyperion, or the Hermit in Greece), a novel heavily laden with autobiographical significance, is concerned above all with working out the experience of revolution and revolutionary war. The political insight achieved in the novel by no means precludes involvement in a future revolution. The protagonist's closing words, "more soon," circumscribes quite precisely the still unfinished historical process, the epochal events which are not as yet intelligible to the observing subject. But the contradiction between a political, external revolution and a spiritual, internal revolution could not be overcome and was bound to reassert itself in ever new form. In Hölderlin's terminology the task was to bring about in Germany a "future revolution in sentiments and ways of perceiving things" (4:257), which should by no means be identified with Schiller's understanding of the task of aesthetic education. One should rather point to Herder's ideas on palingenesis and his interpretation of the Tithon/Aurora myth, and to the fact that the journal that Hölderlin worked so earnestly to get off the ground was named *Iduna*. Something else must also be kept in mind when discussing the Wars of the First Coalition, namely, the fact that simple enthusiasm for French victories (for example Mons, Lodi, and Arcole[4]) was by no means all there was to it for Hölderlin. In his native Württemberg and in Frankfurt Hölderlin had ample opportunity to experience the hardships and difficulties caused by the war. This is the historical origin of his utopia of peace, and the theoretical basis for it is to be found in a work by the man he considered the "Moses of our nation" (*Werke* 4:337): Kant's philosophical draft *On Eternal Peace*, which was inspired by the Treaty of Basel in 1795. Hölderlin's unique synthesis of revolution, war, and peace would be well worth a more detailed investigation. I can do no more than simply mention the ode "Der Frieden" (Peace) and the hymn "Friedensfeier" (Celebration of Peace). The conclusion of "Germanien," echoing Kant, expresses the conviction that Germany has a special role to play in a general European peace: "... Germania, wo du Priesterin bist / Und wehrlos Rat gibst rings / Den Königen und den Völkern" ("... Germania, you who are the priestess and stand, defenseless, advising kings and peoples around you" [*Werke* 1:466]).

Is it really necessary to say that Hölderlin was anything but a poet of war, especially of a war of conquest? Still, one asks how it could come about that German soldiers went off to die for the fatherland in both World Wars with his poems in their backpacks. It seems to me that this is a consequence of his psychic and spiritual individuality. His hypersensitivity and his exalted conception of the purpose of human existence made it impossible for him to perceive the ordinariness of concrete social and political reality, to accept its mundane existence, or to give poetic form to it. What he admitted with regard to natural and geographic reality—that he was "usually content to get an overall impression of it" (*Werke* 4:193)—applies to his perception and experience of historical events in general. As far as possible both his poetry and the statements of political belief laid down in his letters avoid the "accidental" (see *Werke* 4:375). This is one of the main reasons why attempts to identify this poet with any particular political faction or to interpret his poetry as political poetry in the narrow sense were always doomed to failure. The high level of abstraction with which contemporary events are mirrored in his letters and poetry—the political is always only one moment among others—together with the heroic-revolutionary component of his ideal of humanity opens the door to contradictory interpretations: to reactionary distortion of his conception of war and sacrifice, on the one hand, and to onesided concentration on the "Jacobin" elements on the other.

Hölderlin created odes, but no folk songs; he wrote elegies, but no ballads; he composed hymns, but no revolutionary manifestos. We can't imagine him writing travel books like Georg Forster or George Friedrich Rebmann. And something else should be noted, in view of the heated controversy about Hölderlin's political credo: Hölderlin's poetry is not addressed to potential readers among the German "folk" at the end of the eighteenth century, especially not to members of the lower classes. Although, to be sure, Hölderlin thoroughly believed in the idea that the poet had a social responsibility, his own works in no way aimed to rouse the peoples from their slumber, as he demanded in his poem "An unsere großen Dichter" (To our Great Poets). Understanding his poetry requires, at the least—in addition to a detailed knowledge of the classical tradition and a highly sensitive moral-political and poetic consciousness—a capacity for dialectical thinking. If the concept of revolutionary democratism is to be meaningfully applied to his world view at all, then only on the understanding that he is talking about an ideal people, one that is capable of living the "higher life," capable of refined religious practice and a "higher enlightenment."[5] This state of affairs can perhaps best be expressed by saying that the distance between Hölderlin and the lower classes remained in fact, while being bridged in the ideal over and over again. To put it succinctly: should it really be necessary to find a literary-historical concept for integrating the uniqueness of a Hölderlin into the framework of world literature, then we will perhaps have to make do with the term "revolutionary classicism." Even this label, however, would fit only up until the year 1801: Hölderlin's stay in Switzerland and the Peace of Lunéville, which was concluded while he was in Switzerland and affected him so deeply, stimulated in him a new wave of enthusiastic hopes and expectations. He now expressed the hope that "all forms of egotism" would "submit to the holy regime of love and goodness, that public spirit would prevail in all things," and that political considerations would no longer play the dominating role in human affairs.[6] It is in this context that Hölderlin makes the striking claim: "I think that that moral Boreas, the spirit of envy, will cease to exist, along with war and revolution, and then a more beautiful form of living together can develop than what we had in the strict old civil society!" (*Werke* 4:457). He yearns for a new kind of sociability ("Geselligkeit") far superior to all alienated forms of human communication, a form of living together in which people will express their innermost thoughts because others are interested in them. "Friedensfeier" contains the following beautiful verses:

> Und vor der Türe des Hauses
> Sitzt Mutter und Kind,
> Und schauet den Frieden
> Und wenige scheinen zu sterben,
> Es hält ein Ahnen die Seele,
> Vom goldnen Lichte gesendet,
> Hält ein Versprechen die Ältesten auf. (*Werke* 1:471)

[And before the door of the house sit mother and child; she sees the peace and not many seem to die. Anticipation, sent by the radiant light, anticipation fills the soul, a promise claims the attention of the elders.]

I repeat most emphatically: any study of Hölderlin's relationship to the French Revolution that stops at Thermidor, or even at the Eighteenth Brumaire, will arrive at misleading conclusions. His most basic historic experience, from the very outset, was the indivisible unity of revolution, war, and peace. That is to say: in this respect, too, he took an all-encompassing view of an epochal period of transition, of a becoming that arose out of decline. But precisely for this reason the heroic character is a prerequisite for his philosophy of humanity, and the heroic phase is an essential component of individual development as well as a chief ingredient of harmonious human existence. At the level of poetological reflection the heroic has its dialectical place between the naive and the idealistic.

And then came the journey to France, the country to which Hölderlin had originally attached his expectations for the future of mankind. This is not the place for a new attempt to resolve the questions that still remain unanswered about that trip, which I have addressed elsewhere.[7] But even though it is quite inexcusable to simplify complex historical and biographical relationships so drastically, I would like at least to hint at one of the results of the trip: during his stay in France Hölderlin was continuously exposed to the intellectual prehistory of the French Revolution, reminders of the course it had followed, and its sobering results. Inseparable from this—demonstrably so—are his constant remembrance of his own earlier experience of the Revolution and the revolutionary wars, of his sojourns in Tübingen, Frankfurt, and Homburg, of Rousseau (who had provided his basic intellectual orientation), of Robespierre, and of Bonaparte, the revolutionary general who had won his total admiration and whom he had almost encountered at Lyon. Such almost forced remembrance of the Revolution of 1789 and of his own idealization of it, present to his mind in the form of signs and images, helped transform revolutionary transition into historical fact for him—but this had not become possible until now. The state of affairs in France and Europe in the first half of 1802—most notably the Treaty of Amiens and those sometimes spectacular events that gave tangible expression to the transformation of the Republic into a monarchy—had to seem like a definitive end to the period of "war and revolution," even if in a completely different sense than such an expression had held for him as recently as the year before. It is therefore necessary to reject attempts by previous Hölderlin scholars to apply the term "postrevolutionary" to earlier lulls in the military action—quite apart from the fact that the dichotomy revolutionary/postrevolutionary would seem to be quite meaningless for German literary history anyway. But however we may try to get a theoretical handle on concrete developments in the history of literature, one thing can now be considered philologically certain: the late poetry, as demonstrated above all in the Homburg Folio, the important manuscript collection that was begun only after the poet's return from France and has only recently become available to scholars—and only the late poetry!—represents the lyric summation of Hölderlin's painful experience of the epochal transition set in motion by the events of 1789. There we find the following fascinating declaration:

> Bald aber wird, wie ein Hund, umgehn
> In der Hitze meine Stimme auf den Gassen der Gärten,
> In denen wohnen Menschen,
> In Frankreich. (*Werke* 1:532)

[Soon, however, my voice, like a dog, will go around in the heat on the streets of the gardens in which men dwell in France.]

Friedrich Hölderlin's uniqueness in world literature, to put it briefly and abstractly, consists in the fact that he was the German poet of the bourgeois-democratic revolution of another nation, whose historical path was different from that of his own. A hundred and fifty years later, while German soldiers were "marching with Hölderlin in their packs" in foreign countries, one of the Germans who belonged to the "other Germany"—Stephan Hermlin, hunted as a member of the Resistance and hiding in a hayloft in France— read to peasants the letter Hölderlin had written to his sister in 1792 urging her to pray for French victory. In 1943, during his exile in America, Hanns Eisler, later the composer of the GDR national anthem, set Hölderlin fragments to music. Perhaps the goal of my lecture is now clear: I have aimed to show Friedrich Hölderlin as a German poet who was a genuine participant in the period of revolutionary transition at the end of the eighteenth and the beginning of the nineteenth century. Admittedly, the French Revolution, the revolutionary wars, and the longing for peace only mark the historical coordinates of his poetry. His understanding of the historical transition—which first he confidently expected, then only hoped and finally longed for—is far more complex, transcending not only concrete political conditions, but every actual and possible form of social relationship. In this sense Hölderlin's poetry is utopian, nurtured not only by his philosophy of history but also by his religiosity. To be sure, he was bound to be disappointed. In the course of the historical process that seemed to signal, or even claimed to show, progress and regression at the same time, in view of the personal experiences that shook and moved him, the utopia fractured and absorbed ever more of the resistant nature of reality. This was particularly true after Hölderlin's trip to France, in those late texts which elude all genre classification—they present us with experience become form—and, anticipating the lyric poetry of the twentieth century, assure his lasting impact. In the late poetry both aspects are preserved, the utopian hope and the radical disappointment, often enough together in the same poem, in the same stanza, in a single verse, metaphor or sign. The poem "Patmos," which Hölderlin dedicated to Landgrave Friedrich V of Hesse-Homburg, begins as follows:

Nah ist
Und schwer zu fassen der Gott.
Wo aber Gefahr ist, wächst
Das Rettende auch.
Im Finstern wohnen
Die Adler und furchtlos gehn
Die Söhne der Alpen über den Abgrund weg
Auf leichtgebaueten Brücken.
Drum, da gehäuft sind rings
Die Gipfel der Zeit, und die Liebsten
Nah wohnen, ermattend auf
Getrenntesten Bergen,
So gib unschuldig Wasser,
O Fittiche gib uns, treuesten Sinns
Hinüberzugehn und wiederzukehren. (*Werke* 1:481)[8]

[The god is close by and difficult to grasp. But where there is danger, there grows salvation as well. Eagles dwell in darkness, and the sons of the Alps cross the abyss fearlessly on lightly constructed bridges. Therefore, where all around us are the crags of time and our loved ones dwell nearby, languishing on far-flung peaks, give us refreshing water, give us wings, with brave hearts to go over and to return.]

NOTES

1. Georg Wilhelm Friedrich Hegel, *Vorlesungen über die Philosophie der Geschichte* in *Werke in zwanzig Bänden* (Frankfurt/Main: Suhrkamp, 1970) 12:529.
2. See Günter Mieth, "Krise und Ausklang der deutschen Aufklärung? Gedanken zur Periodisierung der deutschen Literatur am Ausgang des 18. Jahrhunderts," *Ansichten der deutschen Klassik*, eds. Helmut Brandt and Manfred Beyer (Berlin/Weimar: Aufbau, 1981) 301–12; Mieth, "Tangenten zwischen der Literaturwissenschaft und der historischen Kulturbeziehungsforschung im Zeichen historisch-politischer Zeitschriften," *Zeitschriften und Zeitungen des 18. und 19. Jahrhunderts in Mittel- und Osteuropa*, Studien zur Geschichte der Kulturbeziehungen in Mittel- und Osteuropa, vol. 8, eds. István Fried, Hans Lemberg and Edith Rosenstrauch-Königsberg (Berlin, 1986) 85ff.
3. Friedrich Hölderlin, *Sämtliche Werke und Briefe*, ed. Günter Mieth, 4 vols. (Berlin/Weimar: Aufbau, 1970) 4:105. Hereafter cited as *Werke*.
4. See *Werke* 4:100, 1:651.
5. See the theoretical draft which goes under the title "Über Religion."
6. Thus Hölderlin in his often-quoted letters from Switzerland. See *Werke* 4:446 and 457.
7. See Günter Mieth, "Friedrich Hölderlin und die Französische Revolution: Einige Anmerkungen zu seinen historisch-politischen Erfahrungen während seines Aufenthaltes in Frankreich," *Acta Universitatis Wratislaviensis, No 1115, Germanica Wratislaviensia LXXX* (Wrocław 1989): 75–83.
8. Additional material can be found in the annotation to my edition of the *Sämtliche Werke und Briefe* (note 4) and in my monograph *Friedrich Hölderlin: Dichter der bürgerlich-demokratischen Revolution* (Berlin: Rütten & Loening, 1978). For additional material on the period, see Günter Mieth, *Vom Beginn der großen Französischen Revolution bis zum Ende des alten deutschen Reiches 1789–1806* (Berlin: Rütten & Loening, 1988).

JEFFREY L. SAMMONS

Heinrich Heine: The Revolution as Epic and Tragedy

MANY OF US WHO TEACH SUCCESSIVE cohorts of young people come to make sometimes disconcerting observations on the recession of historical memory. In the course of time we have been able to watch the changes in presence, vividness, and subjective relevance of the Second World War and the postwar years, the Korean War, the assassination of President Kennedy, and now the clearly fading trauma of the war in Vietnam. This recession is not always, as it sometimes may appear to us, a flow into a black hole of oblivion; rather it undergoes phases. In my early years of teaching I was frequently disturbed by what seemed to me a vagueness in student memory of World War II in general and Nazism in particular; names such as Göring or Himmler would regularly be met with blank looks. Many of today's students appear to have a sharper sense of these matters, and the reason for this, I believe, is the development in the meantime of a broad historiographical base. In fact, I suspect that the renewed interest in the Holocaust may be as much a consequence as a cause of the growth of reliable historiographical resources. On the other hand, the mythopoeia surrounding the Kennedy family, which those of us who lived through the 1960s will vividly recall, and a mild recrudescence of which we witnessed in the spring of 1988 on the occasion of the twentieth anniversary of the assassination of Robert Kennedy, has, it seems to me, pretty much vanished in today's student generation, and in its place are signs of retrospective and critical history of the Kennedy epoch.

It is with these unsystematic observations in mind that I should like to venture a speculation concerning Heinrich Heine's chronological relationship to the French Revolution. Heine was born approximately eight and a half years after the outbreak of the Revolution and around three or four years after the Terror. This means that, when he reached the age of burgeoning awareness of the larger world around him—let us say, around age twelve— these events lay some fifteen to twenty years in the past. I submit that a person who stands in that sort of distance from a complex of great events will tend to read it differently from those both older and younger. Older persons will experience the events forwards, in chronological sequence, because that is the way they live through them, and they will remain in that order in memory. In regard to the French Revolution, one could think of, along with many others, Goethe and Schiller. The younger person, too, will perceive the events in forward order, for they will have been mediated largely by historiography, which generally tends to imitate the chronology of experience. Here one might think of Georg Büchner. The person in Heine's position, on the other hand, will tend to read the events backwards, from their most recent phases, and particularly from the effects that have extended into one's own life.

For the generation of Goethe and Schiller, the effect of living through the events was to find their significance—in most cases negatively charged—in the Terror, as the most intense level of contemporary experience. Interestingly, the same is true of the younger Büchner, who set his dramatic representation of the French Revolution on the threshold of the climactic moment of the Terror, the execution of Robespierre. Heine, on the other hand, focuses most intensely on the culminating and most recent phase of the Revolution: the rise and fall of Napoleon. The systematic historiographical works of the Revolution—for example, those of Thiers and Mignet—which were available to Büchner from his earliest youth, were for Heine adult reading of his early thirties.[1] His formative experiences, however, were derived from an exceptionally energetic body of mythography, "as it is written in the gospels of Las Cases, O'Meara, and Antommarchi" (DA 6:195); to those evangelical texts may be added the sacred books of Paul-Philippe Ségur, Captain Maitland, and Napoleon's own memoirs (DA 6:162–63, 157–58; 7/1:219).

Heine's fixation upon Napoleon is so pronounced that it has been obvious for a long time. What remains the most thorough examination of the topic, Paul Holzhausen's of more than eighty-five years ago, also made the point that Heine's chronological age predisposed him to his reception of Napoleon.[2] In recent times, however, the need to shape Heine into a particular political configuration, believed to be relevant to our times, of a radical, revolutionary, directly activist democrat, has tended to blur the significance of the Napoleonic myth in his consciousness and self-understanding. Only quite recently have there been some signs that this may be changing.[3] In any consideration of his relationship to the French Revolution and to revolution in general, it must be taken as axiomatic that he viewed the Revolution through its Napoleonic phase, that for him Napoleon was incomparably the most important figure of the international epoch of revolution from 1776 to 1848, and that such revolutionary hopes as he may be said to have entertained are often involved with utopian visions of a new Messiah of Napoleonic cast.

It is regularly asserted that his admiration of Napoleon was owing to the relative emancipation of the Jews in the Rhineland under his sovereignty.[4]

But he nowhere indicates this, and there are reasons for doubting that it was a central motivation. Leaving aside the ambiguity of Napoleon's own policy toward the Jews, Heine and his family seem, on the whole, to have experienced little discrimination in his youth by the standards of the time. Furthermore, Napoleonic rule was a decidedly mixed blessing for the Grand Duchy of Berg. While the territory profited from the modernization of political administration, it suffered grievous economic dislocation and depression. It is not improbable that the difficulties leading eventually to the inglorious bankruptcy of Heine's father, who was, after all, an importer of English goods, were initially rooted in Napoleon's economic blockade of the Continent.[5] These consequences of Napoleonic rule bore much more directly upon Heine's life and fate than the alleged emancipation of the Jews; yet he completely ignored them, as in general he attached secondary importance at best to matters of practical politics. Ascribing such a personalized motivation to him actually has the effect of deflecting attention away from the centrality and pervasiveness of the Napoleonic image in his order of mind.

The basic formula for this image would be that he saw Napoleon as the French Revolution incarnate. This formula is to be taken quite literally. Napoleon incarnates the power, the glory, the sublimity, and the potential energy of the Revolution in the shape of a man. Here lies the logic of Heine's constant representations of Napoleon as a god or a Christ figure. Like a pagan god, Napoleon's iconic significance is immortal, but his appearance, though lofty, and his consciousness, though that of original genius, are those of a mortal man. Like Christ, Napoleon is both human and divine, at once worldly savior and supernal redeemer, with the added consideration that, having been cynically duped and condemned by the British in the role of Pontius Pilate, he has suffered a Passion and holds out the hope of a Resurrection and a Second Coming—a theme enunciated in Heine's earliest Napoleonic utterance, the well-known poem, "The Grenadiers" (DA 1:77–78; D 31–32).

A major effect of this deification is to highlight attributes of power. In terms of the historical moment the power is a matter of syncretistic representation. The new age is mirrored in Napoleon in a way that the retrograde elegist Sir Walter Scott is unable to grasp (DA 6:161–62). Napoleon's spirit is infallible in its perception because it is intuitive; thus he was able to meld the revolutionary with the counterrevolutionary and develop "the art of comprehending and guiding the masses" (DA 6:160). This divine syncretism is particularly evident in the famous account in *The Book of Le Grand* of Napoleon's appearance in Düsseldorf. On the one hand, he is the incarnation of revolutionary élan:

> His countenance also had that color that we find among Greek and Roman heads, its features similarly were nobly apportioned, like those of antiquity, and on this face stood written: Thou shalt have no other gods before me. A smile that warmed and calmed every heart hovered on his lips—and yet we knew that these lips needed only to whistle—*et la Prusse n'existait plus*—these lips needed only to whistle—and the whole clerisy had rung its last bell—these lips needed only to whistle—and the whole Holy Roman Empire danced.

At the same time, his "sunny, marmorean hand" was "a mighty hand, one of the two hands that had subdued the many-headed monster of anarchy and put order into the civil war among the peoples" (DA 6:194). Owing to external constraints, this power was not even exercised to the limit of its true potential. Heine imagined that, if Napoleon had commanded such a naval force as France possessed in 1840, he could have invaded England without resistance and liberated it from aristocracy (B 5:307). Since Napoleon's power is the incarnation of a historical force, it survives his mortal degradation and death. If the radical rebels in the Cloître Saint-Méry, Heine tells us, had cried "Vive Napoléon" instead of "Vive la République," the National Guard would not have fired on them (DA 12/1:197). When, nineteen years after Napoleon's death, the government gingerly undertook the experiment of returning his remains to Paris—in the winter, in the hope that revolution would not occur in cold weather—it was gratifying to Heine's iconic imagination that a sunbeam broke through the cloud cover and gleamed on the imperial standard (B 5:277, 299, 340).

The charisma is also inheritable. In 1832 he reported the opinion that the second Napoleon, the Duke of Reichstadt, would need but to appear and the government of the July Monarchy would collapse (DA 12/1:126). Upon the death of that unfortunate youth later that year Heine tells us of general if not universal grief (DA 12/1:216–17). The charisma was inheritable also by the third Napoleon, another feature of Heine's attitude that has been rather played down in recent years but is not insignificant. While Marx regarded Louis Napoleon as a ninny and a marionette of forces beyond his understanding, and, in fact, regularly referred to him by the name of one of Heine's satirical figures, "Crapülinski,"[6] Heine signalled to Marx the opinion that the coup d'état of December 1851 might be a progressive event.[7] To his editor Kolb, Heine wrote before the coup that "as Louis-Philippe had been, so Louis Bonaparte, too, is a miracle for the benefit of the French."[8] In his *Confessions*, presumably written after the coup d'état, Heine amused himself with the conceit that Louis Napoleon was his legitimate sovereign, since he was the rightful heir of his brother, Napoleon Louis, to whom Napoleon had transferred sovereignty over the Grand Duchy of Berg in Heine's boyhood and who had never abdicated (DA 15:22). Even the farce of Louis Napoleon's invasion of the Channel coast and subsequent arrest in 1840 did not seem to dim his luster very much in the eyes of Heine, who gleefully reported the panic of the English in Boulogne at the event (B 5:310).[9] To what extent he was acquainted with Louis Napoleon's pseudo-socialist writings is not known, but it is likely that he would have been aware of them.[10] Such things were, in any case, not his chief consideration; rather it was, as he put it in the suppressed "Waterloo fragment" of around 1853, that the Emperor does not die in France (DA 15:193). In other paralipomena to this passage he praises himself for having revived the Napoleon cult, the "cult of genius," and for having raised up the "divine image," and he adds how much he would like to praise Napoleon III if it were not for the oppressive state of siege and denial of freedom of expression (DA 15:180–83). This enforced abandonment of the Bonapartist allegiance toward the end of Heine's life is a point to which we shall return.

All things considered, the endurance of his Napoleonic allegiance is quite remarkable. "Basically," Ernst Loeb wrote some years ago, "Heine will always see the emperor as his image impressed itself on 'his own highly blessed eyes' as a childhood experience on the occasion of Napoleon's entry into Heine's home town of Düsseldorf."[11] There has been some misunderstanding about this continuity, as though he had at some stage abandoned the mythopoeic apotheosis of Napoleon in favor of a more sober, realistic view of the emperor's limitations and faults. Those who hold this view like to cite the remark in *Journey from Munich to Genoa*: "I beg of you, dear reader, do not consider me an unconditional Bonapartist; my veneration is directed not to the actions, but only to the genius of the man. I love him unconditionally only until the eighteenth of Brumaire—then he betrayed liberty. And he did it not out of necessity, but out of secret predilection for aristocracy" (DA 7/1:68)—a view that might have been influenced by Ludwig Börne, whom Heine had recently visited, and which in fact is ascribed to Börne in Heine's book on his great competitor (DA 11:15–16). The fact is, however, that he constantly and quite consciously distinguished the mythical from the historical Napoleon, so that his commentary runs on two parallel tracks of the imagination, one mythopoeic, the other critically ideological.[12]

His awareness of this duality of vision is apparent in his remark that what he likes best about Napoleon is that he is dead, "for, if he were still alive, I would, after all, have to help fight him." It is true that Bonapartism is a religion, but "in the end this religion gets boring like any other" (DA 12/1:91). Taken altogether, his critique of Napoleon as an apostate to the Revolution is fairly severe. He could have become the Washington of Europe if he had not become a renegade to the Revolution by having himself crowned (DA 12/1:41). In contrast to his earlier view that Napoleon had united the revolutionary and counterrevolutionary tendencies of the age, Heine later concluded that he had been able to unite only persons and interests, not ideas (B 5:250). He lacked a grasp of philosophy, especially German philosophy, and thus could only comprehend the past; he had neither eyes nor ears for the future (B 5:403). The imperial period's pursuit of glory and militarism killed all "civic simplicity and love of liberty" and cost too many lives (DA 12/1:98). Heine recurred to this cost in several places. The age of Napoleon, he wrote, was not so beautiful and happy as it seems in the memory of the Bonapartists: "The fields lay fallow and human beings were led to the slaughter" (DA 12/1:251–52). In Normandy, he reported, "in every cottage hangs the portrait of 'the man,' and, to be sure, as the *Quotidienne* remarks, on the same wall where the portrait of the son of the house would hang if he had not been sacrificed by that man on one of his hundred battlefields" (DA 12/1:217). Yet even here, he reports, Napoleon is honored; the real Napoleon has vanished, punished for his disloyalty to the Revolution, and Bonapartism has become just a name for an ideological location. In general, Heine was critical of French Bonapartism as a political mode, for he saw in it primarily a lust for nationalist imperialism.[13]

Nevertheless, despite all this logical and observant analysis, he was insistent that the myth was more important than the reality and should be kept intact. Thus he wrote under the date of May 30, 1840, in response to a speech of Lamartine that he thought perfidiously disrespectful of Napoleon:

> It is true, it is a thousand times true, that Napoleon was an enemy of liberty, a despot, crowned egotism, and that glorifying him sets a bad, dangerous example. It is true, he lacked the civic virtues of a Bailly, a Lafayette, and he trod the laws underfoot and even the lawmakers, of which there are still some living examples in the Luxembourg Hospital. But it is not this liberticide Napoleon, not the hero of the eighteenth of Brumaire, not the thunder god of ambition to whom you should dedicate the most magnificent funerary games! No; it is the man who represented young France against old Europe whose glorification is in question: in his person the French nation was victorious, in his person it was humiliated, in his person it honors and celebrates itself—and all Frenchmen feel this, and therefore they forget all the dark sides of the deceased and pay homage to him *quand même* (B 5:279–80).[14]

This passage defines Heine's own standpoint fairly well. As has been observed: "It would not be incorrect to see in Napoleon a kind of ideological construct, a mythic projection and embodiment of everything the narrator seeks and considers desirable."[15]

Thus Heine, perhaps in part out of sheer contrariness to his public, gathered together and hyperbolized all the strains of the myth; as has been acutely pointed out, this hyperbolized pathos is not undercut by irony, but supported by it.[16] Repeatedly Napoleon is associated with Christ; indeed, he has replaced Christ as someone in whom the masses can still believe (DA 8/1:243). At other times he figures as a pagan god: he is identified with Prometheus (DA 7/1:67); he is a Classic figure, defeated by puny Romantics (DA 8/1:141–42); he lives on in the memory of the people as a god (DA 12/1:91). At the same time he is a figure in history, a giant of the century (B 5:270), the demonic despoiler of obsolete dignities who "with boots and spurs and spattered with the blood of the battlefield, climbed into the bed of an imperial blonde and stained the white sheets of Habsburg" (DA 11:142). At times the iconography seems pictorial, so that it can be plausibly associated with the heroizing painting of Louis David and Jean-Antoine Gros.[17] Elsewhere the associations are literary. In Napoleon the French have a living epic literature (DA 6:162–63); to the multitudinous faults of August Wilhelm Schlegel belongs his view of the French people as unpoetic, "at a time when so many choristers of the Convention, the great titanic tragedy, were bodily walking about before his eyes; at a time when Napoleon improvised a good epic every day, when Paris swarmed with heroes, kings, and gods . . ." (DA 8/1:171).

In his realistic mode, Heine once claimed it a good thing that Napoleon's statue had been removed from the Vendôme column, and if it is to be restored, "then he will stand there no longer as imperator, as Caesar, but as a representative of the Revolution, atoned for by misfortune and purified by death, as a symbol of the victorious power of the people" (DA 12/1:126–27). In his mythic mode, however, Heine seems to have been attracted a great deal more by Caesar than by the power of the people, so much so that his own political posture has been identified as "Caesarism."[18] He himself observed that when the real Napoleon had vanished from the memory of the common people, what remained was a new Caesarism (DA 12/1:217). The same seems to be true of Heine's consciousness, though in a more self-reflexive way. All the images of power, marble hands taming anarchy and the like, suggest that in Napoleon Heine saw an ideal of government *for* the people much more than *of* or *by* the people. In an interview late in life with an English journalist, Heine is reported to have said: "I have never swerved from my faith in the Emperor. I have never ceased to doubt of his advent—My Emperor—the ruler of the people for the people."[19] "The best democracy," he wrote in his book on Shakespeare, "will always be one where a single man stands at the head of the state as the incarnation of the popular will, like God at the head of the governance of the world" (B 4:201). This thought was generated by a portrayal of Julius Caesar that strongly implies an assimilation to Heine's image of Napoleon:

> We gladly excuse emperors the bloodiest despotism with which they treated a few hundred patrician families and scorned their privileges; we recognize in them, and thankfully, the destroyers of that aristocratic dominance that allowed the people for their hardest labors but a meager wage; we praise them as secular redeemers who, by lowering the high and elevating the low, introduced civic equality. Let the advocate of the past, the patrician Tacitus, describe the private vices and madnesses of the Caesars with the most poetic poison, we know better of them: they fed the people.
> It is Caesar who led the Roman aristocracy to its destruction and prepared the victory of democracy. (B 4:200)

The French, Heine observed, not without a certain malice, as a more social than private people, value equality more than liberty, and thus "soon were happy and content under the rule of their great emperor, who, acknowledging their immaturity, put all their liberty under strict guardianship and allowed them only the joy of a full, glorious equality." This is the case because "the striving for equality was the main principle of the Revolution" (DA 7/1:210).

It is such aspects of his image of Napoleon that lead us back to the image of the Revolution the emperor is alleged to have incarnated. As I have suggested, Heine perceived the first French Revolution backwards. The differentiated detail characteristic of his various representations of Napoleon is less characteristic of his representations of pre-Napoleonic phases. While very occasionally he might focus on one or another event of the course of the Revolution, in general his allusions to it are rhetorical, cast in global and, of course, highly ideological categories. Primarily, he ascribed to the Revolution two achievements that, as constituting a watershed in human history, were in principle irreversible and also touchstones of true progressive allegiance: emancipation from religion and from aristocratic inequality. These issues are linked. The destruction of the institutions and doctrines of traditional religion was not only an achievement of the Revolution; it was, to a certain extent, the prerequisite of revolution, the change of consciousness that makes revolutionary action possible. Thus he argued that Voltaire's attack on religion was a necessary prelude to the French Revolution (DA 8/1:14). That the profoundly revolutionary "secret" of German philosophy, the overthrow of theism, had not yet been effectively communicated to the people at large was the main reason Heine thought the Germans unready for revolution, so that he consistently opposed and scorned all revolutionary activism among German radicals. Time would take care of it, for, as he wrote to Baron Cotta on March 1, 1832, the revolution "is there in the idea, and the Germans have never given up an idea" (HSA 21:31). The downfall of Christianity was the wave of the future; Heine believed that it was irreversible in France, one of his numerous short-sighted perceptions. He was obliged to admit that Napoleon, in fact, had restored the French

Church, but that was all right, since, "after all, his iron pride of will sufficiently guaranteed that the clergy under his government would not presume too much, even less mount to dominance: he kept it on a tight rein as he did the rest of us, and his grenadiers, who marched along beside the processions with rifles at the ready, seemed to be less the honor guard than the prisoner escort of religion" (B 5:486–87). This passage clearly counterpoints an observation on a Catholic procession Heine had made earlier in *The City of Lucca*: "There were almost more soldiers than clergy, but today the support of religion requires many bayonets" (DA 7/1:170). Napoleon is the difference between supporting religion with secular force and disciplining it.

It is via Napoleon, with his inexhaustible qualities, that a link between the issues of religion and equality can be forged, in a passage where he is denominated a "Saint-Simonian emperor" (DA 12/1:217). The phrase naturally associates Napoleon with the new social and secular religious surrogate of Saint-Simonianism that attracted Heine's allegiance for a time. But the passage in fact perpetuates the legend that under Napoleon one was rewarded exclusively on grounds of merit:

> ... as he himself was entitled to the supreme power by reason of his intellectual superiority, so he encouraged the dominance of talents, and sought the physical and moral welfare of the more numerous and poorer classes. He ruled less for the benefit of the third estate, the middle class, the *Juste-milieu*, than for the benefit of the men whose property consists only in heart and hand; and even his army was a hierarchy whose steps of honor were climbed only through intrinsic worth and ability. The meanest son of a peasant there could, just as well as the aristocratic scion of the oldest family, acquire the highest honors and obtain gold and decorations. (DA 12/1:217–18)

The Saint-Simonian attribute can be associated with the Caesarist attribute: "As Caesar gave his name to mere sovereign power, so Napoleon gives his name to a new Caesarism, to which only he is entitled who possesses the highest ability and the best will" (DA 12/1:217). These utterances, however, lie partly on the plane of myth. On the plane of reality the issue was primarily one of the abolition of aristocratic privilege and the displacement of the aristocracy by the middle class, not so much the *Juste-milieu*, the notorious bourgeoisie of property and capitalism, but the educated, cultured, progressive citizens of Heine's own type; in this regard he replicates a familiar pattern of German liberalism. Beyond these specific issues of religion and aristocracy, he drew from the potential of the French Revolution a more general vision of "a certain mode of intellectual and social existence, made up of tolerance, the opening of the spirit, of exchanges among differing persons and cultures, that is to say, the exact contrary of the narrow life of the

Teutomanic, Francophobic, and anti-Semitic philistines of his German homeland, with their nightcaps carefully pulled over their ears in order to hear nothing of the external world."[20] With regard to the "more numerous and poorer classes."—a Saint-Simonian phrase—the egalitarian task of revolutionary government was to relieve their material miseries and thus to neutralize their potential for justifiable violence. Nowhere does Heine support the notion that the source of sovereignty should be located in the common people, and the very thought of it seems to have made him extremely nervous. It is this Caesarist predilection that led him into one of his most embarrassing howlers, his characterization of Tsar Nicholas I as a "standard-bearer of liberty" partly because (in characteristically absolutist manner) he combatted the privileges of the nobility (DA 7/1:71–72). This misjudgment Heine was obliged to repudiate (DA 11:143).

In the course of time, Caesarism and egalitarianism were melded in his imagination into a darker vision of the future. He is often praised for having coined the term *Weltrevolution*, but the apprehensions he associated with world revolution are less often stressed.[21] "The second act," he wrote, "is the European, the world revolution, the great duel of the propertyless with the aristocracy of property, and then there will be no question of nationality or religion: there will be only one fatherland, namely, the earth, and only one faith, namely, happiness on earth." So far, so good, but then Heine asks himself what this regime might look like: "Perhaps there will then be only one shepherd and one flock, a free shepherd with an iron crook and an equally shorn, equally bleating flock of men!" (B 5:406–07). The positive Napoleonic image has reversed into a negative; Heine has imagined, so to speak, a metaphorical transition from Napoleon to Stalin.

Considering the Revolution from the point of view of popular sovereignty and spontaneous political action naturally leads to the question of the Terror that had so preoccupied the older generation. On the relatively rare occasions when Heine thought historically about the Revolution, he was inclined to accept the Terror as necessary, not so much in the specifically political context of the beleaguerment of revolutionary France in 1792 and 1793, but as a stage in the social upheaval. He paired it to the ascetic Christian spiritualism following upon the excesses of Roman decadence as "a necessary medicine" (DA 8/1:127). For all his sympathy with the "good-humored and philanthropic Louis XVI," his "disgraceful execution" was nevertheless necessary: "this line had become impossible and sooner or later, like an abscess, had to be cut out of the French body politic, just as happened to the Stuarts in England . . ." (DA 15:188). While one might suppose Heine, like Büchner, to have been attracted to Camille Desmoulins as a kindred spirit, his execution is deemed necessary on account of his untimely and dangerous moderation, and Heine sketches a rather sentimental vignette of Robespierre privately weeping at the death of his friend (DA 12/1:19).[22]

The guillotine itself was a welcome, gleefully employed image for Heine's most belligerent rhetoric. The most familiar passage is probably the one from the *Winter's Tale* where the narrator catches up Emperor Barbarossa, isolated in his Kyffhäuser retreat, on recent history:

> "Du Barry's life was merry and gay
> While Louis was there to support her,
> But she was already pretty old
> When the guillotine cut her shorter.
>
> "King Louis the Fifteenth died in bed
> With a peaceful disposition;
> The Sixteenth, however, was guillotined,
> And Queen Antoinette in addition.
>
> "The queen showed courage as was right,
> And nothing she did was demeaning;
> Du Barry, however, wept and shrieked
> When it came to the guillotining."— —
>
> The kaiser suddenly stopped stock-still,
> And eyed me with fixed attention,
> And said, "For heaven's sake, explain
> What's this guillotine you mention?"
>
> "The guillotine," I explained to him,
> "Is for people of any position;
> It's a new method found to change their state
> From a living to a dead condition.
>
> "To bring this about by modern means
> They use a new machine now;
> Mr. Guillotin invented it,
> So it's called the guillotine now.
>
> "They strap you tightly to a board,
> Then lower it and shove you
> Between two posts in half a wink;—
> A three-cornered blade hangs above you;—

> "They pull a cord, and so the blade
> Shoots right down, brisk and merry;—
> In consequence your head will drop
> In a sack, all ready to bury." (DA 4:127–28; D 512)

The menace implied by the second-person singular address, duly noted by the kaiser, is characteristic of Heine's use of this motif. In an unpublished poem he imagined the Germans guillotining their princes with customary deference:

> The French and British lack sentiment;
> It's only the Germans have this bent;
> They'll stay sentimental even while
> They act in terroristic style.
> Germans will treat Their Majesties
> With piety and if-you-please.
> In handsome coach and six, bedraped
> With sable plumes, and horses creped,
> The coachman weeping and distraught:
> Thus will a German king be brought
> To execution pious-miened,
> And be obsequiously guillotined. (B 6/1:272; D 766)

This poem is undated but is probably to be located in the 1850s, a very late date for such imaginings. Heine did publish a recommendation to the English working class in 1842 that it begin guillotining its oppressors, starting with the Duke of Wellington (B 5:419).

However, the fear that Heine meant to inspire in others with this rhetoric was in his own heart also.[23] In the first place, like other observers, he was aware of the tendency of the revolution to destroy its own makers. Mother Revolution, he remarked in a veiled threat directed toward Adolphe Thiers, has no sympathy for her sons and has "always murdered the best of them" (B 5:351–52). After the July Revolution of 1830 he began to worry: "Perhaps France is approaching a terrible catastrophe. Those who begin a revolution are usually its victims, and such a fate may perhaps strike nations as well as individuals. The French nation, which began the great revolution of Europe, will perhaps perish, while subsequent nations harvest the fruit of its initiative" (DA 12/1:248–49). Later he quoted an unidentified ally: "Whether the revolution succeeds or fails, men of great heart will always be their victims" (DA 11:168). Among these potential great-hearted victims he clearly numbered himself. In a draft for a preface to the second edition of *Travel*

Pictures IV he complained: "When one observes the people with whom the revolution is supposed to be made, one's courage melts. ... If there is a violent alteration, the first friends of the people are also the first victims" (DA 7/1:525). While expressing his sympathy for the tragic republican rebels in Paris, he asserted: "I am, by God! no republican, I know that if the republicans are victorious, they will cut my throat, because I do not admire everything that they admire" (DA 12/1:197).

One consideration underlying his skepticism about violent revolution is no doubt his suspicion that popular uprising was likely to turn in a dangerous anti-Jewish direction, as he had occasion to observe during his own lifetime, in 1819 and again in 1830. But more general considerations are involved also, including those of common sense. "I couldn't stand to be guillotined every day," he wrote reasonably, "and no one else was able to stand it" (DA 12/1:175). Despite his own propensity to call upon the language of terror for his rhetorical purposes, he argued that it was an anachronism in modern French politics; the radical republicans, he argued, no less than the reactionary Carlists, were "plagiarizers of the past" (DA 12/1:97). While the revolution of 1789 had been "bloody and horrible," he wrote, that of 1830 was "humane and considerate" (DA 11:135). The reason was that in 1789 the lower classes had been ignorant and therefore barbarous, but in the meantime had been elevated by political education. The point of the argument is that freedom of thought and expression in Germany might make a revolution without terror possible.

An unprejudiced examination of Heine's political attitudes in the context of French politics and society of the 1840s has yet to be undertaken. It is a difficult task, partly because his revisions of his articles in the Augsburg *Allgemeine Zeitung* for *Lutezia* have still not been fully analyzed, nor has his still obscure but presumably in some degree opportunistic relationship to the French government and its chief ministers Thiers and Guizot, and partly because of his own claims of self-censorship, which have been taken in some quarters as a warrant for exegetical irresponsibility.[24] But the result of such an analysis would eventually show, I believe, that, while he never abandoned his hopes for and allegiance to liberty, equality, and the relief of material misery, and thus consistently regarded himself as a frontline revolutionary spokesman, he feared rather than hoped for a general revolutionary upheaval in France and in Europe, and supported policies that he thought would inhibit it. His immediate response to the Revolution of 1848 was not only a recrudescence of his Bonapartism; he also, for the moment, praised Lamartine, who in his book on the Girondins had so colorfully depicted the bacchanal of the Revolution and now was a "standard-bearer [of the Republic] with the tricolor banner that he loyally protected when people tried to force upon him the red flag of blood, from which may heaven long preserve us" (B 5:212); in other words, Lamartine replicates Napoleon's role of taming revolutionary anarchy while maintaining revolutionary tradition. (Of course, events were soon to force Heine off this position.)

Thus his view of the Revolution seems to be somewhat entangled, and, if we look for the source of this entanglement, we are likely to find it, as others have, in his projected persona as poet. The axiom from Schiller's *Maid of Orleans*, that "the singer should walk with the king; both dwell on the heights of mankind," ironic in Schiller, as it is put into the mouth of the incompetent and irresponsible King Charles VII, was taken literally by Heine. When speaking of Napoleon in his essay *The North Sea III*, where the emperor is linked with Goethe, Heine remarks that "the great men of all times live in a mystical communion, they nod to one another across the millennia..., they understand and love one another." He then goes on to say that "we little ones" can only admire the great and expand our souls in contemplation of them (DA 6:159). But this self-diminishment is a rhetorical flourish, for normally Heine ascribed to the poet and therefore to himself exceptionally elevated dignity. "The great progressive ideas of mankind are constantly present in their most magnificent clarity and greatness to the mind of the poet," he wrote in the preface to *Atta Troll*, so that "he is all the more irresistibly overcome by hilarity when he sees how coarsely, crudely, and awkwardly those ideas can be conceived by his obtuse contemporaries" (DA 4:11). In one of his polemics against the radical poets he asserted: "The truly great poets have always grasped the great interests of the day otherwise than in rhymed newspaper articles and worried little when the slavish crowd, whose crudeness disgusts them, reproaches them with elitism" (B 5:438). He repeatedly stressed the peculiarly accurate veridical insight that is vouchsafed to the poet more than to other men.[25] Inevitably the dignity of the poet acquires aristocratic and even royal attributes. After what he regarded as his execution of the poet Count Platen, in a letter to Immermann of December 26, 1829, he compared himself to Napoleon in his regal calm (HSA 20:373–74). In attempting to distinguish his own views from what he interpreted as Börne's plebeian repressiveness, he wrote: "For beauty and genius there will be no place in the commonwealth of our new puritans, and both will be blighted and oppressed even more grievously than under the older regime. For beauty and genius are also a kind of monarchy, and they do not fit into a society in which everyone in the ill-feeling of his own mediocrity tries to devalue all higher giftedness down to the banal level" (DA 11:129).

It is from this perspective that we can most intelligibly approach the often discussed and more often evaded question of Heine's repeated claim to have been a monarchist. He was able to distinguish the hated aristocracy from the idea of a king as an icon of excellence and of authority exercised for the benefit of the people. His preoccupation with the concept of populist monarchy, at once commanding and benefiting the people, is interestingly exhibited in his complex fascination with Louis-Philippe, another topic that has been rather evaded in contemporary Heine studies.[26] He could, of course, be very critical of the king, but if one compares his strictures with, for example, the relentlessly savage caricatures of Daumier,[27] his attitude will seem mild and sympathetic. Of Louis-Philippe, he wrote, not without irony, that, like Napoleon, he had saved monarchy in Europe, and it was amazing that the princes of Europe were unable to understand this: "Oh, you are right to call yourselves kings by the grace of God! It was a particular grace of God that he once again sent to the kings the man who saved them when Jacobinism again had the ax in its hands and threatened to smash ancient royalty; if the princes kill this man, too, God cannot help them any more" (DA 12/1:61). Thus it is not surprising that, on the spectrum of French political journalism, Heine was most positively received by the moderately conservative newspapers supportive of the July Monarchy.[28] At the rhetorical level his monarchism is closely linked with his wish-dreams of the social stature and efficacy of the genius-poet. Repeatedly he associates his poetic persona with figurations of power: soldier, knight, king. The parallelism of poet and monarch occurs frequently in the late poetry and is made explicit in "Jehuda ben Halevy":

>   Both in poetry and life,
>   It's the gift of grace that governs—
>   He who has this highest good can
>   Never sin in prose or verse.
>
>   Any poet who possesses
>   This, God's grace, we call a genius:
>   Monarch in the realm of thought, he
>   Is responsible to no man.
>
>   He accounts to God, God only,
>   Not the people; both in art
>   And in life, the people can
>   Kill us but can never judge us. (B 6/1:135; D 659)

Heine's intense rhetoric and elaborate self-stylization as a revolutionary fighter have tended to obscure the fact that there is much that is conventional in his outlook on the French Revolution. The imagery with which he surrounds his icon of Napoleon was already a cliché in his time; the comparisons of Napoleon with Christ and of his fate with the Passion were familiar from French writers.[29] As Paul Michael Lützeler has pointed out, these conventions had largely been fixed during Napoleon's lifetime:

> Already in the first decade of Napoleon's rule the perceptions of his admirers and opponents had consolidated: the emperor is seen simultaneously as Hellenic hero and oriental despot, as Roman Caesar and Attila, as radiant young god and oppressor, as an elemental force of nature and a vain dictator.[30]

Though admiration of Napoleon was doubtless a minority standpoint among Germans in his time, Heine was not alone in taking this position. He was not the only one to take offense at Sir Walter Scott's hostile biography of Napoleon.[31] Even by 1814, before the memoir literature had begun to appear, an improved opinion of Napoleon had emerged in some quarters; it was expressed, for example, by the nationalist liberal Hoffmann von Fallersleben.[32] Heine's friend Varnhagen von Ense; his co-editor of the *Politische Annalen*, Friedrich Ludwig Lindner; his editor at the *Allgemeine Zeitung*, Gustav Kolb; and his publisher of both of these periodicals, Baron Cotta, all seem to have shared his Bonapartism to some degree. Of no mean significance was his discipleship to Goethe in this matter. Jochen Schmidt has written recently:

> Both [Goethe and Heine] apotheosize Napoleon as a genius of action as Stendhal did at the same time in his *Charterhouse of Parma*. Napoleon embodies the youthful dream of greatness and creative power in an epoch perceived as petty and sterile. Thus emerges one of the main myths of the cult of genius in the nineteenth century. It still maintains its force in Nietzsche. It has a compensatory character.[33]

Lützeler has interestingly pointed out how many French writers of Heine's generation were caught up in the Napoleonic myth, either taking the nostalgic view of the days of glory, like Hugo, Lamartine, Vigny, and Balzac, or contributing to the perpetuation of the myth, like Béranger, Barthélemy and Méry, Nerval, Delavigne, and Quinet.[34] With the exception of the older Béranger and the younger Nerval, all were born within seven years of Heine. A number of German Bonapartists, such as Wilhelm Hauff, Baron von Zedlitz, and Baron von Gaudy also fall into this age group.[35]

The religious view of the French revolution and of Paris as a place of pilgrimage had been articulated in the previous generation, for example, by the uncle of Heine's publisher Julius Campe, Joachim Heinrich Campe.[36] Thomas P. Saine's recent study of the response of German intellectuals to the French Revolution defines a number of themes that, adjusted and transformed, reappear in Heine's thinking: the unripeness of Germany for revolution; the resistance to sovereignty and participation in government by the unenlightened masses; the fear that the continued oppression and misery of the exploited lower classes, if not relieved, would eventuate in a cataclysm of civilization.[37] The preference for monarchy, constitutional or otherwise, was characteristic of the majority of German progressives from the beginning to the end of the revolutionary epoch; it was initially Börne's inclination, and his eventual abandonment of monarchism for republicanism is one of the ways in which he bifurcated from Heine.

Apart from the pitch, aggressiveness, and occasional crudity of his rhetoric and satire, there were, it seems to me, three aspects of Heine's thinking that were less conventional and therefore tended to estrange him from his potential public. One was his intensely anti-Christian affect, his insistence that the French Revolution and, in its underground, encrypted way, German philosophy, had put a final end to the history of Christianity and especially Catholicism. In this he was much mistaken, and the error, in my opinion, caused him to misread important elements of French society and politics in his own time and made him a poor prophet of the future. A second aspect, clearly related to the first, was his identification of the fundamental issue of the Revolution as the revolt of sensualism against spiritualism, of the emancipation of the flesh and sexuality as a metonymy for material plenitude—an allegiance not likely to have much fortune on the threshold of the international Victorian Age. The third aspect was his adamant and little differentiated hostility to nationalism, despite the fact that it was his hero Napoleon who had ignited modern nationalism both in France and among the peoples he invaded. All three of these aspects are widely admired today and play a large role in the propagation of Heine as a revolutionary model; however that may be, in his own time they limited the efficacy with the public for which he himself was ambitious.

Finally we may note a psychological subtext in the incarnation of the Revolution in the figure of Napoleon. For Napoleon's career is not only a heroic epic; it is also a tragedy. It can be paralleled with the Christian Passion only so long as the hope for the Resurrection and the Second Coming can be maintained; otherwise it acquires a dark tone of defeat and finality. In my opinion Heine struggled for much of his life with a psychologically originary tendency to melancholy and pessimism. This tendency came to infect his politics as experiences and events caused him to despair of a congruence of reality with his vision. I have tried to show elsewhere that this pessimistic inclination lies at the root of his sociopolitical satire and distinguishes his political verse from that of his despised liberal and radical contemporaries.[38] In fact, it is curious how poetry tends to bring out this tone in him. When he described the return of Napoleon's remains in his report to the *All-*

gemeine Zeitung, he stressed the sunbeam that had penetrated the clouds and shone upon the imperial standard; but when he returned to the scene three or four years later in Caput VIII of the *Winter's Tale*, the atmosphere is one of unrelieved gloom:

> The Emperor's risen up since then,
> But those English worms finally made him
> A very grave man and well-behaved,
> And back in the tomb they laid him.
>
> I saw his funeral rites myself,
> Saw the golden hearse go faring
> Bedecked with golden Victories,
> The golden coffin bearing.
>
> Along the Champs Elysées they marched,
> Through mist and snowfall blended,
> And through the Arch of Triumph too
> The slow procession wended.
>
> The music was playing all out of tune;
> Stiff with cold, the musicians.
> The eagles on the banners looked
> Like doleful apparitions.
>
> The people looked lost in memory,
> Like ghosts of another era—
> The dream of Empire rose again,
> The fairy-tale chimera.
>
> I wept that day. My eyes filled up
> With tears, my heart was pounding,
> When I heard that long-dead cry of love
> "Vive l'Empereur" resounding. (DA 4:110–11; D 499–500)

One of the wiser students of his politics has remarked: "the world proved impervious to his vision and Heine could not escape the fear that the Golden Age was past and its disappearance could only be mourned."[39] In *The Gods in Exile* he mused: "on every greatness on this earth the secret rats are gnawing, and in the end the gods themselves must ignominiously perish" (DA 9:145). As usual, he was thinking of himself in his own kinship, as poet, with the great of the earth. When Louis Napoleon after the coup d'état finally succeeded in making Heine's Bonapartism irrelevant for good and all, he wrote with characteristically tragic self-stylization to his editor Kolb: "The beautiful ideas of political decency, lawfulness, civic virtue, liberty, and equality, for which our fathers so heroically died, and which we dreamed after them, no less addicted to martyrdom—there they now lie at our feet, trampled, smashed" (HSA 23:181).

The more than twenty-year-old project in literary scholarship to make of Heine a successor to the Revolution and a prophetic continuator of it into the present and future has been, in my opinion, misdirected. To be sure, in certain moods he liked to present himself in this way. "I am the son of the revolution," he cried out in his desperate attempt to repel Börne's reproaches of elitism and aestheticism, "and reach again for my charmed weapons. Flowers! Flowers! I will crown my head for the fight to the death. And the lyre, too, hand me the lyre, that I may sing battle songs" (DA 11:50).[40] Who but a Western European university student of our time would be persuaded by such an utterance? Hardly anyone in his own time took Heine seriously as a revolutionary, not even the governments, which, while banning his works and threatening him with arrest, came to regard him largely as a nuisance and a polluter of public discourse. However, the contrary view of him, as primarily aesthetic in his affects and confusedly inadequate in his political thinking does not meet the case, either. His mode of apprehension was primarily synthetic rather than analytic. But the world in which he lived, as he lucidly perceived, was riddled with contradiction and inchoate, ill-defined potentiality, and thus resisted synthesis. When he was ultimately unable to impose his synthetic resolutions upon the world of reality, he was prey to despair. But to us he may appear as a multi-faceted crystal, glittering from its very flaws, absorbing and reflecting with remarkable fidelity all the ambiguities, the contraries, the irreconcilable desiderata of the age of revolution, and leaving to us, not solutions, not leadership, but a context for meditation on and rethinking of the conundrums of modern politics.

NOTES

All quotations from works that have so far appeared in Heinrich Heine, *Historisch-kritische Gesamtausgabe der Werke*, ed. Manfred Windfuhr et al. (Hamburg: Hoffmann und Campe, 1973–), are cited as DA with volume and page number. All others are cited from *Sämtliche Schriften*, ed. Klaus Briegleb et al. (Munich: Hanser, 1968–76) as B. Letters are cited from *Heinrich Heine Säkularausgabe*, ed. Nationale Forschungs- und Gedenkstätten der klassischen deutschen Literatur in Weimar and Centre National de la Recherche Scientifique in Paris (Berlin and Paris: Akademie-Verlag and Editions du CNRS, 1970–) as HSA. Verse passages are cited to the German text in DA or B but quoted from *The Complete Poems of Heinrich Heine: A Modern English Version*, tr. Hal Draper (Boston: Suhrkamp/Insel, 1982), cited as D with page number.

1. Heine read Adolphe Thiers's *Histoire de la révolution française* in the spring of 1830, as he wrote to Varnhagen on April 5 (HSA 20:393). According to Ludolf Wienbarg, Heine read François Mignet's *Histoire de la révolution française* in the fall of that year; see *Begegnungen mit Heine*, ed. Michael Werner (Hamburg: Hoffmann und Campe, 1973) 1:209. On the question of Heine's reading about the French Revolution, see Lucien Calvié, "La révolution française dans l'oeuvre de Henri Heine," *Littérature et révolution française*, ed. Daniel Minary (Annales littéraires de l'Université de Besançon, No. 354), (Paris: Les belles lettres, 1987): 234–35, in general an especially thoughtful consideration of Heine's attitude to the French Revolution, although in my opinion Calvié understresses the importance of the figuration of Napoleon, assimilating it to Heine's perception of the Revolution as a whole.

2. Paul Holzhausen, *Heinrich Heine und Napoleon I.* (Frankfurt/Main: Diesterweg, 1903) 59.

3. E.g., Volkmar Hansen, "Johannes der Täufer. Heines bedingter Bonapartismus," in *Der späte Heine 1848–1856: Literatur—Politik—Religion*, ed. Wilhelm Gössmann and Joseph A. Kruse (Hamburg: Hoffmann und Campe, Heinrich Heine Verlag, 1982) 69–96; see also Lucienne Netter, *Heine et la peinture de la civilisation parisienne 1840–1848* (Frankfurt/Main, Bern, and Cirencester: Peter D. Lang, 1980) 162–74.

4. Thus Holzhausen 63, and often thereafter; e.g., Paul Michael Lützeler, "Napoleon-Legenden von Hölderlin bis Chateaubriand (1798–1848)," in Lützeler, *Geschichte in der Literatur: Studien zu Werken von Lessing bis Hebbel* (Munich and Zurich: Piper, 1987) 291. It has been argued that Heine established December 13, 1799, as his birth date because that was the date of the

completion of the Napoleonic constitution that extended civil rights to the Jews: Otto W. Johnston, "Miszelle. Heinrich Heine and the Thirteenth of December," *Colloquia Germanica* 6 (1972): 196–202. This argument is purely speculative.

    5. See Jeffrey L. Sammons, *Heinrich Heine: A Modern Biography* (Princeton: Princeton University Press, 1979) 31–32.

    6. See S.S. Prawer, *Karl Marx and World Literature* (Oxford: Clarendon Press, 1976) 181.

    7. Richard Reinhardt to Marx, December 30, 1851, *Begegnungen mit Heine* (note 1) 2:294.

    8. Heine to Gustav Kolb, April 21, 1851, HSA 23:97. Joseph Dresch, *Heine à Paris (1831–1856) d'après sa correspondance et les témoinages de ses contemporains* (Paris: Didier, 1956) 115, argued that he accepted the coup because he failed to understand French republicanism and saw in Louis Napoleon a representative of past glories and a principle of order.

    9. See Hansen, "Johannes der Täufer," 79–80, 83.

    10. See Hans Hörling, *Heinrich Heine im Spiegel der politischen Presse Frankreichs von 1831–1841* (Frankfurt/Main, Bern, and Las Vegas: Peter Lang, 1977) 154, and Hansen, "Johannes der Täufer," 81–83. Hansen concludes his analysis with the assertion that Heine's Bonapartism was an integral part of his radical socialism (92). I believe this judgment is an example of the common error of confusing his *prediction* of the coming victory of radical socialism, what he called "communism," with an *allegiance* to it, which he by no means felt, for this outlook was part of his gloomy vision of the world in his last years.

    11. Ernst Loeb, "Zwiespältige Einheit: Heines Luther- und Napoleonbild," *Heine-Jahrbuch* 12 (1973): 126; also in Loeb, *Heinrich Heine: Weltbild und geistige Gestalt* (Bonn: Bouvier, 1975) 55. Loeb is citing the passage from *Ideas: The Book of Le Grand*, DA 6:193.

    12. The dual imaging of Napoleon as reality and myth has already been discussed by Otto W. Johnston, "Signatura Temporis in Heine's *Lutezia*," *German Quarterly* 47 (1974): 220–25. However, Johnston appears to see the contrast as chronological, with the distinction "between the man of history and the hero of legend" (222) emerging clearly in *Lutezia*. But I believe that the distinction is implicitly present throughout Heine's career, merely, as so often with him, shifting its stress at various times. For example, the depiction in *Ideas: The Book of Le Grand* of Napoleon's entry into Düsseldorf as a parodistic post-figuration of Christ's entry into Jerusalem is so self-consciously mythopoeic as to suggest that Heine was rationally conscious of the distinction from the outset.

    13. Hansen, "Johannes der Täufer," 81–83.

14. Cf. Fritz Mende, "Zu Heines politischer Terminologie," in Mende, *Heinrich Heine: Studien zu seinem Leben und Werk* (Berlin: Akademie-Verlag, 1983) 198: "His critique of Napoleon I begins . . . where he betrayed liberty on the eighteenth of Brumaire 'out of secret predilection for aristocracy' and became an 'enemy of liberty' out of egotism. But it ends where he comprehends him as a symbolic figure of the French Revolution, as 'savior of the ideology,' where he sees him as 'standard-bearer of democracy,' as representative of the 'interests of liberty, equality, fraternity, truth, and reason.' "

15. Edward A. Zlotkowski, *Heinrich Heines Reisebilder: The Tendency of the Text and the Identity of the Age* (Bonn: Bouvier, 1980) 117.

16. Burghard Dedner, "Politisches Theater und karnevalistische Revolution. Zu einem Metaphernkomplex bei Heinrich Heine," in *Heinrich Heine und das neunzehnte Jahrhundert: Signaturen*, ed. Rolf Hosfeld (Berlin: Argument-Verlag, 1986) 136. This point is important, as currently Heine's irony is frequently called upon to insist that he means the opposite of what he says.

17. See Jörg Traeger, "Napoleon, Trajan, Heine: Zur Malerei des Ersten Kaiserreichs in Frankreich," *Jahres- und Tagesberichte der Görres-Gesellschaft* (1984): 71–86, expanded with illustrations and notes as "Napoleon, Trajan, Heine: Imperiale Staatsmalerei in Frankreich," *Das antike Rom in Europa: Vortragsreihe der Universität Regensburg*, ed. Hans Bungert (Regensburg: Buchverlag der Mittelbayerischen Zeitung, 1986) 141–206.

18. Giorgio Tonelli, *Heinrich Heines politische Philosophie (1830–1845)* (Hildesheim and New York: Olms, 1975), esp. 109. Heine's friend Heinrich Laube thought that he would have liked best "an imperium à la Caesar" (*Begegnungen mit Heine* (note 1) 1:438).

19. *Begegnungen mit Heine* 2:297.

20. Calvié, "La révolution française," 246.

21. For the more conventional view of this concept, see Wolfgang Kossek, *Begriff und Bild der Revolution bei Heinrich Heine* (Frankfurt/Main and Bern: Peter Lang, 1982) 92–94.

22. On Heine's view of revolutionary terrorism, see Kossek 50–54.

23. The motifs of beheading, execution, or other mutilation are so widespread in Heine's writings that they appear to have psychological as well as political implications, especially as they are as likely to be applied to himself as to others. See Leslie Bodi, "Kopflos—ein Leitmotiv in Heines Werk," *Internationaler Heine-Kongreß Düsseldorf 1972: Referate und Diskussionen*, ed. Manfred Windfuhr (Hamburg: Hoffmann und Campe, Heinrich Heine Verlag, 1973) 227–44.

24. I have long had a suspicion that one reason *Lutezia* has never yet been adequately edited or annotated in a modern edition is that the results would not support the view of Heine propagated by mainstream criticism during the last twenty years. Since the point has not been adequately recognized, I repeat what I have said before of the constantly overpraised Briegleb edition in this regard, that while it "offers a crushingly elaborate and pretentious apparatus on other matters," it "contents itself when it comes to annotating the *Lutezia* text largely with copying a skeleton apparatus out of an East German edition that appeared fifteen years before" (*Heinrich Heine: A Modern Biography*, 322). One need only compare B 5:1051–85 with Heinrich Heine, *Werke und Briefe in zehn Bänden*, ed. Hans Kaufmann (Berlin: Aufbau-Verlag, 1961–64) 6:692–735. For this reason the commentary in DA is anxiously awaited and will be the ultimate touchstone of value of that enterprise. See Hansen, "Johannes der Täufer," 89–92.

25. See Sammons, *Heinrich Heine: A Modern Biography*, 176–77.

26. See my effort to broach it in *Heinrich Heine: The Elusive Poet* (New Haven and London: Yale University Press, 1969) 220–47. For other perspectives, see Rutger Booss, *Ansichten der Revolution. Paris-Berichte deutscher Schriftsteller nach der Juli-Revolution 1830: Heine, Börne u.a.* (Cologne: Pahl-Rugenstein, 1977) 237–44, and Kossek, *Begriff und Bild der Revolution*, 33, 244. Kossek derives Heine's concept of populist monarchy, unconvincingly, as it seems to me, from an argument of Hegel's concerning the emergence of outstanding personalities in a democracy.

27. See, for example, Daumier's caricature of Louis-Philippe laughing up his sleeve while pretending to mourn at Lafayette's funeral, reproduced *Heine-Jahrbuch* 20 (1981), between 160 and 161.

28. Hörling, *Heinrich Heine im Spiegel der politischen Presse Frankreichs*, 39–74.

29. See, e.g., Holzhausen (note 2) 116–19. On the context, see also Otto W. Johnston, "The Napoleon Cult in German Literature," *Revue belge de philologie et d'histoire* 52 (1974): 613–25.

30. Lützeler, "Napoleon-Legenden," 268.

31. Holzhausen (note 2) 127–28.

32. Holzhausen 11–14.

33. Jochen Schmidt, *Die Geschichte des Genie-Gedankens 1750–1945* (Darmstadt: Wissenschaftliche Buchgesellschaft, 1985) 2:63–64.

34. Lützeler (note 4) 289.

35. Lützeler 291.

36. Alain Ruiz, "Heinrich Heines 'arme Vorgänger.' Zur Tradition der deutschen Freiheitspilger und politischen Emigranten in Frankreich seit 1789," *Heine-Jahrbuch* 26 (1987): 92–115, esp. 100.

37. Thomas P. Saine, *Black Bread—White Bread: German Intellectuals and the French Revolution* (Columbia: Camden House, 1988) 44–45, 280–81, 358–59. See also Calvié, "La révolution française," 243–44, 249, on the shared context of Heine's hopes and fears of revolution on the French model.

38. Jeffrey L. Sammons, " 'Der prosaisch bombastischen Tendenzpoesie hoffentlich den Todesstoß geben': Heine and the Political Poetry of the *Vormärz*," *German Quarterly* 51 (1978): 150–59.

39. Nigel Reeves, *Heinrich Heine: Poetry and Politics* (Oxford: Oxford University Press, 1974) 189.

40. On the pervasiveness and ambivalence of his revolutionary rhetoric, see Leslie Bodi, "Heine und die Revolution," *Dichtung, Sprache, Gesellschaft: Akten des IV. Internationalen Germanisten-Kongresses 1970 in Princeton*, ed. Victor Lange and Hans-Gert Roloff (Frankfurt/Main: Athenäum, 1971) 169–77.

HERBERT S. LINDENBERGER

The Literature in History:
Büchner's Danton and the French Revolution

EVERYBODY FAMILIAR WITH THE COMMENTARY on *Danton's Death* will remember seeing the following quotation from one of Büchner's letters in virtually every serious consideration of the play:

> I studied the history of the Revolution. I felt myself crushed under the frightful fatalism of history. I find in human nature a horrifying sameness, in the human condition an inescapable force, granted to all and to no one. The individual merely foam on the waves, greatness a mere accident, the mastery of genius a puppet play, a ridiculous struggle against an iron law: to recognize it is our highest achievement, to control it is impossible.[1]

Even if one were unaware of the play's extensive and controversial interpretive history, one would recognize the documentary importance of a statement such as this one, which appeared in a letter that Büchner wrote to his fiancée some nine or ten months before the composition of the play. Here, after all, one finds the author expressing his *own* attitude toward the French Revolution without the problems one encounters interpreting a drama in which a succession of attitudes, many of them seemingly impossible to reconcile, are voiced toward the same historical event. With whom, for instance, does Büchner expect us to sympathize in his play? With Robespierre and St. Just, to whom he extends so little sympathy, yet who, one might at first think, should be heroes to an activist radical such as Büchner? To Danton and his friends, whose world-weary resignation and refusal to continue the Revolution scarcely seem compatible with the writer's recent political actions—or even with his later radical pronouncements? To the crowd on the streets, for whose economic plight he shows understanding but whose violent sentiments and manipulability hardly entitle them to heroic status?

These questions have proved hard enough for the play's commentators to deal with over the years, and it is no accident that those who have written on *Danton's Death* have reached eagerly for the letter to give them whatever concrete evidence they needed to prove what side Büchner was really taking in the play. Yet even if one ignores the considerable time-span between the letter and the play, or the fact that *between* letter and play Büchner co-authored his radical manifesto *Der hessische Landbote* (The Hessian Country Messenger) and helped lead what turned out to be an aborted uprising of the poor against the Hessian state—even if one ignores these matters, one encounters interpretive difficulties as soon as one tries to accommodate the letter to what one takes to be the meaning of the play. With its fatalistic conception of the individual, above all his helplessness in the face of historical events, it seems most obviously in harmony with only a single, though also quite prominent strand in the play—namely the plight of the title character and his friends as they face the guillotine.

Certainly for those readers who have opted for a conservative or an apolitical view of Büchner and his play the so-called "fatalism" letter has proved a most convenient piece of evidence. When Karl Viëtor, in an essay of 1934, quoted the letter, he used it to separate Büchner decisively from his radical contemporaries: "He [Büchner] thus saw the Revolution quite otherwise from what he had expected and from the way it was presented by his contemporaries who constituted Young Germany."[2] With Büchner's own attitude toward political action defined according to the passivity expressed in the letter, it becomes easy for an interpreter such as Viëtor to claim an antiactivist, indeed a thoroughly apolitical meaning for the play itself: "This drama," Viëtor writes, "has no activist message; it does not glorify the French Revolution or indeed any revolution whatsoever" (174). Behind these statements we note an aesthetic that rigorously separates the realm of art from that of politics: "What we have here is neither propaganda nor polemic; rather it is literature [*Dichtung*], pure literature" (175–76).

Viëtor's once-influential study of *Danton's Death* stands near the beginning of what one might call the passivist interpretation of the play—an interpretation that ascribes a message to the play as a whole by linking the fatalism letter to the eloquent emotional outpourings of Danton and his friends in the play's prison scenes. This interpretation has known a number of variants depending upon what thought systems were in fashion at a particular time. Thus, Robert Mühlher's essay of 1951, significantly entitled "Georg Büchner und die Mythologie des Nihilismus," uses the fatalism letter to place not only the play but Büchner's work as a whole within an antirationalist, anti-democratic tradition for which he invokes such names as Novalis, Schopenhauer, Bergson, and his own contemporary Karl Jaspers.[3] When Mühlher claims that "Büchner's new, deeper, pessimistic insight into the 'frightful fatalism of history' removes him forever from the liberal and democratic camp," (100), one notes how convenient the letter has proven for those who seek to claim Büchner for their own conservative positions. Even my own interpretation of *Danton's Death* (written in 1963), though it argued for a multi-perspectival approach to the play, used the fatalism letter to demonstrate Büchner's anticipation of the absurd view of life encountered in Kafka and other modernist writers.[4]

It is scarcely surprising that the fatalism letter has proved a formidable challenge to critics of the left, especially if they are intent on locating an activist element in *Danton's Death*. Thus, writing for the centenary of Büchner's death in 1937, Georg Lukács, in a head-on confrontation with Viëtor's interpretation of the play, finds two distinct ways to justify the work's revolutionary content. First, though he admits that the letter and the play voice a real philosophical crisis, he attributes this crisis to an earlier, pre-Marxist stage of the historical process: thus, both letter and play reveal the inability of an older, essentially eighteenth-century form of materialism to understand history. Second, to separate Büchner from the "heroic pessimism" that Viëtor had attributed both to the author and his title character, Lukács points to some verbal differences between the sentiments of the letter and those expressed by Danton in the play: whereas Danton echoes only the passive sentiments within the letter, he nowhere displays Büchner's own activist ambition to understand the fatalism of history that Lukács locates in the letter's line "to recognize it is our highest achievement."[5]

Lukács's efforts to defend Büchner as a thinker of the left pale beside those of Thomas Michael Mayer a full generation later, who brings a vast array of philological tools, including considerable archival research, to reassess the meaning of the letter as well as the political import of the play. For example, Mayer cites thinkers from the Enlightenment to Büchner's own time to demonstrate that the term *fatalism* had not yet, when the letter was written, been distinguished from the later, quite separate notion of determinism, that, among other things, it referred to those newer historians who saw history as created by larger forces rather than by individuals.[6] Moreover, Mayer points out the word *fatalité* in a speech of 1832 by the radical thinker Auguste Blanqui, who linked the tragedy of the revolution to the victory of the middle rather than the impoverished class (91–92). Indeed, Mayer's researches yield a new image of Büchner's political affiliations, for by linking him with the followers of Babeuf, especially Buonarroti and Blanqui (68–72), he is able to portray Büchner as a precommunist economic egalitarian and thus to make sense out of Büchner's evident disdain within the play toward the party of Robespierre, who, as portrayed in the play, showed little concern for economic change (108–19).[7]

I have discussed these various attempts to reconcile Büchner's letter to his play not to attempt still another reconciliatory gesture, but rather to ask some questions about the attitude we characteristically take to the process of interpreting individual literary works. Ever since the institutionalization of literary scholarship during the last half of the nineteenth century, a certain distinction has prevailed between the literary work and what has often been labeled its surrounding context. The work itself has enjoyed a privileged status; indeed, literary scholarship has justified its existence over the years through the expertise it has claimed in preserving, elucidating and transmitting the various texts that make up the canon.

The attitudes toward art that prevailed in the Western world during the foundation years of literary scholarship have left an ongoing legacy: thus, the great texts to which scholars devote their custodial efforts can be assumed to possess a certain coherence, and they are often in fact defended by means of organic metaphors derived from the idealist poetics of the early nineteenth century. This coherence has sometimes been defined in terms of what we are to see as the text's meaning: if, that is, we can assign some sort of meaning to the text, then we can also assume that it has a certain coherence. Moreover, the privileged status that the canonical texts have been given often manifests itself as a kind of magical aura—an aura notably lacking in texts of a not specifically literary sort. Thus, the so-called context surrounding the great literary text—the documents attached to the author's biography, the earlier texts (some themselves canonical) that have influenced the great text under consideration, the intellectual and social milieu that the author somehow absorbed—this context, according to the institutional conventions of literary scholarship, must perforce occupy a secondary status.

This secondary status of the contextual materials functions as a necessary part of the institutional arrangements within our field: it guarantees the superior status of the great work under consideration at the same time that it demonstrates the work's coherence. Text and context come to have a kind of symbiotic relationship to one another, each of them, in effect, needing the other to justify the particular attention we pay to them.

Let us return to the relationship between Büchner's fatalism letter and the play that it is claimed to elucidate. Among the items we classify as a literary work's context, a letter by the author on the same subject as the work is considered—at least by accepted institutional rules—to provide special evidence for assessing the work's meaning. Only the author's direct comment on the work (and Büchner has a number of such comments on *Danton's Death* written after the completion of the play) would ordinarily seem of greater relevance. From an institutional point of view it scarcely matters if the contextual evidence is able to elicit quite contradictory results—as the fatalism letter does—when it is applied to the work by different scholars, and in this particular instance by scholars with quite distinct political agendas. What matters most is that the letter seems to provide solid evidence of the author's attitude toward his subject and that, as a result, the letter can help demonstrate the coherence and the meaning, not to speak of the importance, of the work under consideration.

But what if the coherence that we attribute to the work can be demonstrated only at such a cost that the demonstration leaves its readers uneasy about the results? At least one study of Büchner claims several forms of incoherence in *Danton's Death*—for example, the play's inability to reconcile the political Danton with the romantic, *Weltschmerz*-minded Danton, as well as its lack of what the critic calls "real dramatic development"—and simply concludes from this that Büchner must have been suffering from "poetic-dramatic immaturity."[8] One could well imagine this negative judgment taken only a step further to produce a deconstructive reading of the play in the current American mode. Such a reading would exploit the irreconcilable elements that have plagued the play's interpreters to conclude not, like the above condemnation, that the play reveals its author as immature, but rather that, regardless of Büchner's intent or of the social and intellectual milieu out of which *Danton's Death* speaks, its interpretive difficulties become paradigmatic of the tensions and indeterminacies inherent within language itself at all times, in all places.

Must we be tied to a concept of art that demands the demonstration, within a particular work, of total coherence, or of a readily definable meaning, or, if we fail to find such coherence or meaning, must we then use this failure to condemn the work or to celebrate it as representative of some cultural universal? Let me suggest that the difficulties within the interpretive history of *Danton's Death* may have something to do with the genre within which Büchner chose to work—namely the history play, and, in this instance, a loosely organized form of the genre that Büchner took to be Shakespearean. This genre encouraged him to allow a multiplicity of voices to speak without the need of an overriding voice to guide the audience's responses at every point. The more classically organized forms of historical drama—for example, the plays of Corneille or of the later Schiller—go considerably further than *Danton's Death* in providing guidelines to help the audience determine what they supposedly mean, for they are usually explicit about the particular values the audience is expected to admire, even if their heroes carry these values to excess.

The peculiar difficulties that readers have encountered assessing the diverse voices within the play are particularly evident when we set *Danton's Death* next to another work on the revolution in a wholly different genre. I refer to Carlyle's *The French Revolution*, subtitled simply *A History*, though in this instance a historical prose narrative with specifically epic ambitions, indeed with many of the rhetorical conventions that we traditionally associate with the long epic poem. Büchner's little more than month-long labor on his play took place, I might add, at precisely the time that Carlyle was in the middle of his several-year-long labor.

Yet two works could scarcely seem more different than *The French Revolution* and *Danton's Death*: the first an overdetermined narrative whose overbearing, prophetic authorial voice is busily imposing order from above upon the chaos it purports to depict; the second, an underdetermined set of dialogues that, given its genre, eschews a firm guiding framework. One need only note Carlyle's portrayal of Danton during the September massacres: "See Danton enter;—the black brows clouded, the colossus-figure tramping heavy; grim energy looking from all features of the rugged man! Strong is that grim Son of France and Son of Earth; a Reality and not a Formula he too; and surely now if ever, being hurled *low* enough, it is on the Earth and on Realities that he rests."[9] However we choose to assess Büchner's assessment of Danton's role in history, nowhere in the play can we expect the narrative control that Carlyle, in his selfconsciously Miltonic mode, grimly exercises throughout.

Moreover, whereas Carlyle imposes a spiritual meaning upon the often ugly details that he recounts (his condemned figures, whatever their political affiliations, whether king or Jacobin, go to their deaths as Christlike martyrs), Büchner makes little attempt to spiritualize matter, indeed gives the illusion that the historical details he allows to be enacted can and must speak for themselves. The ideological disagreements I have cited among Büchner's commentators would be inconceivable among Carlyle's. When Treitschke, in his history of the nineteenth century, compared these two works, he praised Carlyle for "passionately expressing his moral disgust" at the Terror while expressing his own disgust at Büchner (whose artistic talent he otherwise acknowledged) for "glorifying the Revolution"[10]; although the German historian doubtless understood the political import in the text of his fellow-conservative, his all-too-pat assessment of Büchner's point of view derives more from his knowledge of the German writer's political activities than from the text of his play.[11]

Let us, for the purpose of this argument, think of *Danton's Death* not so much as an enshrined work that stands out as different in kind from other works, but as one among a succession of texts both before and after it—texts that echo, rewrite, absorb one another in a continuing verbal interplay. Thus, the multiple voices within this play become a kind of replay of earlier voices and an anticipation of later voices representing a wide array of historical contexts. Throughout the play, for example, we remain aware of type-scenes common to earlier historical dramas. Robespierre's speech wooing the common people (I, 15–16) restages such familiar scenes as Brutus and Antony vying for the assent of the populace in *Julius Caesar* or Menenius quelling the people at the beginning of *Coriolanus*. The street scenes in which the people express their woes echo scenes in both these plays as well in Goethe's *Egmont* and Grabbe's *Napoleon*. In its dramatic structure the confrontation between Danton and Robespierre (I, 26–27) has less in common with the brief scene depicted in Büchner's immediate historical sources than with the classic confrontation scenes between leaders in a succession of historical plays from *Antony and Cleopatra* to *Maria Stuart*. The echoes we hear from earlier dramas go well beyond those specifically associated with history plays: the suicide of Danton's wife Julie (I, 72–73)—the most conspicuously unhistorical moment in the play, for Danton's widow, actually named Louise, remarried and outlived even Büchner—evokes the love-death by poison of her namesake in *Romeo and Juliet*. Moreover, the Shakespearean dramatic structure that Büchner sought to recapture is one that has been thoroughly mediated by the loosely structured German Shakespearean imitations of the *Sturm und Drang* period—with the result that *Danton's Death* evokes at once the plays of the 1770s and the actual Shakespearean plays that stand behind them.

The earlier dramas that speak to us through *Danton's Death* constitute only one set of voices that we can identify. The historical narratives and documents of the French Revolution that Büchner absorbed within his play create still another set—to the point that in many sections of the play, above all in the political debates, we are never quite sure as we read whether the words originated from Büchner's pen or from his immediate sources. Few literary works of the past two centuries have elicited such detailed source study as has *Danton's Death*. And few—until the advent, in the 1960s, of documentary drama, itself a form shaped by the example of Büchner's play—are so thoroughly suffused with the materials the author read as is this play. At least a sixth of *Danton's Death* consists of literal transfer from or close paraphrase of other texts; it is a critical commonplace, in fact, to refer to the montage technique that Büchner employed in mixing together his source materials within his text.

In view of the present argument, it seems particularly striking to find that the historical materials absorbed within *Danton's Death* themselves derive from quite distinct temporal and even ideological contexts. In the way that materials drawn from different historical moments are juxtaposed, the play resembles certain European cities in which buildings representing diverse architectural styles from many periods stand unselfconsciously next to one another. To illustrate this diversity of materials, I shall move gradually backward in time from the writing of the play. The most recent materials that Büchner employed are several statements on the Revolution from Heine's writings on French politics and art. They include, for example, an apostrophe to Camille Desmoulins and a distinction between the sensualism of the party of Voltaire and the spirituality of Rousseauists—a distinction that Heine employs to castigate Robespierre;[12] in Heine, more than in any other source, Büchner found a means of reconciling hedonism with radical politics.

By far the most extensive sources that Büchner grafted onto his play go back to the decade preceding the July revolution. These consist of three narrative histories, two of them French—a multi-volume version by Adolphe Thiers and a short rendering by his closely allied contemporary François-Auguste Mignet. The two histories represent a "liberal" view within the context of Restoration politics, and both came from authors who were to play a role in instituting the July monarchy.[13] Büchner, a fervent republican during his student years in the France of Louis-Philippe, could not have identified with their politics nor with the crude sensationalism of his third extended source, Karl Strahlheim's *Die Geschichte unserer Zeit*—yet these voices from the 1820s supplied him with most of the concrete historical details he needed, including long passages from Robespierre's speeches quoted in Strahlheim.[14] Certainly the "fatalistic" view of history in their narrative made its way into *Danton's Death* (as well as into the fatalism letter itself)—though Büchner would have been quite aware that the same Thiers who so richly fed his own account of the Revolution was, in his role as interior minister to Louis-Philippe, responsible for putting down a workers' uprising in Paris a month after the writing of the letter and several months before Büchner's own uprising in Hesse. (This was of course the same Thiers who, long after Büchner's death, outdid his earlier acts of repression by destroying the Paris Commune in 1871.)

But Büchner also went back to certain eyewitness accounts of the Revolution dating from the very period about which Büchner was writing. These include, among others, the memoirs of Joachim Vilate, a mysterious figure close to the Dantonists, and Camille Desmoulins's correspondence as well as his periodical *Le vieux Cordelier*,[15] perhaps also a quote from Babeuf.[16] Although the echoes from these early documents are few in number—far less than from the narrative histories of the 1820s—they must have given Büchner the assurance that the language he was evoking was rooted in the very events he sought to render.

Yet the historical echoes that scholars have uncovered go back even further in time than the events Büchner depicted, for they include at least two writers of the Enlightenment, Diderot and Holbach. From Diderot (probably transmitted by means of Goethe's translation) Büchner drew a formulation of realist aesthetics voiced not only in the play (I, 11), but also in the discussion on art in *Lenz* amd in his own letters.[17] In Holbach Büchner found a voice for the materialist sentiments uttered in the play by Thomas Payne and St. Just.[18] It is as though Büchner felt the need to return to the intellectual origins of the Revolution as a means of displaying the play's realist credentials.

Yet the image I have just given of distinct temporal layers embedded within *Danton's Death* may well sound too systematic to fit one's notions of how Büchner used the texts associated with the Revolution within his play. After all, these quotations appear in no particular order, and it is sometimes unclear if Büchner is quoting from an early document or from a much later recounting based on this document. Perhaps I should put the question another way and ask not simply how the text of *Danton's Death* absorbed the texts of the Revolution, but how Büchner himself would have perceived the revolutionary past. Any answer one comes up with would show a jumble of perceptions, many of them irreconcilable with one another in any ordinary way—which may also help us account for that analogous jumble of diverse, seemingly irreconcilable voices we hear in the play.

At the time that *Danton's Death* was composed, Büchner stood forty-one years removed from the events he was depicting—exactly the time-span that separates us from the beginnings of the Cold War and, to cite a particular event in this war, the Berlin airlift of 1948. If one measures Büchner's distance in time from the beginning of the Revolution, an equivalent calculation would take us to the middle of World War II—for example, to the battle of Stalingrad. I mention these modern events only because they could not possibly exercise an effect on any 21-year-old today that the various stages of the French Revolution exercised on Büchner and, indeed, on many others of his generation.

For the French Revolution in the early nineteenth century still maintained the status of an inaugural event, a new birth analogous to the birth of Christ, though an event that also, in view of its later stages, also suggested that the newly created world was flawed, indeed that, perhaps soon after its birth, it was even coming to its end. No event of our own time has exercised as powerful an effect on the general populace—not even the first nuclear bomb, though the Holocaust has doubtless had a similar end-of-the-world effect on Jews, even on contemporary Jews of Büchner's age who did not personally experience it at the time it occurred. (One could well imagine a 21-year-old Jew today reading some books on the Holocaust and then writing a letter very much like Büchner's fatalism letter.)

Moreover, for a young person with Büchner's radical commitments, choosing the French Revolution as the subject of his first play was like choosing an event from one's own national history. For a more nationalist, conservative-minded writer of the early nineteenth century, an analogous act would have been the writing of a Hohenstaufen drama or, to cite an event that Büchner had once celebrated in a school-exercise (II, 7–16), a play about the martyrdom of four hundred Pforzheim soldiers during the Thirty Years War. Just as Shakespeare in his English histories had at once celebrated his nation's triumphs and faced up to its failures, so Büchner could display a significant segment of the Revolution in both its greatness and its horror at once. If the negative aspects of Büchner's portrayal have seemed more prominent than the positive ones in recent times, one must also remember that Shakespeare's histories leave far more powerful traces of failures than triumphs in their readers' memories.

The perceptions of the Revolution that Büchner had stored in his mind must themselves have constituted a jumble, for they came from sources every bit as diverse as the particular sources he echoed in the words of his play. We know, for example, that during his adolescent years he heard his father read from Karl Strahlheim's *Geschichte unserer Zeit* aloud to the family in the evening.[19] Strahlheim (actually a pseudonym for Johann Konrad Friederich) had served in Napoleon's army, just as Büchner's father himself had. As history, his colorfully written and lengthy work, which appeared serially during the 1820s, was directed to a popular audience and would likely have stimulated the imagination of the young Büchner however much the latter may later have disagreed with Strahlheim's often sensationalized treatment of particular events during the Terror.

But Büchner had also absorbed the standard German nationalistic texts of his time. His school essay on the massacre of the Pforzheim troops borrows as liberally from Fichte's *Reden an die deutsche Nation* as *Danton's Death* borrows from its multiple sources.[20] Yet although this text, composed when he was sixteen, celebrates a heroic German event, it also briefly celebrates an analogous event from the French Revolution, namely the refusal of a shipload of French sailors to surrender during Dumouriez's invasion of the Low Countries in 1793 (II, 8–9).

As a result of his participation, during his student years in Strasbourg, in the "Societé des Droit de l'homme et du citoyen," Büchner must have felt that the Revolution could once again renew itself after the long interregnum. Everything that had passed before—the Robespierre dictatorship, the Directory, the Napoleonic regime, the Restoration, the July monarchy—could be swept aside as the Revolution assumed its new course, this time with an emphasis on the economic equality that had eluded its original leaders. Yet the repressive forces that had aborted the uprising he himself had led—forces that resulted in his own arrest and in his writing his play while hiding from the police—must have caused him to reassess his hopes just as the hopes of his play's characters had been shattered as the Revolution moved through its various stages.

The movement from hope to disillusionment was accompanied by another type of movement—this one the shifts in perception that Büchner must have experienced as he moved back and forth between two quite distinct political cultures. The first of these was his native Hesse, a backwater still characterized by the repressions characteristic of Restoration Europe. The second was Strasbourg, site of his university studies and of secret groups that could endow ideas drawn from the French Revolution with a new life. As Büchner moved between Hesse and Strasbourg from 1831 to 1834, he must have felt a temporal dislocation resulting from the ways that each of these cultures viewed the world and postulated the possibilities of change. Indeed, his own attempt to establish a secret society on the French model in Gießen and then to lead a local revolt, together with the catastrophic failure of this attempt immediately preceding the composition of his play, can perhaps help explain the dramatic juxtaposition of divergent voices that have proved so difficult for many of his commentators to reconcile.

The profusion of earlier texts and personal perceptions that nourished *Danton's Death* is matched in variety by a profusion of later texts and interpretations that Büchner's play itself helped to generate. Just as few works of the past two centuries have been fed by earlier texts as thoroughly as this play, few have experienced as wide-ranging and sustained a reception as *Danton's Death*. Its impact upon a long succession of literary movements from the Naturalists through the followers of Brecht has become a commonplace of literary history. The play's various interpretations on the stage over the years themselves could help sketch out a history of the German theater since the beginning of this century. An extensive body of commentary, not only on *Danton's Death* but on Büchner's reception in general, developed well before the study of reception became fashionable within literary study two decades ago.[21]

My concern here is not to rehearse once more the well-known facts about the play's impact, but to stress its ability to speak out on revolution—at once the French and later revolutions—in often unexpected ways over a wide time-span. Let me cite four occasions on which *Danton's Death* has been put to political use. The first is a review of Büchner's *Nachgelassene Schriften* (Posthumous Works) that was written in 1851 by Büchner's close friend Wilhelm Schulz but that remained little noticed by the scholarly community until its republication in 1985. Although Schulz did not meet Büchner until after the completion of *Danton's Death*, he and his wife Caroline were his closest contacts during the writer's period in Zurich; indeed, our close knowledge of Büchner's final days comes from Caroline Schulz's well-known chronicle of his illness.

Wilhelm Schulz's review of his friend's writings was intended above all as a political statement to encourage a renewal of revolutionary hope after the disillusionments of 1848. "May [Büchner's writings] soon be in everybody's hands—to incite wrath in aristocrats and pleasure in democrats!" he writes at the end, leaving no doubt about the firmness of Büchner's revolutionary sentiments.[22] Schulz quotes several passages from *Danton's Death*, among them a speech by the Third Citizen (in I, 15) from which Schulz italicizes the final words of the line "wir hängen sechzig Jahre lang am Strick und zappeln; aber wir werden uns *losschneiden* [we've been hanging on the rope for sixty years and wriggling, but we shall *cut ourselves loose*]" to transfer the revolutionary advocacy of an ordinary citizen to an advocacy that Schulz seeks to hear voiced by the oppressed soldiers of his own time (76).

Drawing upon his personal knowledge of the writer, Schulz quotes Büchner as complaining of the "damnable good nature" of those who worry about sparing individuals when the fate and the hopes of whole peoples and later generations are at stake (78). Schulz even cites the fatalism letter—the very document that was to be used a century later by conservative-minded scholars to demonstrate the apolitical nature of *Danton's Death*—to show that Büchner's despair at the fate of the individual during the Revolution ("the individual merely foam on the waves") must be separated from his far more positive hope for the masses (78). But Schulz does not intend this essay simply for political purposes, in fact does not separate this endeavor from his attempt to enhance his friend's literary reputation. At the start of his essay he defines the qualities peculiar to Büchner's writing, and among these he speaks of something close to what I have earlier called his multi-voicedness: Büchner is notable, according to Schulz, for allowing "each mouth and each thing [to speak] its *own* language" (57—emphasis Schulz's).

My second example of the political efficacy of *Danton's Death* is set a full generation later in a quite distant place. In 1886, before the play had made a major impact on German writers, it was published in its original language both in serialized and book form in the United States under the auspices of German Socialists. This was the year of the Haymarket riots in Chicago and a time that revolutionary hopes were being kindled among American workers, and the play was intended by its German-American advocates to serve a distinctly revolutionary purpose. An article in the journal *Socialist* viewed the play as history rather than literature, in fact calling it "the best history of the first French Revolution."[23] Although this first revolution, according to the article, had failed, the "coming revolution" (256) should profit from its mistakes, many of which would surely become evident to the prospective readers of *Danton's Death*. A central difference between these two revolutions, the article went on, lay in the fact that the new revolution would be able to count on a better educated working class than the first, which had been cursed by "so degenerate a mob . . . over which Danton and his group established their leadership" (256). The lessons that workers in America would gain from a reading of Büchner's play presumably would help steer the coming revolution into a more successful course than its failed predecessor.

Unlike these two nineteenth-century examples of the play's generative potential, the two modern examples try for something less than a renewal of revolution. The first of these is a student production of *Danton's Death* that took place at the University of California, Berkeley, early in 1971. This was, in fact, the only production of the play I have actually been able to attend. And yet the play, once I saw it, was scarcely recognizable to me. The director, William I. Oliver, had edited the text considerably and had added a goodly amount of dialogue on his own. A number of new characters were included in the list of *dramatis personae*, including the executioner Samson, who in Büchner's text is simply mentioned by name. The more introspective speeches in the play, if they appeared at all, were nearly drowned out by the hubbub of the crowd.

After nearly two decades, the chief impression I retain of this production is the chaos of crowds busily and loudly moving about the stage, often threatening, sometimes also committing violence. Although the play kept its original setting, the chief referent to which the action pointed was the chaotic and sometimes violent political atmosphere of the Berkeley campus during the preceding six years—the arrests during the Free Speech Movement of 1964, the demonstrations against the attempted closing of People's Park, frequent tear gas attacks by the police on Telegraph Avenue. Beyond these, one remained aware of the Vietnam War that had been raging for so long that many members of the audience were probably having difficulty maintaining their own rage against it. The production thus became an expression of revolutionary exhaustion in which the meaningless movements of the crowd onstage somehow could be connected with the audience's experience of a political movement that was still persisting yet had lost much of its meaning. Indeed, as one reads accounts of famous past productions of *Danton's Death*—for example, the crowd-centered Max Reinhardt interpretations of 1916 and 1929, each with an emphasis appropriate to its time, or the "depoliticized" Gustav Gründgens version of 1939 that cautiously minimized the crowd's role[24]—one recognizes how readily this play absorbs and transmits the political tensions prevailing at a given moment.

My final example of the play's continuing generative power is Rudi Dutschke's posthumously published essay devoted jointly to Büchner and to his friend, the writer Peter-Paul Zahl, who was still in prison on terrorist charges at the time Dutschke composed this, his final piece of writing, in 1979.[25] Dutschke's obvious purpose in linking Büchner and Zahl was to help free his friend (77–78). From my own point of view, the central interest in this essay lies in Dutschke's particular interpretation of the play. Dutschke stresses the citizens' various complaints about the oppressiveness of work and connects these with the hedonistic sentiments voiced by Danton—a complex of attitudes with which this erstwhile disciple of Herbert Marcuse clearly identifies (50–52). By a strange irony of history the unlikely combination of sensualism and radicalism by which Heine had left his mark on *Danton's Death* now repeats itself in the influence of the author of *Eros and Civilization* on the most celebrated German student radical of the 1960s.

In the comments that he inscribed in his copy of *Danton's Death*, Dutschke wrote the name *Büchner* next to some of Danton's more world-weary pronouncements (113–14). Not only does he identify the play's hero with its author, but Dutschke, near death at this point from wounds inflicted in an assassination attempt on him years before, links himself to both; indeed, it is known that he spoke constantly of Büchner (whom he saw as a fellow persecuted student activist) during his final months and took a particular interest in the circumstances surrounding Büchner's death (133–34), circumstances that themselves had shaped the play *Büchners Tod* by Dutschke's Chilean friend Gaston Salvatore.[26] To complete the story, one might add that Peter-Paul Zahl, reading Dutschke's essay after his death, complained of "a certain lack of radicality" (82).

I have tried thus far to stress the difficulties we encounter when we make too strict a demarcation between a text such as *Danton's Death* and what literary study has conventionally called its context. From an institutional point of view, it ordinarily seems normal and desirable to treat a literary text as an artifact about whose intent and significance the scholarly community (if not necessarily the ordinary reader or the director who prepares it for the stage) can seek to achieve a measure of agreement. Although everybody in the community knows, at some level of consciousness, that this aim is never actually achieved, the very existence of this common aim serves as a stabilizing force to bind the community together at any given time.

The status of a literary text is not altogether different from that of a historical event such as the French Revolution. Literary scholars sometimes entertain the illusion that historians have the advantage of dealing with some "solid" reality different in kind from the unstable verbal fictions that make up the texts on which they work. Certainly Büchner, to judge from those passages in his letters that express his desire to keep his play true to the history of the Revolution (II, 435, 438, 443–44), assumed a stability inherent in the events of the past even if the individual—as the fatalism letter makes clear—often has to struggle to make sense of these events. When Büchner tells us, for instance, that the writer's task is to render "die Geschichte, wie sie sich wirklich begeben [history as it really happened]," we recognize him as a contemporary of Ranke, and when he speaks of the dramatic poet as "nichts, als ein Geschichtschreiber [nothing more than a writer of history]" (II, 443), our own historical sense quickly identifies him with an up-and-coming literary realism. From our present-day vantage-point, what separates *Danton's Death* from other historical narratives of the Revolution is its refusal, perhaps even its inability, to impose a coherence (despite the efforts of the play's interpreters) on events that historians (and even most dramatists) have traditionally felt the need to treat from a single and easily recountable point of view.

If, in Büchner's time, both literature and history gravitated toward what once seemed a stable model of historical reality, in our own time the model for both endeavors has assumed a shape that can perhaps best be described as "textual." Thus, some of the most interesting work that historians have been doing on the Revolution in recent years approaches these much-written-about events in ways similar to those that we use to treat a text such as *Danton's Death*. I do not here refer to the long-standing interpretive conflicts that have marked the historiography of the Revolution since its beginnings. The political battle I cited earlier between Viëtor and Lukács over *Danton's Death* can be matched by a multitude of conflicting views that have struggled against one another for two centuries—between Edmund Burke and Thomas Paine in the first years of the Revolution, between Tocqueville and Michelet in the mid-nineteenth century, between François Furet and the Marxist school in our own day.

I refer rather to the attempts of some recent historians to analyze what a literary scholar would call the textuality of the Revolution. Note, for instance, the following sentence in Furet's critique of the historiography of the Revolution: "So the Revolution was not so much an action as a language, and it was in relation to this language, the locus of the consensus, that the ideological machine established differences among men."[27] This sentence is not simply a polemic against Marxist historians, though it is clearly that as well: it is also an attempt to call attention to the formal attributes that Furet saw giving shape to revolutionary actions. When, in another spot, he declares, "There were no revolutionary circumstances; there was a Revolution that fed on circumstances" (62), he suggests the primacy of plotting much as a literary critic might demonstrate the formative power of plot over character or individual events in a fictional text.

Once we stress the textuality of history, the historian's emphasis and method shift from matters such as causes and effects to explorations of the language, symbols and narrative structures that, to most earlier historians, would have seemed irrelevant to the job of retelling the narratives that long constituted the historian's chief business. For example, in her study of the various festivals that were staged during the Revolution Mona Ozouf, like an anthropologist observing tribal rites or a critic showing how a group of symbols organizes and articulates a poem, demonstrates the centrality of these festivals—traditionally treated peripherally to events such as wars, assassinations, and executions—to an understanding of how the Revolution conceived of and presented itself.[28] In studying the rhetoric and symbolism of the Revolution another recent historian, Lynn Hunt, applies Northrop Frye's definitions of comedy, romance, and tragedy to analyze the generic plots enacted during diverse stages of the Revolution.[29] A literary scholar, Ann Rigney, has recently traced a single episode, the flight to Varennes, through ten historical narratives from Mignet and Thiers to the early twentieth century: she notes, for example, the repetition, with significant variations, of certain *topoi* (for example, the Queen's near-meeting with Lafayette as she left the palace) from text to text, or the fact that what one would think to be an "original" historical source, the *procès-verbal* of the Varennes municipal council, had itself apparently been rewritten for ideological reasons in the version available to historians.[30]

A "literary" reading of the Revolution is by no means unique to our own time: everybody remembers how Marx himself, in "The Eighteenth Brumaire," describes the heroes of the Revolution "performing in Roman costume with Roman phrases" and the "heroes" of 1848 "parodying" their predecessors.[31] Historians, not the least of them Georg Büchner himself in *Danton's Death*, have long emphasized the selfconsciousness with which the figures of the Revolution exploited the parallels they saw between their world and ancient Rome.[32] The prevalence of classical analogy in the speeches and memoirs that have come down to us from the Revolution points to a selfconscious theatricality that breaks down our ordinary notions of the barriers separating the disciplines of history and literary study.

A similar selfconsciousness is itself foregrounded within Büchner's play, not simply by the persistent classical analogies, but also by the characters'—particularly the Dantonists'—emphasis on the role-playing in which all around them are engaged, as for example in the discussions, during the last prison scene, on precisely what poses to put on in the face of death (I, 70–71). Moreover, when I suggested earlier that *Danton's Death* reenacts scenes typical of earlier historical drama, I might just as well have added that these type-scenes—for example, confrontation scenes between political opponents, street squabbles among the common people, speeches of defiance against one's judges—can be found embedded in the documents of the Revolution, doubtless indeed in the behavior patterns of the persons who actually enacted the events of the time. Once we recognize the theatrical element in historical events themselves, we also recognize that literature was (if I may borrow a cliché ever-present in contemporary critical discourse) always already present in the history that literature purports to portray.

NOTES

This paper has also appeared in my recent book, *The History in Literature: On Value, Genre, Institutions* (New York: Columbia University Press, 1990) 109–29, 232–34.

1. Georg Büchner, *Sämtliche Werke und Briefe*, ed. Werner R. Lehmann (Munich: Carl Hanser Verlag), 2 (1972): 425–26. Subsequent quotations from this edition will be cited within the text. Citations from the first volume are from the Wissenschaftliche Buchgesellschaft edition of 1967. Translations here and elsewhere are my own.

2. Viëtor, "Die Tragödie des heldischen Pessimismus: Ueber Büchners *Dantons Tod*," *Deutsche Vierteljahrsschrift für Literaturwissenschaft und Geistesgeschichte* 12 (1934): 182. Subsequent references will be cited within the text.

3. Mühlher, *Dichtung der Krise: Mythos und Psychologie in der Dichtung des 19. und 20. Jahrhunderts* (Vienna: Herold, 1951) 97–145. Subsequent references will be cited within the text.

4. Lindenberger, *Georg Büchner* (Carbondale: Southern Illinois University Press, 1964) 51–53.

5. Lukács, "Der faschistisch verfälschte und der wirkliche Georg Büchner," in *Deutsche Realisten des 19. Jahrhunderts* (Berlin: Aufbau-Verlag, 1952) 79–80.

6. Mayer, "Büchner und Weidig—Frühkommunismus und revolutionäre Demokratie: Zur Textverteilung des 'Hessischen Landboten,' " *Georg Büchner I/II*, ed. Heinz Ludwig Arnold (Munich: text + kritik, 1979) 86–91. Subsequent references will be cited within the text. On the relation of the fatalism letter to what in France was called the "école fataliste" of historians—Thierry, Guizot, Mignet and Thiers, the last two of whom were principal sources for *Danton's Death*—see Gerhard Jancke, *Georg Büchner: Genese und Aktualität seines Werkes* (Kronberg/Ts.: Scriptor Verlag, 1975) 130–35.

7. For a cautionary note on the applicability of Mayer's extensive findings, see Heinz Wetzel, "Ein Büchnerbild der siebziger Jahre: zu Thomas Michael Mayer: 'Büchner und Weidig—Frühkommunismus und revolutionäre Demokratie,' " *Georg Büchner III*, ed. Heinz Ludwig Arnold (Munich: text + kritik, 1981) 247–64. For a critique of Mayer's failure to account for the religious dimension of the play, see William H. Rey, *Georg Büchners 'Dantons Tod': Revolutionstragödie und Mysterienspiel* (Berne: Peter Lang, 1982) 24–26, 65–66.

8. Ronald Peacock, "A Note on Georg Büchner's Plays," *German Life and Letters* 10 (1956–1957): 189–97.

9. Carlyle, *The French Revolution: A History* (New York: Modern Library, n. d.) 490.

10. Heinrich von Treitschke, *Deutsche Geschichte im neunzehnten Jahrhundert* (Leipzig: S. Hirzel), 4 (1889): 434.

11. I do not mean to imply an ideological one-dimensionality to Carlyle's great history. As John D. Rosenberg has demonstrated in his distinguished recent study of *The French Revolution*, Carlyle's narrative contains within its ample borders a generous array of diverse voices that jostle against one another throughout the book. See above all Rosenberg's Bakhtin-influenced chapter entitled "Narrative Voices" in *Carlyle and the Burden of History* (Cambridge: Harvard University Press, 1985) 76–90. Yet Rosenberg also stresses the narrative control that Carlyle exercises throughout: "Although the narrator avoids the first person, the reader everywhere senses his controlling presence, the covert 'I' directing our attention to times and places far removed from the field of action" (59). In the role of epic poet that he has so consciously assumed, Carlyle, like Milton before him, can impose a unity upon the multiplicity he has unleashed—and in a way that a dramatist such as Büchner can refuse to do.

12. See, among other studies of the Büchner-Heine relationship, Henri Poschmann, "Heine und Büchner: Zwei Strategien revolutionär-demokratischer Literatur um 1835," in *Heinrich Heine und die Zeitgenossen: Geschichtliche und literarische Befunde* (Berlin: Aufbau-Verlag, 1979) 203–28; Mayer, "Büchner und Weidig," 69, 126–34; Mayer, "Georg Büchner: Eine kurze Chronik zu Leben und Werk," *Georg Büchner I/II* (note 6) 390–91; Burghard Dedner, "Legitimationen des Schreckens in Georg Büchners Revolutionsdrama," *Jahrbuch der deutschen Schillergesellschaft* 29 (1985): 345–53.

13. For a modern assessment of the role of Mignet and Thiers in the development of historiography in early nineteenth-century France, see Peter Stadler, *Geschichtschreibung und historisches Denken in Frankreich: 1789–1871* (Zurich: Verlag Berichthaus, 1958) 121–28. On the "liberal version" of the Revolution that they and other historians of the 1820s propagated, see Stanley Mellon, *The Political Uses of History: A Study of Historians in the French Restoration* (Stanford: Stanford University Press, 1958) 5–30. For an assessment of Mignet's and Thiers's views of the Revolution with Büchner's play particularly in mind, see Bernd Zöllner, *Büchners Drama 'Dantons Tod' und das Menschen- und Geschichtsbild in den Revolutionsgeschichten von Thiers und Mignet* (Dissertation, University of Kiel, 1972) 17–59. On the continuity of their "fatalism" through Büchner and Marx (including their notions of class conflict), see Bernard Görlich and Anke Lehr, "Materialis-

mus und Subjektivität in den Schriften Georg Büchners," *Georg Büchner III*, ed. Heinz Ludwig Arnold (note 7) 50–54.

14. For an easy-to-follow, line-by-line compilation of Büchner's borrowings from these three narrative sources, see Büchner, *La Mort de Danton*, ed. Richard Thieberger (Paris: Presses Universitaires de France, 1953) 35–52. Thieberger presents the source material in the order in which it appears in the play. For a line-by-line analysis of Mignet and Thiers that starts from these sources and then moves to the play, see Zöllner 60–91. On Büchner's ability to distance himself on occasion from Strahlheim in the very act of borrowing from him, see Thomas Michael Mayer, "Zur Revision der Quellen für *Dantons Tod* von Georg Büchner," *Studi germanici* 7 (1969): 316–17.

15. On Büchner's use of these sources from the early 1790s, see Adolf Beck, "Unbekannte französische Quellen für 'Dantons Tod' von Georg Büchner," *Jahrbuch des freien deutschen Hochstifts*, ed. Detlev Lüders (Tübingen: Max Niemeyer Verlag, 1963) 488–538. Thomas Michael Mayer argues that a number of sources that Beck and others before him had attributed to French documents of the 1790s could have been found by Büchner in German in a supplementary volume of Strahlheim's *Unsere Zeit*. See Mayer, "Zur Revision der Quellen," 297–317. Since the version in Strahlheim is a translation of these documents, one can still attribute them to the decade of the Revolution.

16. See Mayer, "Büchner und Weidig," 110–11.
17. See Mayer, "Büchner und Weidig," 76–82.
18. On Büchner's use of Holbach, see Dedner 367–74.
19. See the memoir by Büchner's brother Wilhelm in Georg Büchner, *Werke und Briefe*, ed. Fritz Bergemann (Wiesbaden: Insel, 1958) 567.
20. See Mayer, "Georg Büchner: Eine kurze Chronik," 363.
21. For a list of reception studies, some of them full-length monographs, up to the late 1970s, see Gerhard P. Knapp, "Kommentierte Bibliographie zu Georg Büchner," *Georg Büchner I/II* (note 6) 453–54. Several have appeared since this bibliography, including the long section entitled "Wirkungsgeschichte" in Jan-Christoph Hauschild, *Georg Büchner: Studien und neue Quellen zu Leben, Werk und Wirkung* (Königstein/Ts.: Athenäum, 1985) 161–288. For a list of stories and dramas about Büchner himself, see Knapp 454–55. For some early reviews of the play, followed by a study of how these reviews anticipate recent conflicts in the play's interpretation, see "Dokumente der Frührezeption von *Dantons Tod*," ed. Volker Bohn, and Bohn, " 'Bei diesem genialem Cynismus wird dem Leser zuletzt ganz krankhaft pestartig zu Muthe': Überlegungen zur Früh- und Spätrezeption von *Dantons Tod*," *Georg Büchner III* (note 7) 99–103, 104–30 respectively.

22. Walter Grab, *Georg Büchner und die Revolution von 1848: Der Büchner-Essay von Wilhelm Schulz aus dem Jahr 1851: Text und Kommentar* (Königstein/Ts.: Athenäum, 1985) 82. Subsequent references will be cited within the text.

23. Quoted by Christine Heiß in "Die Rezeption von *Dantons Tod* durch die deutschamerikanische Arbeiterbewegung im 19. Jahrhundert," *Georg Büchner Jahrbuch 4/1984*, ed. Thomas Michael Mayer (Frankfurt/Main: Europäische Verlagsanstalt, 1986) 256. Subsequent references will be cited within the text.

24. For lengthy accounts, including quotations from contemporary newspaper reviews, see Ingeborg Strudthoff, *Die Rezeption Georg Büchners durch das deutsche Theater* (Berlin: Colloquium Verlag, 1957) 52–56, 105–09, 125–31 respectively. For additional descriptions, including a list of the extensive cuts and changes that Reinhardt made to maintain his focus on the crowd, see Wolfram Viehweg, *Georg Büchners 'Dantons Tod' auf dem deutschen Theater* (Munich: Laokoon-Verlag, 1964) 56–68, 188–90, 213–16 respectively. Viehweg also analyzes the influence of the German revolution of 1918 on various productions of the play during the Weimar Republic (69–98).

25. See Dutschke, "Georg Büchner und Peter-Paul Zahl, oder: Widerstand im Übergang und mittendrin," *Georg Büchner Jahrbuch 4/1984*, ed. Thomas Michael Mayer (Frankfurt/Main: Europäische Verlagsanstalt, 1986) 10–75, and, in the same volume, Ernst-Ullrich Pinkert, "Langer Marsch, aufrechter Gang, Schmerzen verschiedener Art: *Editorischer Kommentar* zu Rudi Dutschke's Büchner-Zahl-Essay," 76–153. Subsequent references will be cited within the text.

26. Salvatore, *Büchners Tod* (Frankfurt/Main: Suhrkamp, 1972). The play stages what Salvatore imagines to be the dying Büchner's hallucinations, among them the persecutions suffered by his comrades who, unlike Büchner, had been imprisoned after the failed Hessian uprising.

27. Furet, *Interpreting the French Revolution*, trans. Elborg Forster (Cambridge: Cambridge University Press, 1981) 178. A subsequent reference will be cited within the text.

28. Ozouf, *Festivals and the French Revolution*, trans. Alan Sheridan (Cambridge: Harvard University Press, 1988). From the point of view of this paper, it seems significant that at one spot Ozouf employs a classic literary text partially about the Revolution, Wordsworth's *Prelude*, in the same way that she uses the archival materials on which her study is based, that is, as an eyewitness account of a festival, in this instance the Festival of the Federation (described in Book VI of the poem) that the English poet experienced while travelling across France in the summer of 1790 (56–57).

Thus, a work that has traditionally been treated as "literature" here serves as the raw material of "history."

29. Hunt, *Politics, Culture, and Class in the French Revolution* (Berkeley: University of California Press, 1984) 34–39. Hunt stresses the relation between conspiratorial and literary plots. For an earlier attempt to link dramatic plot and political plot, see my own book, *Historical Drama: The Relation of Literature and Reality* (Chicago: University of Chicago Press, 1975) 30–38. For another, earlier application by a historian of Frye's (as well as other literary theorists') categories to historical discourse, if not precisely to "history itself," see Hayden White, *Metahistory: The Historical Imagination in Nineteenth-Century Europe* (Baltimore: Johns Hopkins University Press, 1973).

30. Rigney, "Toward Varennes," *New Literary History* 18 (1986): 77–98.

31. Marx, "The Eighteenth Brumaire of Louis Bonaparte," in *Selected Writings*, ed. David McLellan (Oxford: Oxford University Press, 1977) 300, 301.

32. For a detailed study of Büchner's use of classical analogy in the play, see Helmut Koopmann, "*Dantons Tod* und die antike Welt: Zur Geschichtsphilosophie Georg Büchners," *Zeitschrift für deutsche Philologie* 84 (Sonderheft 1965): 22–41.

ARLENE A. TERAOKA

Race, Revolution, and Writing: Caribbean Texts by Anna Seghers

IN EACH STORY OF ANNA SEGHERS'S "Caribbean trilogy" the main characters are Europeans. Michael Nathan in *Die Hochzeit von Haiti* (The Wedding of Haiti, 1948) is a Jewish jeweler from Paris and an enthusiastic supporter of the French Revolution. Called upon by the black Haitian leader Toussaint L'Ouverture to assist him in his correspondence with the French Commissioners, Michael becomes inextricably involved in the Haitian slave revolt. When Toussaint dies years later in a French prison, Michael, nurtured by the same humanistic ideals, dies at the same time in London. In *Wiedereinführung der Sklaverei in Guadeloupe* (The Reintroduction of Slavery in Guadeloupe, 1948), the Frenchman Beauvais and the French-educated mulatto commander Berenger work to restore economic prosperity and to secure the new social order on Guadeloupe by reorganizing agricultural labor among the freed slaves. When slavery is reestablished by Napoleon, both men resist: Berenger blows up his fort and with it himself and his family; Beauvais dies in a local battle against French troops, the single white body in a pile of black corpses. Finally, in *Das Licht auf dem Galgen* (The Light on the Gallows, 1960), three French revolutionaries, Galloudec, Sasportas, and Debuisson, are sent by the Directory to free the slaves in Jamaica. When Napoleon comes to power, the former slaveowner Debuisson forsakes the revolutionary mission and betrays his two comrades. Sasportas dies on the gallows and Galloudec dies in a prison hospital, both loyal to the end to the ideals of the French Revolution and to the slave revolt.[1]

Such narratives practically interpret themselves. If one focuses on the major figures and events of Seghers's texts as I have just done and as most interpreters of these texts do, one is led simply to add another voice to the chorus. Solidarity between black and white, individual commitment and loyalty to revolutionary ideals, the survival of the revolution even in defeat, the universality of the fight for freedom, and the moral and political significance of any individual's death in that fight—these principles are what Seghers's Caribbean texts forthrightly and eloquently demonstrate.[2]

What interests me more, however, is what is left out—not those heroic European or Europeanized revolutionaries who die noble deaths fighting for freedom in the Caribbean, but the shadowy figures in the background who play no recordable role; not the main figures who are vehicles for some more or less explicitly stated political lesson, but those minor ones who are politically unengaged, unaware, and inarticulate. Seghers's revolutionaries and their fates are documented in traditional histories. These others, blacks known only as "Ann," "Suzanne," "Douglas," or "Angela," are Seghers's invention and, along with descriptions of the marketplace and the tropical weather, help to create the Caribbean setting of her stories.[3]

White Men, Black Women

Local color in Seghers's Caribbean texts is presented with vivid sensuality. There are torrential rain storms, the tropical sun, the wild and exotic vegetation of islands whose products—coffee, sugar, rum, cacao, pepper, precious wood—indulge the European nose and palate. The white observer is overwhelmed by the sights, sounds, and smells—the fruits and fish, the colors, the medley of human voices, the screeches and grunts of the live animals for sale—in the marketplace of Port Republicain (L 152–53). The seductive sensual power of the Caribbean world emerges clearly in *Das Licht auf dem Galgen* where Debuisson, drawn by the physical beauty of the land, loses sight of his mission of revolution (L 184).[4]

This pervasive sensuality is also specifically sexual, and it is here that it becomes most interesting. For in the fictional tropical world, black skin seems intimately tied to sexuality. Further, as this world is one seen and experienced by principal figures who are without exception male, it is the black woman who unambiguously exudes the promise of sex.

Two examples come to mind, both striking for their gratuitousness in the narratives. The housekeeper Angela is "no longer very young but also not old enough to break off her chain of lovers, which she strung together as need, whim, or chance would have it" (H 39). The mother of several children with different fathers, Angela has no political convictions of her own but rather adopts the opinions, however contradictory, held by her current lovers. Lucy, another black housekeeper, here seen through the eyes of the black servant Douglas, is "plump and oldish, but with a cheeky look in her eyes and still wild about dancing." Douglas is expected by his master to marry Lucy, but, as he sees it, "he hadn't the least desire to do this. What there was to enjoy in Lucy's skirts and kitchen had always been at his disposal" (L 231). Neither female figure plays a functional role in the revolutionary narratives. Rather, their stories exist as self-contained vignettes illustrating the presumably typical lives of slave women. Lucy and Angela are not unusually beautiful or unusually promiscuous; they are in fact not presented as unusual in any way.

The black woman is simply available for sex: like the climate and the indigenous flora of the islands, she appeals by nature to the senses.

More importantly, the inherent Caribbean sensuality becomes a crucial element of plot in each of the three stories in the sexual relationship between a white male revolutionary and a black female slave. The point of intersection between master narrative and local color is beautifully articulated in the following, first encounter between Michael Nathan and the black slave Margot, who is to become his lover and the mother of his child, in *Die Hochzeit von Haiti*. The weather sets the stage for sex. It is night, in the hot, rainy season, during a heavy downpour. Michael returns home and is intercepted at the door:

> He wanted to enter. Just then a small black woman pressed through under his arm into the doorway. Her young, healthy scent was so strong from the dampness that even Michael could not escape it, although he otherwise avoided temptations of this kind. This same small woman had brushed past him three times already in the past weeks with a slight signal of her hand that probably indicated readiness for love. . . . Now, as he became aware of the small breasts in the wet calico dress, it was clear to him that he had seen correctly. The girl was exceptionally beautiful. The furious jealousy of white women at the sight of her was understandable; understandable, the cruelty that they vented on their female slaves through unthinkable punishments (more imaginative than men) for small offenses. Michael cursed himself for a moment because he couldn't even look at these long legs and hips, this little belly in the slippery dress, these breasts that fit into two cupped hands, without thinking at the same time of the general condition of humankind. She grasped the edge of his sleeve between her thumb and forefinger with a shyness that could not be shyness about love, that much he already understood about this island. (H 28–29)

Michael, shedding hat and coat, follows Margot in the pouring rain through a maze of empty streets, alleys, and courtyards. Finally, just at the moment when he hopes that they have reached some kind of culmination ("one was at a kind of goal," H 31), Margot disappears and is replaced by a black man who steps out from the shadows. Michael is told that Toussaint L'Ouverture needs his help to draft a confidential letter of momentous import, and Margot and the sexual pleasure she promises are immediately, completely, forgotten: "[Michael] felt the pleasure of intellectual adventure, which had a vast expanse and was more enticing than that young thing, whom he had already stopped thinking about" (H 32).

The passage is remarkable in a number of respects. The young Michael Nathan, who usually resists temptations of the flesh and who is, we have learned early in the story, "ugly" and "pensive" (H 11), succumbs instantly to the power of the small, almost childlike black woman, following her with abandon into the night. The sight and smell of Margot's body, enhanced by the rain which plasters her dress to her skin, seem to exude sex, just as her every gesture offers to the man an obvious signal of her "readiness for love." But Michael is unable to look at Margot's body without being led to think of the unjust treatment that blacks suffer from their white masters. The sex of the black woman, in other words, is the vehicle for considerations of a very different sort; it demands the attention of the man only to draw it elsewhere. This is then reinforced at the end of the chase where, at "a kind of goal," Michael arrives not at the place of sexual intercourse with Margot but at the abrupt encounter with a messenger of the slave revolt.

We learn later that it was Margot's task to deliver Michael to Toussaint's messenger. But Michael, who is already predisposed to the black cause and who finds the "intellectual adventure" of the revolt intrinsically much more attractive than the adventures of the flesh, did not need to be—literally—seduced to follow. The sex as such, therefore, is gratuitous. Or rather, in a fascinating and fundamental way, sex and revolution are so intimately connected that one functions as an extension of the other. Michael is drawn to the black woman as to the revolution and follows one as the other; it is telling that he is not attracted to just any woman, or to white women, but specifically and powerfully to Margot. Thus the seeming interchangeability, actually a strange identity, of the two goals: significantly, the meeting with the revolutionary leader Toussaint becomes Michael's anticipated "nocturnal rendezvous" (H 37).

In *Wiedereinführung der Sklaverei* there is the brief affair between the Frenchman Beauvais and the black Suzanne. In order to maintain his commitment to the abolition of slavery, the Frenchman finds that he must renounce his promises to his fiancée in France. When Suzanne nurses him during a self-induced illness, one which is meant to prevent him from sailing back to France and which thereby marks his irreversible choice to remain in Guadeloupe, his emotional focus turns from the white fiancée Claudine completely to the black Suzanne:

> All at once the memory left him. He strained to hold onto something blond and white; then it slipped into darkness as if into water, into a time that was no longer his. Suzanne remained, hard and shiny like the pit of the fruit that she peeled for him. The fruits of the land. Red, yellow, violet, and green, now and then with black pits. He loved the pink palms of her hands more than the blond and white vapor. (W 101-02)

Again there is a peculiar link between the revolution and the black woman, so that Beauvais's commitment to one is experienced simultaneously as passion for the other. Suzanne, one with the fruits of the Caribbean, is identified with the intense tropical colors of the island while Claudine fades into "something blond and white." The two women come to represent opposing aesthetic sensibilities as well as conflicting political commitments. Thus when Beauvais decides to remain on the side of the freed slaves in Guadeloupe, the black woman enters his dreams and phantasies to replace the particular erotics of the white.[5]

Even in *Das Licht auf dem Galgen*, written some twelve years after the first two Caribbean stories, the relationship between Sasportas and the slave girl Ann follows the familiar pattern. At a crucial point after Napoleon's takeover in France, an event that places the mission on Jamaica in serious jeopardy, Sasportas must decide whether to withdraw from the band of blacks who are organizing revolt or to keep his appointed secret meeting with his black liaison. Predictably, it is at this narrative juncture that the black slave Ann is introduced.

We have been told that women find Sasportas attractive (L 139–40) but also that he is generally unresponsive: "[Sasportas] was not interested in girls" (L 155; cf. L 143). Suddenly it seems predetermined that he and Ann will sleep together. We hurriedly learn her name, her physical qualities, and her life story (L 187–88); Ann and Sasportas have met before, but only now do we learn of the earlier encounter and their immediate, mutual attraction (L 191–92). The act of lovemaking occurs without suspense or hesitation: Sasportas lifts up the mosquito net surrounding his bed, Ann climbs in next to him (L 192). What is a matter of suspense, however, namely Sasportas's decision to suspend the mission or to continue with the slave revolt, is silently resolved in the hours spent with Ann. We learn nothing of what goes through Sasportas's mind, a narrative silence emphasized by the hyphen in the text that breaks off the account of the night in bed. Or does the sexual act itself connote Sasportas's answer to the revolution?

Once again the sexual bond occurs simultaneously with the bond to the revolution. Later Sasportas will rise from Ann's bed and climb out the window to keep his meeting with the black slaves, enlisting Ann's assistance in covering up his absence (L 193). Additionally, the woman becomes committed to the revolution as she commits herself to the man. Ann, previously fearful of being punished by her masters (L 192), is now suddenly unafraid as she aids Sasportas's escape. Indeed, this is only the first of many actions she performs for the sake of the slave revolt, at increasingly greater personal risk and with such increasing boldness that she becomes in the end "completely fearless" (L 241). The change in her character and actions is abrupt and irreversible and linked undeniably to her sexual encounter with the white revolutionary;[6] loyalty to the slave revolt is loyalty to her lover, just as for Sasportas the commitment to the black woman is simultaneously a commitment to continued revolution.

(R)evolution: From Black to White

What I have presented lies beneath the surface of the main action of the texts, with their undebatably clear political and ideological intentions. The relationships between white men and black women, in contrast to the main stories of revolution, appear sketchy, unfinished, confusing, and disturbing. The three instances of white-black relationships share the curious consistency that the white men, the revolutionaries, are dispassionate and sexually disinterested.[7] (One might be tempted in this regard to speculate on the hidden meaning of Michael Nathan's lower lip, which hangs characteristically "limp" [H 11] from his mouth!)[8] It is always the black woman who is attracted to the white man, who is at first oblivious to her signals of interest. What attracts the black women, and why are the men so annoyingly passive?

In all three texts the women gain their identity, which is always their place in the revolution, through their men. Margot brings Michael to Toussaint, Suzanne nurses Beauvais back to health, Ann helps Sasportas to escape and becomes a valuable messenger. Two of the three women are named only when the sexual relationship with the white man is about to be established: before that time Margot is only "a small black woman," while Ann is not even present. The very existence of the women in the narratives is determined by the need for their services in the revolution. Accordingly, when separated from the men, the women fade away as figures: Margot dies, and Suzanne and Ann are sold—that is all we are told; apparently that is all that we need to know. A further similarity is the explicitly childlike character of the three women. Margot's smallness and youth are continually emphasized; Suzanne is perceived as "something that suffered and was threatened and that needed more love than a human being was capable of giving" (W 102). Ann, "a very young, small, almost frail Negress," "a child" (L 187), is literally retarded in physical and mental development (L 190). All await a process of physical, intellectual, and political maturation to be initiated by the white male and his revolution.[9]

With the white men the situation is different. Already revolutionaries, they are drawn to the black women (and explicitly not to the white) as extensions of their political commitment. Thus when separated from their lovers the men do not become lost to the revolution. For them, in fact, the women are quite forgettable, and indeed this happens in just so many words: twice Michael Nathan is called to Toussaint, and both times he forgets Margot completely.[10] Beauvais forgets his white fiancée, so that he cannot even recall her in his dreams. Seghers's texts show that the women are seduced into embracing the politics of their lovers, while the men are committed to their politics through (one supposes) principles. Essentially asexual, the men can and do do without the women: the women lack political identity, while the white men are presumably already whole.

The specific whiteness of this view of things is revealed in *Wiedereinführung der Sklaverei* by the story of Paul Rohan, an exemplary black revolutionary who, like the white Beauvais and the mulatto Berenger, remains loyal to his ideals to the very end. Yet the men are not simply three of a kind. Beauvais and Berenger become increasingly distanced from their white bride and mulatto wife as they come to terms with their unqualified commitment to the principles of the revolution. As Beauvais puts it, in the choice between happiness with a woman and the problems of the slave population of a Caribbean island, the woman dissipates like vapor (W 92). For the black Paul Rohan, in contrast, there is no choice between the principle of freedom and the woman he loves.

During his last years in slavery Rohan had not been able to marry his lover, who was sold away to another farm. Subsequently, freedom for Rohan does not entail forgetting one's wife or bride in times of revolutionary crisis but exactly the opposite—freedom means being with the woman one loves: "Freedom for generations to come—that had fused together for him with the girl whom the administrator of the Rohan estate had sold to the Noailles estate" (W 77). While the white Beauvais must learn to sacrifice his own "earthly happiness" (W 92), the black Rohan, in becoming part of the revolution, learns to recognize the importance of his personal desires as a part of what is at stake: "It had taken him a long time to set himself apart as one who had within the common sorrow a particular sorrow, and a separate happiness, and a particular, separate love that concerned him alone" (W 81). For the whites revolution entails self-sacrifice; for the blacks it requires self-assertion. This makes a difference for their women as well: Claire, unlike the lovers of the white men who tend to disappear from view, dies fighting alongside her now-husband Rohan, even more vicious in battle than he (W 121).

What emerges in these various stories is a sense of difference between a white and a black dynamic of revolution. The difference is reinforced first by curious statements in the text regarding a characteristically black sense of time. When Michael Nathan is in Toussaint's camp we read that "he had been up here for days now already, maybe even weeks. It had become the time of the Negroes, the boundless, weightless time of drifting sand" (H 55).[11] A black experience of time as a kind of timelessness, such that one does not experience its duration measured by days, weeks, or months, is articulated also in *Das Licht auf dem Galgen*: Sasportas, once he has broken with Debuisson and committed himself without reservation to the black revolt, "had almost as little understanding for the meaning of time, its measure, its passing, as did his beloved" (L 206). And towards the end of the story Sasportas finally loses all sense of time whatsoever: "One could see that Jean didn't know how much time had passed in the meantime. One could see that he had incessantly waited, listened, hoped for something. . . . Was it days, was it years ago?" (L 220).[12]

Limitless and undefined, the black world exists in silent contrast to the primary world of the whites with its historical clarity and chronology.[13] Not surprisingly, images of darkness and light work further to strengthen the difference. Beauvais's memory of his white bride, once he decides to join his fate to that of the blacks on Guadeloupe, disappears not only into black time, "a time that was no longer his," but into "darkness" as well (W 101). There is also the obvious "light on the gallows" that serves as a beacon for future (European) revolutionaries and that symbolized for the author Seghers enlightenment, historical memory, and reason.[14] But as the concepts of light and darkness themselves suggest, black and white worlds, while contrasted, do not stand in absolute opposition. Rather, their relationship appears to be one of an ideologically laden continuum, a process by which blacks move on several levels from "blackness" to "whiteness"—from slave labor to European culture, from emotions to thoughts, and from illiteracy to literacy.

Crucial here is the depiction of the black leader Toussaint L'Ouverture, whom Seghers considered one of the most important historical figures in the time of the French Revolution.[15] In *Die Hochzeit von Haiti* Toussaint's rise from slavery to become the leader of the black revolution and the military governor of the island is presented rather shamelessly in terms of his becoming "white." Toussaint, having learned to read (which always means reading the works of white men), acquires an unqualified admiration for European culture:

> The white culture seemed to him a radiant, immense castle. A reflection of it had fallen upon his boyhood years, making life worthwhile for him. It shouldn't be despised because it had been thought up by the whites. In a better life all people would be allowed to take part in it. The same reflection would be allowed to fall upon all lives. (H 34)

Emancipation in Toussaint's view is thus the process of making white culture universal—not of preserving difference in equality but of instituting sameness.[16] Skin color therefore does not matter (H 34). Since Christ suffered for all men, the only real difference at stake, in Toussaint's view, is the one between good and bad Christians, between a sufficient or insufficient, complete or incomplete participation in the cultural value of whiteness (H 35).

In a number of ways Toussaint himself is the role model. He has learned from white books. His governor's palace is adorned with lamp shades, carpets, silk wall fabrics, and uniformed servants in the best French tradition (H 47). He earns the servant Angela's respect through his "courtly" demeanor towards her and his connoisseur's eye in choosing among the various delicacies she offers him (H 48). And he has developed a genuine aesthetic appreciation for the fine jewelry of the European aristocracy (H 49). The black slave Toussaint, in short, has grown to become a master of white culture.[17]

Much the same holds true for Paul Rohan who, like Toussaint, learns to read from a sympathetic clergyman: "He had finally overcome the most difficult obstacle in learning: to pull together into words the single letters that he long since knew" (W 90). Learning to read resembles learning to think, in that exceptional blacks who previously recognized only isolated fragments of their world, "single letters," slowly gain the ability to synthesize them into meaningful "words." Rohan is singled out in the narrative as one black who, through his relationship with the whites, has acquired revolutionary insight; as "the favorite of one of these whites" Rohan has learned to think politically, that is, as a white revolutionary, often falling into disagreement with other blacks who are less advanced in their understanding of events in Guadeloupe (W 96–97).[18]

In contrast, "black" blacks cannot read or even think clearly, as Debuisson's loyal servant Douglas demonstrates when he slowly comes to the realization that his master is a revolutionary on the side of the slave revolt:

> [Douglas] did not understand much of the talk. He understood nothing of being free and becoming free. But one thought was fermenting in him, he himself didn't even know where it came from: it swelled and swelled and tormented him, almost made his head burst. . . . Douglas sensed suddenly that the foreign young gentleman, Master Debson's friend, was suspicious, and if he was, then so was Master Debson. Douglas sensed this.
> He didn't astutely put together the details; it was all there together in this feeling he had. . . . (L 232)

A page earlier we are told that Douglas usually forgets what he does not have immediately before his eyes or what he is not immediately hearing (L 231). Now he strains to put together the fragments he remembers, isolated details of his interaction with Debuisson and Sasportas, in order to arrive at the difficult thought that is fermenting inside him. In what reads almost like a caricature, we see the inveterate slave trying to think! The process even gains tragic overtones, as the thought that Douglas formulates after so much effort leads him to betray the very men who are trying to liberate him.

The final consequence of such intellectual underdevelopment is graphically illustrated by the demise of an illiterate black in *Wiedereinführung der Sklaverei*. Learning of the French order to reinstate slavery, Jean Rohan returns to the jungle, a decision that results from his lack of political understanding: "[Jean Rohan] didn't have . . . the bold and wild mind that seldom shrinks back (but when it does, then in despair) when the realization of its unlimited imagination is made impossible in the limited world" (W 108). In the jungle Rohan in fact ceases to think at all—here the (European) narrator must step in to tell us what his thoughts would have been "had he still had thoughts at all in the hot, whistling darkness" (W 110; cf. W 111). Hunted down by a pack of dogs, he is finally shot from his hiding place in the branches of a tree; referred to in the text as "the dead man," then as the "prey" of the dogs, the dead Rohan, who has long since been deprived of his reason, is now stripped rhetorically of his humanity. The dogs must be torn away from the body, and the narrative concludes with images of the corpse being slowly devoured by jungle animals and insects:

> In their wake a migration of insects fell upon the remaining flesh; then came small creatures with teeth and beaks. Finally a large, bushy beast of prey came with its young one, calmly and heavily, frightening off the others, the mother hungry, the young one hungry. (W 111)

We are made to see that it is only the rare, "white" individual who possesses the reasoning power and the strength to recognize what is actually attainable at a given historical moment. Shortly before his arrest and deportation Toussaint's deep sadness is described, "such waves of melancholy, as if he had just measured once and for all the gap between the boundary of everything attainable on earth and the boundlessness of thought" (H 54). Michael Nathan expresses a more pessimistic (and according to the narrative, realistic) view of the situation than even Toussaint:

> Michael understood that these people could not see the situation in the same light as he himself did. He also understood that the gap between what is attainable on earth and the boundlessness of thought, which Toussaint had just brooded over, was a few eons shorter for these people than for himself. (H 54)

For Michael Nathan, the only real white in these excerpts, the distance between what one is capable of achieving in thought and what one is capable of achieving in reality is greatest—"eons" greater than for the blacks. Toussaint, the "whitest" of the blacks, understands the tragedy of this distance.[19] The literate Paul Rohan has some sense of it as well, as do, to a lesser extent, Toussaint's followers. But the illiterate and black Jean Rohan who lacks any understanding of the challenge of ideals is made to die a horrifying, brutal death in which he is reduced—fittingly—to mere flesh in the world of nature.

Writing Revolution

The embellishment of the revolutionary narrative with local color in Seghers's Caribbean stories reveals the encounter of two worlds, black and white, characterized according to familiar Eurocentric dichotomies. The white world represents the epitome of civilization, reason, and thought; the black world, in contrast, is a world of brutal nature, confused emotions, immediate sensations that do not add up. Whites are sexless men of ideals and principles; blacks are represented by oversexed women or by men with befuddled minds, all of whom act on emotion and instinct. The white world is an ordered history of struggle and progress; the timeless black world is one of endless waiting and senseless death.

The most fascinating and disturbing moments in Seghers's narratives occur when these worlds meet. This happens in two typical ways. The white revolutionary becomes sexually involved with a black slave woman; alternatively, blacks learn to read and to think, which means they read the works of white culture and come to think like white men. The Eurocentric and sexist attitudes underlying this conceptual framework are obvious: the blacks enter the world of the whites, which is presented as politically advanced and culturally superior; further, sex is the means of entry for the black women while reading and writing are reserved for the men.[20] It is only a small consolation that Seghers intends to demonstrate not any inferiority of the blacks in the Caribbean, but their committed struggle for emancipation: the black slaves, as Seghers would have it, overcome the color barrier both in their erotic/emotional and in their intellectual lives, to fight for the freedom that belongs to men and women everywhere.[21] The unfortunate paradox of Seghers's writing is that it reasserts the superiority of the white world, and the inferiority of the black, despite its own intentions.

Supreme as their ideals may be, a striking sense of emptiness and impotence marks the white revolutionaries. Except for Margot's daughter who dies of yellow fever, the men in question father no children with their black lovers, leaving nothing, no one, behind.[22] Failure characterizes also their activities as revolutionaries. Michael Nathan dies in London as Toussaint dies in his French prison in the Alps; Beauvais and Berenger both die in a symbolic attempt to resist the counterrevolutionary Napoleonic army; Sasportas dies on the gallows, his efforts to aid the slave revolt betrayed by Debuisson. The black Haitian republic is left in ashes and ruins, slavery is reestablished on Guadeloupe, and the revolt on Jamaica never occurs. Yet if the white revolutionaries leave no legacy in the way of actual heirs, they are remembered—this is Seghers's point, and her own example—through the stories, oral and written, of those who come after. For these men, (black) sex is replaced by (white) writing as a means of binding oneself and others to the revolution.

In the end writing emerges for the whites in the Caribbean narratives as the revolutionary act *par excellence*. It is the means by which the revolution first triumphs in *Die Hochzeit von Haiti*: Michael Nathan, as Toussaint's secretary, writes a letter that joins Toussaint's slave army to the Commissioners sent by the new revolutionary French government, an alliance that leads eventually to the abolition of slavery. In *Das Licht auf dem Galgen* Sasportas, Debuisson, and Galloudec coordinate their efforts to organize the slave revolt by means of written messages which Douglas delivers (but himself is unable to read). On a more important level, writing occurs in the third story of the cycle in the letter that Galloudec sends to Antoine, the French official who had written out the initial order to organize the Jamaican slaves. The letter, which is finally delivered to Antoine in hiding from Napoleon, provides the narrative frame of the story (which is all about passing messages) and thematizes directly the significance of writing. Antoine reflects:

> A letter is worth a lot. Even if it was intended for an office that no longer exists, for a person who no longer holds an office. Such a letter is a true testimonial. The young person [Sasportas] can be easily forgotten. As I had almost forgotten him. How many have already been forgotten! Monuments are built for lesser men. Not for him. Only this bit of paper remains. (L 131)[23]

In a strange way, the act of writing assures that one is remembered, regardless of which former official of which non-existent office ultimately reads the document. The "bit of paper" suffices, though its readership may be unknown or uncertain.[24] The act of writing is important in itself as an act of personal and revolutionary affirmation. Thus even with just one reader, Sasportas's death on the gallows is inscribed in memory as an inspiration to revolutionaries everywhere: "Thus Jean Sasportas had a legacy of sorts, faint and cautious after so many years. Your memory and mine—it is no salute, but it honors him, it sustains him, it preserves him" (L 245). Revolutionary passion is incited finally by seduction through the eyes and ears of an audience. The white world produces no children of the revolution but only its own readers. Through writing, and perhaps only through writing, the failure of the revolution is subsumed and overcome, and the deaths of the revolutionaries gain meaning again. Europe's revolutionaries are saved through words on a page; revolution survives, as text.

NOTES

Initial research for the present essay, taken from a larger work in progress on the discourse of the Third World in postwar German literature, was supported by an American Council of Learned Societies/Social Science Research Council Grant for East European Studies. Translations of Seghers's texts were provided by Karen Storz, University of Minnesota.

1. Anna Seghers, *Die Hochzeit von Haiti: Karibische Geschichten* (Darmstadt, Neuwied: Hermann Luchterhand, 1976). References are given to work and page numbers in this volume, with abbreviations "H" for *Die Hochzeit von Haiti*, "W" for *Wiedereinführung der Sklaverei in Guadeloupe*, and "L" for *Das Licht auf dem Galgen*. For an impassioned account of the history of revolt in the Caribbean see C.L.R. James, *The Black Jacobins: Toussaint L'Ouverture and the San Domingo Revolution*, 2nd ed. (New York: Vintage Books, 1963).

2. There are numerous examples of this kind of scholarship particularly, but not exclusively, from the GDR. See Kurt Batt, *Anna Seghers: Versuch über Entwicklung und Werke* (Frankfurt/Main: Röderberg, 1973) 217–23; Helga Herting, *Geschichte für die Gegenwart: Historische Belletristik in der Literatur der DDR* (Berlin: Dietz, 1979) 17–39; Heinz Neugebauer, *Anna Seghers: Leben und Werk* (Berlin: Das Europäische Buch, 1978) 117–26; Siegfried Streller, "Geschichte und Aktualität in Anna Seghers' Erzählung *Das Licht auf dem Galgen*," *Weimarer Beiträge* 8 (1962): 740–51; Siegfried Streller, "Von verborgener Größe," *Neue Deutsche Literatur* November 1980: 139–42; Siegfried Streller, "Zauber und Leid der Karibik: Lateinamerika im Werk von Anna Seghers," in *Wortweltbilder: Studien zur deutschen Literatur* (Berlin, Weimar: Aufbau, 1986) 187–97; and Frank Wagner, "Selbstbehauptung und ihr geschichtliches Maß: Aus Anlaß der Geschichten *Drei Frauen aus Haiti* von Anna Seghers," *Zeitschrift für Germanistik* 2 (1981): 37–47. Western critics too, to the extent that they have dealt with Seghers's Caribbean stories, discuss the same themes; see for example Manfred Behn-Liebherz, "Der Schriftsteller als Gedächtnis der Revolution: Die *Karibischen Geschichten*," *Text + Kritik* 38 (September 1982): 87–95, and W.F. Tulasiewicz, "Introduction," in Anna Seghers, *Die Hochzeit von Haiti*, ed. W.F. Tulasiewicz and K. Scheible (London: Macmillan; St. Martin's Press, 1970) 7–69. Bernhard Greiner ("Der Bann der Zeichen: Anna Seghers' Entwürfe der Identitätsfindung," *Jahrbuch zur Literatur in der DDR* 3 [1983]: 131–55) begins to question the interpretive clichés of Seghers scholarship: "Phrases like 'sticking with it,' 'coming alive,' 'finding one's identity under the sign of fidelity,' such attempts to transform things into literature are questionable. . . ." (153)

3. For other discussions of blacks in Seghers's texts see Reinhold Grimm, "Germans, Blacks, and Jews; or Is There a German Blackness of Its Own?" in *Blacks and German Culture*, ed. R. Grimm and Jost Hermand (Madison: University of Wisconsin Press, 1986) 150–84; Carolyn R. Hodges, "The Power of the Oppressed: The Evolution of the Black Character in Anna Seghers' Caribbean Fiction," *Studies in GDR Culture and Society 7*, ed. Margy Gerber et al. (Lanham, MD: University Press of America, 1987) 185–97; Maguèye Kassé, "Heinrich von Kleist—Anna Seghers: La Révolution française et le thème de la révolte dans les Antilles françaises," *Etudes Germano-africaines* 2 (1983): 57–71; and John Milfull, "Juden, Frauen, Mulatten, Neger: Probleme der Emanzipation in Anna Seghers' *Karibische Erzählungen*," in *Frauenliteratur: Autorinnen—Perspektiven—Konzepte*, ed. Manfred Jurgensen (Bern, Frankfurt/Main: Peter Lang, 1983) 45–55. Gertraud Gutzmann is the only scholar thus far to tackle head-on the uncomfortable problems of racism and Eurocentrism in Seghers, in "Eurozentristisches Welt- und Menschenbild in Anna Seghers' *Karibischen Geschichten*," in *Frauen—Literatur—Politik*, ed. Annegret Pelz et al., Literatur im historischen Prozeß, Neue Folge 21/22 (Hamburg: Argument, 1988) 189–204.

4. There is undeniably a clichéd quality to Seghers's representation of the Caribbean. Gutzmann points out that Seghers, by her own admission "much too tired to study my surroundings [in Santo Domingo]," began to learn about Haiti and Santo Domingo when finally in Mexico, through books (192–93). Seghers's reminiscences are given in her "[Ein Brief]," in *Aufsätze, Ansprachen, Essays 1954–1979*, Gesammelte Werke in Einzelausgaben, Vol. 14 (Berlin, Weimar: Aufbau, 1984) 252–58; see also the interview with Wilhelm Girnus, 432–43, here 441. Seghers lists Schoelcher's *Esclavage et Colonisation* as a source for her work ("[Ein Brief]," 256); Streller ("Geschichte und Aktualität," 746, n. 10) cites also R.C. Dallas, *Geschichte der Maronen-Neger auf Jamaika*, ed. T.F. Ehrmann (Weimar, 1805). Touristic and nostalgic clichés persist throughout Seghers's essays on various aspects of Latin American culture and history; see "Die gemalte Zeit: Mexikanische Fresken" (1947), "Brief nach Brasilien" (1962), and "Brief über ein Buch" (1969), in Seghers, *Aufsätze, Ansprachen, Essays 1927–1953*, Gesammelte Werke in Einzelausgaben, Vol. 13 (Berlin, Weimar: Aufbau, 1984) 214–20, and in *Aufsätze, Ansprachen, Essays 1954–1979*, 196–200, 341–44.

For information on Seghers's life and activities in Mexico and on its impact on her writing, see Kurt Batt, "Die Jahre in Mexiko," *Neue Deutsche Literatur* October 1973: 16–29; Batt reveals also his own adherence to the usual stereotypes. Marianne O. de Bopp points out that members of the German exile community in Latin America were oriented towards Europe and had little or nothing to do with Latin America or with the Latin American

German colony already in residence ("Die Exilsituation in Mexiko," in *Die deutsche Exilliteratur 1933–1945*, ed. Manfred Durzak [Stuttgart: Reclam, 1973] 175–82). One exception seems to have been Egon Erwin Kisch, "the discoverer of the host country" (Kießling), whom Heinrich Mann likened to Alexander von Humboldt; see Wolfgang Kießling, *Exil in Lateinamerika, Kunst und Literatur im antifaschistischen Exil 1933–1945*, Vol. 4 (Frankfurt/Main: Röderberg, 1981) 471–86. Kießling's is the best general work on the German exile community in Latin America; see also Alexander Abusch, "Landung und Kampf unter Mexikos Sonne," *Sinn und Form* 32 (1980): 547–72, and Kathleen J. LaBahn, *Anna Seghers' Exile Literature: The Mexican Years (1941–1947)*, American University Studies, Series 1, Vol. 37 (New York: Peter Lang, 1986), esp. Chapters 1 and 3.

5. Beauvais's decision to remain in the Caribbean presents an important revolutionary lesson:

> The choice was a cursed one between what one called happiness: a young, snow-white thing who was like pure glass with a cracking in every movement, even in the sound of her voice, who by chance was called Claudine! And between what had nothing in the least to do with happiness: an island in the Caribbean sea that by chance was called Guadeloupe, inhabited by less than ten thousand Negroes, who had won their freedom six years before with his assistance and who were supposed to be slaves again this year. The island could no more fade away than some star. Much more easily Claudine. That is probably the lot of all earthly happiness, to fade away like vapor. (W 91–92)

The revolutionary chooses the revolution above any private "earthly happiness"; personal happiness is fleeting, while the fight for freedom and equality is a universal imperative. R.K. Angress ("Kleist's Treatment of Imperialism: *Die Hermannsschlacht* and 'Die Verlobung in St. Domingo,'" *Monatshefte* 69 [1977]: 17–33) argues that in Kleist's anti-imperialist works the individual's claim to love is incompatible with a total commitment to social change—erotic love is the antithesis of political engagement. For the white revolutionaries in Seghers's Caribbean texts, the same holds true. Seghers, who drew from Kleist's "Verlobung" in her own *Die Hochzeit von Haiti* while criticizing Kleist for his limited understanding of the black revolution, is close to him at least in her presentation of the existential dilemma of the white revolutionary. See her remarks on Kleist in "[Ein Brief]," 255–56.

6. As one critic put it, although I quote here out of context, Ann is won over to the revolution in bed. See Horst Hölzel, "Für Tiefe und Breite ein Beispiel," *Neue Deutsche Literatur* November 1961: 124–28, here 127.

7. Cf. the sexual impotence of the revolutionary in Seghers's "Aufstand der Fischer von St. Barbara" (1927), in *"Aufstand der Fischer von St. Barbara" und andere Erzählungen* (Darmstadt, Neuwied: Hermann Luchterhand, 1981) 16–17, 27, 52, 61.

8. The same physical trait is shared by Michael's ugly sister Mali, who never has a boy friend and never marries, and who devotes her life to caring for her brother.

9. Cf. the discussion of female types in Seghers, in Irene Lorisika, *Frauendarstellungen bei Irmgard Keun und Anna Seghers* (Frankfurt/Main: Haag & Herchen, 1985) 93–98. The physical stature of the women serves to illustrate what appears to be the case in Seghers's texts for their race in general: blacks are not fully developed. In this way Seghers's narratives are heir to the widespread view of nineteenth-century European natural science ("ontogeny recapitulates phylogeny") that placed non-European, non-white peoples at a lower stage of human development. For a discussion see Stephen Jay Gould, "Measuring Bodies: Two Case Studies on the Apishness of Undesirables," in *The Mismeasure of Man* (New York, London: W.W. Norton, 1981) 113–45, esp. 113–19. Milfull explains the "virtues" of the black women (speechlessness, loyalty, self-sacrifice, etc.) in Seghers's texts as a model for "genuine" revolutionaries (53–55). This levels any problems raised by Seghers's depiction of women and blacks.

10. The narrative makes an explicit point of this: "When the memory of Margot left him in Toussaint's quarters, then it was only proper that she should vanish completely like sweet, sometimes stinging, generally painful dreams" (H 57). Michael's wife and child, in fact, have been dead for weeks.

11. Tulasiewicz takes this as evidence of the blacks' inability to seize opportunity, to prepare for the right moment (65).

12. See also the remarks about Bedford (L 173). The lack of sharp definition characterizes not only the sense of time but any sense of order in the black world. Michael Nathan's father sees in Haiti a "tangled, inexplicable, senselessly motley world" (H 11); for the blacks Christophe and Ismael, the world is "too confused" (W 113).

13. The image of a timeless black world is suggested as a positive alternative ideal to the European model of history in Heiner Müller, *Der Auftrag: Erinnerung an eine Revolution*, in *Herzstück* (Berlin: Rotbuch, 1983) 43–70. See my "*Der Auftrag* and *Die Maßnahme*: Models of Revolution in Heiner Müller and Bertolt Brecht," *The German Quarterly* 59 (1986): 65–84, esp. 77. Müller's text is a dramatic reworking of Seghers's *Das Licht auf dem Galgen*.

14. Christa Wolf points out the "im besten Sinn aufklärerische[n] Impuls" in Seghers's writing and thought ("Glauben an Irdisches," in C. Wolf, *Leben und Schreiben: Neue Sammlung* [Darmstadt, Neuwied: Hermann Luchterhand, 1980] 115–43, here 141). See also her comments on the importance of Lessing for Seghers (132). Gutzmann argues that precisely because of Seghers's orientation towards the ideals of the Enlightenment the author was unable to appreciate the unique qualities of a foreign culture: "The humane ideals of

freedom, equality, fraternity which she inscribes in her stories are rather more suited to leveling cultural and racial differences than to working them out and accentuating their importance" (190). Abdul R. JanMohamed and David Lloyd make a similar critique of universalist humanism in another context; see their introductions to two special issues on "The Nature and Context of Minority Discourse," *Cultural Critique* 6 (Spring 1987): 5-12, and *Cultural Critique* 7 (Fall 1987): 5-17.

15. See Seghers, "[Ein Brief]," 254. Seghers writes about Toussaint in "Große Unbekannte," in *Aufsätze, Ansprachen, Essays 1927-1953*, 221-57, here 241-57.

16. As Gutzmann writes, "in Seghers's portrayal equality of the races seems to mean more the raising of blacks to the level of the whites' culture" (195).

17. White history and white culture provide the standard for Seghers's view of Latin American history generally. In her essay honoring the "Große Unbekannte" (Great Unknowns) who fought for freedom in Latin America she writes: "The struggle for freedom, which brings out astonishing capabilities in ... humans the world over, ... has brought forth, here and there on an unknown island or in a jungle village on the Pacific, *a Thomas Müntzer or a Liebknecht or a Dimitroff*" (222, emphasis mine). And later in the same essay Seghers speaks of Toussaint as the only one who, on the basis of his intellectual and moral qualities, would have been capable of overcoming the gap between his people and those who had been free for thousands of years (255-56). Toussaint's greatness, in short, was his ability to catch up to the whites. This view echoes throughout *Die Hochzeit von Haiti*; see H 46, 56.

18. See Gutzmann on the whites assist the Blacks in articulating their revolutionary goals (199). Other examples of blacks educated successfully in white ways are the household manager of Count Evremont, who tells how she became "reasonable" (H 7-8), and especially Bedford, whom Galloudec teaches literally to think (L 173-74). Henry Louis Gates, Jr. discusses the constellation of reason, writing, and race in his "Editor's Introduction: Writing 'Race' and the Difference It Makes," *Critical Inquiry* 12.1 (1985): 1-20:

> After René Descartes, *reason* was privileged, or valorized, above all other human characteristics. Writing, especially after the printing press became so widespread, was taken to be the *visible* sign of reason. Blacks were "reasonable," and hence "men," if—and only if—they demonstrated mastery of "the arts and sciences," the eighteenth century's formula for writing. So, while the Enlightenment is characterized by its foundation on man's ability to reason, it simultaneously used the absence and presence of reason to delimit and circumscribe the very humanity of the cultures and people of color which Europeans had been "discovering" since the Renaissance. The urge toward the systematization of all human knowledge (by which we characterize the Enlighten-

ment) led directly to the relegation of black people to a lower place in the great chain of being. . . . (8)

19. The political and emotional affinity between Michael and Toussaint is underscored here by a sudden and unique physical similarity: Michael notices that Toussaint's chin hangs down like his own when he is deep in thought (H 53).

20. My reading of Seghers, like Gutzmann's, disputes the views of Reinhold Grimm, who sees an "utterly clear, sober, straightforward, and unequivocally progressive" depiction of blacks in Seghers's writing (158). Decisive for Grimm is "the simple fact that blacks, Jews, and mulattoes are depicted together, and that their joint portrayal is meant to bespeak and symbolize the unity of all the wretched of the earth, regardless of race or color" (160). Likewise, Kassé attributes to Seghers "a spirit that is not subject to any ethnocentrism or Eurocentrism" (57). Milfull defends Seghers's model for black emancipation as not "conventional Eurocentrism," but rather a strategy for avoiding "deformations" of the revolutionary mission (52); for Streller, Seghers's encounter with Latin American history "explodes Europe-centered thinking" ("Zauber und Leid der Karibik," 189).

21. Equally, Europeans should feel themselves in solidarity with the struggle for freedom in all parts of the world. See Seghers's remarks in "Aufgaben der Kunst" and "Abschied vom Heinrich-Heine-Klub," in *Aufsätze, Ansprachen, Essays 1927–1953*, 168–74 and 204–08, here 172–73 and 205. In Heiner Müller's treatment of the same material, revolutionaries are bound inescapably by their class and race, thus undercutting the purported universal validity of the French ideals; see the discussion in my "*Der Auftrag* and *Die Maßnahme*." A detailed analysis of Müller's adaptation of Seghers's *Das Licht auf dem Galgen* in his *Der Auftrag* remains wanting. Milfull dismisses Müller's text as a "verzweifeltes Postskriptum" to Seghers (52).

22. Michael Nathan, returning to Europe after Toussaint's capture, marries in London and becomes the father of two sons (H 59–60). In a conventional and non-revolutionary life he is clearly capable of producing progeny, yet there the matter is of no consequence to him (H 59).

23. The written document is meant to save those "who would otherwise have disappeared without a trace in deep waters or in a jungle; their names are not in any book nor on any monument; perhaps they didn't even have real names" (L 245). Writing in books or on monuments is the mark of white history.

24. Heiner Müller again provides a stark contrast. In *Der Auftrag* the betrayal of the revolution is depicted as the symbolic shredding of the written "mission." For Müller the sexual and political bond between white revolutionary and black slave does not find its transposition into a mission of

solidarity and revolt for future generations. Rather, the revolutionary mission is abandoned, while the white revolutionary loses consciousness and all political conscience in the experience of physical ecstasy. Seghers, for whom the task of the author is to function as the "memory of the revolution" (the formulation is Kurt Batt's, in his *Anna Seghers*, 223), writes to preserve the memory of something still very much alive: the revolution lives on, in and through the activity of its writers and readers. For Müller there is only the fading memory of something past. His text ends not with a powerful act of remembering, but with Debuisson, the white European, forgetting the storming of the Bastille prison.

EHRHARD BAHR

Models of the French Revolution and Paradigm Change in Contemporary German Drama: Peter Weiss and Heiner Müller

THERE ARE TWO MODELS OF THE FRENCH Revolution in German literature, constituting a tradition that later authors, writing on the same subject, cannot escape. One strand of presenting the Revolution is Georg Büchner's drama *Dantons Tod* of 1835, the other is Kleist's novella *Die Verlobung in St. Domingo* (The Engagement in Santo Domingo) of 1811. The confrontation between Danton and Robespierre, as dramatized by Büchner, has influenced the representation of the Revolution in German literature throughout the nineteenth and twentieth centuries (Robert Griepenkerl, Karl Bleibtreu, Richard von Kralik, Arthur Schnitzler).[1] Peter Weiss's 1964 drama *Die Verfolgung und Ermordung Jean Paul Marats, dargestellt durch die Schauspielgruppe des Hospizes zu Charenton unter Anleitung des Herrn de Sade* (The Persecution and Assassination of Jean-Paul Marat, As Performed by the Inmates of the Asylum of Charenton under the Direction of the Marquis de Sade) is one of the most recent examples of this tradition. Weiss chose different characters for his drama, but his protagonists cannot escape the model of Büchner's confrontation. De Sade takes Danton's place and Marat that of Robespierre, but the basic confrontation remains the same. What motivated Weiss in bringing together Sade and Marat was, as the author explained, "the conflict between an individualism carried to extreme lengths and the idea of a political and social upheaval."[2] This brief statement could also serve as an analysis of the conflict in Büchner's drama. In writing his play, Weiss was clearly motivated by the insight that the French Revolution had been betrayed by Napoleon and that the political figures of the French Revolution had been misrepresented by the conservative historians of the nineteenth and twentieth century. Weiss stated that "scarcely any other personality of the French Revolution had been depicted in so revolting and bloodthirsty a light by bourgeois historians of the nineteenth century as Marat." As reason for these distortions, Weiss presented the argument that Marat's ideas "led in a direct line to Marxism" (*Marat/Sade* 142). But in spite of the author's declared sympathies for Marat, Weiss could not avoid the takeover of the emplotment of his drama by the dramatic character of the Marquis de Sade, assuming the Danton role.

Peter Weiss's *Marat/Sade* is the prime example of the externalization of the intellectual discourse on the French Revolution in Germany after 1945. The author considered his drama a play, reflecting the current political situation ("ein aktuell-politisches Gegenwartsstück"). This contemporary topicality emphasized the fact that there had never been a revolution in Germany. Weiss compared the development between 1789 and 1815, including Napoleon's betrayal of the French Revolution, with the experience of his own generation between 1918 and 1945.[3] Parallels are drawn in *Marat/Sade* between the restoration period under Napoleon and the Adenauer years of the post-war West German state (1949–1963). These parallels motivated Jürgen Habermas to characterize Weiss's *Marat/Sade* as exposing a nation-wide process of repression. Habermas's defence of the play in 1964 appears in hindsight an anticipation of the infamous "historians' controversy" (*Historikerstreit*) of 1986–88,[4] only at that time Habermas was accusing his contemporaries of denying historical continuity and the French Revolution as part of their unmastered past. Denouncing his contemporaries for their historical bias in holding the French Revolution liable for the crimes of the Nazis and for unmasking Robespierre as a "little Hitler," Habermas took critics to task who tried to praise or dismiss the play as "intellectually embellished circus entertainment." Such designations were designed, he claimed, to prevent people from thinking about their own national history.[5]

The other model, represented by Kleist's novella *Die Verlobung in St. Domingo*, deals with the revolution that spread to France's colonies in the Caribbean. In May, 1791, the Constituent Assembly had extended France's constitutional freedoms to the "free coloreds" in the Colonies, but withdrew them again under pressure from the white plantation owners. In August 1791, the black slaves, under the leadership of François-Dominique Toussaint L'Ouverture, revolted against the rule of the white plantation owners and established their own independent state institutions. After the abolition of slavery in 1794, Toussaint-L'Ouverture entered the service of the French Republic. As its general, he successfully defended Haiti against British and Spanish forces and declared the colony's independence in 1800. In 1801, he became Haiti's president for life, but expeditionary forces, sent by Napoleon, forced his surrender in 1802. Toussaint-L'Ouverture was deported to France and died in 1803 in the same fortress prison where Kleist was later incarcerated as an alleged spy in 1807.[6] The revolt of the black slaves against white rule on Haiti forms the background of Kleist's novella, which centers on the love between a young Swiss officer and a mulatto girl. Their love across the color barrier does not survive the reality of racial prejudice. Enraged over her apparent betrayal, the young officer kills his lover. Her last words are: "You should not have distrusted me!"[7] When he becomes aware of the fact that her betrayal was only a strategy to save him from murder by a gang of black slaves, he commits suicide.[8] Seizing upon the interrelationship of revolution, race, sexuality, and violence, Kleist's novella established a most powerful and modernist model for presenting the French Revolution within a colonial context by transferring the location of the revolutionary action from Paris (and Strasbourg) to Haiti. Furthermore, Kleist's novella is a prime example of the discourse of violence in German literature after the Reign of Terror in France. This discourse of violence was obviously most complex during the period from 1793 to 1815 when Europe was almost continuously at war, thrusting political images of liberty together with those of extermination and terror. Although the war between the races on Haiti had led to indiscriminate mass murder on both sides, Kleist's narrator scrupulously records the violence without taking sides or making a value judgment.[9] The impartiality of his narration appears almost more shocking than the violence it describes.

Anna Seghers, winner of the famous Kleist-Prize in 1928, followed Kleist's model in focusing on the interracial relationships in her "Caribbean trilogy" (*Die Hochzeit von Haiti* [The Haitian Marriage], 1948; *Wiedereinführung der Sklaverei in Guadeloupe* [The Reintroduction of Slavery in Guadeloupe], 1948; *Das Licht auf dem Galgen* [The Light on the Gallows], 1954).[10] The revolutionary thrust of the stories, however, is defeated, despite their best intentions, by the author's eurocentric attitude, as Arlene A. Teraoka has shown.[11] Anna Seghers believed that dead revolutionaries would find successors, but her revolutionaries are failures, leaving no legacy except their "writings" in the widest sense of the word. In *Das Licht auf dem Galgen*, it is a letter written by one of the agitators, sent by the revolutionary government to Jamaica to foment a revolt among the black slaves. The letter is a report about the failure of the mission. Nevertheless, *Das Licht auf dem Galgen* preserved enough of its revolutionary spark to inspire Heiner Müller to write a poem on a theme of Anna Seghers's story in 1958, entitled "Motiv bei A.S." (Theme of A.S.)[12] and twenty years later his play *Der Auftrag* (*The Task*, or "The Mission"). It is noteworthy that already the early poem establishes the relationship between Büchner and Seghers by evoking names from both of their works: Debuisson's name as well as those of Robespierre and Danton. Müller's *Der Auftrag* of 1979 is subject to both traditions, that of Büchner's *Dantons Tod* and that of the Kleist-Seghers novellas about the Caribbean revolution. But although his play uses scenes from Büchner and themes and characters from Seghers's *Das Licht auf dem Galgen*, Müller is not torn between the two traditions. He is able to combine them to achieve a paradigm change by relating the revolution to the self-liberation of the people in the Third World, thereby realizing the dreams of the black revolutionaries of the 1790s and providing a new model for the presentation of revolution in

German literature. As Teraoka has pointed out, "the play treats the failure of the *white* revolution, the revolution of the European man of reason and Enlightenment, of Danton and Robespierre."[13] Simultaneously with the decline of the European revolution, the play features the rise of a new type of revolution, that of the Third World, starting a new type of history.

Although Peter Weiss never acknowledged Büchner's *Dantons Tod* as a model, his "anxiety of influence" becomes evident when he declares the principle represented by Marat to be correct and superior to De Sade's.[14] While Büchner never really took sides in *Dantons Tod*, giving an impartial account of the revolutionary process that inevitably includes the principles represented by both Danton and Robespierre, Weiss developed a special sympathy for Marat because he perceived him as "one of those who were in the process of coining the concept of socialism" (*Marat/Sade* 143). This shift of sympathy counteracts the adopted model. In Büchner's drama, the two major characters are polar opposites of equal strength. Even though Danton is executed, Robespierre is aware of the fact that he faces a similar fate. Without referring to *Dantons Tod*, Weiss admitted that his *Marat/Sade* showed the same dialectic structure which placed the major figures Marat and de Sade in opposition to each other: "The more substance de Sade shows, the more powerful arguments Marat has to muster, in order to counterbalance de Sade's authority."[15]

There were three seminal productions of *Marat/Sade*, yet none of them dealt adequately with the problem of balance: the first, directed by Konrad Swinarski at the Schiller Theater in West Berlin in April 1964, the second by Peter Brook with the Royal Shakespeare Company at the Aldwych Theater in London a little later that year, and the third by Anselm Perten at Rostock in the GDR in 1965. While Swinarski's and Brook's productions were biased in favor of de Sade's point of view, the East German production favored Marat as the positive hero of the play.[16] In spring, 1965, Weiss identified with the latter interpretation, declaring that any production of his play in which Marat does not emerge as the moral victor will be mistaken.[17] Later, in September, 1965, Weiss declared his solidarity with the socialist world order and the liberation movements in the colonial states.[18] Yet the text of the play is in conflict with the declared authorial intention. Although Weiss assigned Marat's political philosophy a privileged position in his comments on the play, the text of the play denies Marat this position. Weiss's comments constitute a "willful revision" not only of his own play, but also of *Dantons Tod*.[19] But Weiss's reversal came too late to "correct" his own text (despite the numerous changes between the first and fifth version), not to speak of correcting Büchner's text.

The plot of *Marat/Sade* evolves from a play-within-a-play, taking place on three spatio-temporal levels: 1) the murder of Marat by Charlotte Corday in Paris in 1793 during the French Revolution; 2) the theatrical re-enactment of this historical event by the inmates of the insane asylum at Charenton under the direction of the Marquis de Sade in 1808 during the First French Empire under Napoleon; and 3) the "present-day" performance of this production between 1964 and now, addressing the modern audience with numerous illusions to the German *Wirtschaftswunder* and the capitalist welfare state after 1945. This three-level plot is based on some historical facts: de Sade was confined to the asylum at Charenton from 1801 to 1814, and during that time he directed a kind of amateur theater among the patients for therapeutic reasons. This enterprise was encouraged by the asylum director, Coulmier. In exclusive circles in Paris, it was considered a favorite entertainment to attend de Sade's productions at Charenton. A personal meeting between Marat and de Sade never took place nor has a Marat play by de Sade been identified, but de Sade delivered the eulogy at the Marat memorial in 1793.

At the center of the play is the ideological debate between de Sade and Marat, modelled after the confrontation between Danton and Robespierre in Büchner's drama. As Weiss explained in 1964, de Sade

> ... supports, on the one hand, the social change that Marat demands, yet, on the other hand, he sees the dangers of a socialism degenerating into a totalitarian state. He does not know how to bring these changes about; he is afraid that the ideal socialistic state as Marat imagines it is not possible. Like a modern representative of a third point of view, he is between the socialist and individualist camp.[20]

Marat figures as a precursor of Marxism, far ahead of his time. He is "the only real revolutionary."[21] The first version of *Marat/Sade* focused on the ambivalence between these two points of view: "on the one hand, extreme individualism and on the other the changing of society in this madhouse world." At that time, the insane asylum served as a valid metaphor for Weiss's perception of politics. His only alternative was to show his doubts: "I cannot do more. Because I do not believe in political forms of society—as they are today—I do not dare to propose new forms. . . . I represent the third viewpoint, which I do not like myself."[22] Therefore, in the first version of the play, de Sade arrives at the following conclusion in the epilogue:

> SADE: Es war unsre Absicht in den Dialogen
> Antithesen auszuproben
> und diese immer wieder gegeneinander zu stellen
> um die ständigen Zweifel zu erhellen
> Jedoch finde ich wie ichs auch dreh und wende
> in unserm Drama zu keinem Ende
> . . .
> So sehn Sie mich in der gegenwärtigen Lage
> immer noch vor einer offenen Frage. (*Marat/Sade* 133–34)
>
> [SADE: It was our intent to test antitheses
> in our dialogues
> and to place them into opposition to each other
> in order to enlighten our constant doubts
> Yet, whichever way I turn
> I cannot find a conclusion to our drama
> . . .
> Therefore you see me in the present situation
> still facing an open question].[23]

Meanwhile, Weiss had identified with Marxist socialism and liberation movements in the Third World. Therefore this conclusion, reflecting Weiss's point of view in 1964, was revised for the London and the Rostock productions. But despite numerous revisions, Marat's role remained a part in a play that was written and directed by de Sade. It was impossible to deny de Sade's authorship without changing the basic structure of the play.

As the first and the subsequent versions of *Marat/Sade* show, de Sade's authorship does not constitute a handicap for Marat. Beside him De Sade places the former priest Jacques Roux, "who surpassed Marat in his rabble-rousing," as Marat's *alter ego* (*Marat/Sade* 143). The point of view of the Revolution is well represented. Although de Sade expresses the opposite of Marat's arguments, he needs him as a sounding board for his ideas. Marat and de Sade function as representatives of external and internal revolution:

> SADE: Marat
> diese Gefängnisse des Innern
> sind schlimmer als die tiefsten Verliese
> und solange sie nicht geöffnet werden
> bleibt all euer Aufruhr

nur eine Gefängnisrevolte
die niedergeschlagen wird
von bestochenen Mitgefangenen. (*Marat/Sade* 123–24).

[*SADE*: Marat
these cells of the inner self
are worse than the deepest dungeons
and as long as they are not opened
all your revolution remains
only a prison mutiny
to be suppressed
by bribed fellow prisoners].

Both Marat and de Sade are opposed to the restoration under Coulmier/Napoleon, but this opposition does not negate their differences. While de Sade maintains that life is meaningless, expressing his disgust with the total indifference of nature, Marat goes to the opposite extreme:

MARAT: Gegen das Schweigen der Natur
stelle ich eine Tätigkeit
In der großen Gleichgültigkeit
erfinde ich einen Sinn
Anstatt reglos zuzusehn
greif ich ein
und ernenne gewisse Dinge für falsch
und arbeite daran sie zu verändern und zu verbessern.
(Marat/Sade 38–9)

[*MARAT*: Against nature's silence
I use action
In the vast indifference
I invent a meaning
Instead of watching unmoved
I intervene
and say that this or that is wrong
and I work to change and improve them].

Written by de Sade, this statement and other speeches accurately reflect Marat's position, whose words in *Marat/Sade* correspond in content to his writings. But in order to function within the play, as it was originally conceived, Marat's words need the opposition of de Sade. Otherwise, they would not have the revolutionizing effect on the inmates of the insane asylum demonstrated at the end of the play, when they have to be clubbed into submission. The opposition between de Sade and Marat affects neither the truth nor the effectiveness of their respective statements. It is a structure of "stable antinomies," which cannot be changed without changing the play as a whole.[24] A play that figured Marat as the moral victor would presuppose a rational world, and the madhouse of the asylum would become an inappropriate metaphor. The structure of *Marat/Sade* did not allow for an accommodation of Weiss's changed political viewpoint. Weiss must finally have realized this aporia. When he selected the protagonists for his later revolutionary plays—Friedrich Hölderlin and Leon Trotsky—he avoided a closed antinomic structure. But Weiss was never able to achieve a paradigm change in his dramatic work, even though his political views pointed in that direction. His plays *Gesang vom Lusitanischen Popanz* (Song of the Lusitanian Bogey) of 1967 and *Viet Nam-Diskurs* (Discourse on Vietnam) of 1968 did not go far enough to effect such a change.

Heiner Müller's *Der Auftrag* (*The Task*, or "The Mission"),[25] written and published in the East German journal *Sinn und Form* in 1979 and first produced in East Berlin in 1980, is a collage of dramatic scenes, burlesque theater, monologues, prose narratives, and documents. There is no clear division between the various segments of the text of the play nor are they numbered. Arlene A. Teraoka has identified twelve separate scenes or segments.[26] Among other models, Müller's *Auftrag* is based on Anna Seghers's novella *Das Licht auf dem Galgen*, which supplies the story, on Büchner's *Dantons Tod*, which provides one of the central scenes and metaphors of the play, and finally on Bertolt Brecht's *Die Maßnahme* (The Measures Taken). The play's subtitle "Erinnerung an eine Revolution" (Memory of a Revolution) is an obvious reminder to read the text as reconstruction of a story. There is no conventional plot, but only fragments of an action, primarily set in Jamaica in the late 1790s and featuring three Jacobin agitators—Debuisson, Galloudec and Sasportas—and their aborted mission. They have been sent from France to lead a slave revolt against the British in the name of the Republic of France. But before they have even begun to organize the slaves for a revolt, they receive the message that Napoleon has dissolved the Directory and taken over the government by a coup d'état in Paris. The revolution in France is finished and the mission in Jamaica has become meaningless. While Sasportas, a former black slave, and Galloudec, a French peasant, continue to fight oppression, Debuisson betrays the revolution by returning to his former life as a slaveholder.[27] Seghers's original novella is a story with a "frame," relating the central story by way of a letter to Antoine, a former Jacobin, a few years later. Maintaining that part of the frame, Müller's play opens with the text of the letter and its delivery to Antoine in France after 1804, reporting the failure of the mission: Sasportas has been hanged and Galloudec has been detained by the Spanish in Cuba and died in prison. Then the fragments of the main plot are presented in scenes 4–11. At the end of the play, however, the latter half of the narrative frame is deleted. Debuisson becomes identical with Antoine, the addressee of the letter of the first three scenes, because both of them have betrayed the revolution. The play ends on the theme of betrayal rather than on the note of hope projected by the closure and the title of Seghers's novella *Das Licht auf dem Galgen*. *Der Auftrag* is thus a re-writing of Anna Seghers's novella against its original intent. Because of his analysis of the revolution betrayed, Müller antithetically concludes the original story by retaining its plot, while changing its meaning.[28]

The scene, based on Büchner's *Dantons Tod*, is at the center of *Der Auftrag* and is introduced as "Das Theater der Revolution" (The Theater of the Revolution). Galloudec and Sasportas dress up as Danton and Robespierre, putting on the heads of the respective historical figures. Büchner's drama takes on the quality of a play-within-a-play in *Der Auftrag*, employing the metaphor of revolution as theater.[29] But the confrontation between Galloudecdanton and Sasportasrobespierre is reduced to an imbecilic exchange of insults, somewhat reminiscent of Hitler's denunciation of Roosevelt:

> *SASPORTASROBESPIERRE*: Parasit Syphilitiker Aristokratenknecht
> *GALLOUDECDANTON*: Heuchler Eunuch Lakai der Wallstreet
> *SASPORTASROBESPIERRE*: Schwein
> *GALLOUDECDANTON*: Hyäne. (*Auftrag* 56)

> [*SASPORTASROBESPIERRE*: Parasite Syphilitic Aristocrat's flunkey
> *GALLOUDECDANTON*: Hypocrite Eunuch Lackey of Wall Street
> *SASPORTASROBESPIERRE*: Swine
> *GALLOUDECDANTON*: Hyena.] (Scene 8)

With these words, the two characters figuratively "behead" each other by striking the heads from each other's shoulders. This slapstick comedy is a parody of the classic confrontation between Danton and Robespierre in Act I, Scene vi of Büchner's drama. The burlesque contrafacture of this scene in Müller's *Auftrag* renders the traditional Eurocentric "Theater der Revolution" as the ineffectual bickering of a few privileged intellectuals, who are parading as revolutionaries. In the following scene, this "Theater der Revolution" is condemned by Sasportas:

> The Theater of the white Revolution is over. We sentence you to death, Victor Debuisson. Because your skin is white. Because your thoughts are white under your white skin.] (*Auftrag* 56)

The French Revolution is declared not only obsolete as a model of European revolution, but also inherently colonialist. Debuisson is condemned to death as "Besitzer" ("property owner") and "Herr" ("master"). The issue of the revolution is no longer based on the inequality between classes, but on the sexual, racial and cultural differences between European colonialists and the oppressed masses of the Third World. Sasportas condemns the white revolution, because it is devoid of "Rausch" ("ecstasy") and "Geschlecht" ("sex"). The Communist revolution, represented by the peasant Galloudec, cannot serve here as a model either, as it did in Brecht's *Die Maßnahme*, where the Moscow revolution is exported to China. In *Der Auftrag*, genuine revolutions are to be found only in the Third World, which extends not only to Africa, Asia and the two Americas, but also to the ghettos of the modern metropolises in Europe and North America. Sasportas declares that he will find his supporters among "Neger aller Rassen" ("blacks of all races"). Galloudec can support this revolution, but not lead it.

As Teraoka has shown in her seminal study of Heiner Müller's postmodernist poetics, *Der Auftrag* is structurally and thematically based on one of Brecht's early *Lehrstücke* or "learning plays."[30] But the Brechtian *Lehrstück*, as dramatic model, is undermined and deconstructed by Müller's text collage. The didactic function is purposefully abandoned. In terms of an emancipatory intellectual discourse, there is neither a lesson to be learned, nor a judgment to be pronounced. As Teraoka concludes:

> The "control chorus" [of the Brechtian *Lehrstück*], who directs the . . . remembered, reconstructed action. . . , merges with the [protagonist] as he finally betrays the revolution. . . . The action of the play thus completes a full circle, as [the protagonist] in Scene 12 becomes the counter-revolutionary [control chorus] . . . in Scene 2.[31]

The abandonment of rationality in favor of the corporeality espoused by Sasportas constitutes the rejection of the Hegelian/Marxist perspective of a rational world order and historical progress. In its place, the figure of Sasportas offers the perspectives of a sexual, racial and cultural revolution, independent from the European models of the French Revolution and Marxist Communism.

This paradigm change does not allow for the label of historical pessimism that has often been applied to Heiner Müller's plays.[32] In the re-writing of literary material on the revolution, *Der Auftrag* presents a new model, the Third World Revolution, "recognizing its uniqueness and its necessary independence from the historical and ideological categories of Europe," as Teraoka has shown.[33] Peter Weiss was approaching such a paradigm change in his plays on Angola and Vietnam, but he was not yet able to effect it despite his declaration of solidarity with the revolutionary movements of the

Third World. As a dramatist, he "had failed to go far enough."[34] In this respect, Heiner Müller "completed" what Peter Weiss began.

NOTES

1. See Elisabeth Frenzel, *Stoffe der Weltliteratur: Ein Lexikon dichtungsgeschichtlicher Längsschnitte*, 2nd. rev. ed. (Stuttgart: Kröner, 1963) 542–44. For a comparison of Büchner's *Dantons Tod* and Schnitzler's *Der grüne Kakadu* see Walter Hinderer,"Der Aufstand der Marionetten: Zu Arthur Schnitzler's Groteske *Der grüne Kakadu*," *Zeitgenossenschaft: Zur deutschsprachigen Literatur im 20. Jahrhundert: Festschrift für Egon Schwarz zum 65. Geburtstag*, ed. by Paul Michael Lützeler (Frankfurt/Main: Athenäum, 1987) 12–32.

2. Peter Weiss, "Anmerkungen zum geschichtlichen Hintergrund unseres Stückes," *Die Verfolgung und Ermordung Jean Paul Marats dargestellt durch die Schauspielgruppe des Hospizes zu Charenton unter Anleitung des Herrn de Sade: Drama in zwei Akten*. 8th ed. (Frankfurt/Main: Suhrkamp, 1967) 140. The play will be quoted hereafter in the text as *Marat/Sade*.

3. "Gespräch mit Peter Weiss, Frühjahr 1965," *Materialien zu Peter Weiss' Marat/Sade*, ed. by Karlheinz Braun (Frankfurt/Main: Suhrkamp, 1967) 101. Quoted hereafter as *Materialien*.

4. See *"Historikerstreit": Die Dokumentation der Kontroverse um die Einzigartigkeit der nationalsozialistischen Judenvernichtung* (Munich/Zurich: Piper, 1987); Charles S. Meier, *The Unmasterable Past: History, Holocaust, and German National Identity* (Cambridge: Harvard University Press, 1988).

5. Jürgen Habermas, "Ein Verdrängungsprozeß wird enthüllt," *Materialien* 120–24.

6. See Hans Christoph Buch, *Die Scheidung von San Domingo: Wie die Negersklaven von Haiti Robespierre beim Wort nahmen* (Berlin: Wagenbach, 1976), and C.L.R. James, *The Black Jacobins: Toussaint L'Ouverture and the San Domingo Revolution*, 2nd ed. (New York: Vintage Books/Random House, 1963).

7. Heinrich von Kleist, *Sämtliche Werke und Briefe*, ed. Helmut Sembdner, 2 vols, 4th, revised ed. (Munich: Hanser, 1965) 2:193.

8. For a brief discussion see Robert E. Helbling, "The Engagement in Santo Domingo," *The Major Works of Heinrich von Kleist* (New York: New Directions, 1975) 100–05.

9. Ruth K. Angress, "Kleist's Treatment of Imperialism: *Die Hermannsschlacht* and *Die Verlobung in St. Domingo*," *Monatshefte* 69 (1977): 16–33; Ilse Graham, *Heinrich von Kleist: Word into Flesh. A Poet's Quest for the Symbol* (Berlin, New York: de Gruyter, 1977) 128–34.

10. Anna Seghers, *Die Hochzeit von Haiti: Karibische Geschichten* (Darmstadt/Neuwied: Luchterhand, 1976).

11. See her article in this volume.

12. Heiner Müller, *Germania Tod in Berlin* (Berlin: Rotbuch Verlag, 1977) 80.

13. See *The Silence of Entropy or Universal Discourse: The Postmodernist Poetics of Heiner Müller*, New York University Ottendorfer Series, N.S. vol. 21 (New York/Berne: Lang, 1985) 124. I am indebted to Teraoka for my discussion of Heiner Müller.

14. "Gespräch mit Peter Weiss, Frühjahr 1965," *Materialien* 101. See also Harold Bloom, *The Anxiety of Influence: A Theory of Poetry* (London, Oxford: Oxford University Press, 1975).

15. "Peter Weiss über die Inszenierungen des *Marat/Sade*," *Materialien* 112.

16. See Darko Suvin, "Weiss's *Marat/Sade* and its Three Main Performance Versions," *Modern Drama* 31 (1988): 395–419.

17. "Gespräch mit Peter Weiss, Frühjahr 1965," *Materialien* 101.

18. Weiss, "10 Arbeitspunkte eines Autors in der geteilten Welt," *Materialien* 114–19.

19. See Bloom, *The Anxiety of Influence* 30.

20. "Gespräch mit Peter Weiss, Frühjahr 1964," *Materialien* 94.

21. *Materialien* 93.

22. *Materialien* 99.

23. The English version by Geoffrey Skelton, verse adaptation by Adrian Mitchell (New York: Atheneum, 1980), does not contain these lines.

24. Hans Mayer, "Peter Weiss und die zweifache Praxis der Veränderung," *Theater heute* 13.5 (May 1972): 18–20.

25. Heiner Müller, *Herzstück* (Berlin: Rotbuch Verlag, 1983) 43–70. The play is quoted hereafter in the text as *Auftrag*. For an English translation see Heiner Müller, *The Task, Hamletmachine and Other Texts for the Stage*, ed. and transl. by Carl Weber (New York: Performing Arts Journal Publications, 1984) 81–101.

26. See *The Silence of Entropy* 125, and "*Der Auftrag* and *Die Maßnahme*: Models of Revolution in Heiner Müller and Bertolt Brecht," *Monatshefte* 59 (1986): 65–84, esp. 79–80.

27. Heiner Müller has changed Sasportas from a Spaniard in Seghers's novella into a black slave and left Debuisson to an uncertain fate as the son of a slaveholder who has returned to the fold of the family, while in Seghers's novella Debuisson admits his participation in the conspiracy and is deported to England.

28. See Bloom, *The Anxiety of Influence* 14.

29. See Hans-Thies Lehmann, "Dramatische Form und Revolution: Überlegungen zur Korrespondenz zweier Theatertexte: Georg Büchners *Dantons Tod* und Heiner Müllers *Der Auftrag*," *Georg Büchner: Dantons Tod. Die*

Trauerarbeit im Schönen: Ein Theaterlesebuch, ed. by Peter von Becker (Frankfurt/Main: Syndikat, 1980) 106–21; and *The Silence of Entropy* 143–51.

30. *The Silence of Entropy* 123–69. See also "*Der Auftrag* and *Die Maßnahme*" (note 26) 65–84.

31. *The Silence of Entropy* 165.

32. "*Der Auftrag* and *Die Maßnahme*" 80; Lehmann, "Dramatische Form und Revolution" 114; Wolfgang Müller, " 'Erblasten': Zur Rezeption der Französischen Revolution in der DDR-Literatur," *Schreckensmythen—Hoffnungsbilder: Die Französische Revolution in der deutschen Literatur. Essays*, ed. by Harro Zimmermann (Frankfurt/Main: Athenäum, 1989) 329–30; Genia Schulz, *Heiner Müller*, Sammlung Metzler 197 (Stuttgart: Metzler, 1980) 21–22.

33. "*Der Auftrag* und *Die Maßnahme*" 80.

34. *The Anxiety of Influence* 14.

EHRHARD BAHR

Bibliography: A Select Checklist

1. Germany and the French Revolution:

Gooch, George Peabody. *Germany and the French Revolution.* London: Longmans, Green & Co., 1920.

Stern, Alfred. *Der Einfluß der französischen Revolution auf das deutsche Geistesleben.* Stuttgart: Cotta, 1928.

Droz, Jacques. *L'Allemagne et la révolution française.* Paris: Presses Universitaires de France, 1949.

Träger, Claus, ed. *Mainz zwischen rot und schwarz: Die Mainzer Revolution 1792-1793 in Schriften, Reden und Briefen.* Berlin: Rütten & Loening, 1963.

Scheel, Heinrich, ed. *Jakobinische Flugschriften aus dem deutschen Süden Ende des 18. Jahrhunderts.* Berlin: Akademie-Verlag, 1965.

Grab, Walter. *Norddeutsche Jakobiner: Demokratische Bestrebungen zur Zeit der Französischen Revolution.* Frankfurt/Main: Europäische Verlagsanstalt, 1967 (Hamburger Studien zur neueren Geschichte, vol. 8).

Hermand, Jost, ed. *Von deutscher Republik 1775-1795.* 2 vols. (Frankfurt/Main: Insel, 1968).

Griewank, Karl. *Der neuzeitliche Revolutionsbegriff: Entstehung und Entwicklung.* Frankfurt/Main: Europäische Verlagsanstalt, 1969.

Jäger, Hans-Wolf. *Politische Metaphorik im Jakobinismus und im Vormärz.* Stuttgart: Metzler, 1971.

Lautzas, Peter. *Die Festung Mainz im Zeitalter des Ancien Régime, der Französischen Revolution und des Empire (1736-1814).* Wiesbaden: Franz Steiner, 1973.

Blanning, T.C.W. *Reform and Revolution in Mainz 1743-1803.* Cambridge: Cambridge University Press, 1974.

Garber, Jörn, ed., *Revolutionäre Vernunft: Texte zur jakobinischen und liberalen Revolutionsrezeption in Deutschland 1789-1810.* Kronberg/Ts.: Scriptor, 1974 (Skripten Literaturwissenschaft 5).

Grab, Walter. "Eroberung oder Befreiung? Deutsche Jakobiner und die Franzosenherrschaft im Rheinland 1792-1799." *Studien zu Jakobinismus und Sozialismus,* ed. Hans Pelger. Berlin, Bonn, Bad Godesberg: Dietz, 1974, 1-102.

Scheel, Heinrich, ed. *Die Mainzer Republik.* 3 vols. Berlin: Akademie-Verlag, 1975–1989.
Blanning, T.C.W. "German Jacobins and the French Revolution." *The Historical Journal* 23.4 (1980): 985–1002.
Deutsche Jakobiner: Mainzer Republik und Cisrhenanen 1792–1798 (catalogue of the 1981 Mainz exhibit) vol. 1: *Handbuch;* vol. 2: *Bibliographie;* vol. 3: *Katalog.* Mainz: Bundesarchiv und Stadt Mainz, 1981.
Blanning, T.C.W. *The French Revolution in Germany: Occupation and Resistance in the Rhineland 1792–1802.* Oxford, New York: Oxford University Press, 1983.
Gilli, Marita. *Pensée et pratiques révolutionnaire a la fin du XVIIIe siècle en Allemagne.* Paris: Les Belles Lettres, 1983.
Voss, Jürgen, ed. *Deutschland und die Französische Revolution: Achtzehn Beiträge.* Munich: Artemis, 1983.
Gilli, Marita. "Le Mouvement révolutionnaire Allemand à la fin du dix-huitième siècle." *Annales Historiques de la Révolution Française* 56.255–56 (1984): 7–23.
Grab, Walter. *Ein Volk muß seine Freiheit selbst erobern: Zur Geschichte der deutschen Jakobiner.* Frankfurt/Main: Büchergilde Gutenberg, 1984.
Gilli, Marita, "Images, metaphores et comparaisons dans les discours des Jacobins de Mayence." *Annales Historiques de la Révolution Française* 269–70 (1987): 291–313.
Vierhaus, Rudolf. "Politisches Bewußtsein in Deutschland von 1789." R.V., *Deutschland im 18. Jahrhundert.* Göttingen: Vandenhoeck & Ruprecht, 1987, 183–201.
———. " 'Sie und nicht wir!' Deutsche Urteile über den Ausbruch der Französischen Revolution." Ibid., 202–15.
Berding, Helmut, ed. *Soziale Unruhen in Deutschland während der Französischen Revolution.* Göttingen: Vandenhoeck & Ruprecht, 1988 (Sonderheft Geschichte und Gesellschaft, No. 12).
Günther, Horst, ed. *Die Französische Revolution: Berichte und Deutungen deutscher Schriftsteller und Historiker.* Frankfurt/Main: Deutscher Klassiker-Verlag, 1988.
Saine, Thomas P. *Black Bread—White Bread: German Intellectuals and the French Revolution.* Columbia, SC: Camden House, 1988.
Stammen, Theo and Friedrich Eberle, eds. *Deutschland und die Französische Revolution 1789–1806.* Darmstadt: Wissenschaftliche Buchgesellschaft, 1988.
Abdelfettah, Ahcène. *Die Rezeption der Französischen Revolution durch den deutschen öffentlichen Sprachgebrauch, untersucht an ausgewählten historisch-politischen Zeitschriften (1789–1832).* Heidelberg: Winter, 1989.

Eberle, Friedrich and Theo Stammen, eds. *Die Französische Revolution in Deutschland: Zeitgenössische Texte deutscher Autoren.* Stuttgart: Reclam, 1989.
Forum für Philosophie Bad Homburg, ed. *Die Ideen von 1789 in der deutschen Rezeption.* Frankfurt/Main: Suhrkamp, 1989.
Harpprecht, Klaus. *Die Lust der Freiheit: Deutsche Revolutionäre in Paris.* Reinbek: Rowohlt, 1989.
Herzig, Arno, Inge Stephan and H.S. Sachs, eds. *"Sie und nicht wir": Die Französische Revolution und ihre Wirkung auf Norddeutschland und das Reich.* 2 vols. Hamburg: Dölling & Galitz, 1989.
Hoffmeister, Gerhart, ed. *The French Revolution and the Age of Goethe.* Hildesheim, Zürich, New York: Georg Olms Verlag, 1989.
Krauß, Henning, ed. *Folgen der Französischen Revolution.* Frankfurt/Main: Suhrkamp, 1989.
Kuhn, Axel, et al. *Revolutionsbegeisterung an der Hohen Carlsschule.* Stuttgart-Bad Cannstatt: Frommann-Holzboog, 1989.
Neugebauer-Wölk, Monika. *Revolution und Constitution. Die Brüder Cotta: Eine biographische Studie zum Zeitalter der Französischen Revolution und des Vormärz.* Berlin: Colloquium, 1989.
Akademie der Wissenschaften der DDR, ed. *Die Französische Revolution von 1789 und ihre weltgeschichtliche Bedeutung,* Sbb. Gesellschaftswissenschaften, 1990 (3/G). Berlin: Akademie-Verlag, 1990.
Timm, Eitel, ed. *Geist und Gesellschaft: Zur deutschen Rezeption der Französischen Revolution.* Munich: Fink, 1990.
Weis, Eberhard. "Ländliche und städtische Unruhen in den linksrheinischen deutschen Gebieten von 1789 bis 1792." *Deutschland und Frankreich um 1800: Aufklärung—Revolution—Reform.* Eds. Walter Demel and Bernd Roeck. Munich: Beck, 1990, 110–24.
Albrecht, Wolfgang. "Aufklärung, Reform, Revolution oder 'Bewirkt Aufklärung Revolutionen?' Über ein Zentralproblem der Aufklärungsdebatte in Deutschland." *Lessing Yearbook* XXII (1990): 1–75.
Middell, Katharina and Matthias, eds. *200. Jahrestag der Französischen Revolution: Kritische Bilanz der Forschungen zum Bicentenaire,* Beiträge zur Universalgeschichte und vergleichenden Geschichtsforschung, vol. 1. Leipzig: Leipziger Universitätsverlag, 1991.

2. The French Revolution and German Philosophy:

Ritter, Joachim. *Hegel und die Französische Revolution*. Frankfurt/Main: Suhrkamp, 1965.

Scheel, Heinrich. *Die Begegnung deutscher Aufklärer mit der Revolution*. Berlin: Akademie-Verlag, 1973.

Burg, Peter. *Kant und die französische Revolution*. Berlin: 1974.

Schmitt, Eberhard and Matthias Meyn. *Ursprung und Charakter der Französischen Revolution bei Marx und Engels*. Bochum: Brockmeyer, 1976.

Sauerland, Karol. "Goethes, Schillers, Fr. Schlegels und Novalis' Reaktionen auf die neuen politischen, konstitutionellen und sozialphilosophischen Fragen, die die Französische Revolution aufwarf." *Daß eine Nation die ander verstehen möge: Festschrift für Marian Szyrocki*. Eds. Norbert Honsza and Hans-Gert Roloff. Amsterdam: Rodopi, 1988 (Chloe, Beihefte zum Daphnis, 7), 615–37.

Batscha, Zwi. *"Despotismus von jeder Art reizt zur Widersetzlichkeit": Die Französische Revolution in der deutschen Popularphilosophie*. Frankfurt/Main: Suhrkamp, 1989.

Buhr, Manfred, et al. *Republik der Menschlichkeit: Französische Revolution und deutsche Philosophie*, Studien zur Dialektik. Köln: Pahl-Rugenstein, 1989.

Mah, Harold. "The French Revolution and the Problem of German Modernity: Hegel, Heine, and Marx." *New German Critique* 50 (Spring/Summer 1990): 3–20.

3. The French Revolution and German Literature:

Voegt, Hedwig. *Die deutsche jakobinische Literatur und Publizistik 1789–1800*. Berlin: Rütten & Loening, 1955.

Weiland, Werner. *Der junge Friedrich Schlegel oder Die Revolution in der Frühromantik*, Studien zur Poetik und Geschichte der Revolution, vol. 6. Stuttgart: Kohlhammer, 1968.

Bertaux, Pierre. *Hölderlin und die Französische Revolution*. Frankfurt/Main: Suhrkamp, 1969.

Hermand, Jost. *Von Mainz nach Weimar (1793–1919): Studien zur deutschen Literatur*. Stuttgart: Metzler, 1969.

Steiner, Gerhard, ed. *Jakobinerschauspiel und Jakobinertheater*. Stuttgart: Metzler, 1973 (Deutsche revolutionäre Demokraten, vol. 4).

Brinkmann, Richard, ed. *Deutsche Literatur und Französische Revolution*. Göttingen: Vandenhoeck & Ruprecht, 1974.

Krüger, Christa. *Georg Forsters und Friedrich Schlegels Beurteilung der Französischen Revolution als Ausdruck des Problems einer Einheit von Theorie und Praxis.* Göppingen: Kümmerle, 1974.

Segeberg, Harro. "Literarischer Jakobinismus in Deutschland: Theoretische und methodische Überlegungen zur Erforschung der radikalen Spätaufklärung." *Deutsches Bürgertum und literarische Intelligenz 1750–1800,* ed. Bernd Ludz. Stuttgart: Metzler, 1974 (Literaturwissenschaft und Sozialwissenschaften 3), 509–68.

Mattenklott, Gert and Klaus R. Scherpe, eds. *Demokratisch-revolutionäre Literatur in Deutschland: Jakobinismus.* Kronberg/Ts.: Scriptor, 1975 (Literatur im historischen Prozeß 3/1).

Träger, Claus, ed. *Die Französische Revolution im Spiegel der deutschen Literatur: Eine Dokumentation.* Leipzig: Reclam, 1975 (3rd. ed. 1988).

Stephan, Inge. *Literarischer Jakobinismus in Deutschland (1789–1806).* Stuttgart: Metzler, 1976 (Sammlung Metzler, 150).

Borchmeyer, Dieter. *Höfische Gesellschaft und Französische Revolution bei Goethe: Adliges und bürgerliches Wertsystem im Urteil der Weimarer Klassik.* Kronberg/Ts.: Athenäum, 1977.

Fink, Gonthier-Louis. "Das Frankreichbild in der deutschen Literatur und Publizistik zwischen der Französischen Revolution und den Befreiungskriegen." *Jahrbuch des Wiener Goethe-Vereines* 81–83 (1977–1979): 59–87.

Schneider, Manfred. *Die kranke schöne Seele der Revolution: Heine, Börne, das "Junge Deutschland," Marx und Engels.* Frankfurt/Main: Syndikat, 1980.

Chiarini, Paolo and Walter Dietze, eds. *Deutsche Klassik und Revolution: Texte eines literaturwissenschaftlichen Kolloquiums.* Rome: Edizione dell' Ateneo, 1981.

Pillau, Helmut. *Die fortgedachte Dissonanz. Hegels Tragödientheorie und Schillers Tragödie: Deutsche Antworten auf die Französische Revolution.* Munich: Fink, 1981.

Koßeck, Wolfgang. *Begriff und Bild der Revolution bei Heine.* Frankfurt/Main, Bern: Lang, 1982.

Eibl, Karl, ed. *Französische Revolution und deutsche Literatur.* Hamburg: Meiner, 1986.

Dau, Rudolf. *Berührungspunkte zweier Zeitalter: Deutsche Literatur und die Französische Revolution.* Berlin: Dietz, 1989.

Fink, Gonthier-Louis, ed. *Les Romantiques Allemand et la Révolution française/Die deutsche Romantik und die französische Revolution: Actes du colloque international, Strasbourg, 2–5 novembre 1989.* Strasbourg: UFR des Langues, U.S.H.S. [1989] (Collection recherches germaniques, No. 3).

Karthaus, Ulrich. "Schiller und die Französische Revolution." *Jahrbuch der deutschen Schillergesellschaft* 33 (1989): 210–39.

Koopmann, Helmut. *Freiheitssonne und Revolutionsgewitter: Reflexe der Französischen Revolution im literarischen Deutschland zwischen 1789 und 1840.* Tübingen: Niemeyer, 1989.

Rietzschel, Thomas, ed. *Revolutionsgedichte: Von Hölderlin bis Fried.* Zürich: Arche, 1989.

Roethe, Wolfgang. *Deutsche Revolutionsdramatik seit Goethe.* Darmstadt: Wissenschaftliche Buchgesellschaft, 1989.

Steiner, Gerhard. *Das Theater der deutschen Jakobiner: Dramatik und Bühne im Zeichen der Französischen Revolution.* Berlin: Henschel, 1989.

Streller, Siegfried, ed. *Literatur zwischen Revolution und Restauration: Studien zu literarischen Wechselbeziehungen in Europa zwischen 1789 und 1835.* Berlin/Weimar: Aufbau, 1989.

Träger, Claus, ed. *"—Ihr seid dabeigewesen": Deutsche Schriftsteller zur Französischen Revolution.* Leipzig: Insel, 1989.

Volke, Werner, Ingrid Kussmaul and Brigitte Schillbach, eds. *"O Freyheit! Silberton dem Ohre..." Französische Revolution und deutsche Literatur 1789–1799.* Marbacher Kataloge, 44. Marbach am Neckar: Deutsche Schillergesellschaft, 1989.

Zimmermann, Harro, ed. *Schreckensmythos—Hoffnungsbilder. Die Französische Revolution in der deutschen Literatur: Essays.* Frankfurt/Main: Athenäum, 1989.

Cape, Ruth I. *Das französische Ungewitter: Goethes Bildersprache zur Französischen Revolution.* Heidelberg: Winter, 1991.

Hinderer, Walter. "Deutsches Theater der Französischen Revolution." *German Quarterly* 64 (1991): 207–19.

4. The Modern Reception of the French Revolution:

Bouvier, Beatrix W. *Französische Revolution und deutsche Arbeiterbewegung: Die Rezeption des revolutionären Frankreich in der deutschen sozialistischen Arbeiterbewegung von den 1830er Jahren bis 1905.* Bonn: Neue Gesellschaft, 1982.

Hippel, Wolfgang von, ed. *"Freiheit, Gleichheit, Brüderlichkeit?": Die Französische Revolution im deutschen Urteil von 1789–1945.* Munich: Deutscher Taschenbuch-Verlag, 1989.

Hettling, Manfred, ed. *Revolution in Deutschland? 1789–1989: Sieben Beiträge.* Göttingen: Vandenhoeck & Ruprecht, 1991.

Notes on the Contributors

EHRHARD BAHR is Professor of German at the University of California, Los Angeles. He has published books on irony in the late works of Goethe (1972), on Georg Lukács (1970), Ernst Bloch (1974), and Nelly Sachs (1980). He is the author of articles on eighteenth- to twentieth-century German literature, literary theory, and exile literature, and is the editor of a three-volume history of German literature (1987–1988).

ZWI BATSCHA is Professor of Political Science at the University of Haifa. He is the author of *Gesellschaft und Staat in der politischen Philosophie Fichtes* (1970), and *Studien zur politischen Theorie des deutschen Frühliberalismus* (1981), among others. He is the editor of numerous editions of texts of German eighteenth-century political theory. His most recent book is entitled *"Despotism von jeder Art reizt zum Widerspruch": Die Französische Revolution in der deutschen Popularphilosophie* (1989).

KLAUS L. BERGHAHN is Professor of German and member of the Humanities Institute at the University of Wisconsin, Madison. He is the author of *Formen der Dialogführung in Schillers klassischen Dramen* (1970), *Am Beispiel Wilhelm Meisters: Einführung in die Wissenschaftsgeschichte der Germanistik* (1980, with Beate Pinkerneil), and *Schiller: Ansichten eines Idealisten* (1986). He is the editor of several books and editions and has published numerous articles and essays on eighteenth-century literature, especially on Schiller.

GONTHIER-LOUIS FINK is Professor of German at the Université des Sciences humaines in Strasbourg. His publications include *Naissance et apogée du conte merveilleux en Allemagne (1740–1800)* (1966), *L'Allemagne face au classicisme et à la révolution* (1972), and *Goethe et l'Alsace* (1972). He is the editor of *Cosmopolitisme, Patriotisme et Xénophobie en Europe au Siècle des Lumières* (1986) and *Les Romantiques allemands et la Révolution française* (1989).

JENS KRUSE, Associate Professor of German at Wellesley College, is the author of a book on the representation of history in Goethe's *Faust II*, and has published on Goethe and the French Revolution, Goethe and Martin Walser, Georg Lukács, and Kafka.

HERBERT S. LINDENBERGER is Avalon Foundation Professor of Humanities in Comparative Literature and English at Stanford University. His publications include *On Wordsworth's "Prelude"* (1963), *Georg Büchner* (1964), *Georg Trakl* (1971), and *Historical Drama: The Relation of Literature and Reality* (1975). His most recent book is *The History in Literature: On Value, Genre, Institutions* (1990).

GÜNTER MIETH, Professor of German at the University of Leipzig, is the author of *Friedrich Hölderlin: Dichter der bürgerlich-demokratischen Revolution* (1978) and the editor of Hölderlin's collected works. His most recent book is entitled *Vom Beginn der großen Französischen Revolution bis zum Ende des alten deutschen Reiches 1789–1806* (1988).

THOMAS P. SAINE is Professor of German at the University of California, Irvine. He is the author of articles and books on Enlightenment and the eighteenth century, including *Die ästhetische Theodizee: Karl Philipp Moritz und die Philosophie des 18. Jahrhunderts* (1971), *Georg Forster* (1972), *Von der Kopernikanischen bis zur Französischen Revolution: Die Auseinandersetzung der deutschen Frühaufklärung mit der neuen Zeit* (1987). He was one of the editors of the Suhrkamp/Insel English Goethe edition in twelve volumes (1980–1989). His most recent book is *Black Bread—White Bread: German Intellectuals and the French Revolution* (1988).

JEFFREY L. SAMMONS is Professor of German at Yale University. He is the author of *The Nachtwachen von Bonaventura: A Structural Interpretation* (1965), *Heinrich Heine: The Elusive Poet* (1969), *Six Essays on the Young German Novel* (1972), *Literary Sociology and Practical Criticism* (1977), and *Heinrich Heine: A Modern Biography* (1979). He was one of the editors of the Suhrkamp/Insel English Goethe edition in twelve volumes (1980–89). His most recent book is entitled *Wilhelm Raabe: The Fiction of the Alternative Community* (1987).

ARLENE A. TERAOKA is Associate Professor of German at the University of Minnesota. Her publications are concerned especially with contemporary German literature and include a monograph on the postmodernist poetics of Heiner Müller entitled *The Silence of Entropy or Universal Discourse* (1985).

W. DANIEL WILSON is Associate Professor of German at the University of California, Berkeley. His books include *The Narrative Strategy of Wieland's Don Sylvio* (1981) and *Humanität und Kreuzzugsideologie: Die Türkenoper im*

18. Jahrhundert (1983), and *Geheimräte gegen Geheimbünde: Ein unbekanntes Kapitel der klassisch-romantischen Geschichte Weimars* (1991).

BERND WITTE is Professor of German at the Technische Hochschule at Aachen and is the editor of the critical edition of the works of Christian Fürchtegott Gellert. His books include *Walter Benjamin. Der Intellektuelle als Kritiker: Untersuchungen zu seinem Frühwerk* (1976), and *Walter Benjamin: An Intellectual Biography* (Detroit: Wayne State University Press, 1991). He is a co-editor of the new *Goethe-Handbuch* (projected to appear 1993–1995).

Index of Names

Abegg, Johann Friedrich 77
Achenwall, Gottfried 65
Adenauer, Konrad 240
Alxinger, Johann Baptist 20, 42, 55, 56
Angress, R.K. (see Ruth Kluger)
Anna Amalia, Duchess of Saxe-Weimar 35, 47, 54
Aris, Reinhold 75, 77
Ayrenhoff, Kornelius Hermann 26

Babeuf, François 199, 204
Baggesen, Jens 51
Bahr, Ehrhard 8, 94, 95
Bailly, Jean 178
Baioni, Guiliano 96
Balsamo, Joseph (Cagliostro) 39–41, 54
Balzac, Honoré de 188
Barbarossa (Friedrich I, Holy Roman Emperor) 183
Barner, Wilfried 94, 95 96, 161
Barruel, Augustin de 44, 49, 57
Barthelémy, François de 188
Batscha, Zwi 7, 74, 75
Batt, Kurt 231, 232, 237
Beaumarchais, Pierre Augustin Caron de 6
Beethoven, Ludwig van 116
Behler, Ernst 159, 160, 162
Benjamin, Walter 160
Béranger, Pierre Jean de 188

Berghahn, Klaus L. 8, 118
Bergson, Henri 198
Bertuch, Friedrich Justin 52
Bieberstein, Johannes Rogalla von 33, 36, 48–50, 54, 56–58
Biester, Johann Erich 37
Blanqui, Auguste 199
Bleibtreu, Karl 239
Blessin, Stefan 96
Bode, Johann Christoph 34, 35, 37, 40, 43–45, 48–50, 52–54, 56, 57
Böhmer, Georg Wilhelm 126, 127, 129, 131, 141, 144, 146
Bonaparte, Napoleon (see Napoleon I)
de Bopp, Marianne O. 232
Borchmeyer, Dieter 96
Börne, Ludwig 177, 186, 189, 191
Böttiger, Karl August 43, 44, 47, 56, 57–58
Brandes, Johann Christian 21
Brecht, Bertolt 207, 234, 246, 248, 251
Briegleb, Klaus 192, 195
Brinkmann, Richard 58, 159, 160
Brook, Peter 242
Brown, Jane K. 95, 96
Brunswick (see Karl Wilhelm Ferdinand)
Büchner, Georg 5, 8, 26, 174, 182, 197–218, 239, 241, 242–43, 246, 247, 250, 251
Büchner, Wilhelm 216

Buonarroti, Filippo 199
Bürger, Gottfried August 28, 163
Buri, Isenburg von 26
Burke, Edmund 20, 211
Byron, George Gordon (Sixth Baron Byron of Rochdale) 6

Caesar, Gaius Julius 179f.
Cagliostro (see Joseph Balsamo)
Calvié, Lucien 192, 194, 196
Campe, Joachim Heinrich 14, 57, 102, 117, 188
Campe, Julius 188
Carl August, Duke of Saxe-Weimar 35, 36, 42, 43, 48, 50, 55, 88, 102
Carlyle, Thomas 201, 202, 215
Charles VII, King of France 186
Claudius, Matthias 30
Clauer, Carl 22
Clemenceau, Georges 11
Condorcet, Jean-Antoine-Nicolas de Caritat, marquis de 12
Conz, Karl Philipp 16
Corday, Charlotte 5, 26, 243
Corneille, Pierre 201
Cotta, Friedrich 126, 128, 142, 143
Cotta, Johann Friedrich 180, 188
Custine, Adam-Philippe de 24, 122–26, 128–30, 132, 137, 141, 142, 144

Dalberg, Karl Theodor von 132

Danton, Georges (also dramatic figure) 4, 5, 8, 197–212, 214, 216, 239, 241–43, 247
Danton, Louise 203
Daumier, Honoré 187, 195
David, Jacques-Louis 179
Delavigne, Casimir Jean François 188
Desmoulins, Camille 4, 182, 204
Diderot, Denis 204
Dorsch, Anton Joseph 130, 135, 145
Dülmen, Richard van 34, 35, 50, 52, 53
Dumont, Franz 142
Dumouriez, Charles François 206
Dutschke, Rudi 209, 210, 217

Ebel, Johann Gottfried 3
Edelsheim, Georg Ludwig von 58
Edinhard, Gustav 26
Ehlers, Martin 41, 42, 51, 55, 58
Eichendorff, Joseph Freiherr von 7
Eisler, Hanns 169
Engel, Leopold 48, 49, 50, 51
Engels, Friedrich 4, 7, 99, 100
Epstein, Klaus 45, 46, 48, 49, 52, 55, 56, 57
Erhard, Johann Benjamin 70
Ernst II, Duke of Saxe-Gotha 35, 36, 52
Erthal, Friedrich Karl von, Elector of Mainz 122, 129, 132

Fallbacher, Karl-Heinz 35, 50

Fehn, Ernst-Otto 34, 35, 50, 52
Ferguson, Adam 66, 76
Feuchtwanger, Lion 6, 7
Fichte, Johann Gottlieb 3, 4, 7, 36, 50, 51, 99, 151, 164, 206
Fink, Gonthier-Louis 7, 9, 58, 161
Forster, Johann Georg Adam 18, 24, 25, 29, 101, 115, 118, 119–47, 166
Forster, Therese (see Therese Huber)
Foucault, Michel 39
Francis II, Holy Roman Emperor 23, 41, 122
Frederick II, King in Prussia 36, 67
Frederick William II, King in Prussia 36, 41, 51, 55, 128
Frenzel, Elizabeth 10, 250
Friedrich V, Landgrave of Hesse-Homburg 169
Friedrich Christian, Duke of Schleswig-Holstein-Augustenburg 36, 51, 102, 107
Fritsch, Jakob Friedrich von 35
Frye, Northrop 212, 218
Furet, François 211, 217

Gates, Henry Louis, Jr. 122, 235
Gaudy, Franz von 188
Gellert, Christian Fürchtegott 86
Gentz, Friedrich 18, 25, 43
Girnus, Wilhelm 232
Girtanner, Christoph 21
Gleim, Johann Wilhelm 20, 26
Glucksmann, André 4
Göchhausen, Ernst August Anton von 34, 37, 41, 49, 52, 53, 54, 55
Goebbels, Joseph 6
Goethe, Johann Wolfgang von 3, 4, 8, 11, 20, 24, 25, 27, 34, 35, 46, 48, 50, 54, 55, 58, 79–97, 99, 100, 102, 151–57, 161, 162, 164, 165, 174, 186, 188, 203, 204
Göring, Hermann 173
Görres, Joseph 24, 29, 30
Gottsched, Johann Christoph 95
Grabbe, Christian Dietrich 203
Graßl, Hans 49, 50, 51
Grégoire, Gabriel 134, 138
Greiner, Bernhard 231
Griepenkerl, Robert 5, 239
Grimm, Reinhold 232, 236
Grolmann, Ludwig Adolf Christian von 49
Gros, Jean-Antoine 179
Gründgens, Gustav 209
Guizot, Guillaume 185, 214
Gutzmann, Gertraud 232, 235, 236

Habermas, Jürgen 6, 7, 10, 240, 250
Hamilton, Alexander 102
Hansen, Volkmar 192, 193, 195
Hardenberg, Friedrich von (Novalis) 8, 30, 51, 150–59, 161, 162, 198
Harpprecht, Klaus 140
Hauff, Wilhelm 188
Hauptmann, Gerhart 5
Haussmann, Nicolas 146

Hegel, Georg Wilhelm Friedrich 3, 4, 7, 101, 117, 163, 171, 195
Heine, Heinrich 3, 4, 8, 173–96, 203, 204, 210, 215, 236
Hennings, August von 56
Herder, Johann Gottfried 3, 19, 23, 29, 30, 35, 50, 54, 84, 111, 118, 164, 165
Hermand, Jost 232
Hermlin, Stephan 169
Hertzberg, Ewald Friedrich, Graf von 18
Heym, Georg 5, 10
Heyne, Christian Gottlob 121, 129, 141
Himmler, Heinrich 173
Hinderer, Walter 250
Hitler 5, 6, 7, 247
Hobbes, Thomas 65
Hoffmann, Jochen 34
Hoffmann, Leopold Alois 22, 33, 34, 35, 40, 41, 42, 43, 44, 54, 55, 56, 57
Hoffmann von Fallersleben, August Heinrich 188
Hofmann, Andreas Josef 131, 134–35, 136, 143, 145, 146
d'Holbach, Paul Heinrich Dietrich 204, 216
Hölderlin, Friedrich 3, 8, 15, 18, 30, 101, 115, 117, 163–71, 246
Holzhausen, Paul 174, 195
Horkheimer, Max 6
Huber, Ludwig Ferdinand 18, 24, 29, 129, 130, 133, 140
Huber, Therese (Therese Forster) 27, 129, 133, 136, 137, 140, 146
Hufeland, Gottlieb 42, 55
Hugo, Victor 50, 188
Humboldt, Alexander von 233

Hume, David 66, 76
Hunt, Lynn 212, 218
Hutcheson, Francis 66

Iffland, August Wilhelm 26
Immermann, Karl Leberecht 186

Jagemann, Christian Joseph 54
JanMohamed, Abdul R. 235
Janz, Rolf-Peter 96
Jaspers, Karl 198
Jenisch, Daniel 16
Jeßner, Leopold 5
Johnson, Christa 9
Johnston, Otto W. 193, 195

Kafka, Franz 199
Kalb, Heinrich von 165
Kant, Immanuel 4, 7, 24, 29, 31, 61–77, 90, 102, 117, 164, 165
Karl Eugen, Duke of Württemberg 103
Karl Wilhelm Ferdinand, Duke of Brunswick 23, 41, 117
Kassé, Maguèye 236
Kennedy, Robert 173
Kießling, Wolfgang 233
Kisch, Egon Erwin 233
Kleist, Heinrich von 7, 8, 233, 239, 240–41, 250
Klopstock, Friedrich Gottlieb 4, 13, 15, 16, 19, 23, 26, 30, 101, 102
Kluger, Ruth 233, 250
Knebel, Karl Ludwig von 47
Knesebeck, Karl Friedrich 24
Knigge, Adolph Freiherr von 16, 17, 23, 43, 128
Kobuch, Agatha 51

Index of Names

Kolb, Gustav 176, 188, 191, 193
Kollwitz, Käthe 5
Kolmar, Gertrud 5, 6
Körner, Christian Gottfried 53, 101, 107
Koselleck, Reinhart 49, 53, 88, 96
Kossek, Wolfgang 194, 195
Kotzebue, August von 27
Kralik, Richard von 239
Kruse, Jens 8, 161
Kurrelmeyer, Wilhelm 53, 54, 55, 56

L'Ouverture, François-Dominique Toussaint (also fictional character) 219, 221, 222, 224–29, 231, 235, 236, 240
Lafayette, Marie Joseph de Motier, marquis de 88, 178, 195, 212
Lafontaine, August Heinrich J. 27
Lamartine, Alphonse de 178, 185, 186, 188
Lassalle, Ferdinand von 5
Laube, Heinrich 194
Laukhard, Christian Friedrich 24, 29
Lauth, Reinhard 48, 49, 50, 52, 53
Lavater, Johann Caspar 26
Leibniz, Gottfried Wilhelm von 66
Lengefeld, Charlotte von 102
Lenthe, Ernst Ludwig Julius von 57
Leopold II, Holy Roman Emperor 12, 20, 41

Lessing, Gotthold Ephraim 235
Lichtenberg, Georg Christoph 18
Lindenberger, Herbert S. 8, 214
Lindner, Friedrich Ludwig 188
Lloyd, David 235
Locke, John 65
Loeb, Ernst 177, 193
Louis XVI, King of France 13, 14, 20, 23, 26, 27, 39, 46, 72, 79, 81, 86, 100, 101, 107, 182
Louis Napoleon (see Napoleon III)
Louis-Philippe, King of the French 187, 195, 204
Lukács, George 94, 100, 117, 150, 199, 211, 214
Luther, Martin 14, 193
Lützeler, Paul Michael 117, 188, 192
Lux, Adam 127

McAnear, Michael Frank 9
Madison, James 102, 232
Maitland, Sir Frederick Lewis 174
Maniquis, Robert M. 9
Mann, Heinrich 5, 7, 233
Marat, Jean-Paul (also dramatic character) 5, 26, 239, 242–46
Marcuse, Herbert 118, 210
Marie Antoinette, Queen of France 23, 212
Martini, Fritz 44, 52, 53, 57, 58
Marx, Karl 4, 7, 61, 99, 100, 109, 112, 117, 176, 193, 212, 215
Mayer, Thomas Michael 161, 199, 214, 215, 216, 217, 251

Mehring, Franz 100
Meidner, Ludwig 5
Meilhan, Senac de 21
Meiners, Christoph 46
Mende, Fritz 194
Mercier, Louis-Sébastien 19
Merlin de Thionville, Antoine-Christoph 134
Méry, Joseph 188
Metternich, Matthias 126, 131, 143
Michelet, Jules 4, 211
Mieth, Günter 8, 9, 171
Mignet, François-Auguste 174, 192, 204, 212, 214, 215, 216
Milfull, John 232, 234, 236
Milton, John 215
Montesquieu, Charles de Secondat 65, 66
Moritz, Karl Philipp 79
Möser, Justus 63
Mühlher, Robert 198
Müller, Adam 96
Müller, Heiner 8, 234, 236, 237, 241, 246–49, 251
Müller, Johannes von 131, 144
Müller-Seidel, Walter 94
Münter, Friedrich 59

Napoleon I (Bonaparte), Emperor of the French 5, 6, 8, 44, 168, 174–82, 186–91, 192, 193, 194, 195, 206, 219, 223, 230, 239, 240, 243, 245, 246
Napoleon II (Duke of Reichstadt) 176
Napoleon III, Charles Louis, Emperor of the French 176–77, 191, 193

Napoleon Louis, Grand Duke of Cleves and Berg 176
Nehring, Wolfgang 8
Nerval, Gérard (Gérard Labrunie) 188
Neumayr, Clemens 39, 40, 54
Nicholas I, Czar of Russia 96, 182
Nietzsche, Friedrich 4, 188
Novalis (see Friedrich von Hardenberg)

Oliver, William I. 209
Ozouf, Mona 212, 217

Paine, Thomas 102, 205, 211
Pape, Friedrich Georg 128
Perten, Anselm 242
Pfeffel, Gottlieb Conrad 15, 16, 20, 27
Platen, August von 186
Popper, Karl 61, 74
Posselt, Ernst Ludwig 12

Quinet, Edgar 188

Ranke, Leopold von 211
Rebmann, Andreas Georg Friedrich 28, 29, 128, 166
Rehberg, August Wilhelm 21, 46, 63, 70, 96
Reichard, H.A.O. 12, 49
Reichardt, Johann Friedrich 14, 102
Reinhardt, Max 209, 217
Reinhardt, Richard 193
Reinhold, Karl Leonhard 35, 37, 38, 48–50, 52, 53, 55, 56, 75, 232, 236
Reubel, Jean-François 146
Riem, Andreas 29

Index of Names

Rigney, Ann 212
Robespierre, Maximilien François Marie Isadore de (also dramatic figure) 4, 5, 6, 28, 29, 87, 105, 168, 174, 183, 197, 199, 202, 203, 204, 206, 239–43, 247
Robison, John 44, 57
Roosevelt, Franklin Delano 247
Rosenberg, John D. 215
Rossberg, Adolf 49, 51, 53, 58
Rousseau, Jean-Jacques 29, 51, 65, 66, 71, 109, 111, 163, 168
Roux, Jacques 244
Rowe, Nicholas 96

Sade, Donatien Alphonse François, comte, called marquis de (also dramatic figure) 91, 239, 242–46
Saine, Thomas P. 8, 9, 188
Saint-Just, Louis Antoine Léon de (also dramatic figure) 4, 25, 197, 205
Salvatore, Gaston 210, 217
Sammons, Jeffrey L. 8
Scheel, Heinrich 120–21, 125, 127, 128, 141, 143, 144
Schelling, Friedrich Wilhelm 101, 164
Scherpe, Klaus 103
Schiller, Friedrich 8, 24, 27, 30, 34, 37, 53, 54, 79–80, 81, 82, 83, 84, 87, 99–118, 161, 163, 164, 165, 174, 186, 201
Schlaffer, Hannelore 95, 97
Schlegel, August Wilhelm 7, 179

Schlegel, Friedrich 3, 7, 24, 50–51, 99, 100, 117, 150–52, 157–58, 159, 161, 162
Schlosser, Johann Georg 145
Schmidt, Jochen 54, 56, 75, 188, 195
Schmitt, Carl 150
Schmitt, Eberhard 58
Schneider, Eulogius 16, 163
Schnitzler, Arthur 8, 239, 250
Schoelcher, Victor 232
Schoenberg, Arnold 6
Schopenhauer, Arthur 198
Schubart, Christian Friedrich Daniel 15, 18, 23, 163
Schulz, Caroline 207–08
Schulz, Wilhelm 207–08
Schüttler, Hermann 58
Schütz, Friedrich Wilhelm von 28
Scott, Sir Walter 175, 188
Seghers, Anna 8, 219–37, 241, 246, 247, 251
Shaftesbury, Anthony Ashley Cooper, Earl of 66
Shakespeare, William 84, 179, 206, 242
Sieveking, Georg Heinrich 101
Sieyès, Emanuel Joseph 12, 16
Simon, Johann Friedrich 134, 138
Smith, Adam 66, 76, 89, 96
Sömmerring, Samuel Thomas 122
Staël-Holstein, Anne Louise Germaine de 99
Stalin, Josef 182
Starck, Johann August 49
Starnes, Thomas C. 53
Stäudlin, Gotthold Friedrich 163
Stein, Heinrich Friedrich Karl Reichsfreiherr von und zum 19, 96

Stendhal (Henri Beyle) 188
Strahlheim, Karl (Johann Konrad Friederich) 204, 206, 216
Swinarski, Konrad 242

Teraoka, Arlene A. 8, 219, 241, 242, 246, 248, 249, 251
Thieberger, Richard 216
Thierry, Augustin 214
Thiers, Louis-Adolphe 174, 184, 185, 192, 204, 212, 214, 215, 216
Tocqueville, Alexis de 30, 211
Tolstoi, Alexander 9
Treitschke, Heinrich von 202, 215
Trotsky, Leon 246
Tulasiewicz, W.F. 231, 234

Usteri, Paul 18

Varnhagen von Ense, Karl August 188, 192
Viehweg, Wolfram 217
Viëtor, Karl 197–98, 210
Vigny, Alfred comte de 188
Vilate, Joachim 204
Voigt, Christian Gottlob 35, 42, 55, 58
Voltaire (François Marie Arouet) 180, 204
Voß, Christian Friedrich 120, 128, 129, 142, 143

Washington, George 6, 102, 177
Wedekind, Georg 126, 131
Weischedel, Wilhelm 74, 75, 76, 77

Weishaupt, Adam 30, 33, 35, 36, 43, 51, 52, 53, 54
Weiss, Peter 6, 8, 239–40, 242–44, 246, 249, 250, 251
Wellington, Arthur Wellesley, Duke of 184
Wieland, Christoph Martin 4, 7, 17, 18, 21, 24, 25, 26, 29, 30, 33–59
Wienbarg, Ludolf 192
Wilson, W. Daniel 7, 48, 50, 51, 55
Witte, Bernd 7, 9, 94, 95
Wolf, Christa 234
Wolf, Friedrich 6
Wolff, Christian 62, 63, 66, 74
Wordsworth, William 217
Würzer, Heinrich 28, 29

Zahl, Peter-Paul 210, 217
Zedlitz, Joseph Christian von 188

For Product Safety Concerns and Information please contact our EU
representative GPSR@taylorandfrancis.com
Taylor & Francis Verlag GmbH, Kaufingerstraße 24, 80331 München, Germany

www.ingramcontent.com/pod-product-compliance
Lightning Source LLC
Chambersburg PA
CBHW070638160426
43194CB00009B/1496